GENDER AND CONTEMPORARY HORROR IN FILM

EMERALD STUDIES IN POPULAR CULTURE AND GENDER

Series Editor: Samantha Holland, Leeds Beckett University, UK

As we re-imagine and re-boot at an ever faster pace, this series explores the different strands of contemporary culture and gender. Looking across cinema, television, graphic novels, fashion studies and reality TV, the series asks: what has changed for gender? And, perhaps more seriously, what has not? Have representations of genders changed? How much does the concept of 'gender' in popular culture define and limit us?

We not only consume cultural texts, but share them more than ever before; meanings and messages reach more people and perpetuate more understandings (and misunderstandings) than at any time in history. This new series interrogates whether feminism has challenged or change misogynist attitudes in popular culture.

Emerald Studies in Popular Culture and Gender provides a focus for writers and researchers interested in sociological and cultural research that expands our understanding of the ontological status of gender, popular culture and related discourses, objects and practices.

Titles in this series

Samantha Holland, Robert Shail and Steven Gerrard (eds.), *Gender and Contemporary Horror in Film*

Steven Gerrard, Samantha Holland and Robert Shail (eds.), *Gender and Contemporary Horror in Television*

Robert Shail, Steven Gerrard and Samantha Holland (eds.), *Gender and Contemporary Horror in Comics, Games and Transmedia*

Samantha Holland, *Screen Heroines, Superheroines, Feminism and Popular Culture*

GENDER AND CONTEMPORARY HORROR IN FILM

EDITED BY

SAMANTHA HOLLAND
Leeds Beckett University, UK

ROBERT SHAIL
Leeds Beckett University, UK

STEVEN GERRARD
Leeds Beckett University, UK

United Kingdom – North America – Japan – India – Malaysia – China

Emerald Publishing Limited
Howard House, Wagon Lane, Bingley BD16 1WA, UK

First edition 2019

Reprints and permissions service
Contact: permissions@emeraldinsight.com

British Library Cataloguing in Publication Data
A catalogue record for this book is available from the British Library

ISBN: 978-1-78769-898-7 (Print)
ISBN: 978-1-78769-897-0 (Online)
ISBN: 978-1-78769-899-4 (Epub)

ISOQAR certified
Management System,
awarded to Emerald
for adherence to
Environmental
standard
ISO 14001:2004.

Certificate Number 1985
ISO 14001

INVESTOR IN PEOPLE

Contents

List of Contributors

Emilio Audissino (University of Southampton), a film scholar and a film music-ologist, holds one PhD in History of Visual and Performing Arts from the University of Pisa, Italy, and one PhD in Film Studies from the University of Southampton, UK. He specialises in Hollywood and Italian cinema, and his interests are film analysis, screenwriting, film style and technique, comedy, hor-ror, and film sound and music. He has published journal articles, book chapters, and encyclopedia entries on the history and analysis of films from the silent era to contemporary cinema. He has taught film history, technique and theory at the Universities of Genoa, Southampton, West London, and UNINT Rome. He is the author of the monograph *John Williams's Film Music: 'Jaws', 'Star Wars', 'Raiders of the Lost Ark' and the Return of the Classical Hollywood Music Style* (University of Wisconsin Press, 2014), the first book-length study in English on the composer, and the editor of the collection of essays *John Williams. Music for Films, Television and the Concert Stage* (Brepols, 2018). His book *Film/Music Analysis. A Film Studies Approach* (Palgrave Macmillan, 2017) concerns a method to analyse music in films that blends Neoformalism and Gestalt Psychology.

Irene Baena-Cuder graduated in Media and Communication from the University of Extremadura, Spain, in 2008, and after gaining some professional experience in this field, she achieved an MA in Gender Studies at the University of Huelva, Spain. She has recently completed her PhD in Film Studies at the University of East Anglia, UK, where she explored contemporary Spanish horror film from a gender perspective. Her research contributions include academic chapters and published articles studying issues of historical memory and Spanish Gothic, Spanish fascist identities, masculinity, representation of women as possessed monsters in contemporary Spanish horror film or the wider problematic representation of strong, independent women as monsters within this genre. She has worked as a Guest Lecturer at Glasgow Caledonian University, UK, and she currently teaches Film and Media studies at the University of East Anglia.

Fernando Gabriel Pagnoni Berns works at the Universidad de Buenos Aires (UBA) – Facultad de Filosofía y Letras (Argentina), as Professor in 'Literatura de las Artes Combinadas II'. He teaches seminars on international horror film. He is director of the research group on horror cinema 'Grite' and has published articles on Argentinian and international cinema and drama in the following publications: Imagofagia, Vita e Pensiero: Comunicazioni Sociali, Anagnórisis, Lindes and UpStage Journal among others. He has published chapters in the books *Horrors of War: The Undead on the Battlefield*, edited by Cynthia Miller, *To See the Saw Movies: Essays on Torture Porn and Post 9/11 Horror*, edited by John Wallis, *For His Eyes Only: The Women of James Bond*, edited by Lisa

Funnell, *Dreamscapes in Italian Cinema*, edited by Francesco Pascuzzi, *Reading Richard Matheson: A Critical Survey*, edited by Cheyenne Mathews, *Time-Travel Television*, edited by Sherry Ginn, *James Bond and Popular Culture*, edited by Michele Brittany, and *Deconstructing Dads: Changing Images of Fathers in Popular Culture*, edited by Laura Tropp, among others. Currently, he is writing a book about Spanish horror TV series *Historias para no Dormir*.

Hannah Bonner is in the PhD program in Film Studies at the University of Iowa, USA. She has an MA in Film Studies from The University of Iowa and a BA in English and Honors in Creative Writing from UNC-Chapel Hill. Finally, her chapter on the HBO show *Girls* in the anthology *HBO's Original Voices: Race, Gender, Sexuality and Power* from the publisher Routledge was published in 2018.

Joseph Brennan is an Independent Scholar working in Sydney, Australia. He writes on male sexuality in the fields of porn, fan, and celebrity studies, and his work has been published in leading scholarly journals. Joseph is currently editing a special issue on 'queerbaiting', to appear in the *Journal of Fandom Studies* in 2018, and is also assembling a book collection on the topic for a university press. He has worked previously as Lecturer of Media and Communications at the University of Sydney, where he received his PhD. He is editorial board member on the Routledge journal *Psychology & Sexuality*. Selected journals in which his work has appeared include: *International Journal of Cultural Studies, Porn Studies, Sexualities, Psychology & Sexuality, Sexuality & Culture, Disability & Society, Continuum, Celebrity Studies, Popular Communication, Discourse, Context & Media, Media International Australia, Journal of Fandom Studies* and *M/C Journal*.

Niall Brennan received his PhD from the London School of Economics and Political Science, UK, where he focused on representations of national culture, values and identity in the Brazilian television mini-series. His research continues to focus on Latin American television and film, as well as on representations of gender and sexuality in fiction and reality TV globally. Niall is an Assistant Professor in the Department of Communication at Fairfield University, USA.

Wickham Clayton is a Lecturer in Film History and Theory at the University for the Creative Arts in Farnham, UK. He is an editor of *Style and Form in the Hollywood Slasher Film* (2015) and a co-editor of *Screening Twilight: Critical Approaches to a Cinematic Phenomenon* (2014). Wickham's work focuses on film form and aesthetics, film genre (with some specialization in horror), the Biblical Epic and auteurist perspectives on the historical poetics of the films of Woody Allen.

Matthew Denny is a Teaching Fellow in the Department of Film and Television Studies at the University of Warwick, UK. He has recently completed a PhD on theories of authorship and postmodernism, and has previously conducted research on Hammer Horror.

Kath Dooley is a filmmaker and academic in the School of Media, Creative Arts & Social Inquiry at Curtin University, Australia. She completed a creative PhD exploring portrayals of the body in the work of contemporary French directors Claire Denis, Catherine Breillat and Marina de Van at Flinders University, South Australia, in 2014. Kath has written a number of short and feature length screenplays and has directed several award-winning short films and music videos. Her research interests include French cinema, screen production methodology, screenwriting and screen education.

Louise Flockhart graduated from the University of Dundee, UK, with an MA (Hons) in English Literature in 2013, and then with an MLitt in Gender, Culture and Society in 2014. She was awarded the Mary Ann Baxter award for excellence in the GCS MLitt. She was then awarded AHRC DTP funding to carry out her PhD at the University of Stirling, UK. Louise is currently in the middle of her doctoral studies, writing her thesis on representations of female cannibals in contemporary literature and film.

Diego Foronda is MA in Literature graduated at the Universidad de Buenos Aires (UBA) – Facultad de Filosofía y Letras (Argentina)-. He has published in *Representations of the Mother-in-Law in Literature, Film, Drama, and Television*, edited by Jo Parnell and *Critical Essays on Arthur Machen*, edited by Antonio Sanna.

Steven Gerrard is Senior Lecturer at The Northern Film School, Leeds Beckett University, UK. A firm fan of all things Low Culture, Steven has written two monographs entitled *The Carry On Films* (Palgrave Macmillan) and *The Modern British Horror Film* (Rutgers University Press). He is a co-editor of *Crank it up! Jason Statham – Star* and a series of books for Emerald Publishing on gender in horror.

Samantha Holland is a Senior Research Fellow at Leeds Beckett University, UK. Her research interests include gender, leisure, subcultures and popular culture. Her publications include *Alternative Femininities* (Berg, 2004); *Body, Age & Identity*; *Pole Dancing, Empowerment & Embodiment* (Palgrave Macmillan, 2010); and *Modern Vintage Homes & Leisure Lives: Ghosts & Glamour* (Palgrave Macmillan, 2018).

Frances A. Kamm is the Co-founder and Organizer of the Gothic Feminism project at the University of Kent, UK, and the co-editor of the forthcoming *Gothic Heroines on Screen*. Frances completed her PhD last year with her thesis entitled: 'The Technological Uncanny and the Representation of the Body in Early and Digital Cinema'. Her research interests include theories of the uncanny, the filmic body and visual effects technologies.

Zeynep Koçer is an Assistant Professor in the Department of Communication and Design at Istanbul Kültür University, Turkey. She teaches visual culture, film history and cultural studies. Koçer received her PhD in Visual and Cultural

Studies from I.D. Bilkent University. Her research areas are Turkish modernization and politics, cultural studies, reception studies and gender.

Maddi McGillvray is a PhD student in Cinema and Media Studies at York University, where she writes extensively on the horror genre. Maddi's other research interests include feminist film theory, transmedia studies, and exploitation cinema. Continuing her interest in gender and horror, Maddi is completing her doctoral dissertation on contemporary female horror filmmakers. In addition to her current research, Maddi is also writing a chapter titled "'Softness Have You Seen My Film?': The Women of the New French Extremity" for the edited collection *Women Make Horror*. She is also the Editorial Assistant at *Rue Morgue*, the world's leading horror in culture and entertainment magazine.

Shellie McMurdo is currently in the third year of doctoral research at the University of Roehampton, UK. Her thesis, titled 'Blood on the Lens: Found Footage Horror and the Terror of the Real' uses close critical analysis influenced by trauma theory to examine the rise in popularity of the found footage horror subgenre. In addition to her current research, Shellie has a forthcoming chapter in an edited collection on *American Horror Story* and is currently working on the proposal for a co-authored book on the mediation of the West Memphis Three case. Her wider research interests are trauma theory, torture horror, fandoms and transmedia.

Francesca Sobande is a Lecturer in Marketing and Advertising at Edge Hill University, UK, and is interested in the manifestation of intersecting issues concerning race and gender in popular culture. Her research foregrounds digital diasporic dynamics amidst the media marketplace experiences of Black women in Britain. Francesca has been involved in the organization of symposia, including *Examining Normativity in Consumer Culture and Labour Markets* (University of St Andrews) and is on the editorial team behind the forthcoming collection *To Exist is to Resist: Black Feminism in Europe*.

Introduction

Samantha Holland

At the very start of this project, I met my colleague Rob Shail for morning coffee and asked him if he would like to edit a book with me about gender in horror; specifically about what − if any − changes in gender representation in
horror films there have been. My idea was that such a book would tie in with
the themes of the new book series *Emerald Studies in Popular Culture and
Gender*, and its publication would launch the series. Shortly afterwards, we
recruited our friend and colleague Steve Gerrard as our third editor because of
his love for and knowledge of the horror genre. I tweeted a call for chapters and
we were overwhelmed by the positive response, receiving more than 80 abstracts
and expressions of interest, as well as supportive messages. This was many more
than we had anticipated (in fact, we had worried about whether we would
receive enough) and resulted in us being able to work on three separate volumes,
with each of us acting as lead editor for one volume: film, television and fandom
and other media. This, then, is the first volume which concentrates on film. The
books offer an overview of what is happening currently with gender in the horror genre; hopefully, they also begin a conversation. The reader can choose to
read just one of the three, or all three, in any order.

All three volumes focus on the horror genre since 1995, the year that the first
Scream film was released and the year that, arguably, horror films 'came back'.
Horror fans had suffered something of a drought in the 1980s, displaced by
action movies and 'musculinity', although admittedly this epoch resulted in
some strong iconic screen heroines such as Ellen Ripley, Sarah Connor and
Charlie Baltimore. But the *Scream* franchise (1996, 1997, 2000, and 2011) signalled a fruitful and lucrative new life for the genre, which still flourishes to
date. The horror genre is thriving because it is able to remain current. Film franchises such as *Saw*, *The Conjuring* and *The Purge* speak to different aspects of
our fears: horror is always based on contemporary anxieties and so will always
find new ways to tell those stories and new styles to do so. The conventions and
even the aesthetics of the horror movie will always be recognizable, such as the
lighting and the score, but horror will always be up to date. The slasher films of
the 1970s reflect perfectly the anxieties of the time, for example in the time of

Gender and Contemporary Horror in Film, 1−3
© **Samantha Holland**
All rights of reproduction in any form reserved
doi:10.1108/978-1-78769-897-020191001

the women's liberation movement there was *Black Christmas* (1974); and the rise of consumption and consumerism prompted *Dawn of the Dead* (1978). More recently, *The Blair Witch Project* (1999) was arguably the first film to use the format of found footage, combining the very modern (film cameras and smart-mouthed University students in grunge-inspired plaid) with the very ancient: the fear of the wilderness, of being lost and of being threatened by something unseen and evil. It doesn't matter how much tech you have if you have no signal for your GPS and you never learnt to read a map. Found footage has become a staple in the genre partly because horror has always responded to our fears and mapped them onto narratives about the domestic and the everyday.

The chapters in this book owe a great debt to Carol J. Clover and her conceptualization of the 'Final Girl' character in horror films – in fact, eight chapters out of 15 refer to Clover's work. As Clover (1992, p. 42) points out, in a horror film, we will fear for a woman more than for a man. Men are killed in horror films but are less likely to face the torture, the chase, the 'graphic detail' (Clover, 1992, p. 35) of the terror that the female protagonist has to face, because she is 'abject terror personified' (Clover, 1992) and in order to identify with her plight we must watch her endure it. Nonetheless, endure it she does and her survival – and the audience's identification with her, whether they are male or female – is a key element of the success of the horror genre.

Clover's concept of the Terrible Place is also an important theme in the chapters which follow, whether explicitly or implicitly, that place of nightmares where there is no escape. Horror begins by establishing normality, a house, a school, where daily life is uneventful. Very quickly that safe place becomes a place of terror, where the most homely space can no longer be trusted – who is in the closet? What is under the bed?

The chapters examine all the mainstays of the horror genre, with subjects ranging from werewolves and cannibals to ghosts and zombies – all using a 'gender lens' and interrogating what, if anything, has changed in representations of gender in contemporary horror. Is horror really all about a blonde girl trying to escape capture and torture? Sometimes, it is; often it is much more than that. Indeed, the authors discuss torture, and alongside that feminism, Black or ageing masculinities, social media and new technologies, patriarchy, gay porn and the Gothic, amongst many other things, proving that the term gender encompasses just about all things for all people. A mixture of world horror cinema is included, for example, from the US, Spain, France, Turkey and Latin America. As editors, we were keen to include established scholars but also emerging writers, and we wanted to ensure a fair mix of male and female authors.

The book is structured in three parts, which broadly capture the overarching concerns of the chapters within them, and the horror genre itself: they are "Bodies," "Boundaries" and "Captivity." These are subjects that reflect the danger, pain, change, challenge and suffocating terror experienced in horror, and without which horror could not function. Laura Mulvey (1989, p. 17) argues that film, especially the horror film, will 'focus attention on the human form'. In doing so we see how vulnerable our bodies are. So in Part I "Bodies," the chapters deal with the Final Girl (threats to her body and her physical agency), with masculinities (including the challenges of the aged body) and with the cannibal (who literally eats human bodies).

Part II "Boundaries" is about physical and imagined boundaries, which both are central to the horror genre. Horror films are full of people crossing boundaries, going places they shouldn't and doing things they will regret. How many times have you shouted at the screen 'don't go in there!' This part, then, includes chapters about ghosts, hauntings and vampires — but also about porn and social media, two spaces where boundaries are frequently crossed.

Finally, Part III "Captivity," looks at ideas about being trapped — whether in a place, or in your own body, reflecting decades of feminist work about the captivity of gender roles.

The authors set out to address the challenges and changes to be found in modern horror films around gender, and in doing so, they demonstrate the breadth and richness of the genre, and how it precisely mirrors our anxieties and preoccupations.

PART I
BODIES

Chapter 1

'It's So Easy to Create a Victim': Subverting Gender Stereotypes in the New French Extremity

Maddi McGillvray

> Man endures pain as an undeserved punishment; woman accepts
> it as a natural heritage.
> — Anonymous

The female victim has been a reoccurring cinematic image since the development of the medium. Not only has the female form become the conventional site of pain and suffering in film, but this correlation has also become particularly quintessential in the horror genre. Linda Williams notes this in 'Film Bodies: Gender, Genre, and Excess' (1991), arguing that genres such as horror, pornography, and melodrama hinge on the spectacle of a sexually saturated and victimized female body (Williams, 1991). Women have been at the centre of the horror genre since its origins (Dani, 2017). They are the last ones standing at the end, hunted and slaughtered by psychopathic killers, haunted and/or possessed, give birth to the monsters of such films, and in some rarer cases, they are even the monsters themselves. Nevertheless, misogynistic depictions of women have frequently appeared within the horror genre since its emergence. Starting with *Le Manoir du Diable* (Méliès, 1896), which is often cited as the first horror film, and continuing until today, the presence of gendered specific violence has been a recognizable trope throughout the history of horror cinema.

Despite such narratives, horror is one of cinema's most consistently popular and lucrative genres (Prince, 2004). Not only is horror experiencing what many are calling its 'golden age' with the critical success of films like *Get Out* (Peele, 2017), *It* (Muschietti, 2017), and *Hereditary* (Aster, 2018), but the popularity of television shows such as *The Walking Dead* (2010—present) and

Gender and Contemporary Horror in Film, 7—22
© **Maddi McGillvray**
All rights of reproduction in any form reserved
doi:10.1108/978-1-78769-897-020191002

American Horror Story (2011–present) also suggests that horror and images of violence and gore have become normalized elements of our media and viewing culture. As a result, more is required in order to shock and stimulate today's audiences. The last decade has seen the birth of extreme cinema, which is defined in the *Oxford Dictionary of Film Studies* as, 'a group of films that challenge codes of censorship and social mores, especially through explicit depictions of sex and violence, including rape and torture' (Kuhn & Westwell, 2012). This trend has not only seeped its way onto North American screens, but has also gained prominence among international markets as well. For instance, in North America, torture porn films such as *Saw* (Wan, 2004) and *Hostel* (Roth, 2005) have become contemporary franchises comparable to the *Friday the 13th* and *A Nightmare on Elm Street* series. Similarly, so-called 'Asia Extreme' films including *Audition* (Miike, 1999), *Ichi the Killer* (Miike, 2001) and *Oldboy* (Park, 2003), as well as 'European Extreme' shockers such as *A Serbian Film* (Spasojevic, 2010) and the American co-production *The Human Centipede* (Six, 2009), have also gained prominence in the global film market (Jennings, 2008, p. 5).

However, as scholar Erin Jennings states, 'nowhere is the surge of excess sex and violence in film more apparent than in France' (Jennings, 2008, p. 6). *Artforum* critic and programmer James Quandt coined the term 'New French Extremity' to describe the growing presence of extreme violence and sexual brutality in French films at the turn of the twenty-first century.[1] Referring to a series of transgressive films by French auteurs such as Gaspar Noé, Claire Denis, Bruno Dumont, and Catherine Breillat, Quandt cites the New French Extremity as, 'a cinema suddenly determined to break every taboo, to wade in rivers of visceral and spumes of sperm, to fill each frame with flesh, nubile or gnarled, and submit it to all manner of penetration, mutilation, and defilement' (Quandt, 2004). While Quandt initially wrote about the New French Extremity as an arthouse movement, in the years that followed, the title quickly become synonymous with horror films. Consequently, the New French Extremity has earned a reputation for eliciting excessive reactions from critics and audiences, including mass walkouts, fainting, and vomiting. Despite the vociferous reactions and controversies these films have elicited, they have had an undeniable impact on French cinema, as these films have both flourished nationally and continue to gain popularity beyond French borders.

At the centre of this cycle, as scholar Tim Palmer states, is an emphasis on human sexuality rendered in stark and graphic terms (Palmer, 2006a, 2006b, p. 58). The correlation between sex and violence is not exclusive to the New French Extremity, as France has a unique history of representing such themes in art. The New French Extremity extends a libertine tradition that includes the

---

[1]At the time of his article, Quandt labelled the New French Extremity as an art house 'movement'. That being said, the title has since been applied to an ongoing list of startling and deeply upsetting French horror films. This has led many critics and scholars to contend whether or not the New French Extremity is in fact a cinematic movement or a genre in and of itself.

writings of the Marquis de Sade and the films of Luis Buñuel, which used transgressive depictions of sexual violence to rouse society from its complacency. The New French Extremity's origins can also be traced back to a long history of violent theatrical performances, including the Grand Guignol — also known as the French Theatre of Horror — from Pigalle, Paris, which featured explicit, stomach-turning portrayals of carnage, sex, and death. More recently, the New French Extremity is also comparable with a wide range of horror subgenres including slasher, rape-revenge, and home invasion narratives. Scholars like Steve Jones and Alexandra West have also traced the relationship between the New French Extremity and torture porn[2] based on their shared themes of violence. Despite their overt similarities, West makes a point to differentiate the two subgenres by explaining that while similar, '[the former] are not violent films, but rather films about violence' (West, 2016, p. 6). Most influential, however, is the body horror subgenre and the work of Canadian filmmaker David Cronenberg.[3]

Despite its growing popularity among fans of the horror genre, the New French Extremity is not traditionally celebrated among critics and is often criticized for sensationalizing physical and sexual violence. As writer James Walker proclaims, 'The New French Extremity has no home in modern cinema, that much is clear. Speculation of the New French Extremity transforming into a European Extremity, and a subsequent new breed of horror movies altogether is an idea nothing short of farfetched in my mind' (Walker, 2013). Quandt is also among many who consider this display of sex and violence to be of little substance, summarizing this group of films as, 'aggressiveness that is really a grandiose form of passivity' (Quandt, 2004). Palmer also sheds light on the condemning attitudes towards the New French Extremity claiming, 'Contemporary French cinema is today catalysing a new wave of controversy. In particular, a part of recent French films that deal frankly and graphically with corporeal transgressions has provoked an international scrutiny at times bordering on hysteria' (Palmer, 2006a, 2006b, p. 171). These unfavourable critiques are problematic because as Jennings posits, 'issues of gender and

---

[2]Since David Edelstein's 2006 *New York* article 'Now Playing at Your Local Multiplex: Torture Porn', the term has been applied to a wealth of films since the early 2000s. While the title itself has been heavily debated, the subgenre is marked by its gratuitous imagery of violence, gore and bodily torture. Edelstein contends that torture porn films relish in the sensational sights they can provide audiences, comparing the splatter of blood to the 'money shot' in pornography.

[3]The films of the New French Extremity are often compared to Cronenberg's films and their similar fascinations with the horrors of bodily corporeality. However, one of the largest departures between the New French Extremity and Cronenberg's filmography is the treatment of women and the female body. Unlike the New French Extremity, which places strong emphasis on the female experience, Cronenberg's narratives focus heavily upon male protagonists. While Cronenberg's earlier films such as *The Brood* (1979) and *Dead Ringers* (1988) deal with the monstrous female body as a site of disgust, his protagonists are almost always men, resulting in the subordination of female agency to the male perspective.

representation are almost never discussed, as critics often become too engrossed in the spectacles of violence to imagine anything else going on' (Jennings, 2008, p. 6). My chapter will therefore address this gap in literature by examining the potential feminist implications of two of the most popular titles to emerge out of the New French Extremity catologue: Alexandre Bustillo and Julien Maury's *Inside* (2007) (original French title: *À L'intérieur*) and Pascale Laugier's *Martyrs* (2008).[4]

In the New French Extremity, severe acts of violence are commonly inflicted upon women. In some cases, these are even performed by the female characters themselves. As a result, the New French Extremity often provokes fierce responses, leading some to claim that they are just spectacles of sexism. For instance, in an online review of *Martyrs* R.J. Sayer posted a comment claiming, 'MARTYRS is a FASCIST film. A MISOGYNIST, FASCIST film' (Hall, 2008). *Inside* and *Martyrs* both push the limits of obscenity and present dizzying images of violence performed upon the female body. What is specific to these two films are their particular representations of victimhood, which explicitly centre upon the wounded and suffering female body. Through a close textual analysis of *Inside* and *Martyrs*, my discussion will demonstrate that while collectively these films are preoccupied with female suffering, their narratives also offer internal criticisms of the misogynistic portals of victimhood that are prevalent in the genre. The violence performed on or by the women of these films is not pleasurable nor is it designed to excite the spectator. Rather, these works can be understood as pushing the limit of what the female body can tolerate in order to situate the female protagonists in a position of power to overwhelm and consume patriarchy.

1.1. Yuletide Terror: *Inside* (2007)

Inside opens with an image of a foetus inside of a womb. Suddenly, it is disturbed by an outside force, which is revealed to be a car crash involving expectant mother Sarah (Alysson Paradis) and her husband Matthieu (Jean-Baptiste Tabourin), who is killed on impact. The film cuts to several months later where Sarah is spending Christmas Eve alone preparing for an induced birth the next day. Her loved ones all try to support her, but she refuses their offers of help, instead asking her employer Jean-Pierre (François-Régis Marchasson) to drive her to the hospital the following morning. That evening, a mysterious woman credited only as La Femme (Béatrice Dalle) arrives at Sarah's door asking to

---

[4]Quandt associates films such as *Sombre* (Grandrieux, 1998), *Pola X* (Carax, 1999), *Baise-moi* (Despets and Thi, 2000), *Trouble Every Day* (Denis, 2001), *Intimacy* (Chéreau, 2001), *Irreversible* (Noé, 2002), *In My Skin* (de Van, 2002), *Secret Things* (Brisseau, 2002), *La Chatte à Deux Têtes* (Nolot, 2002), and *Haute Tension* (Aja, 2003) as a representative sample of films that fall into the New French Extremity. More recent films such as *Calvaire* (Du Welz, 2004), *Sheitan* (Chapiron, 2006), *Frontier(s)* (Gens, 2007), *Inside* (Bustillo & Maury, 2007), *Martyrs* (Laugier, 2008), *Raw* (Ducournau, 2016) and more also fall into the New French Extremity category.

use her phone. When Sarah refuses, La Femme announces that she knows Sarah's name and about the death of her husband. Sarah calls the police who arrange to have a patrol car visit throughout the night. When Sarah falls back to sleep, La Femme appears in her bedroom and tries to remove her unborn baby with scissors. Sarah manages to escape and locks herself in the bathroom, where La Femme torments her throughout the night. When police officers arrive as promised, La Femme answers the door and convinces them that she is Sarah and that everything is fine.[5] Just as they are about to leave, an officer realizes the woman who answered the door was not pregnant as was described by the dispatcher. They enter the home, but are swiftly murdered one by one by La Femme. In a surprise twist, La Femme reveals that she was in the other car during the accident and lost her unborn child. Desperate to take Sarah's baby as her own, La Femme performs a caesarean section on Sarah, who dies in the process. The film closes on a chilling image of a badly bruised and burned La Femme, having been successful with the delivery, cradling the newborn in her arms.

Inside begins with a narrative that is common to the horror genre: a woman being hunted by a psychopathic killer. Yet, Bustillo and Maury do not present the typical male aggressor/female victim dichotomy that one might expect. Instead, they deviate from this trope by offering a violent frenzy of female on female violence.[6] In keeping with the home invasion subgenre, there are several unsettling moments where the audience witnesses La Femme's figure slip in and out of view of Sarah's windows without her noticing. La Femme embodies all of the characteristics of a typical horror villain: she hunts and stalks her prey, she torments Sarah with physical and psychological violence, and she even penetrates Sarah's body with a sharp, phallic weapon. However, to have them delivered by a woman is one of the film's most subversive achievements (Burton, 2014). In a 2008 interview with *Rue Morgue*, Bustillo cited his friend's experience with pregnancy as the inspiration for the film, stating:

> A friend of mind was pregnant and I asked myself what a pregnant woman alone at home at night would feel [...] My first idea

---

[5] Politics are embedded within the background of *Inside*, and centre around this plot point. Police officers arrive at Sarah's house, despite the race related riots that are occurring in the Paris suburbs. The film makes brief references to the riots throughout, especially through Sarah's occupation as a journalist. When the squad car arrives to check on Sarah after La Femme's attacks, they have a young Muslim man in their custody who they arrested during the riots.

[6] While *Inside* is a fictional narrative, there has been a measurable increase in real world foetal abductions in which an attacker (typically a woman) attempts to remove a child from its mother by performing a makeshift/impromptu caesarean section, often killing the mother in the process. These types of horrific crime stories are more common than one might think. Unheard of before 1987, there have now been over 13 such cases recorded in the United States alone and the number continues to rise. Research is currently being conducted to understand the motivations and psychological reasons for the phenomena and the surge of these gruesome crimes in recent years.

was to have a struggle between the pregnant woman and a serial
killer who hunted her to eat her placenta. But it was too basic;
like every slasher movie with a fucking bad guy on one side and a
poor innocent girl on the other. Changing the sex of the boogy-
man was more interesting, more original, a struggle for real life.
(Andrews, 2008, pp. 16–21)

In having a female perpetrator, *Inside* not only rejects common horror film conventions, but Bustillo and Maury also dissociate the violence portrayed in the
film from the very real and problematic discourse of domestic abuse and male
violence against women.

In spite of this, Sarah is by no means a likeable character that the audience
could emotionally identify with or perhaps even root for. At first glance, one
might want to identify with her in a similar vein as the 'Final Girl' (Clover,
1992).[7] She is the film's victim-hero and the audience watches her as she repeatedly tries to fight back against La Femme's attacks; but Sarah is cold and distant
throughout the film, preferring to isolate herself from friends and family – as
well as the audience. One particularly disturbing moment is when Sarah accidentally kills her mother. Wanting to check up on her daughter before her delivery,
Sarah's mother enters the home to find Jean-Pierre, who has just been convinced
that La Femme was Sarah's mother. Concerned, she runs up the stairs to look
for Sarah, who is hiding in the bathroom. Assuming the footsteps belong to La
Femme, Sarah blindly stabs the figure behind the door only to realize that it is
her mother. Surprisingly, Sarah does not shed a single tear in this heartbreaking
moment. In fact, she does not cry for the entirety of the film. Instead, she faintly
mutters the word 'Mommy' under her breath as she witnesses her mother's
blood spatter across the wall (West, 2016, p. 167). This moment creates a sense
of unease for the viewer, as it unclear whether Sarah is in shock or if this
moment is indicative of her aloof demeanour.

Bustillo and Maury further emphasize Sarah's unlikeability by presenting her
as a mother who does not want her own child. As West notes, 'Sarah's physicality epitomizes the desired mother. She is financially stable, attractive, and
gainfully employed. She is exactly the type society desires to be a mother'
(West, 2016, p. 167). Nevertheless, Sarah appears disinterested and even resent-
ful towards her unborn child. Something as routine as a doctor's visit seems like

---

[7]Carol Clover's influential *Men, Women, and Chainsaws: Gender in the Modern Horror
Film* examines the representation of the surviving female character in the horror genre,
otherwise referred to as the 'Final Girl'. The Final Girl is easily identifiable as the film's
protagonist, as the audience follows her as she fights back against the monster that
threatens her. Clover identifies several characteristics that are attributed to the Final
Girl, arguing that she is often more resourceful, levelheaded, watchful, mechanical, masculine and, most importantly, not sexually active. Despite the fact that slasher films
seem to offer sadistic pleasure to the viewer, Clover argues that they are structurally
engineered to align spectators not with the male monster, but with the Final Girl.

a nuisance to Sarah, and her pregnant belly merely serves as a haunting reminder of her deceased husband and the life she wanted to create with him. In *The Monstrous-Feminine: Film, Feminism, Psychoanalysis* (1993), theorist Barbara Creed critiques the gender politics of the horror film. One of Creed's central arguments is that feminine monstrosity in horror is directly linked to the reproductive and mothering female body. Using psychoanalysis, Creed reflects upon the conflict that exists within the mother–child relationship and argues that while the child typically struggles to break free from the maternal hold, the mother is often reluctant to release it (Creed, 1993, p. 11). *Inside* takes this notion a step further by presenting Sarah as a mother who rejects her child before it is even born. This is highly unimaginable, since society commonly associates the maternal figure as a site of unconditional love. In this way, Sarah embodies the societal pressures women face to fulfil their desired roles as mothers. It is Sarah's body and her choice to do with it what she wants, and yet, her disinterested feelings about her pregnancy also make her a cold-hearted monster. Patriarchal society may desire her to be a mother, but why should she?

Instead, it is the film's supposed villain that desperately wants the child. Eliot Burton notes that it is exceptionally rare that a horror villain, whether male or female, is portrayed with more tangible emotions than the protagonist (Burton, 2014). The film's twist ending reveals that La Femme's psychotic behaviour stems from the trauma she *also* experienced in the car accident. Although Sarah and La Femme are both grieving the loss of their loved ones, they are opposites in almost every other way. One is a villain and the other is a victim; one is cloaked in black and the other dons a white nightgown; one is without a child and the other is heavily pregnant; and finally, one desperately wishes to be a mother and the other does not. The spectator, therefore, becomes more inclined to sympathize with La Femme because she is a mother who is unable to cope with the loss of her child. In this sense, the extreme violence perpetrated by La Femme seems to be more meaningful and almost rationalized. Le Femme is everything a modern woman is not supposed to be, and yet, under patriarchal culture, she may end up the hero for killing the 'unnatural' non-maternal woman.

As the battle rages between Sarah and La Femme, *Inside* investigates what the female body as the site of life can tolerate. One of the ways Bustillo and Maury approach this is by visually illustrating the liminal space between the mother's body and the foetus. *Inside* begins within the maternal body and transitions outwards. The opening credits roll over red fluids, which transitions into a shot of a gestating foetus accompanied by a voice-over saying, 'No one can take you away from me.'[8] From this moment on, the camera is able to penetrate the boundary between the inside and outside of Sarah's womb throughout the rest of the film. This connection is solidified

---

[8]In the film's opening, the audience is lead to believe that the voiceover belongs to Sarah, as the camera quickly transitions to the outside world and the interior of her car during the accident. However, once the film's twist is revealed, the voice could also be interpreted as belonging to La Femme, who is the more maternal figure.

when Sarah experiences violent trauma that directly affects the inside of her womb. In the first scene where La Femme tries to take Sarah's baby, the camera shows her piercing Sarah's stomach with the blade of her scissors. The camera then cuts to a shot of the foetus struggling inside her during the assault. This act reveals the notion that the two are united. Any harm or damage that is done to Sarah may also directly impact the life of the unborn child. As West states, 'Sarah is not merely an incubator for the unborn child, but its only chance at survival' (West, 2016, p. 166). In the film's climax, Sarah goes into labour after hours of prolonged abuse. Although she attempts to give birth naturally, Sarah comes to the realization that she must allow La Femme to cut the foetus out of her. It is at this moment that Sarah's attitude towards motherhood appears to shift: she is now willing to sacrifice her own life in order to give her unborn child a chance at survival. Sarah makes a martyr of herself; an act that restores the film's balance by freeing both women from their grief. La Femme now has the child she believes to be rightfully hers, and in doing so, Sarah is no longer suffering with the pain she was carrying − both literally and figuratively.

Despite being directed by two male filmmakers, *Inside* centres entirely upon female characters. Although some men are present in the film, they are either positioned as secondary characters or are quickly expelled from the narrative completely. For instance, the film begins with a substantial dismissal of patriarchal norms with the death of Sarah's husband who dies in the car crash in the opening sequence and only appears in the rest of the film through brief flashbacks. While Matthieu's absence lingers over the film, the male character with the most screen time is Sarah's employer Jean-Pierre. The two share some sort of ambiguous romantic relationship, and he even stops by Sarah's home after La Femme's initial visit to ensure she is all right. However, La Femme easily manipulates Jean-Pierre and proceeds to stab him to death before he can do anything about it. *Inside* is also one of the few horror films where police officers are not only present, but they show up multiple times to ensure Sarah's protection. Nevertheless, La Femme simply murders anyone who comes to Sarah's aid. Not only is La Femme disposing of all of the male characters in the film, but they are police officers and corporate businessmen. This works to present an erasure of the most extreme form of patriarchy: the authoritative male. Rather than simply forwarding the damsel in distress trope, which is still heavily utilized in mainstream cinema, *Inside* is progressive in the way it removes all of Sarah's safeguards (West, 2016, p. 168), forcing her to fight back on her own against her aggressor.

The degree of Sarah's fight is visually illustrated through her physical transformation during the film. In the beginning, Bustillo and Maury emphasize Sarah's beauty and innocence, positioning her as a kind of contemporary Virgin Mary archetype. Scholar Ashley Nunes highlights the significance of Sarah's nightgown in these early moments: 'she wears a white a nightgown. The white signifies her cleanliness, her purity [...]' (Nunes, 2012). Yet as the film progresses, Sarah's body transforms into an abject and unclean space. For instance, Sarah has a grotesque nightmare where she starts profusely vomiting milky white fluids and an infant-like figure. Shortly thereafter, when La Femme is tormenting Sarah from outside of the bathroom, her water breaks and causes a clear discharge to pour onto the floor. In her discussion of the maternal body as the site of abject horror, Creed suggests that it is the mother who educates the child about practices of defilement and the proper and improper body (Creed, 1993, p. 12). Creed relates this to toilet training as a primal mapping of the body, which teaches children about waste and excrement. By the end of the film, Sarah's porcelain white skin is coated in bright red blood and fluids; her internal organs are now visible. Her suburban home transforms into a living womb, much like the one in the opening credits, with its blood-soaked walls and darkened interior (West, 2016, p. 168). This not only rejects the basic orders and rules that are established by the mother in infancy through toilet training, but signifies Sarah's agency. Although Bustillo and Maury present a narrative that is common to the genre, Sarah has not been made into a victim in the traditional sense. She confronts and almost defeats her oppressor, and the only reason why she finally capitulates to La Femme is to safely deliver her child.

1.2. Manufacturing Victims: *Martyrs* (2008)

Martyrs premiered during the 2008 Cannes Film Festival and sparked media outrage for its unflinching depictions of violence and gore. News stories widely reported that during the 2008 Toronto International Film Festival's Midnight Madness screening, at least one moviegoer passed out during the film and another vomited in the lobby.[9] *Martyrs* begins with the story of Lucie (Jessie Pham), a young girl who escapes from an abandoned warehouse where she is being abused and tortured by a group of unidentified French elites. After being placed in an orphanage by authorities, she befriends a young girl named Anna (Erika Scott). During their friendship, Anna discovers that Lucie is tormented by a demon (Isabelle Chasse) that is only visible to Lucie. The film then transitions to fifteen years later, where Lucie (Mylène Jampanoï) believes she has found her previous torturers living in the French countryside; she barges into their home and brutally murders everyone with a shotgun, including two children. After committing the murders, Lucie calls Anna (Morjana Alaoui) and convinces her to help bury the bodies in the family's backyard. While Anna hides the corpses, the demon reappears and torments Lucie to the point that she commits suicide. As Anna is left alone to deal with Lucie's crimes, she uncovers

---

[9]This controversy also impacts the film's distribution. The French Commission de Classification des Oeuvres Cinématographiques granted *Martyrs* an 18+ rating, which defined the film as unsuitable for children under 18 or forbidden in cinemas for under 18. The producers of the film appealed and the French Society of Film Directors (SRF) asked the French ministry of culture to examine the decision, remarking that, 'this is the first time a French genre film has been threatened with such a rating'. The Minister of Culture, Christine Albanel, eventually asked the Commission of Classification to change its rating, which was done in July 2008. *Martyrs* was finally rated 16+, which allowed for wider distribution and circulation.

an underground corridor where she finds a horribly disfigured woman credited as 'The Creature' (Emilie Miskdjian) wearing a metal helmet drilled into her skull. Anna attempts to save the woman, but strangers enter into the home and immediately shoot her. Anna then becomes captured by the strangers, who belong to a secret Society controlled by the leader they refer to as Mademoiselle (Catherine Bégin). Mademoiselle informs Anna of their goal to discover the secrets of the afterlife through the process of transfiguration. Anna is then held captive by the society and after days of relentless torture, a doctor surgically removes Anna's skin and places her alive under a heating vent. Anna miraculously survives and achieves transfiguration. Upon realizing this outcome, the overjoyed Mademoiselle asks her if she has seen the other world. Anna whispers into Mademoiselle's ear, but the audience is unable to hear what she says. As the society gathers to hear Mademoiselle's account of the event, she commits suicide as she whispers her final words, 'keep doubting'.

Laugier explicitly incorporates female victimization into the diegesis of his film. Mademoiselle determines that transfiguration can only be achieved through the young female body, all of which attempts failed with Lucie. When Anna is first captured by the society, Mademoiselle shows her several pictures of historical accounts of martyrdom. She then states, 'We've tried everything. Even children. It's proven that women are more sensitive for a transformation. Young women. It is that way.' *Martyrs* has been frequently linked to the torture porn subgenre and films such as *Hostel* and *Saw*. Despite this, Laugier contends that *Martyrs* as anti-*Hostel*, stating, 'the film doesn't talk about torture - it talks about the pain' (Carnevale, 2008). While visceral, *Martyrs* does not present torture as a spectacle for the eyes in the same vein as its torture porn counterparts. *Martyrs* is profoundly despairing and nihilistic in tone, and it never encourages viewers to relish or enjoy its painful scenes (Hawkes, 2016). Instead, it focuses on the experiences of these women and how they are dealing with the pain of their situations. Each woman has her own psychosis or reactions to the violence: Lucie sees a demon, the woman in the cellar believes that bugs are crawling on her skin, and as we later find out, Anna hears Lucie's voice speaking to her (West, 2016, p. 160–161). Such an approach does not relish in their victimization, nor does it make a spectacle of it. Instead, *Martyrs* depicts the very real psychological trauma that comes from being a victim of violence (West, 2016, p. 159).

Carol J. Clover was one of the first to identify the limited number of roles available for women in horror, which according to Molly Langill in turn have 'created stereotypes around gender and sexuality' (Langill, 2014). That being said, *Martyrs* contains no sexuality, and any female nudity that occurs in the film is not intended to excite or titillate. Lucie and Anna are both racialized characters that do not fit the typical dumb big-breasted blonde tropes that one might expect to find in a slasher film. Instead, guilt and compassion emerge as the film's prominent themes and female character traits. For instance, through the use of objective and subjective shots, it is revealed that the demon who haunts Lucie is not real, but a manifestation of her guilt for not being able to save another girl who was enslaved with her as a child. This theme of guilt forms a crucial link to the French film *Les Yeux Sans Visage* (Franju, 1960), which is about a physician who kidnaps young women and performs medical experiments on them in an effort to find a successful facial transplant donor for his daughter (Totaro, 2009). The extreme acts the doctor takes, much like Lucie's murderous rage against the family, stems from his guilt over an accident he caused that disfigured his daughter. Writer Donato Totaro ties Lucie's guilt to France's National guilt over the Vichy regime and their collaboration with the Nazis (Torato, 2009). Whereas women in horror have been frequently represented as screaming, crying, cowering, and, above all, weaker than their male counterparts, Lucie distorts previous misogynistic gender binaries. Not only is the monster that torments her female, but also she has manifested this creature in her mind purely out of guilt. Rather than simply admitting defeat, Lucie takes action to tries to rid herself of her past traumas, even if that action is to ultimately commit suicide.

By the same token, Anna's character can be read in correlation with Nancy Chodorow's book *The Reproduction of Mothering: Psychoanalysis and the Sociology of Gender* (1999). Chodorow contends that there is an important difference between the processes of identification in female and male infants. For boys, the process of identification is based on differentiation and separation. Initially the boy identifies with the mother, but when the boy becomes aware of the sexual difference and is forced by the father to separate from his mother, he must reject her as an object of identification (Chodorow, 1999, p. 174). In contrast, the identity of the girl is formed through a process of multiple identifications. The girl initially identifies with the mother, but when she shifts her attention towards the father, she can continue to identify entirely with her mother, whom she recognizes as being like her and unlike her (Chodorow, 1999, p. 100). Chodorow argues that the woman's sense of self is based on a continuity of this relationship that ultimately prepares her for an empathic role of a mother who can identify with all of her children (Chodorow, 1999, p. 174). Anna is arguably one of the most empathetic women to emerge in the genre in recent years. She finds herself in the cult's home because she holds feelings for Lucie and wants to help her escape her troubled past. It is not just her friend that she cares for, but complete strangers as well. After Lucie commits suicide, Anna finds The Creature in the home's cellar. She cares for her and even attempts to relieve her of her pain by removing the helmet drilled into her skull. It is this desire to help Lucie and the woman that directly results in Anna's capture. This defies traditional representations of femininity in horror because Anna becomes more than a one-dimensional victim. Anna is not dimwitted, nor does she do anything to warrant what happens to her in the film's final act. Instead, she is a genuinely good person whose compassion and care for other women that directly seals her fate.

Martyrs also departs from the subgenre in its treatment of torture as a means of achieving what Mademoiselle calls 'transfiguration'. Transfiguration is the moment when the body, through extreme physical suffering, moves beyond awareness of the physical world to see what lies beyond death (Torato, 2009). The martyr, according to Mademoiselle, gives themselves up to the pain to transcend themselves and achieve transfiguration (Torato, 2009). This concept is heavily explored in the second half of the film. Before Anna is skinned alive and eventually reaches transfiguration, the members of the society shackle her to a chair, shave her head, force her to excrement into a bucket, eat green slop, and subject her to daily beatings. This leaves her face horribly bruised and disfigured. The most difficult scene to watch in the film is when a male member of the society repeatedly punches Anna in the face. All of the previous torture sessions are handled in brief sequences followed by a cut to black (Tobias, 2010). This sequence, in contrast, feels like it is the longest of all of the stages Anna must overcome before the removal of her skin. The camera is fixed on Anna and solely focuses on what she is going through. As the unnamed man is assaulting her, melodic music begins to play. Anna then hears Lucie's voice, which tells her that she does not need to be afraid anymore. It is here where the connection to an object or purpose starts to disappear and the distinction between subject and object no longer exists. Any resemblance to human life or femininity is shattered. Anna no longer resists her abusers, nor does she seem to be affected by the pain. Instead, she succumbs herself to the fate that awaits her. She is alive, but has completely let go. The departure of the subject and object divide brings about a collapse in meaning, one that is particularly engendered by masculine subjectivity.

The formal elements of the film's climax where Anna is skinned alive also confront the audience about their voyeuristic tendencies in relation to gore, violence, and representations of human suffering on screen. This sequence begins when one of the members of the Society calls Mademoiselle and states, 'I have never seen an expression like it. She's let go, completely let go. Her face is like […] her eyes […] I swear she no longer sees anything around her.' Anna's face is framed through a close up at eye-level, causing her to stare directly into the eye of the camera for several seconds. This moment serves to complicate traditions of the oppressive male gaze, which is detailed in Laura Mulvey's iconic essay 'Visual Pleasure and Narrative Cinema' (1975). Mulvey determines that pleasure in looking in Hollywood cinema is split between active males and passive females. She argues that the female appearance in cinema is coded for, 'strong visual and erotic impact and connotes a to-be-looked-at-ness', whereas the camera and the male viewer are constituted as the 'bearer of the look' (Mulvey, 1975, p. 11). In this moment, Anna addresses the viewer, viewing them as they view her. Her returned gaze in this sequence disrupts traditional horror cinema conventions and offers a critical feminist stance. While the second half of the film documents Anna's abuse and the surrender of her subjectivity, the film pauses and returns the gaze on the spectator in a moment of extreme violence and anguish. Since this image of Anna's face and piercing blue eyes is held for several seconds, it creates the impression that Anna herself is begging the audience to stop watching. Anna's look becomes a vehicle to indirectly confront the viewer and question their desire to voyeuristically observe such disturbing and graphic imagery from a safe distance.

The removal of Anna's hair and skin also defeminizes her, making her appear more monstrous than human. Although Anna is still coded as the object of the gaze, she is not represented as having erotic impact for the pleasure of the male viewer. Instead, her appearance induces disgust and repulsion. Rather than enjoying the gore and violence from a safe masochistic distance, the audience is forced into close proximity with Anna and indirectly experiences the torture alongside her. As writer Rebecca Hawkes states, 'audiences are encouraged to identify wholly with Anna, responding to her humanity and suffering along with her' (Hawkes, 2016). This serves to position the audience as both victim of and complicit in the violence being entrusted upon her. This climactic scene also defuses Mulvey's argument that the way the female body is '[...] stylized and fragmented by close-ups [making her] the direct recipient of the spectators look' (Mulvey, p. 14). Although the female body is captured through close-ups, it is precisely through this framing that Anna, as well as the film, transitions from an object to be looked at, to the bearer of the look. This framing offers feminist potential because, as Linda Williams determines, the woman's look in horror is threatening to male power (Williams, 1996, p. 36). As the spectators, and especially male viewers, witness Anna's martyrdom as anguish that forces her to give up on subjectivity, they too lose their comfortable sense of self. This causes the traditionally stable masculine position to crumble and dissolve under the pressure of the reversed gaze of the defeminized female body.

Martyrs is similar to *Inside* in the way it works to present a form of erased patriarchy. Since the release of films like *The Exorcist* (Friedkin, 1973), *The Omen* (Donner, 1976) and *Rosemary's Baby* (Polanski, 1968), horror seemed like the ideal setting for the dismantling of religion (West, 2016, p. 160). However, West argues that more often than not these religious-themed horror films tend to reaffirm the importance of Christianity and its patriarchal structure as a tool to restore order (West, 2016, p. 160). The images of Anna's shaved head recall France's most famous heroine, that of martyred Joan of Arc. However, *Martyrs* is not only a condemnation of religion, but also of its patriarchal systemic order (West, 2016, p. 160–161). As West states, 'the audience sees the before, after, and current effects of the lengths to which this secret society will go to achieve their goal' (West, 2016, p. 160). Lucie also eradicates a similar patriarchal condition when she murders the bourgeois family she believes are her previous torturers. Her victims reflect the stereotypical nuclear family and consist of a mother, father and two children. We know nothing about them and they become objectified in the sense that they act as superficial symbols of the family. Laugier also avoids populating his film with patriarchal male characters. It is not a man who is able to save Anna and help her overcome the pain she is enduring, but her love and friendship with Lucie. Much like *Inside*, the few men who are included in the narrative die almost immediately. The characters in the film are also all operating under the control of Mademoiselle's authority. This is significant because although there are male characters within the society, they also act under the control of a god-like woman. *Martyrs* offers feminist potential by presenting a female centred world that interrogates conventional gender hierarchies. The film illustrates a battle between the will of both Mademoiselle and Anna, emphasizing the power and determination of the female form. Laugier chooses not to cut away from the abuse, but instead to present it through closeness. He distorts the female body itself, until it loses all hints of the feminine and its connotations and ability to give life (Green, 2011).

The film contains images analogous to those associated with the monstrous-feminine, but they do not exist to pleasure the viewer.

1.3.   Conclusion

While audiences may have become comfortable with images of violence and gore in film and television, the methods used in the New French Extremity are still highly controversial. In particular, the filmic texts I have discussed depict the defilement of the female form in ways that are commonly deemed unacceptable in mainstream cinema. Although at first glance *Inside* and *Martyrs* focus upon wounded and suffering female bodies, I have argued that such texts also offer empowering tendencies because they interrogate tropes of female victimhood in the genre. Horror films, particularly those about masked men wielding deadly weapons, often have a roster of stereotypical female victims. Filmmaker Jean Wexler lists some of these tropes in an interview with BBC. She states, 'The bimbo, the party girl [...] who is one of the characters who's going to get slashed and killed right away [...] And then one that's reading a book so she's going to be the Final Girl who survives to the end' (BBC, 2015). Moreover, in an online forum, 'Tired Hiker' provided the typical misogynistic explanation for the phenomenon stating, 'females are good lead roles for horror films, probably because mostly guys go to see horror films, and guys usually want to see hot chicks. Plus, chicks can scream better than guys, they are more vulnerable than guys, and they tend to have nicer breasts and asses than guys' (*Killer Movies*, 2006). Although *Inside* and *Martyrs* seemingly begin with a narrative that is common to the horror genre, both offer a glaring departure from Wexler and Tired Hiker's descriptions.

Both films deviate from the male monster/female victim dichotomy by offering ultra-violent scenes of female on female violence that removes gender hierarchies altogether. Although the women of these films may start off vulnerable, they take charge of their situations, while also complicating the nature of feminine identity. At the same time as these films present upsetting images of women being victimized, tortured, and killed, they are also strong, compelling, and non-normative characters. Neither Sarah nor Anna barely let out a scream during their violent ordeals, something that is highly uncommon in the genre. They have not been made into a victim in the traditional sense. Both women confront and almost defeat their oppressors, and the only reason why they succumb to their fate is to take on the role as martyr figures. Both films use the stereotyping of female victims in horror and offer an internal criticism of it. Male characters are either absent or dispelled at the beginning of the narratives, presenting a systematic erasure of patriarchy. While the victimization of women is made a spectacle of in the horror genre through facial close-ups of terrified women, these texts collectively challenge such misogynistic filmic techniques in the ways they interrogate modes of visuality. *Inside* and *Martyrs* offer a reappropriation of victimhood, and thus, their cinematic approaches to female corporeality cannot simply be dismissed as masochistic female victimization.

References

American Horror Story. Creators Brad Falchuk and Ryan Murphy. 20th Century Fox Television. [Television]. 2011–present.

Andrews, S. (2008). Enfants terribles. *Rue Morgue*, 16–21.

Audition. Dir. Takashi Miike. *Basara Pictures.* 1999.

A Serbian Film. Dir. Srdjan Spasojevic. *Contra film.* 2010.

Baise-moi. Dir. Virginie Despentes and Coralie Trinh Thi. Canal+. 2000.

Burton, E. (2014). Control of the knife: Transgressing gender stereotypes in Bustillo and Maury's inside. *Offscreen*, *18*(6–7). Retrieved from http://offscreen.com/view/control-of-the-knife

Calvaire. Dir. Fabrice du Welz. La Parti Productions. 2004.

Carnevale, R. (2008). Martyrs – Pascal Laugier interview. *Indie London*. Retrieved from http://www.indielondon.co.uk/Film-Review/martyrs-pascal-laugier-interview.

Chodorow, N. (1999). *The reproduction of mothering: Psychoanalysis and the sociology of gender.* Los Angeles, CA: University of California Press.

Clover, C. J. (1992). Her body, himself. *Men women and chainsaws: Gender in the modern horror film* (pp. 21–64). Princeton, NJ: Princeton University Press.

Creed, B. (1993). *The monstrous-feminine: Film, feminism, and psychoanalysis.* New York, NY: Routledge.

Frontier(s). Dir. Xavier Gens. Cartel Productions. 2007.

Get Out. Dir. Jordan Peele. Blumhouse Productions. 2017.

Green, A. M. (2011). The French horror film martyrs and the destruction, defilement, and neutering of the female form. *Journal of Popular Film and Television*, *39*(1), 20–28.

Hall, P. (2008). Review: MARTYRS. *Horror's not dead.* Retrieved from http://horrorsnotdead.com/wpress/2009/review-martyrs/.

Haute Tension. Dir. Alexandre Aja. Alexandre Films. 2003.

Hawkes, R. (2016). Why Pascal Laugier's Martyrs is the greatest horror film of the 21st century. *The Telegraph*. Retrieved from https://www.telegraph.co.uk/film/what-to-watch/martyrs-2008-pascal-laugier/

Hereditary. Dir. Ari Aster. PalmStar. 2018.

Hostel. Dir. Eli Roth. Hostel LLC. 2005.

Ichi The Killer. Dir. Takashi Miike. Omega Project. 2001.

Inside. Dir. Alexandre Bustillo and Julien Maury. La Fabrique de Films. 2007.

Intimacy. Dir. Patrice Chéreau. Téléma. 2001.

In My Skin. Dir. Marina de Van. Canal+. 2002.

Irreversible. Dir. Gaspar Noé. 120 Films. 2002.

It (I). Dir. Andy Muschietti. New Line Cinema. 2017.

Jennings, E. (2008). Erotic body horror: Dangerous female corporealities in contemporary French cinema. Master's Thesis. Carleton University.

Kuhn, A., & Westwell, G. (2012). *Oxford dictionary of film studies.* Oxford: Oxford University Press.

La Chatte à Deux Têtes. Dir. Jacques Nolot. Elia Films. 2002.

Le Manoir du Diable. Dir. Georges Méliès. Star-Film. 1896.

Les Yeux Sans Visage. Dir. Georges Franju. Champs-Élysées Productions. 1960.

Martyrs. Dir. Pascal Laugier. Canal Horizons. 2008.

Langill, M. (2014). Issues of gender in the horror genre, Part 1. *Offscreen, 18*(6–7). Retrieved from http://offscreen.com/issues/view/volume-18-issues-6-7.

Mulvey, L. (1975). Visual pleasure and narrative cinema. *Screen, 16*(3), 6–18.

N.A. (2015). Are horror films inherently sexist? *BBC Culture*. Retrieved from http://www.bbc.com/culture/story/20150805-are-horror-films-inherently-sexist

Nunes, A. (2012). Running with scissors: Abjection and the Archaic Mother in *À l'intérieur (Inside)*. Inter Disciplinary. Retrieved from http://www.inter-disciplinary.net/at-the-interface/wp-content/uploads/2012/04/nunesewpaer.pdf

Oldboy. Dir. Chan-wook Park. Egg Films. 2003.

Palmer, T. (2006a). *Brutal intimacy: Analyzing contemporary French cinema.* Middletown, CT: Wesleyan University Press.

Palmer, T. (2006b). Under your skin: Marina de Van and the contemporary French Cinema du Corps. *Studies in French Cinema, 6*(3).

Pola X. Dir. Leos Carax. Arena Films. 1999.

Prince, S. (2004). *The horror film*. London: Rutgers University Press.

Quandt, J. (2004). Flesh & blood: Sex and violence in recent French cinema. *Artforum*. Retrieved from http://www.artforum.com/inprint/id=6199.

Raw. Dir. Julia Ducournau. Petite Film. 2016.

Rosemary's Baby. Dir. Roman Polanski. William Castle Productions. 1968.

Saw. Dir. James Wan. Evolution entertainment. 2004.

Secret Things. Dir. Jean-Claude Brisseau. Centre National de la Cinématographie. 2002.

Sheitan. Dir. Kim Chapiron. 120 Films. 2006.

Sombre. Dir. Philippe Grandrieux. Arte. 1998.

The Human Centipede. Dir. Tom Six. Six entertainment. 2009.

The Walking Dead. Creator Frank Darabont. American movie classics. [Television]. 2010-present.

The Exorcist. Dir. William Friedkin. Warner Bros. 1973.

The Omen. Dir. Richard Donner. Twentieth Century Fox. 1976.

Tobias, S. (2010). Martyrs. *AV Club*. Retrieved from https://film.avclub.com/martyrs-1798223075

Tired Hiker (2006). *Females as lead roles in horror movies? Killer Movies*. Online forum comments. Retrieved from http:www.killermovies.com/forums/archive/index.php/t-401131-females-as-lead-roles-in-horror-movies.html.

Totaro, D. (2009). Martyrs: Evoking France's cinematic and historical past. *Offscreen, 13*(15). Retrieved from http://offscreen.com/view/martyrs_historical.

Trouble Every Day. Dir. Claire Denis. Arte. 2001.

Walker, J. (2013). The new French extremity: An endeavour into excessive violence. *The Artifice*. Retrieved from http://the-artifice.com/new-french-extremity/.

West, A. (2016). *Films of the new French extremity: Visceral horror and national identity*. Jefferson, NC: McFarland & Company Inc.

Wexler, J. (2015). Are horror films inerhently sexist? BBC culture. Interview piece by Nada Tawfik. Retrieved from http://www.bbc.com/culture/story/20150805-are-horror-films-inherently-sexist

Williams, L. (1991). Film bodies: Gender, genre, and excess. *Film Quarterly, 44*(4), 2–14.

Williams, L. (1996). When the woman looks. *The dread of difference: Gender and the horror film* (pp. 17–36). Austin, TX: University of Texas Press.

Chapter 2

Elegiac Masculinity in *Bubba Ho-Tep* and *Late Phases*

Fernando Gabriel Pagnoni Berns and Diego Foronda

In this chapter, we propose to read two (overlooked) horror films; *Bubba Ho-Tep* (Don Coscarelli, 2002) and Adrián García Bogliano's *Late Phases* (2014), to address the ways in which cultural politics of ageing operate together with masculinity. In doing so, we examine how popular culture and media start to negotiate with (1) the cultural meanings of growing old and how that is interpreted and (2) the shifts taking place in the stable model of masculinity in Western representation. We necessarily discuss what 'masculinity' is, in terms of gender role and gendered representation. Interestingly, both films end in a contradictory note that blends together a return to hegemonic masculinity with the acceptation of the fact that the traditional macho image is undergoing a process of reconfiguration. This contradiction is what made these horror films interesting case studies about male ageing as depicted in popular culture.

Bubba Ho-Tep revolves around an aged Elvis Presley (Bruce Campbell) living within a retirement community. There, he must face a walking, soul-sucking mummy. In turn, *Late Phases* tells about Ambrose (Nick Damici), an ageing war veteran living within a retirement community. There, he must face a blood-thirsty werewolf who predates on the residents. In both films, the protagonists must compensate a failing sense of hegemonic masculinity with a last act of heroism. Though this last action, they both contradictorily recuperate some norms of hegemonic masculinity (like bravado) while, in turn, negotiating with more nuanced dimensions of gender representation that exceed the logic of traditional, fixed forms of masculinity and virility. This simultaneity situates the concept of masculinity as transitory and mobile rather than one that is historically stable and univocal, producing a reading that highlights the fact that masculinity can be performed in 'another way'.

Gender and Contemporary Horror in Film, 23–37
doi:10.1108/978-1-78769-897-020191003

2.1.   Hegemonic Masculinity in an Ageing World

Both *Bubba Ho-Tep* and *Late Phases* are part of a cycle of production of popular culture beginning at the new millennium 'that posit masculinity as a flexible category from which multiple versions of gender and sexuality emerge' that 'work to contain masculinity in a post-feminist context' (Albrecht, 2015, p. 4). Michael Albrecht follows Diane Negra (2006) when she states that this new context is 'preoccupied with distinctions of age and generation and it is adept at searching out and 'rehabilitating' those who do not fit the 'proper' heteronormative, script. Women were the common target but, as Negra asserts, men are increasingly becoming 'redeemed' in their 'alternative' forms of masculinity. Dysfunctional masculinity, that that opposed 'hegemonic' masculinity, is now worthy of interrogation, as the former points to the fact that the traditional depictions of manhood are socially and culturally constructed. Although terms such as 'masculinity' and 'manhood' defy unambiguous definitions, they are highly useful tools for the study of the dimensions of men's gendered subjectivity. In this chapter, we have preferred to work with a notion of masculinity that gives precedence to the cultural, symbolic, political and social meanings that Western thought attaches to the social category of men (what men are and what they should do and what not). As Anders Ahlbäck states:

> Gender can be defined as an ideological process that organizes human beings into different gender groups and produces knowledge about the perceived differences and relationships between these groups. Masculinity is knowledge about a particular category in the resulting gender order. It ranges from what people think is typical and 'normal' for men, to what they think characterizes the ideal man, and what they find problematic and undesirable in a man. [...] Manliness is an older and narrower concept that refers to notions of ideal manhood, of what is noble and admirable in a man. (2014, p. 20)

This 'older and narrower' concept responds the gendered divisions between men and women that establish an order on the world based on sexual difference connected to power, patriarchy and 'essences' that standardize social relationships and behaviours as normal or abnormal through constant reactualization. Because our aim is to analyse ageing men in contemporary horror film, we need to acknowledge that the dominant form of masculinity was, up to the 1990s, conceptualized through the notion of 'hegemonic masculinity', a term 'largely unable to deal with aging men's shifting and contradictory realities' (Jackson, 2016, p. 173) but in negative ways. The concept of hegemonic masculinity was derived from Raewyn Connell who points to masculinity as a social and discursive construction, rather than a set of given biological facts. Masculinity, as a text, is produced and reproduced through a 'reproductive arena' , that is, 'the various practices, performances, and social processes that get culturally attached to reproductive differences' (Pascoe & Bridges, 2016, p. 12). For Connell, hegemonic masculinity legitimates 'the dominant position of men and the subordination of women' (1995, p. 77). Even if the concept is 'historically and contextually mobile' (Pascoe & Bridges, 2016, p. 18), hegemonic masculinity 'refers to the most culturally exalted forms of masculinity configurations that justify dominance and inequality' (Pascoe & Bridges, 2016, p. 18) such as a supposedly superior rational intellect, emotional control or strength, all issues perceived as forms of eminence over women. Expelled from hegemonic masculinity are 'less manly' things such as interest in arts or sensibility, thus sustaining a strong and clear line dividing men from their 'weaker' counterpart, women. Also, hegemonic masculinity rejects as abhorrent any kind of help-seeking behaviour (Galdas, 2009, p. 63). At least, up to entering old age.

Traditional visions of masculinity are inextricably linked to some tropes believed as 'essential' in men: valour, strength, intelligence, aggression, etc., all necessary parts on the construction of 'normal' masculinity. If a man fails to comply with these 'essences', then he fits into a form of what Kaja Silverman calls 'deviant masculinity' abnormal not so much in the sense of moral as to a phallic system (1992, p. 1). These 'deviant' masculinities can be labelled as subordinate. 'Subordinated masculinities, like ageing and disabled men, exist outside the oppressively, dominant regime of men and masculinities that often displays the values of achievement, aggression, toughness and domination over women' (Jackson, 2016, p. xv). Forms of subordinate masculinity are related to inferior statuses of class, race and sexual orientation, a positioning that constitute a loss of hierarchical position at least in comparison to 'normal' (i.e. hegemonic) maleness. 'If hegemonic masculinity is predicated on the absence of impairment, therefore the presence of disability in cultural representations is easily recognized as a loss of masculinity' (Rodan, Ellis & Lebeck, 2014, p. 16).

Furthermore, 'hegemonic masculinity is particularly invested in phallic authority' (Loue & Sajatovic, 2008, p. 529) so the natural declination that comes with age disturbs the image of the self-sufficient man with the threat of emasculation or feminization, understanding these terms in negative ways according the cultural productions of patriarchy: feminization implies the debilitation of a hierarchical apex which now runs the risk of becoming somehow 'less'. 'Some gerontologists believe that old men are emasculated by aging while others believe that aging men adapt to a new, similar, ideological experience of masculinity' (Kolb, 2014, p. 84). Trying to conform the rigidity of hegemonic masculinity at old age can be traumatic and stressful, (Loue & Sajatovic, 2008, p. 529). Role changes such as retirement, loss of primary role (i.e. caretaker of the family), widowhood and moving to a nursing home or retirement community can be traumatic aspects to the rigid traditional depictions of masculinity (Krout & Wethington, 2003; Loue & Sajatovic, 2008; Victor, 2005). Ageing implies need for care, medical examinations, fragility, dependence and, sometimes, feelings of loneliness. Both women and men cannot escape from at least some of these new circumstances shaping ageing. Thus, men 'fell' into 'subordinated masculinity' the configurations of masculinity with the least social status and power. As argued, 'any movement away from a more dominant form of masculinity and toward, say, open expression of pain, fear, and need, or the regular provision of care, serves as a sign of aging and emasculation' (King, 2013, p. 296) and, thus, an antithesis of hegemonic masculinity.

In this scenario, the masculinities represented in both *Bubba Ho-Tep* and *Late Phases* belong to the scenario of subordinate, deviant masculinity. It is not by chance that both films begin with the ageing hero living or moving to a nursing home, an institution popularly associated with decay, frailty and death. 'The images of long-term care are images of frailty and despair, loneliness and destitution, and above all a profound sense of loss, a loss not only of things, but of who and what we are' (Agich, 2003, p. 2). Nursing homes, in fact, share imagery with horror cinema in general: the main revulsion awaken by these places are shaped by a potent image rife with horrific overtones: 'a blabbering, incoherent, dishevelled elder strapped into a geri-chair, withdrawn or beckoning for attention, but invariably ignored by staff who, without emotion, expression, or enthusiasm, perfunctorily perform the onerous tasks of daily bed and body work' (Agich, 2003, p. 2). Even if nursing homes are also places for autonomy, care, companionship, assistance, and entertainment (Agich, 2003, p. 3), the horror images prevail, mostly because we are afraid of 'giving in' to ageing and death (Dunlop, 2004, p. 33). Thus, getting old can be seen as traumatic, unexpected, the scenario to start to bid goodbye to everything that was good in life.

It is in this sense that both films can be read as elegies for a bygone era and ideology: that of youth but also of hegemonic masculinity. In this chapter, we will read both films as elegiac texts that engage with the last days of masculinity understood in rigid, fixed ways in a post-feminist era that invites men to break free from the responsibilities, visual depictions and cultural (re)productions of traditional hegemonic masculinity. *Bubba Ho-Tep* and *Late Phases* negotiate this passage from a hegemonic masculinity (both male protagonists are coded as heroes – the King himself and a war veteran) – to a negative sense of self as 'deviant' men who are defined by 'feminine' characteristics such as frailty or dependence. This elegiac sense of loss is framed through a fantastic story that narrates the battle against forms of monstrosity: supernatural creatures and age anxieties. Some hegemonic masculinity is recovered at the end of the films, but while doing so, the male heroes must retreat into oblivion, their deaths signalling the end of an era. This contradiction mostly follows the 'contradictory mixture of some legacies of gender privilege interacting with the threat of loss, bodily fragility and defeat' (Jackson, 2016, p. 39) felt by many men. In this sense, both films work as elegies for the heroes but also for the notion of hegemonic masculinity as well.

2.2.   Horror Elegies: Bubba Ho-Tep and Late Phases

Late Phases opens with Ambrose shopping for a headstone for his own grave. He senses death approaching, especially after the passing of his wife. Ambrose asks an employer about possible discounts for senior citizens. Of course, there is none. As the employer says, 'If I sell headstones at a senior citizen discount, I won't last long.' In a later scene, Ambrose mentions the real meaning of the retired community: 'people don't come to places like this to live. They come here to die.' These little pieces of conversation are a good example of the way in which ageing equals dying. At least, it did until some time ago. In our close past, reaching 65 years was signpost of retirement (from jobs and, to some extent, from active life). Now, a person of 65 years is still considered young (Hayutin, 2012, p. 36). This is due mostly to medical, pharmaceutical and technological developments, 'but also to the recognition that the rate of ageing has become partly controllable' (Weale, 2010, p. xi); in brief, life-expectancy has increased faster than ever in the last decades.

Still, we all live in a world heavily fighting ageing and denying death. We deeply fear ageing. We deeply fear the loss of beauty and control of our bodies and senses. And, paradoxically, this fear takes place in an ageing world, where old people represent a large percentage of the world population to the point of threatening the whole system of pension (Kruse, 2010, p. 64).

Ambrose is starting his process of mourning, not meaning his death but his loss of hegemonic masculinity. *Late Phases'* opening, thus, can be read as an elegiac passage. An elegy is a text that works as a public display of private grief while helping us to cope with the subject of the inevitability of death (Kennedy, 2007, p. 11). It is basically a funereal process of mourning directed to those who left us behind, but also to our own frail existence. It is also an artistic form of dealing with the topic of death as inevitable and 'the reinterpretation of convention and a broad scepticism about how to figure and represent loss' (Kennedy, 2007, pp. 21–22).

Mainstream films are hardly seen as elegies since the engagement with traditional forms of narratives and spectacle leave little space to intimate meditations on death, rather favouring formulaic narratives. Experimental or avant-garde film could be read as more suitable, as them avoid any form of well-structured logic while privileging a poetic form. The performance of elegy, however, also implies a process of spiritual heal through 'a movement from incoherence to coherent self' (Kennedy, 2007, p. 25). Narrative cinema, as intelligible narrative forms, can be suitable vehicles to visual meditations in passing away, as both *Late Phases* and *Bubba Ho-Tep* can testify. Arguably, the linkage between horror cinema and death should give interesting spaces for the formulation of meditations on passing away; it can be argued, however, that the current rely in FX and 'jump scares' derail any possibility of access a zone of meditation and mourning. In this sense, it is interesting that both films follow a similar narrative structure: after an initial attack performed by the titular monster (the mummy or the werewolf), the rest of the film relies not so much on further duels against the supernatural monster but on the hero's dealing with a failing hegemonic masculinity. Both films have little action, privileging rather a meditation on grief for a lost masculinity turned horror film.

As David Kennedy argues, 'the elegist, ever watchful of himself, must move out of the world in order to move into the space of elegy' (2007, p. 27). Meditation in grief and death needs a contemplative state. An elegy 'occurs in a place and at a time divorced from everyday reality. These places and times are often simultaneously conceptual and literal' (Kennedy, 2007, p. 26). As stated

earlier, the action of both films takes place in nursery homes, spaces here literally detached from urbanity: the nursing homes of the films reside in suburban
areas, far from the noise, movement and life of the city. *Bubba Ho-Tep* opens
with Elvis (or a man who believes himself being the King. The film leaves this
question unanswered) already living in a nursing home, while Ambrose begins
his adventures after moving to a community of residential homes for senior citizens, the Crescent Bay's Retirement Community. Unlike Elvis, who is far past
his best years – Bruce Campbell covered in heavy ageing make-up – Ambrose
is depicted as a man still active and physically strong. Ambrose is first depicted
in the film busy making the arrangements for his own funeral. This representation is slightly contradictory: on the one hand, he is seen as a man close to
death, as he is making the preparative for his own funeral. On the other hand,
he is depicted as a man with agency who, rather than denying death, faces the
inevitable. To further expel Ambrose from hegemonic masculinity, Bogliano
and writer Eric Stolz chose to make their main ageing hero blind, as a way to
enhance his dependence towards others. Like ageing, disability challenges masculine privilege. Through disability, Bogliano furthers downplay his hero's
'proper' masculinity.

Both films open with a mediation in ageing and death. Ambrose's actions in
the opening of *Late Phases* are very telling in this respect. As he shops for a
headstone for his own grave, Ambrose is coded as a man actively coping with
his own ephemeral nature. However, he is reluctant to speak with his son Will
(Ethan Embry) about his own situation as an ageing man when both drive to
the retired community where Ambrose will move in. Through the trip, Ambrose
seems angry and uncommunicative. Arguably, Ambrose is willing to embrace
death and the finitude of his life; however, he is reluctant to address his ageing
state as a man moving to a nursery home. Death seems not to be a problem for
him since it means finitude of existence ('the only thing precious about life is
that it ends', he says). Ageing, however, really bothers him, a veteran of the
Vietnam War who is now dependent on the care and surveillance of others.
What Ambrose really fears is the loss of his masculinity. Moving into a nursing
home implies the acceptance of his physical decay, a farewell to his hegemonic
masculinity. Living within a nursing home is, arguably, an elegiac time.

Old age and blindness mean for Ambrose an emasculation of his body that
he is not willing to accept; so, he transfers this process of emasculation to his
son Will. While moving to the retirement community, Will phones his wife to
apologize since everything is taking more time than expected and, therefore, he
will be late for dinner. This annoys Ambrose who, through a gesture, implies
that his son is dominated by his wife, a form of emasculation. When Will asks
his father about the constant cry of Shadow, Ambrose's guide dog, the old man
replies: 'It's you. You have your mother's scent.' Ambrose emasculates his son
through a symbolic act of castration overlapping a maternal (feminine) image
onto his son. After arriving at the community, Ambrose rejects his son's help to
come out of the car or accommodate his belongings to the new house. In a later
scene, when Will mentions the absurdity of Ambrose's steadfast attitude of carrying with him all his savings all the time, his father dryly retorts: 'It's my

money. I'm keeping it. Stop acting like your mother.' To secure his own masculinity, Ambrose needs to construct a negative reverse, a feminine opposite to which he can act as a superior.

Elvis' sense of faltering masculinity is not enacted through actions but voice-over. *Bubba Ho-Tep* opens with an aged Elvis reflecting on his current state of bodily decadence: 'I was dreaming. Dreaming my dick was out and I was checking to see if that infected bump on the head of it had filled with pus again.' He follows: 'How could I have gone from the "King of rock and roll" to this? Old guy in a rest home in East Texas with a growth on his pecker. And what is that growth. Man? Cancer? Nobody's talking.' The obsession with his genitalia indicates a preoccupation with the loss of masculinity. As argued, 'anxieties about the performance of masculinity may also lie behind the male elegist's turning aside' (Kennedy, 2007, p. 27) since loss and grief 'are inextricable from anxieties about appropriateness, decency, normality and timeliness' (Kennedy, 2007, p. 38). The process of suffering and traumatic loss of virility that some men undergo 'emasculate' them, thus underlining politics of 'proper' forms of masculinity and how to act manly enough (and retain some virility) through ageing and frailty. Further, 'the aged body has been (re)marginalized within prostate cancer discourses' (Kampf, 2013, p. 55), a process that has had direct relationship with issues of male sexuality. 'Given that the prostate is a gland that produces nourishing and protecting sperm fluid, it has a profound impact on male virility and sexuality - both of which are considered to be dominant markers of masculine identity' (Kampf, 2013).

Like Ambrose, Elvis' reliance on forms of hegemonic masculinity such as virility is ancillary to his masculine subjectivity. When Elvis meditates about his wife Priscilla, he does so in terms of sex rather than love: 'Would we still wanna fuck? Or would we merely have to talk about it?' Later, when a young pretty woman comes to the nursing home to remove her father's belongings, she does so without noticing Elvis' sexualizing gaze, who intently looks at her butt after she bends over to get things from a low drawer: 'the revealing of her panties wasn't intentional or unintentional. She just didn't give a damn. She saw me as someone physically and sexually non-threatening.' In the films' opening scenes, the conflict does not pivot around the fear of ageing men approaching death, but about the inner stress caused by the ageing heroes' acknowledgement of their own vulnerability.

Moving to a nursing home is seen as a further step towards emasculation. When the female neighbours come to welcome Ambrose, he shows them one of his weapons. When one of them complains about the legality of a blind man carrying weapons, Ambrose says it is legal: 'perhaps you were thinking in retards?' When Will tries to help him through the moving, Ambrose rejects the help: 'I can take care of myself. What do I look like? An idiot?' When James Griffin (Lance Guest), the official driver of the community, wants to help him to get into the car to go to church, Ambrose tells him 'I'm blind. I'm not crippled.' Ambrose's blindness, which is both internal and external ('I was not blind in my eyes, I was blind in my heart'), takes him away from the world.

Nursing homes tend to be hospital-like spaces in which elders often have limited opportunities to control their schedule, which is usually determined by the personnel. Constraints on autonomy, the latter one of the most important signposts of hegemonic masculinity, could lead to feelings of helplessness and loneliness. Elvis' nursing home is a dark, wide house filled with boring beige corridors that looks all alike. There is a huge green park circling the house, but nobody seems to use it. In the film, the residents are always depicted walking through the corridors or resting in their beds. Elvis' main antagonist besides the supernatural presence of the mummy is a nurse (Ella Joyce) who addresses all the residents in condescending or commanding tones, disrupting male agency after reducing it to a child-like level. Unlike *Bubba Ho-Tep*, the community for senior citizens where the action of *Late Phases* take place is a long row of pretty white houses with plenty of backyards and green areas. All the residents, however, seems to be old ladies whose main goal is to intrude into Ambrose's life and home. Former Vietnam soldier Ambrose is now circled and *haunted* by femininity in the form of senior women wearing bonnets and aprons. Wherever Ambrose goes, he only finds women, his masculinity tainted by this underlining of his condition as an emasculated man. The only man close to him is a mute elder living within a mechanical lung, whose life depends exclusively on his wife's surveillance. It is not rare then that Ambrose main emotional attachment is towards his male dog (which moves with him). Neither is by chance that the dog is one of the first victims of the werewolf's attack, thus deepening Ambrose's sense of isolation within a world of ageing and femininity. Through the film, Ambrose is reluctant to bury his dog, a way to put the reality of his loneliness to a halt.

The spaces produced by the nursing homes are pervaded with loneliness and abandon. It is interesting to note that the first on-screen killing in both films have a resident suffering from familiar abandon as victim. In *Late Phases*, Delores (Karen Lynn Gorney) the first victim, is an elderly woman who is attacked by the werewolf as she talked to her daughter Victoria (Karron Graves) on the phone. Scattered through the conversation, there are pieces of information that shapes an image of abandon. Victoria is an estranged daughter who calls just to apologize about missing a meeting with Delores. She blames the misunderstanding in dates on her mother's senility (senility that Delores strongly denies). Later, Victoria asks her mother to buy a dog to keep her company, allegedly a replacement for the family's absences in the life of the elderly woman. It is implied that Victoria only calls her mother late at night with the hope of finding the latter deeply sleep, so she only has to leave a message without actually having to talk to her. The day after the killing of Delores, Victoria wants to finish the entire bureaucratic process as quickly as possible: 'I just want to get this over with and move on with my life, okay?'

The first victim in *Bubba Ho-Tep* is Bull (Harrison Young), who shares a room with Elvis. The morning after his passing, Elvis is shocked by the presence of Bull's daughter (Heidi Marnhout) in the nursing home; he simply assumed that Bull had no family since nobody came to visit him ever. It is after these first killings that both ageing heroes start to deal with their deviant, counter-hegemonic masculinity. Ambrose and Elvis slowly begin to shape plans to end the supernatural menaces, even knowing that their bodies will not resist the final confrontation. Still, it is the setting of a plan to end the uncanny menaces that promotes a more active approach to life; Elvis get up from bed (he is depicted in the first scenes always resting) while Ambrose's investigation on who the werewolf is in human form gives him a goal. Rather than continuing their commiserate rejection of ageing, Ambrose and Elvis begin a process of mourning, producing their own elegy.

Ambrose and Elvis slowly start to piece together the puzzles indicating the presence of supernatural creatures. It is not by change that the werewolf and the mummy both choose retirement communities as their targets: the people living there are invisible, expendable and physically weak. Griffin, the official driver of the community, is actually the werewolf brutally mauling the residents. Arguably, he has chosen this particular job as a way to pass unnoticed within a community of invisible people who are close to death anyway. The mummy, however, does not leaves behind him a bloody mess (like the werewolf does) but a dead body, as his actions passes unnoticed. The ancient mummy actually sucks the soul from the elderly, so the deaths are seen as natural, just a normal event in a nursing home. Jack (Ossie Davies), one of the inmates who will help Elvis track down the mummy, states this fact in an explicit way: 'that's what they brought us here for, to get us out of the way until we die. And those who don't die first from disease or just plain being old, he [the mummy] gets.'

The realization that something supernatural is taking place within the community came with responsibilities for both Ambrose and Elvis. The two aged heroes know that they would not be taken seriously if they attempt to warn the authorities about a werewolf or a mummy roaming through the retirement community. Ambrose actually tries to warn about the presence of a killer lurking in the retirement community; the only answer he gets, however, is condescending cops who make fun of him. For them, it is all about animal attacks and the main problem in the community is that 'the elderly can't defend themselves.' When Ambrose inquires about why those deaths are not investigated, one of the cops tells him 'death at old age is not on our list of this town's biggest problems.' Moving people working for the nursing home even mock the smell of old people: 'I can smell this old folk smell from all the way up here. [...]. It's following me.' Similarly, in *Bubba Ho-Tep*, the stretcher-bearers in charge of the ambulance mock the deaths taking place within the residence: one of them mentions 'what kind of life he had, you know, his kids, his grandkids and his legacy. Look at him now.' The other one only answers: 'Oh, who gives a shit?' In a later scene, the mocking continues:

> Stretcher-bearer one. 'What? You gonna get all weepy on me again?'
>
> Stretcher-bearer two: 'No. I was just gonna suggest that you use some of this here deodorizer and spray it in that corpse because she's smelling pretty ripe.'

In this scenario of invisibility, Ambrose and Elvis realize that the welfare of the community depends exclusively on them. Only they, as witnesses of the supernatural killings, can track down the monsters and destroy it, putting the killing spree to an end. The rest of the film until the climatic confrontation is dedicated to these two men preparing a final battle that, they know, will take their life. That Ambrose chooses a shovel as a blind stick not only metaphorizes his condition as a hunter who is always digging (literal and methaporical) the truth out of the community, but also illustrates the fact that a large part of the film is spent in him digging his own grave and farewell. For Ambrose, the only thing he can really control, under his conditions, is the moment of his death.

This shift towards the final confrontation comes in a complex manner: first, it involves a resurface of some resemblance of hegemonic masculinity. Ambrose is in charge of taking care of a community mostly composed by elderly women, thus returning to a traditional form of masculinity. One of the first actions performed by Elvis after realizing that he is in charge of stopping the mummy, is to roughly dismiss his nurse, up to that moment his (feminine) nemesis. After she asks him to take his nap, Elvis loses his patient: 'You fuck off, you patronizing bitch! I'm sick of your shit! I'll lube my own crankshaft from now on. You treat me like a baby again, I'll wrap this goddamn walker right around your head!' This first piece of resistance against dominant femininity comes with traditional traits associated with the figure of the macho: pejorative treatment towards women and threats with physical force. Further, both men know that the climatic confrontation will require huge amounts of physical force, a recuperation of one of the traits underlining hegemonic masculinity.

Still, this regaining of some male supremacy comes with the realization that nuance forms of masculinity, more attuned with 'soft' forms of manliness, must be accepted. Rather than acting alone, Elvis hunts and confronts the mummy with the help of another inmate, Jack, a black man who claims to be John F. Kennedy, explaining that he was 'fixed' up after the assassination, dyed black, and abandoned. It is clear that before the beginning of the killing spree, Elvis had kept the other patients at distance. Only after the killings and with the need of help and companionship, Elvis take care in meet his peers and open himself to the world. Ambrose, however, takes the responsibility to protect people that he seems to despise. Further, before the climatic confrontation with the werewolf (a pack of werewolves, in fact, as the main one has bitten and produced contagion within the community), Ambrose's last action is that of making amends with his son. He does so addressing his own vulnerability after acknowledging he had made a mistake: Ambrose leaves his son a voicemail, revealing that he had lost his deceased wife's ring, rather than sold it, as implied before. He apologizes and says his goodbyes, as he knows he will not survive the night.

These displays of vulnerability, however, are arguably downplayed with images of traditional masculinity. Ambrose kills the werewolf with a phallic shotgun while Elvis receives help from another figure associated with masculinity (even if a soft one): J.F.K. Before *Bubba Ho-Tep*'s final confrontation, one of the last victims was Kemosabe (Larry Pennell), an elderly man who believes himself a cowboy, another historical figure associated with manliness and bravery. Kemosabe was the name Tonto used to address the Lone Ranger, a renowned figure of national heroism. Kemosabe is even murdered by the werewolf while wearing the traditional costume associated with the Lone Ranger. The climax, then, presents three historical figures dead: the heroic cowboy, Elvis and John Kennedy. In other words, part of the American history has passed away.

2.3.   Elegy for National Masculinity

The last few years have had seen deep shifts in the conceptualization of masculinity. First, there have been changes on how masculinity plays within the family, since many men now go beyond being just financial support to the family to actively participate in the process of nurturing and housekeeping, a fact unthinkable just some years ago. Even if women still do the vast majority of housework and childcare, 'increasing number of fathers are actively, albeit generally not equally, involved in caring for babies and little children' (Myers, 2006, p. 215). Further, men, in the classical conception of fatherhood, were emotionally unavailable or mostly absent at the moment of childcare. That was explained because fathers' main function was that of breadwinners. Now, this responsibility of childcare is shared with the mother in some homes. Moreover, the threat of unemployment destabilizes the solid figure of the father as the one in charge of granting welfare to their children. Since men cannot guarantee the futures of their sons and daughters, they supplanted this failure with nurturing (Donaldson, 1993, p. 651).

However, Hannah Hamad argues that the 9−11 attacks led to the fact that masculinity has to be rebuilt into what could be called 'protective paternalism' (2013, p. 52) in which men must protect the family from external threats, in horror films metaphorized into supernatural threats. Contradictorily, however, United States is 'feminized' through the recurrence of terrorist attacks. As argued, the stereotypes shaping women and men's behaviour can be also assigned to states or institutions (Cox & Stokes, 2012, p. 185). Thus, nations can be gendered according the aggressive/colonialist bias or neutral/pacifist approach they take in the global scenario. A strong militarization, inclination to foreign intervention and strong rejection to give the presidency to a woman recreates United States as a masculine nation of manly protectors. Carine Mardorossian argued that 'the opposition of (a masculinized) agency and (feminized) victimization that grounds this conceptualization is the process through which the nation generates "other" (abject) bodies and posits itself as their opposite, namely as an inviolable, unimpeachable, and homogenous entity' (2014, p. 34). The terrorist attacks of September 11 and those which follow, however, produced new discourses which 'metaphorically dressed the nation in a skirt' (Lemelle, Jr, 2010, p. 13) as the United States were coded as 'raped' and, therefore, feminized when stripped from its sense of invulnerability.

As noted, then, the first decade of the new millennium showed new forms of masculinity which, even if not totally dethrone hegemonic masculinity, at least weakened its status.

The elegiac masculinities of *Late Phases* and *Bubba Ho-Tep* function as an elegy that extends beyond the characters to frame the ideology of hegemonic masculinity as well. Further, one of the characteristics of the modern elegy is its 'unwillingness or refusal to give up their dead' (Kennedy, 2007, p. 57). 'We are fascinated and seduced by mortality and decay because they are so deeply imbricated into the world' (Kennedy, 2007, p. 80). The new forms of elegy 'presupposes a reader who is lost, dejected and overwhelmed by a world that appears to be filled with the potential for disaster and punishment' (Kennedy, 2007, p. 131). David Kennedy argues about the end of traditional history, where 'endless repeats of news footage of 9/11 and 7/7, negates any sense of a sequential narrative linking past, present and future' (2007, p. 133). The world as we know it, together with the ideologies that shaped it, is changing before our eyes. We are obliged to say goodbye.

Ambrose and Elvis are representations of the masculine America. Ambrose is a veteran returning from Vietnam triply wounded. First, he returns with eye trauma. His illness gets worse as time pass by and, being too proud, he ends up blind and misanthropic: 'By the time I went blind I could not stand to look at the world any way.' Secondly, he returns transformed, with his 'good side dead', as he tells Father Roger (Tom Noonan). When he became a soldier, Ambrose only thought on saving lives. However, one of the first things he had to do was to kill a six-year-old boy, a traumatic moment in his life to which he returns again and again: 'That moment was like a full transformation.' Third, he returns defeated, the war lost. After learning Ambrose serve in Vietnam, the ladies of Crescent Bay are impressed. Ambrose, however, grudgingly retorts: 'Didn't you hear? We lost that one.' To that triple 'lacking' (of health, of spirit, of national identity) a fourth is added: old age. Ambrose is a beaten nation, his masculinity crumbling away, sinking down by the weight of defeat and age. The country that sent him to war does not even pay his headstone, the piece that bears his name: the state wants to forget him, as he is a reminder of national defeat.

The other two main men of the film do not fare much better. Father Roger — the man in the charge of the community's church — hides a bleak past. He felt his entry into the religious as a period of transformation and repression. James Griffin, a man doomed to turn into a werewolf, only wants to 'live and worship and kill in solitude and die in peace.' James Griffin accepts his new state almost a self-flagellation. He knows that his attacks have to be fatal because, if not, he would propagate the werewolf condition to his victims. The men of *Late Phases*, then, are deeply scarred: the misanthrope (Ambrose), the one who cages his demons (father Roger) and the one who lets them flow freely (James Griffin) represent the three interacting agents in the Freudian psychic apparatus, Id, ego and super-ego in an oedipal community in which the Father (the State) abandons their children and submits them to the castrating and feminizing mother (the feminine community). In this scenario, the only male character unscarred is Will, the one who shares responsibilities with his wife and who apologizes for coming late for dinner. Even Ambrose seems to appreciate this new form of masculinity at the end, thus communicating with his son to apologize before the fatal confrontation with the werewolf. Later, Will and his wife stand at his father's military funeral at dusk, where Will accepts the tri-folded flag and gives it to his wife, a rite of passage from hegemonic masculinity (the military funeral) to a new one, softer (the inclusion of the wife).

A passé form of national masculinity is illustrated in *Bubba Ho-Tep* as well. Cleaning up his father's belongings, Bull's daughter throws away old sepia photos taken in the battlefront and even a purple heart. Those things do not have meaning for her; it is just military stuff. She, standing for the new generations (she is the only really young character in the film), does not share the ideals of manly heroism. Elvis and Kennedy put on their respective suits (Elvis 'traditional' outfit and a dark suit for the man who believes himself J.F.K) to face the mummy at the end of the film (Ambrose also wears his military outfits to confront the werewolf in the film's climax). The last words of Elvis before passing away are very telling: 'I was going down for the last count and I knew it. But I still have my soul [...]. And the folks up there at Shady Rest they have theirs too. And they're gonna keep them. Every single one.' He has acted as the manly protector but he did so to defend people who he previously just dismissed. His act of heroism involved manliness but also empathy and openness of emotions. Killing the mummy, he has saved the nursing home; the confrontation, however, has taken away Elvis, J.F.K and, previously, the Lone Ranger. The supernatural menace has been defeated, but not before it took with it a huge part of American masculinity.

We can see that the endings are contradictory, a complex amalgam of hegemonic masculinity framed with an elegiac chant for times quickly receding into oblivion. The use of a nursing home as the main space is, then, fitting, as the old age means the passing of traditional forms of thinking that a nation previously embraced with gusto.

While politics of masculinity may shift and adapt to endure in new times, older legacies of masculinity still weave in and out of fictional narratives, as both Ambrose and Elvis die recuperating some trace of hegemonic masculinity. Machismo, objectification of women and sense of superiority are, sadly, not a thing of the past, but, arguably, are not ageing well. Also fitting is the fact that the chosen monsters are representative of the old pantheon of supernatural horror: a mummy and a werewolf. Images from the past are dying, but still walk and haunt the new millennium, lurking in unexpected places such as nursing homes or horror movies.

References

Agich, G. (2003). *Dependence and autonomy in old age*. Cambridge: Cambridge University Press.

Ahlbäck, A. (2014). *Manhood and the making of the military: Conscription, military service and masculinity in Finland, 1917–39*. Farnham: Ashgate.

Albrecht, M. (2015). *Masculinity in contemporary quality television*. New York, NY: Routledge.

Connell, R. (1995). *Masculinities*. Berkeley, CA: University of California Press.

Cox, M., & Stokes, D. (2012). *US Foreign policy*. Oxford: Oxford University Press.

Donaldson, M.. (1993). What is hegemonic masculinity? *Theory and Society, 22*(5), Special Issue: Masculinities, 643–657.

Dunlop, J. (2004). A geriatrician's perspective. In C. B. Mitchell, R. D. Orr, & S. A. Salladay (Eds.), *Aging, death, and the quest for immortality* (pp. 33–42). Grand Rapids, MI: William B. Eerdmans Publishing.

Galdas, P. (2009). Men, masculinity and help-seeking behavior. In A. Broom & P. Tovey (Eds.), *Men's health: Body, identity and social context* (pp. 63–82). Chichester: Wiley & Blackwell.

Hamad, H. (2013). *Postfeminism and paternity in contemporary US Film: Framing fatherhood*. New York, NY: Routledge.

Hayutin, A. (2012). Changing demographic realities. In H. Cisneros, M. Dyer-Chamberlain & J. Hickie (Eds.), *Independent for life: Homes and neighborhoods for an aging America* (pp. 35–44). Austin, TX: University of Texas Press.

Jackson, D. (2016). *Exploring aging masculinities: The body, sexuality and social lives*. New York, NY: Palgrave Macmillan.

Kampf, A. (2013). There is a person here: Rethinking age(ing), gender and prostate cancer. In A. Kampf, B. L. Marshall, & A. Petersen (Eds.), *Aging men, masculinities and modern medicine* (pp. 52–68). New York, NY: Routledge.

Kennedy, D. (2007). *Elegy*. New York, NY: Routledge.

King, N. (2013). Battles and balloons: Old manhood in film. In J.-A. Sutherland & K. Feltey (Eds.), *Cinematic sociology: Social life in film* (pp. 286–298). Los Angeles, CA: Sage.

Kolb, P. (2014). *Understanding aging and diversity: Theories and concepts*. New York, NY: Routledge.

Krout, J., & Wethington, E. (Eds.). (2003). *Residential choices and experiences of older adults: Pathways to life quality*. New York, NY: Springer.

Kruse, A. (2010). A stable pension system: The eighth wonder. In T. Bengtsson (Ed.), *Population ageing – A threat to the welfare state? The case of Sweden* (pp. 47–64). New York, NY: Springer.

Lemelle, Jr, A. (2010). *Black masculinity and sexual politics*. New York, NY: Routledge.

Loue, S., & Sajatovic, M. (Eds.). (2008). *Encyclopedia of aging and public health*. New York, NY: Springer.

Mardorossian, C. (2014). *Framing the rape victim: Gender and agency reconsidered*. New Brunswick, NJ: Rutgers University Press.

Myers, J. (2006). *Child protection in America: Past, present, and future*. Oxford: Oxford University Press.

Negra, D. (April 2006). Where the boys are: Postfeminism and the new single man. *Flow: A Critical Forum on Television and Media, 4*(3). Accessed via http://www.flowjournal.org/2006/04/wedding-crashers-failure-to-launch-feminism-postfeminism-masculinity/

Pascoe, C. J., & Bridges, T. (2016). Exploring masculinities: History, reproduction, hegemony, and dislocation. In C. J. Pascoe & T. Bridges (Eds.), *Exploring masculinities: Identity, inequality, continuity, and change* (pp. 1–34). New York, NY: Oxford University Press.

Rodan, D., Ellis, K., & Lebeck, P. (2014). *Disability, obesity and ageing: Popular media identifications.* New York, NY: Routledge.

Silverman, K.. (1992). *Male subjectivity at the margins.* New York, NY: Routledge.

Victor, C. (2005). *The social context of ageing: A textbook of gerontology.* New York, NY: Routledge.

Weale, R. (2010). *Youth prolonged, old age postponed.* London: Imperial College Press.

Chapter 3

Game of Werewolves: XXI Century Spanish Werewolves and the Conflict of Masculinity

Irene Baena-Cuder

3.1. Spanish Recent Past and Masculinity

On 17th and 18th of July 1936 General Francisco Franco initiated a military coup d'état against the democratic and legitimate government of the Second Republic in Spain, which resulted on a Civil War (1936–1939) between those loyal to the Republican government and those who supported the military uprising. The aftermath of this Civil War was Franco's Fascist Dictatorship, from 1939 to 1975.

After the war, Franco tried to justify his actions as a 'righteous crusade against atheism, communism and freemasonry' (Archibald, 2012, p. 21). A crusade against the anti-Spain that the government of the Second Republic, and everyone loyal to it, represented to him. Accordingly, Franco's *National-Catholic* regime's main goal was the 'reconstruction of the fatherland'.[1]

This goal involved re-shaping both male and female identities into new roles based on Phalange's and Roman Catholic's principles and, in order to do so, 'Phalange used a specific language that, in relation to masculinity, it was based on sport and youth. The aesthetic and ideology of its project was conceived in relation to that youth (healthy, clean, cheerful, heroic [...]) which would lead to men with very specific values (obliging, sacrificed, patient, heroic, virile, honest, strict [...]) promoted by Franco's regime and the Roman Catholic church (Blasco Lisa, 2013, p. 11). Thus, whereas the Phalange's Female Section promoted 'those activities, knowledge and abilities that were considered intrinsically feminine, which were linked basically to children upbringing, home care and men's pleasure' (Pérez-Samaniego & Santamaría-García, 2008, p. 3), the so-called *Frente de*

---

[1]Quoted in a study by Morcillo (2008, p. 3).

Gender and Contemporary Horror in Film, 39–51
© Irene Baena-Cuder
All rights of reproduction in any form reserved
doi:10.1108/978-1-78769-897-020191004

Juventudes (Youth Front) promoted a male role 'characterized by virtues such as sacrifice, loyalty or service to the nation'.[2] As a result, 'masculine attributes encompassed not only courage, heroism, and a sense of adventure but also stoicism, discipline, and an idealized sense of that camaraderie' (Vincent, 1999, p. 73). Moreover, whereas the aim of these practices was 'to educate men who are able to use their patriarchal power for the defence and development of the nation. Women, however, must be to their service'.[3]

As a result, Spanish cinema during the first half of Franco's regime (1940s–1950s), reproduced this type of hegemonic masculinity through male characters attributed with 'strength, courage, dominance, and Catholicism' (Cívico-Lyons, 2012, p. 4), as films from this period were used by the regime as a tool to legitimize these 'newly imposed definitions on the family and gender roles through endless recycling of the same stories and narrative resolutions which tended to reinforce the status quo and close off any alternative readings' (Jordan & Morgan Tamosunas, 1998, p. 18).

However, after the autarky policy from the first half of the regime failed, Franco decided to open the country to the world in order to attract foreign investments. Consequently, the second half of Francoism, from the 1960s to the dictator's death in 1975, was marked by the *aperturismo* (opening up). This new policy had a significant impact on Spanish cinema since the dictator relied on it as a tool to inform the world that 'Spain at least culturally was no longer the retrograde, fascist, backwater of Europe' (Higginbotham, 1998, p. 60). Indeed Spain experienced a major change as the country 'developed as a capitalist, consumerist society throughout the 1960s' (Faulkner, 2013, p. 81). As a consequence of this deep change, censorship relaxed and alternative representations of femininity, masculinity and the family were available at the screens. As Mary T. Hartson explains, 'Filmic representations of men from the 1970's reflect the confusion that this change effected in masculine subject formation with the result that male characters are often seen as self-destructive, confused, violent or un-manly as they struggle (and fail) to master their environments' (Hartson, 2008, p. 153).

The Spanish horror genre emerged during this second half of Francoism, as authors of Spanish horror cinema, like Lázaro-Reboll, Javier Pulido, Víctor Matellano, Diego López and David Pizarro, among others, agree to establish a Spanish horror boom at the end of the 1960s. 'Between 1967 and 1976 more than a hundred horror films were filmed in Spain' (Pulido, 2012, p. 38). *Hell's Creatures* (aka *La Marca del Hombre Lobo* or *The Mark of the Wolfman*),[4] starring Paul Naschy as werewolf Waldemar Daninsky, is 'considered as a key milestone and starting point of the Spanish horror boom'[5] and achieved a great

---

[2]Pérez-Samaniego and Santamaría-García (2008, p. 4).
[3]Pérez-Samaniego and Santamaría-García (2008, p. 6).
[4]*The Mark of the Worlfman*, dir. by Enrique López Eguiluz (MaxPer PC, 1968).
[5]'Para muchos, la carta fundacional del cine de terror español' (Pulido, 2012, p. 38).

success both at national and international box offices, particularly in Germany and the United States.

More importantly for this article, *Hell's Creatures* supposed the introduction of Waldemar Daninsky, 'a werewolf with a complex personality that will star in thirteen films to the date, from *Hell's Creatures* to *Tomb of the Werewolf*.[6] The lycanthrope persona was explored in more depth and established as a success in *The Werewolf Versus the Vampire Woman* aka *La noche de Walpurgis*,[7] 'one of the most successful films of the genre' (Hartson, 2015, p. 129), and *Curse of the Devil* aka *El Retorno de Walpurgis*.[8]

For the construction of a Spanish version of the myth, Naschy combined the aesthetic from both the classic Universal monsters and the British Hammer with recognizable Spanish elements such as the landscapes or the folklore (Sala, 2010).

Regarding the personality of the monster, 'Daninsky has many characteristics, depending on the moment, from perversion to kindness, as well as ambiguity, torment, mystery, sexuality or melancholy.'[9] Naschy named his creature Waldemar Daninsky after 'an Edgar Allan Poe character (The Facts in the case of M. Valdemar) and a Polish weightlifting champion, Waldemar Baszanowsky' (Lázaro Reboll, 2012, p. 69). When he was cast to embody the werewolf, Naschy gave Daninsky his athletic appearance, linking the Spanish werewolf myth to a hyper-masculine identity. 'As a weightlifting competitor in the 1950s and 1960s, Naschy had developed an athletic and muscular body which he proudly displayed in his first role as Waldemar Daninsky, whether he was wearing a tight T-shirt or other garments which accentuated his musculature and strength, or showing his naked torso.'[10] Moreover, in addition to the athletic monster, Naschy also played the part of the seductive *galán*, a la Don Juan, providing another screen depiction of the *macho ibérico* (Iberian macho). 'Daninsky's masculinity is defined in relation to female characters: commanding and manly, gallant and passionate.'[11]

Although Tim Snelson states that 'lycanthrope narratives have been typically read in scholarship as an analogy for the simultaneous horror and fascination experienced by adolescent males at the physical and mental transformations of

---

[6]'Un hombre lobo de personalidad compleja que va a aparecer en trece películas hasta la fecha, que van desde *La marca del hombre lobo* dir. by *Enrique López Eguiluz* (MaxPer PC, 1968) a *Tomb of the Werewolf* dir. by Fred Olen Ray (American Independent Productions. 2004)' (Víctor Matellano, 2009, p. 41).

[7]*La Noche de Walpurgis*, dir. by León Klimovsky (Plata Films, 1970).

[8]*El Retorno de Walpurgis*, dir. by Carlos Aured (Lotus Films and Producciones Escorpión, 1973).

[9]'El personaje de Daninsky tiene muchos matices según el momento, que van de la perversión a la bondad, pasando por la ambiguedad, el tormento, el misterio, la sexualidad o la melancolía' (Víctor Matellano, 2009, p. 41).

[10]Lázaro-Reboll (2012, p. 77).

[11]Lázaro-Reboll (2012, p. 77).

puberty' (Snelson, 2015, p. 84). I would argue that the specificities of the Spanish social and historical context, still under Franco's repressive dictatorship, helped Naschy create a very particular lycanthrope who is, at the same time victim of a repressive dictatorship and an imposed masculine identity very hard to meet, and a monster, free to release the tension against its victims. Naschy himself referred to Spanish Horror of this time as a materialization of shared anxieties and tension in an interview in which he stated that 'When you hacked an axe into a skull, what you were really doing was to break a system that had provoked you a great unconscious frustration.'[12]

In this sense, although 'Spanish horror boom was certainly synchronous with a variety of horror products emerging from other national contexts, in particular Great Britain, Italy and the United States',[13] the Spanish horror films released under Franco's dictatorial regime differ from other national products as it 'might come to reflect an 'ideology of repression, terror and silence',[14] offering an escape or catharsis to the repressive social reality of the time, as 'the long years of fear policy and repression had to be somehow materialised in the cinema screens: the real catalysts of a vertically imposed and horizontally self-learnt repression'.[15] Javier Pulido explains how 'In such a controlled society as the Francoist one, filmmakers projected their frustrations onto celluloid as a way to release tensions, which resulted on a bloody cocktail of violence and sex, celebrated and cheered by the audience.'[16]

In 1975, after the dictator's death, Spain started a process of transition to Democracy which supposed the beginning of many political and social changes, including radical changes in gender politics as 'the Francoist legislation that stipulated that men should be the breadwinners and dominate the public arena, while women should stay at home, raising children' (Estrada, 2006, p. 268) was abolished, opening the way to new and more progressive gender identities.

However, although Estrada states that the 'monolithic model of masculinity imposed by the Francoist regime gradually disappears from the Spanish screen after the dictator's death'[17], other scholars in Spanish film argue that this model

---

[12]'Cuando pegabas un hachazo a una cabeza, lo que estabas haciendo era, en realidad, romper un sistema que te había provocado una gran frustración inconsciente' (Pulido, 2012, p. 43).

[13]Lázaro-Reboll (2012, p. 12).

[14]Lázaro-Reboll (2012, p. 11).

[15]'Los largos años de políticas de miedo y represión tenían que traducirse de alguna manera en las pantallas de cine, auténticos catalizadores de una represión impuesta verticalmente y autoaprendida horizontalmente' (Ivan Gómez and Fernando de Felipe', 2013, p. 202).

[16]'En una sociedad tan controlada como la franquista, los cineastas proyectaban sus frustraciones en el celuloide a modo de mecanismo de liberación, dando como resultado un sanguinolento cocktail de violencia y sexo, celebrado y jaleado por los espectadores' (Pulido, 2012, p. 43).

[17]Estrada (2006, p. 266).

can still be felt in Spanish contemporary society and fiction. As Triana-Toribio explains, 'If we look at the actors that have recently represented Spanishness and maleness for foreign and local audiences, we find that the most common type is that of the photogenic lead exemplified by Antonio Banderas, or Javier Bardem' (Triana-Toribio, 2004, p. 152) who embody the hyper-masculine stereotype of 'man as provider and taker of erotic initiatives' (Perriam, 2003, p. 97).

Consequently, it could be said that, although women started a process of liberalization and empowerment and men were free to adopt more progressive masculine identities, the macho masculine stereotype did not disappear from Spanish society and screens.

In addition, these major changes in gender roles and identities took place in a very short period of time, generating some collective gender anxieties, particularly those related to the emergent role of women in society and the consequent crisis of masculinity. This left men struggling to move from Francoist fascist strong masculine identity to new alternative types of masculinity. The film *Lobos de Arga*, aka *Game of Werewolves*,[18] offers an interesting confrontation between two groups of personae embodying very different types of masculinity that could be read as a materialization of the conflict of masculine identity in contemporary Spain.

3.2. Lobos de Arga

The film starts with an introduction formed by a succession of dark drawings which work as a comic,[19] while a male narrator explains, through a voice-over, the origins of the lycanthrope curse and sets the story. Although the plot in this introductory sequence takes place in the past, it already includes two key aspects that will determine the story.

On the one hand, the narrator sets the location in Arga, a small rural village located in Ourense, Galicia, in North-West Spain. This region is known in the rest of Spain as a land of supernatural folklore and superstition. Among their traditional myths, we can find la *Santa Compaña* (ghosts), *Meigas* (witches) and *lobishome*[20] (werewolves).

More significantly, the first documented case of lycanthropy in Spain was set in Allariz, a small village in Ourense, Galicia, just like *Lobos de Arga*. This documented case was focused on serial killer Manuel Blanco Romasanta,[21] whose

---

[18]*Lobos de Arga* aka *Game of Werewolves*, dir. by Juan Martínez Moreno. (Telespan/ Vaca Films/TVE, 2011).

[19]Lobos de Arga was in fact adapted to a comic with the same title by Hernán Migoya, Ruben del Rincón and Man. It was published by Glénat in 2012.

[20]See J.L. Garrosa Gude (2009): *Unha Inquietante Presenza: Lobos e Lobishomes no Imaxinario Galego e universal: do Lobo ao Lobishome*.

[21]See Simón Lorda, Flórez Menéndez and González Fernández *El Hombre Lobo Blanco Romasanta* (Galicia, 1852–1854). *Nuevos y viejos datos en torno a un caso de leyenda*.

story and trial have been adapted to film in *The Ancines Woods*, aka *El Bosque del Lobo*[22] and, more recently, in *Romasanta, The Werewolf Hunt.*[23]

On the other hand, this introduction sets the origin of the lycanthropy in a gypsy curse, thrown at the beginning of the twentieth century by a gypsy woman, over the Duchess of Mariño's son, as a revenge for the murder of a whole gypsy community.

Thus, unlike other werewolf narratives in which lycanthropy is inherited from father to son or transmitted via saliva after being bitten, *Lobos de Arga* follows the Spanish referent of the successful *La Noche de Walpurgis*/*The Werewolf Versus the Vampire Woman*, where lycanthropy is also the result of a gypsy curse.

Accordingly, it could be argued that the comic-like introductory sequence's function is to position the film within the specificities of the Spanish context and to differentiate it from other coetaneous, international lycanthropic narratives. In addition, thanks to the introduction, a link could be established between this film and the tradition of Spanish werewolves' films from the seventies, as one of the comic creators explained: 'The amazing werewolves [...] are a mix between a homage to classic (Spanish) horror [...] and a touch of *españolada*.'[24]

After the credits and introductory sequence, the film brings us back to the present, where the story takes place, and introduces the main characters and the storyline. The protagonist, Tomás, is a writer in his mid-thirties, who, after many years living in Madrid, decides to go back to the rural, isolated village in Galicia where he was born, as the villagers have invited him to a ceremony in which he will receive an award to celebrate his success as a writer, although his only novel published to the date was not that successful.

Tomás is introduced driving his car from the capital to the village, Arga, and talking on the phone with his grandmother. This scene let us know that the village is really isolated, as there are frequent long shots of woods and lonely roads and he loses the phone signal. Moreover, he is already portrayed as too dependent from his grandmother which, given his age, already seems to position him as immature. These two aspects would be very relevant and further developed throughout the film.

In addition, this physical journey could be understood as a metaphor of a deeper, emotional journey and memory exercise experienced by the protagonist. This parallelism is encouraged when, during the phone conversation in the opening sequence, he tells his grandmother his intention of staying in the village for some time in order to write a new novel about 'going back to my roots'.

---

[22]*Ancines Wood* aka *El Bosque del Lobo*, dir. by Pedro Olea (Amboto, 1970).
[23]*Romasanta the Werewolf Hunt*, dir. by Paco Plaza (Castelao Productions, 2004).
[24]'Los increíbles hombres lobo [...] una mezcla de homenaje al terror clásico [...] y un toque de españolada' Hernán Migoya, In Jesús Jiménez 'Los Lobos de Arga También aúllan en el comic' RTVE.es. Retrieved from http://www.rtve.es/noticias/20120127/lobos-arga-tambien-aullan-comic/488676.shtm. Accessed on 25 October 2015.

Moreover, the shots of the car are accompanied by active pop-rock music with lyrics and strong drums and electric guitars that changes significantly to an instrumental, mainly string instruments such as violins and harps, slower, more melodic and dramatic music with a that emphasizes the emotional charge and nostalgic feelings that Tomás experiences as he arrives to his childhood home after 20 years away. The lighting also changes to a warmer, natural light coming into the old pazo, a traditional Galician construction, from the windows, contributing to this feeling too.

In the pazo, he encounters his old childhood friend Calisto, a coarse shepherd obsessed with sheep. Together, they walk around the village, remembering their childhood and teenage years in Arga still with nostalgia. As they do so, there are frequent mentions to the Spanish Civil War and, more specifically, to the anarchists who hid in the village during said war. These historical references are repeated throughout the film, as if we were looking back to both Tomás' and Spain's neglected past. This process of remembering the past is even contemplated in the dialogue, when the two friends even mention to feel like travelling through time back to the past as they walk through one of the tunnels used by the anarchists in search of the beast.

By doing this, particularly at the beginning of the film, the narrative seems to be establishing a connection between Spanish Francoist past and the present in which the story takes place.

Among these referential connections, I'd point out the fact that the dynamite left behind by said Anarchists is used by the protagonists to blow up the church in an attempt to escape from the werewolves in what could be interpreted as a reference to some anarchists who burnt churches during the Spanish Civil War.

As the story continues, the film introduces the rest of the characters who are almost entirely male and, although we have a glimpse of one or two female villagers and Tomás' grandmother appears towards the end of the film, the weight of the narrative falls exclusively on the male characters. As Bernárdez Rodal explains, 'Spanish comedy is constructed over a specific type of humour related to violence and male action, where women have no place and other types of humour are not explored.'[25]

Furthermore, the characters in *Lobos de Arga* could be divided into two different groups, the villagers and Tomás and his friends. More importantly, these two groups appear to be constructed in opposition to each other.

On the one hand, we find Tomás and his editor Mario. They are in his mid-late 30s and they represent Spanish present. They both come from Madrid and embody new kinds of masculine identity that differ considerably from the macho ideal of traditional strong masculinity promoted under Francoism. Calisto,

---

[25]'La comedia española se articula sobre un tipo particular de humor que tiene que ver con la violencia y con la acción masculina, donde las mujeres no tienen cabida y otras formas de entender el humor no están contempladas' (Asunción Bernárdez Rodal, 2007, p. 10).

Tomás' childhood friend, is also included in this group as, although he lives in the village, he does not belong with the rest of the villagers, who are also significantly older than him. He is of the same age as Tomás and Mario and his behaviour is also different from the rest of the villagers. It could be said then that Calisto also embodies a different type of masculinity.

These characters are not brave nor strong, Instead, they are weak, scared and in distress. They don't know how to fire arms and they are not agile or athletic. Unlike the macho identity, they show their emotions freely and thus, they are frequently seen crying, screaming or visibly scared. Moreover, they are frequently portrayed stumbling, falling, running from the enemy and asking shamelessly Tomás' granny for help when they feel their lives are in danger, showing an immaturity that is patent whenever they interact, resulting in childish fighting. They are also single and have no children or a job, behaving more like teenagers than the men in the mid-late 30s that they are.

Accordingly, Tomás' grandmother is constructed as the only real adult of this group, when she join it at the end of the film. She is portrayed as a mother, who tells off the men, puts an end to their childish arguments and, ultimately, tries to save them. As pointed out by Bernárdez Robal. In Spanish cinema, 'Female characters are usually more intelligent, mature and are better prepared than their male counterparts [...] they are better prepared to face difficulties and are more trustworthy.'[26]

This portrayal is part of a major trend in Spanish fiction constructing '*soft* male characters' (Jiménez-Varea, Guarinos, Gordillo, Cobo-Durán, & López-Rodríguez, 2013, p. 44) usually depicted as 'clumsy, dumb, ignorant, ridiculous, unable, weak, incompetent or frustrated'.[27] The comic element of the film relies deeply on this ridiculous construction of 'men whose masculinity is taken to the extreme of the absurd'.[28]

In addition, although their sexuality is not discussed in the film, they mention that they are 'not very lucky with women', breaking as well with the Don Juan side to the macho stereotype that played a relevant part in the construction of Naschy's lycanthropic persona of Waldemar Daninsky, as it has been mentioned above. Tomás was 'dumped' by his girlfriend, who also left him the dog, which is used by Calisto to make fun of him. Calisto himself is 'obsessed with sheep', also sexually, as it is revealed that he had sexual intercourse with at least one sheep in the past. This is also used as a constant source of jokes in the film. Furthermore, the actor who plays Mario, Secun de la Rosa, is widely known among Spanish audiences for playing homosexual characters, such as Toni

---

[26]'Los personajes femeninos suelen ser más inteligentes, maduros y preparados que sus contrapartes masculinos [...] ellas están major preparadas para asumir las dificultades y son personas más íntegras' (Bernárdez Rodal, 2007, p. 13).

[27]'Torpes, bobos, ignorantes, ridículos, incapaces, débiles, incompetentes, o frustrados' (Guarinos, p. 43).

[28]'Su masculinidad llevada a los límites de lo ridículo' (Sergio Cobo, Durán, Guarinos, and López, 2012, p. 8).

Colmenero in the popular sitcom *Aída* (2005–2014) or Pacheco in the horror comedy *Witching and Bitching*.[29] As a result, these characters not only fail to meet the *galán* stereotypical Spanish masculine identity but also challenge it, suggesting even alternative types of sexualities.

On the other hand, we find the villagers who are mainly male, although, as mentioned above, we can see one or two women among the group. They are rural, and they are considerably older than Tomás and his friends. This fact is explained in the film by Calisto, who tells Tomás that all the young people left the village for big cities in order to find a job. These characters are constructed within the village and they are portrayed in old houses, wearing old-fashioned clothes and using equally old theatrical properties. Even the village per se, with its old houses made of stone and its narrow silent streets takes the audience back to the past as the camera explores it with the arrival of Tomás. A member of the production team explained in the film's making off a documentary that, in order to find the perfect location for the film, they searched for a village that 'looked stuck in the past'. and they represent Spain's past. As a result, it could be said that these characters represent Spain's past.

Unlike the previous group, the villagers are organized following a strong vertical structure which is also reminiscent of Spain's Francoist past, placing the priest on the top of the patriarchal hierarchy. He is Evaristo, Tomás' uncle, and he is also the leader of the wolf pack. He is the most powerful person in the village but, more significantly, he repeatedly disguises his commands under god's will, such as: 'Leave no witnesses [...] It's god's will!' Evaristo is the main representative of the villagers. He is always assertive and speaks with a deep, low voice.

The first time Evaristo and Tomás meet, Tomas is clearly scared by his uncle to the point of running from him until he clumsily trips on a stone and falls. In this scene, Evaristo is portrayed from a low angle and he is carrying a sharp hoe, which positions him as a man of power, whereas Tomás, on the ground, is shown from a high angle, with an expression of fear, positioning him as weaker. Once Evaristo recognizes his nephew, his strong expression relaxes and he friendly punches Tomás on the shoulder. Nevertheless, Tomás reacts to this in pain, as if Evaristo was too strong. Moreover, immediately after this, Evaristo takes Tomás to the village pub to celebrate their reencounter after so many years. There, he introduces him to the rest of the village and taps him on the back harshly again, displaying once more his strength. Then, Tomás orders a tonic, as he explains that he does not drink alcohol but Evaristo insists on him drinking and *orujo*, a traditional Galician strong liquor. After drinking the shot, Evaristo's expression is impassive but Tomás reacts as if he had just swallowed fire. He coughs repeatedly and makes an expression of deep disgust. Evaristo then taps him

---

[29] *Witching and Bitching* aka *Las Brujas de Zugarramurdi*, dir. by Alex de la Iglesia (Enrique Cerezo P.C./ La Ferme! Productions, 2013).

hard on the back again and he almost falls to the ground. This scene seems to portray both men in opposition to each other and it also constructs the two characters embodying very different kinds of masculinity. Thus, while Evaristo, a strong, powerful man who can *drink like a man*, embodies a traditional strong type of masculinity, Tomás, who is weak, scared, and clumsy and who *can't hold his liquor*, embodies a softer type of new masculinity.

Thus, as Evaristo, the villagers are strong, tough, used to hard work and weapons and who are never scared. These men are usually portrayed holding old shotguns and agricultural tools, as a symbol of their power and strength. I could be said then that there characters not only embody the past but also the type of traditional strong masculinity linked to that past. More importantly, only these characters, those who were born in the cursed village and seem stuck in the past, become werewolves.

Regarding the transformation and the wolves' appearance, it can be observed that the film takes Naschy's Waldemar Daninsky as a reference, using costume and make-up effects instead of modern digital special effects. This is an aspect of the film that has not been missed by Spanish horror fans and critics, as seen in the film magazine *Fotogramas*' review of the film: 'Nostalgia of the Terror Fantastic and the myths of Iberian *fantaterror* (mainly of the greatly missed Paul Naschy and his Waldemar Daninsky).'[30]

As weightlifter Naschy, *Lobos de Arga's* werewolves are very strong, muscular and agile. They move really fast and are depicted jumping great distances and heights, exhibiting their physical power. Their eyes are red, injected with blood, and the strong abdominal and chest muscles, unlike the rest of their body, are not covered by hair, leaving them exposed as a mark of their strength. Furthermore, these muscles grow abnormally in the process of transformation, outstanding from the rest of the body as if they were being inflated in different close-ups. It seems then that the director wanted to emphasize this muscular aspect of the lycanthropes.

Accordingly, it could be argued that both the village and its inhabitants are constructed as reminders of the past, including references to the Civil War and Francoist Spain. More significantly, this particular construction involves the lycanthrope myth, which works in the narrative as another element to relate Spain's past and its influence in the present. More specifically, by creating a Spanish lycanthrope or *lobishome* so deeply rooted in the past and with a clear reference and physical resemblance to Waldemar Daninsky, the myth seems to be used in the narrative as a symbol of the old Francoist masculine identity and its influence in the present.

---

[30]'Nostalgia de Terror Fantastic y los mitos del fanterror ibérico (el añorado Paul Naschy y su Waldemar Daninsky a la cabeza) Jesús Palacios 'Para Amantes de la Comedia de Terror Gamberra' *Fotogramas*. Retrieved from http://www.fotogramas. es/Peliculas/Lobos-de-Arga. Accessed on 16 August 2015.

Finally, these two groups of characters appear in confrontation to each other since the beginning of the film, when the villagers capture and try to kill Tomás and Mario. The filmmaking helps to increase this feeling of division and opposition with long shots both frontal or from a high angle, in which the groups are portrayed facing each other. The camera seems to mark the line that separates these groups, leaving the villagers/werewolves on the left, always showing Evaristo one step ahead of the rest, leading them as the alpha male, and the urban visitors on the right of the screen, frequently scared, screaming or even crying.

Thus, the fight between werewolves and the young urban men could be interpreted as a Trope of a fight between the imposed Francoist strong masculine identity, based on the principles of strength, heroism, love for the fatherland and Roman Catholicism and the new masculinities emerged in the last years in democratic Spain. It could be argued then that the film responds to collective anxieties shared by Spanish men and their struggle to move from the strong macho male identity, still present in contemporary Spain, to more progressive and gender equal masculinities.

Finally, at the end of the film, after the final fight in which they defeat the werewolves, there is a final scene in which Tomás and Mario ask Calisto why he did not become a werewolf as the rest of the villagers, to what he replies that he was not actually born in the village. Suddenly, Tomás remembers that he was indeed born there and, consequently, he turns into a werewolf. While he is in the middle of the becoming-wolf process, Calisto and Mario discuss their possibilities but they decide to stoically accept their fate and live a life of lycanthropy from now on, instead of running for their lives.

Although this epilogue scene works as a comic plot twist, it could be also interpreted as an extension, and now also an embodiment, of the conflict of Spanish masculinity. It seems that Tomás cannot escape from his past and the roots he came to research for his novel and, after defeating the werewolves and rejecting the masculine identity they represent, he is finally turning into a lycanthrope and soon will be Mario and Calisto too, after being bitten by Tomás.

3.3. Conclusion

To conclude, the myth of the werewolf seems to function in *Lobos de Arga* as a reminiscent of the Spanish Francoist past in which this myth was created and developed and as an embodiment of the imposed hyper-masculine identity of that time. The attack of the lycanthropes leads to a fight between this old Spanish masculinity and the new contemporary ones, materializing the struggle of the new Spanish contemporary masculinities through a comic catharsis and using the lycanthrope Trope.

Moreover, as Tomás walks the streets of this village in which the time seems to have stopped long ago, he looks back at his past and he progressively rediscovers his long forgotten memories and roots, including references to the

Spanish Civil War. As he does so, the audience is encouraged to look back at their own Spanish recent past and to remember it. This memory exercise is very significant because, at the end of the film, after the fight with the werewolves, Tomás cannot escape this past. This could be conceived as a symbol of the strong influence that this type of masculinity still holds today in Spain. The protagonist cannot fight against his roots and change his heritage and, consequently, he becomes a werewolf too as, despite everything, he is a villager too. He bears *The Mark of the Wolfman.*

References

Archibald, D. (2012). *The war that won't die: The Spanish Civil War in cinema.* Manchester: Manchester University Press.

Bernárdez Rodal, A. (January 2007). Representación Cinematográfica de la Violencia de Género: Femenino y Masculino en el Cine Comercial Español. *Circunstancia*, 12. Año V. Retrieved from http://eprints.ucm.es/10476/2/violencia_y_cine._circunstancia.pdf. Accessed on December 2015.

Blasco Lisa, S. (Junio 2013). El Ideal de Masculinidad en el Fascismo Español. *Intelectuales y política en la Europa de entreguerras.* (Junio, 2013), p. 11.

Cobo, S., Durán, V., Guarinos, V., López, F. J. (2012). Las Masculinidades Histriónicas en la Ficción Televisita Española: Los Hombres de Paco (Antena 3 TV). *La construcción de la nueva masculinidad en las series televisivas de ficción en España.* University of Seville, Madrid: Editorial Fragua pp. 3–18. Retrieved from http://www3.udg.edu/publicacions/vell/electroniques/congenere/2/comunicacions/Francisco%20Javier%20Lopez.pdf. Accessed on 23 January 2016.

Cívico-Lyons, I. (2012). Representing masculinities in Spanish film: Introduction. *Post Script.* Summer, *30*(3), 3–7.

Estrada, I. (2006). Transitional masculinities in a Labyrinth of solitude: Replacing patriarchy in Spanish Film (1977–1987). *Bulletin of Spanish Studies, LXXXIII*(2), 265–280.

Faulkner, S. (2013). *A history of Spanish film. Cinema and society 1910–2010.* London: Bloomsbury.

Garrosa Gude, J. L. (2009). Unha inquietante presenza: lobos e lobishomes no imaxinario galego e universal. O mito que fascina: do lobo ao lobishome. *Asociación de Escritores e Escritoras en Lingua Galega, II Xornadas de literatura de tradición oral,* 113–143.

Gómez, I., & de Felipe, F. (October 2013). Alegorías de Miedo. El Cine Fantástico en los Tiempos de la Transición. *Studies in Spanish & Latin American Cinemas, 10*(2), 197–211.

Hartson, M. T. (2008). *Masculinity in Spanish film: From prohibition to commanded enjoyment.* East Lansing, MI: Michigan State University.

Hartson, M. T. (2015). Voracious vampires and other monsters: Masculinity and the terror genre in Spanish cinema of the transición. *Romance Notes, 55*(1), 125–136.

Higginbotham, V. (1998). *Spanish film under Franco.* Austin, TX: University of Texas Press.

Jiménez, J. Los Lobos de Arga También aúllan en el comic. *RTVE.es.* Retrieved from http://www.rtve.es/noticias/20120127/lobos-arga-tambien-aullan-comic/488676.shtm. Accessed on 25 October 2015.

Jiménez, J. Para los Amantes de la Comedia de Terror Gamberra. *Fotogramas*. Retrieved from http://www.fotogramas.es/Peliculas/Lobos-de-Arga. Accessed on 16 August 2015.

Jiménez-Varea, J., Guarinos, V., Gordillo, I., Cobo-Durán, S., López-Rodríguez, F. J. (2013). Estereotipos Masculinos en las Series de Ficción Española: Torpes e Inútiles. In V. Guarinos (Ed.), *Hombres en Series. Construcción de la Masculinidad en los Personajes de Ficción Seriada Española de Televisión*. Madrid: Editorial Fragua.

Jordan, B., & Morgan-Tamosunas, R. (1998). *Contemporary Spanish cinema*. Manchester: Manchester University Press.

Lázaro-Reboll, A. (2012). *Spanish horror film*. Edinburgh: Edinburgh University Press.

Matellano, V. (2009). *Spanish horror*. Madrid: T & B Editores.

Morcillo, A. G. (2008). *True Catholic womanhood. Gender ideology in Franco's Spain*. DeKalb, IL: Northern Illinois University Press.

Pérez-Samaniego, V., & Santamaría-García, C. (2008). 'Educación, Currículum y Masculinidad en España'Gobierno-Vasco (ed.). Retrieved from http://www.gri-mus.or.at/helden/outcome/spain1.pdf. Accessed on 15 July 2015.

Perriam, C. (2003). *Stars and masculinities in Spanish cinema: From Banderas to Bardem*. New York, NY: Oxford University Press.

Pulido, J. (2012). *La Década de Oro del Cine de Terror Español. 1967–1976*. Madrid: T & B Editores.

Sala, Á. (2010). *Profanando el sueño de los Muertos*. Potevedra: Scifiworld.

Simón Lorda, D., Flórez Menéndez, G., & González Fernández, E. (2008). El Hombre Lobo Blanco Romasanta (Galicia,1852–1854). Nuevos y viejos datos en torno a un caso de leyenda. In J. Martínez Pérez, J. Estévez, M. del Cura, & L. V. Blas (Coord.), *La Gestión de la Locura: Conocimientos, prácticas y escenarios. (España, Siglos XIX-XX)* (Cuenca: Ediciones de la Universidad de Castilla la Mancha, pp. 265–272). Cuenca: Castilla La Mancha University Press.

Snelson, T. (2015). *Phantom ladies. Hollywood horror and the home front*. London: Rutgers University Press.

Triana-Toribio, N. (2004). *Live flesh: The male body in contemporary Spanish cinema*. London: Tauris.

Vincent, M. (1999). The martyrs and the saints: Masculinity and the construction of the Francoist Crusade. *History Workshop Journal, 47*, 68–98.

Films Cited

Ancines Wood aka *El Bosque del Lobo*, dir. by Pedro Olea (Amboto, P.C., 1970).

El Retorno de Walpurgis, dir. by Carlos Aured (Lotus Films and Producciones Escorpión, 1973).

La Noche de Walpurgis, dir. by León Klimovsky (Plata Films, 1970).

Lobos de Arga aka *Game of Werewolves*, dir. by Juan Martínez Moreno (Telespan/Vaca Films/TVE 2011).

The Mark of the Wolfman, dir. by Enrique López Eguiluz (MaxPer PC., 1968).

Romasanta. The Werewolf Hunt, dir. by Paco Plaza (Castelao Productions, 2004).

Tomb of the Werewolf, dir. by Fred Olen Ray (American Independent Productions, 2004).

Witching and Bitching aka *Las Brujas de Zugarramurdi*, dir. by Alex de la Iglesia (Enrique Cerezo P.C./ La Ferme! Productions, 2013).

Chapter 4

Navigating the Mind/body Divide: The Female Cannibal in French Films *Grave* (*Raw*, 2016), *Dans ma peau* (*In My Skin*, 2002) and *Trouble Every Day* (2001)

Kath Dooley

4.1. Introduction

A lone and distant human figure walks at the side of an empty, tree-lined street in the deserted and silent countryside. When a single car approaches, the figure appears to have vanished, but then suddenly she reappears, running onto the road in front of the fast-moving vehicle. The startled driver swerves to avoid her and loses control. The car smashes into a nearby tree at full force, leaving smoke to drift from its mangled engine. The lone figure lies sprawled on the empty road as a shrill and sinister non-diegetic soundtrack starts to build. After a moment, she stirs and slowly rises, uninjured, then moves to inspect the damage to the car and its driver. It seems that the car crash has been planned. The soundtrack continues to build, before the film cuts to its title, *Grave* (English title: *Raw*).

This jarring sequence opens the 2016 feature film debut of French writer/director Julia Ducournau. While the subject matter of this scene is in itself shocking, the motivation of the lone figure is somewhat more disturbing. A later scene from the film reveals that this act of inducing fatal car accidents in an isolated setting is a tactic regularly used by one of the film's cannibalistic central characters as a means to deliver fresh human flesh on which to feast. It is a drastic measure, to be sure, which reinforces the film's central themes of survival, uncontrollable urges and unstable bodies.

Grave is a body horror that explores cannibalism in a contemporary setting. The narrative follows the journey of vegetarian student, Justine, who develops cannibalistic desires after she is forced to eat rabbit kidneys as part of a hazing ritual in her first week at a prestigious French veterinarian school. As Justine's bodily impulses become increasingly uncontrollable, she is coached by her older

Gender and Contemporary Horror in Film, 53–66
doi:10.1108/978-1-78769-897-020191005

sister Alex, a more advanced student who is afflicted with the same disease. Both of the sisters display moments of lost cognition when experiencing cravings for flesh, which results in injury to their classmates, to each other, and gruesome murder.

This film's exploration of a mind/body divide and uncontrollable carnivorous desire echoes earlier portrayals of the female cannibal the French films *Trouble Every Day* (2001, dir. Claire Denis) and *Dans ma peau* (*In My Skin*, 2002, dir. Marina de Van). Like *Grave*, these two feature film predecessors also feature graphic scenes of characters nibbling at human flesh, be it their own or that of their unfortunate victims. These earlier films are identified with the early twenty-first-century trend known as the 'New French Extremity' (Quandt, 2004) or the French *cinéma du corps* (cinema of the body) trend (Palmer, 2007), which involves disturbing and horrific portrayals of alienated protagonists, sexual debasement and transgressive urges. Set amongst a backdrop of capitalistic and corporate oppression, both *Trouble Every Day* and *Dans ma peau* portray the cannibal as an unstable body who loses the ability to maintain close relationships and exist in 'normal' society. *Grave* displays some of the characteristics of the *cinéma du corps*, considering the film's brutal University setting and its scenes of graphic and bloody sexual contact. In particular, one can draw parallels with the Justine's journey and that of Esther, protagonist of *Dans ma peau*, who searches for subjectivity and a sense of identity as she is overcome by urges to mutilate her own body.

In this chapter I will argue that while the earlier films display characters that are isolated and alienated from others, *Grave*'s protagonist actively seeks out close, meaningful relationships. As such, her journey is a coming of age that ultimately sees her fit in, rather than drop out, of university life. Unlike the cannibals in T*rouble Every Day* and *Dans ma peau*, Justine seeks connection rather than disconnection from those around her, with varying levels of success. In this respect, the film breaks away from the tendencies of the *cinema du corps*, and ends with a suggestion that there is a hope for the management of Justine's condition and her successful integration into the world at large.

While the graphic offerings of the *cinéma du corps* feature an array of imagery that is associated with the horror film, past critiques of this cinematic tendency or 'mini-movement' have resisted this categorization, instead aligning films with art-house cinema. For example, Hainge writes that while *Dans ma peau* and *Trouble Every Day* 'do indeed present transgressive bodies, unruly bodies, bodies attacked, and bodies invaded', they are not horror films, and as such, 'they cannot be explained in terms of diversion or social commentary' (2012, p. 568). For Haigne, these texts call for a reconsideration of 'the relational modes that are brought into play in the creation and deployment of the cinematic object itself' (2012, p. 568). Certainly, the two films cited here do feature and explore the aesthetics of European art cinema, in that they feature narrative ambiguity, limited insight into character psychology and loose causal relationships when considering plot developments. Like Haigne, I consider that that the handling of such elements in the two films calls for a rethinking of cinematic codes and methods of audience engagement.

However, Coulthard and Birks make the point that 'the tendency to stress new extremity as a form of art cinema fails to recognize the ways in which these films engage with genre tropes and with the gendered implications and expectations associated with generic formulas' (2016, p. 462). For these authors, a consideration of the gendered tropes of cinematic horror is essential to the analysis of these films' impact (2016, p. 462). I agree with their argument that 'by appropriating tropes from the horror film, but refusing them the closure and recuperation customary to narrative conventions of the genre, new extremism calls attention to the paradoxes and contradictions inherent in the gender politics of horror' (2016, p. 462). As such, my analysis of *Grave, Trouble Every Day* and *Dans ma peau* will consider the gendered tropes of horror that are present within each film, as well as the interplay of these factors with the art-house aesthetics of the *cinéma du corps*. I'll interrogate the two earlier films, before then moving on to compare Ducournau's portrayal of the female cannibal in the more recent film. In doing so, I argue that the three films explored in this chapter display both generic horror and art house film characteristics, allowing them to break away from the limitations of the traditional cannibal film.

4.2. Loss of Bodily Control in *Trouble Every Day*

Claire Denis' *Trouble Every Day* was launched at the Cannes Film Festival in 2001, where its gory, cannibalistic subject matter immediately raised controversy. Reports suggested that several audience members had fainted during the film's more graphic scenes, earning the film a '*Prix Très Spécial* and a dubious reputation as a *film à scandale*' (Met, 2003). Indiewire critic Peranson described the film's subject as 'the body and the fluids that flow from inside it', and also noted that the film's 'few gory and cannibalistic scenes' were likely to attract attention (2001). The film's narrative follows the journeys of two troubled characters with cannibalistic urges, the active cannibal, Coré (Beatrice Dalle), and the resistant cannibal, Shane (Vincent Gallo). Both characters struggle with urges to wound, kill and feast on other humans, which manifest during moments of sexual desire and contact. While the newly married scientist, Shane, takes medication and seeks a cure for his condition, Coré appears to be completely out of control, attracting and killing male suitors whenever opportunity allows. Meanwhile her long-suffering scientist husband, Léo (Alex Descas), tidies her crime scenes and attempts to control her behaviour by locking her into the house. The film's backstory suggests that both Shane and Coré were infected with a plant-based disease as a result of shared experience in one of France's former territories. When Shane returns to Paris on honeymoon with his new bride (Tricia Vessey), he seeks to track down Coré and his former colleague, Léo, as well as other scientific acquaintances, in the search for a cure that will save him, and his new marriage, from destruction. When he finally crosses paths with Coré towards the end of the film, she exclaims 'I want to die', her only line of dialogue in the film. This wish is granted soon after in a raging house fire. The film ends with a final transgression from Shane, where his murderous urges take over during a sexual encounter with a hotel chambermaid.

As I've reported elsewhere, the characterization featured in *Trouble Every Day* is typical of Denis' work in that both Shane and Core are portrayed without psychological depth; rather Denis maintains a focus on the physicality of their bodies, achieved through repeated close-up and extreme close-up shots of their skin (Dooley, 2015). This stylized camerawork keeps the spectator close to the film's graphic and gory action in scenes of killing, and blurs the line between victim and attacker, object and subject, as body parts become indiscernible. For example, one scene from the film sees Core lure a teenage male neighbour into her bed, where after moments of rough sexual foreplay, she bites him to death. In close-up and extreme close-up, the camera captures a series of shared kisses before Coré moves in for the kill, biting and then chewing the neck of her seemingly paralysed and hapless victim. Minutes later, the neighbour is dead but Denis does not seek to judge Coré's behaviour. As Morrey notes, Denis' cinema searches for an ethical representation, one that 'would seek not to penetrate the sense of its subject from an external position of authority, but rather to open representation as a question by sliding across the surfaces of sense' (2008, p. 30). In this way, one can feel some sympathy for Coré, who is completely alienated from other humans as a result of her affliction. The director presents the two killers Coré and Shane, not so much as evil monsters, but as human subjects who are plagued by the problem of dealing with their irrational and transgressive urges.

This graphic display of bodily contact and corporeal transgression is somewhat typical of the French films labelled *cinéma du corps*, a cycle of films that Palmer describes as consisting of 'arthouse thrillers with deliberately discomfiting features: dispassionate physical encounters involving filmed sex that is sometimes unstimulated; physical desire embodied by the performances of actors or non-professionals as harshly self-gratifying; the sex act itself depicted as fundamentally aggressive, devoid of romance or empathy of any kind; and social relationships that disintegrate in the face of such violent compulsions, (2007, p. 171). The mise-en-scène of *Trouble Every Day* is also typical of the *cinéma du corps* tendency, which sees films unfold in cold corporate or sterile environments, such as office spaces, laboratories and hospitals. As Beugnet notes, these are settings that utilize 'the abstraction and dehumanization of the late-capitalist world as a foil for the deployment of their "aesthetics of sensation" (2007, p. 33). One can observe this tendency in *Trouble Every Day* as Shane searches for an old colleague in a Paris medical laboratory, seeking a cure for his deadly affliction. Here, we are offered close-ups of a brain in a water container as well as other scientific contraptions that remind us of human attempts to transcend mortality. Moreover, the film's ending, in which Coré dies and Shane finally succumbs to his disease, is typical of the film cycle, as it offers little hope for any of the characters portrayed in the film. One can imagine that Shane's marriage is now over, but this thread is left unresolved as the film's credits roll.

Moving on to an analysis of horror film conventions, one can note that the narrative of the film described above shares some of the concerns of the traditional American horror film, in its portrayal of monster characters whose behaviour is tied to 'sexuality, repression and psychosis' (Tudor, 1989, p. 47). Coulthard and Birks offer an excellent summary of the work of scholars such as Robin Wood (1979), Carol Clover (1992), Linda Williams (1984) and Barbara Creed (1986), all of whom explore gender and repression in the genre (2016, p. 462). Coulthard notes that 'stressing gender and its repressions, abjections and monstrous deformations, these scholars insisted on a reconsideration of horror, in particular the denigrated and discarded trash cinema of horror called slasher films, a group of films characterized by exceedingly formulaic plots involving gory murders of teens and young adults' (2016, p. 462). While the European art house styled plot of *Trouble Every* Day can be described as anything but formulaic, Creed's theorization of the monstrous-feminine provides a useful lens through which to unpack the portrayal of Coré as out-of-control monster, as I'll now explore.

Creed refers to Kristeva's theory of abjection, viewed as description, to provide a basis for the analysis of the monstrous-feminine in the horror film (1986, p. 70). This approach sees the feminine constructed within a patriarchal discourse, in which the figure of an archaic maternal figure represents an 'all-devouring womb [...] which generates horror' (1986, p. 63). For Creed, this ideological project within the horror film is 'an attempt to shore up the symbolic order by constructing the feminine as an imaginary 'other', which must be repressed and controlled in order to secure and protect the social order' (1986, p. 70). As Coulthard and Birks rightly suggest, the 'blood-soaked' Coré 'is a clear expression of Creed's monstrous-feminine', evidenced during the sex/murder scene described earlier (1986, p. 471). One could posit that by murdering her naïve teenage lover, Coré exercises her will as a maternal force who has the power to give or take life. As Creed's analysis posits, as monstrous feminine figure she represents 'the blackness of extinction' and 'a force that threatens to re-incorporate what it once gave birth to [...]' (1986, p. 63). The scene following, in which a blood smeared Coré paints the walls of her abode with her young victim's blood, gives further weight to this hypothesis.

As a fellow cannibalistic monster, the portrayal of Shane sits in sharp contrast with that of Coré, with gender providing the point of difference. Coré is associated with an animalistic, natural world in that she kills an earlier victim in bushes at the side of a highway and is largely portrayed without speech, so that animalistic, sexual desires and murderous urges, rather than a cognitive process, appears to be driving her behaviour. By contrast Shane is present within a professional and technical world as scientist, a backdrop associated with increased rationalism and control. Whereas Coré's sexual appetite and attractiveness seems infinite, Shane remains largely impotent throughout the film, refusing his wife's sexual advances, and preferring masturbation in an attempt to control his cannibalistic urges. Coulthard and Birks observe that this gendered difference in behaviour between Shane and Coré as monster is typical of the horror genre: 'what makes the female monster sexy tends to make the male monster less so, a fact that can be explained by horror's traditional role as a site of negotiation for masculine sexual anxieties' (p. 471).

Coré's eventual death can be read as a conclusion that restores normative social order, as is typical of the conventional American horror film; however, Shane's final action – the sexual encounter and murder of a hotel chambermaid – leaves the audience with a more problematic and ambiguous ending. As monster, Shane seems to only to have 'begun' at the end of the film, and as such, he poses a much greater threat than the policed and imprisoned Coré. Shane's sexual appetite is unleashed, rather than re-contained or re-repressed, leaving the audience without a clear resolution. One can align this narrative end point with the type of shock ending that appeared in American cinema in the 1970s, (see *Carrie* (dir. Brian De Palma, 1976), *Halloween* (dir. John Carpenter, 1978) and *Friday the 13th* (dir. Sean Cunningham, 1980)). According to Kawin, this type of ending aims 'to send the audience out with the shock of unresolved fear, to carry the chill outside' (2012, p. 13). Specifically, this ending sees Shane, as the film's main protagonist, *become the monster*, so that there is little hope for 'the core of the norm, reproductive sexuality' to flourish, and a return to order' (Kawin, 2012, p. 12). In this sense *Trouble Every Day* interrogates the structure of the traditional horror film and also exposes the contradictions associated with gendered portrayals of the monster. Denis' portrayal of the two cannibals suggests an uncontrollable urge as driver of murderous behaviour, which manifests itself differently when considering the gender of the two monster characters.

4.3. The Mind/Body Divide in *Dans Ma Peau*

The year following the controversial reception of Denis's *Trouble Every Day* saw the release of Marina de Van's debut feature film *Dans ma peau* (*In My Skin*, 2002). This film features a female protagonist who, following an accident, becomes obsessed with the mutilation of her own body. Most notably for this chapter, the film's 20-something protagonist, Esther, is observed nibbling and biting at her own flesh in fits of compulsive behaviour. As such, the narrative and character portrayals featured in the film stand as an interesting point of comparison with that of the more recent *Grave*.

With scenes of graphic mutilation and bodily disorder, *Dans ma peau* was quickly compared to the films of de Van's *cinéma du corps* counterparts. In a similar fashion to the work by Denis described above, de Van frames the body in extreme close-up, drawing attention to wounds and scars on the skin's surface. In *Dans ma peau*, the camera frequently pans along arms and legs with movement following human form, and the fracturing of the body into separate body parts contributes to the viewer's awareness of the protagonist's loss of a sense of unified self. As with Denis' film, de Van's protagonist is unable to control her bodily urges; the director's corporeal images explore feminine psychology with a particular focus on a perceived divide between mind and body.

The film opens with split screen images of Paris business district La Défense, some of which are inverted so that they resemble a film negative, intercut with shots of office stationery. This title sequence suggests a split between the surface and inner realities of this corporate world, suggesting disorder. The first scene then introduces protagonist Esther (de Van), a successful marketing executive, and her husband Vincent (Laurent Lucas), an upwardly mobile couple who are considering an upgrade to a larger apartment (and larger mortgage). The world is thrown off-balance, however, when Esther trips and falls in the rear yard at a party, not immediately realizing the severity of an injury to her leg. She visits a doctor and receives several stitches to repair a deep cut in her calf, but much to both her and the doctor's amazement, Esther cannot feel the pain of this wound. So begins a process of experimentation and transgression where Esther digs at her wound, eventually alienating herself from her husband and colleagues. The act of self-mutilation becomes an embodiment of her 'corporeal malaise' (Palmer, 2006, p. 175), and could also be read as an internalization of the pressures involved with 'business' ideals and mundane corporate life. Esther becomes increasingly obsessed with self-mutilation until she is no longer able to continue with her career. The film's final scenes show her alone in a rented hotel room, nibbling at her own skin as if compelled by a desire to consume her own flesh.

One could view Esther's problem as representative of a mind/body divide: required to be 'all mind' in the corporate world, she lacks the ability to feel the pain of her serious and graphically presented wound as her body is literally disconnected from her brain. Her body's nerve centre, one that registers and processes such sensations, has broken down. According to this reading of the film, the narrative involves a drive to overcome this problem and reconcile Esther's position as both object (body) and subject (mind).

As much as she appears to be cognitive of her acts of self-mutilation, there are many moments when the body itself appears to have taken control. Close-up and medium shots of Esther's wounded body often appear separately to shots of her head, indicating that her bodily impulses are occurring involuntarily, or independent of thought. This mind/body divide occurs most explicitly when Esther lunches with work colleagues in a busy restaurant. Fighting urges to disfigure her body under the table, at one point Esther looks down to find that her disobedient arm has literally become disconnected from the rest of her body. It sits on the tablecloth; isolated, but strangely, no one seems to notice. A pattern of shot-reverse-shot sees her looking down, the disconnected arm, and then back to her face for a contained response. Similar shot framing and editing occurs in an earlier scene when a surprised Esther first discovers her leg wound. In separate shots we see blood on her leg, on the carpet, before then cutting to a shot of her reacting face. Esther is both an object (reduced to body parts) and the active viewer of her own body parts, the agent with whom the audience identifies. One could read her state of being as a metaphor for a devastating division brought about by the demands of corporate life, with her drive to mutilate being a symptom of this disorder, rather than a cure.

De Van reinforces this uncomfortable mind/body disturbance when Esther first checks into a hotel room to indulge in further mutilation of her wounds. This rented room setting allows her anonymity; a space for an encounter with the self. With her body contorted so that her face is pressed against her bleeding arms and legs, the camera frames these moment of self-biting as it would a meeting of lovers. Medium close-ups reveal Esther's somewhat obscured, desiring expression as she licks and kisses her bleeding wounds with a lover's gaze cast upon her own body. At this moment, like Coré, the blood smeared Esther appears to be a clear expression of Creed's monstrous-feminine, being a figure of bloody abjection, who in this case, seeks to consume herself. The protagonist's problem is not unlike that of Shane and Coré in *Trouble Every Day*: how to control and manage an unstable body. The failure or inability to do so means alienation from friends, colleagues and loved ones, as well as from the self.

The last shot of *Dans ma peau*, in which Esther lies disfigured on a bed in an anonymous hotel room with a vacant expression on her face, suggests that she may have achieved the goal of remaking herself but that this is undertaken at the expense of her future as wife, mother and money earner, having abandoned the corporate and domestic/family world. In sync with the final shots of *Trouble Every Day*, where Shane murders the hotel chambermaid during a sexual encounter, this final scene rejects the conventional ending of the horror film, in which fertility and reproduction are reset as core values, and 'the world once again a safe place for humanity' (Kawin, 2012, p. 12). Like Shane, Esther has now rejected a conventional future of marriage and children in favour of an unknown, alienated path.

Writing on this final scene, Hainge makes the point that after a series of close-up, split screen shots 'in which there is a total sensory and corporeal identification between Esther and the viewer, these final shots, in which the camera tracks back and rotates, allow the viewer to regain a more distanced perspective in which s/he is returned to his/her own body' (2012, p. 573). He rightly notes, however, that they do not allow for the 'work of intellectual synthesis and hermeneutic closure that final shots often allow', but rather encourage a feeling of vertigo due to the camera's rotation (2012, p. 573). As with the work of Denis, the focus remains on the surface of the skin, rather than a psychological understanding of character, as Esther's final emotional state is left a mystery.

4.4.   Unruly Bodies in *Grave*

When *Grave* was released on the festival circuit in 2016, it garnered both positive critical reviews and sparked controversy on account of its subject matter. Like *Trouble Every Day*, screening of the film reportedly led to audience members fainting in cinemas, this time at the Toronto film festival (Heller-Nicholas, 2017, p. 32). In sync with the earlier films discussed in this chapter, the movie displays graphic scenes of bodily dysfunction and gore, and is described by Ducournau as a 'body horror' (Heller-Nicholas, 2017, p. 32). However, it breaks away from the narrative tendencies of the *cinéma du corps* through its exploration of warm character relationships and its hopeful ending. As such, the film both deploys and subverts generic horror film conventions, which I'll now explore further.

In *Grave*'s early scenes, the protagonist Justine, an exceptional student and 'good girl', is delivered to her new Veterinarian School home by her cagey parents, neither of whom is interested in spending time on the stark, concrete campus. This cold, sterile environment echoes the setting of *Dans ma peau* and *Trouble Every Day*, featuring imposing architecture and a scientific backdrop for the narrative. Justine locates her dorm room and attempts to settle in but her efforts are quickly undermined by a group of militant older students (the 'veterans') who are on a mission to force new recruits through a punishing process of induction. Her bed mattress is thrown out of her dorm room window, and like the other novices, she is forced along the hallway in shots of chaos and disorientation, still dressed in her nightwear. Several of the new recruits are crammed silently into a steely metal elevator, where they exchange nervous glances in a brief moment of calm. The next scene begins with a wide shot that shows the masses of students crawling in a dark, enclosed space on their hands and knees. Eventually they arrive at a door — the entrance to an elaborate underground party where new and old students alike drink, dance and interact. It is here that Justine locates her sister, Alex (Ella Rumpf), who is one year ahead of her in her studies.

The punishing nature of the novice students' 'rush week' continues in the scenes that follow. Justice and other new recruits are drenched in animal blood and made to continue their induction in soiled lab coats and with matted, blood-soaked hair. Like the other novices, Justine is forced to consume rabbit kidneys, with protests of her vegetarian status ignored by both the veterans and her sister. This is an oppressive environment where the importance of ritual overrides personal circumstance and the following of orders is paramount. These early scenes are intercut with an introduction to veterinarian studies, in particular, an alarming scene that shows a horse being anaesthetized in a padded room. Students watch as a tube is forced into the paralysed horse's clamped mouth and the beast's legs are hoisted into the air, to be constrained by a medical device. The treatment of the horse and of Justine is an apt comparison, as both are overcome by an institution that seeks to regulate, control and order its human and animal bodies.

Shortly afterward, Justine's body displays a disturbing reaction to the situation. In class, she starts to itch, and then we see her tossing and turning in bed, scratching herself compulsively, but unable to find relief. Frustrated, she throws off her bed sheets and switches on the light, illuminating the extent of her bodily distress. Justine shrieks at the sight of an uneven, blotchy red rash that covers much of her body. Close-up shots of her skin are difficult to view, made more distressing by the sound of chaffing as fingers continue to scratch away at the distressed surface. This close-up depiction of marked and broken skin echoes portrayals of Coré's bodily carnage in *Trouble Every Day* and of Esther's self-gouging in *Dans ma peau*. Before long, Justine's urge to consume flesh sets in, and she is seen rabidly consuming meat kebabs and raw chicken breast, before turning to human flesh. The graphic scenes that follow, in which flesh-seeking Justine nibbles on her sister's accidentally severed finger, and later, discovers the body of her mutilated and deceased roommate, certainly can be compared to the *cinema du corps* offerings in their unsettling and realistic depiction of gore.

However, the film moves away from portrayals of the cannibal in the two earlier films, as we now observe a female protagonist who is actively engaged in meaningful relationships with others. Like Coré and Esther, Justine appears to be suffering from a mind/body divide that leads to uncontrollable physical urges but she seeks to control these through connection (rather than disconnection) with those around her, with varying levels of success. This approach to Justine's characterization stops the film from being a 'faithful replication of the (earlier "extreme cinema") the tendency with its underlying humanity' (Barton-Fumo, 2017, p. 45). Whereas Esther and Coré's cannibalistic tendencies alienated them from their partners and society in general, Justine is concerned with maintaining relationships, most notably, with her erratic and rebellious older sister, Alex, and her sympathetic roommate, Adrien (Rabah Nait Oufella).

When Justine arrives at the campus, she seeks out her sister for advice and guidance. Depending on her mood, Alex is either warm and inviting, or more often, cool and punishing. A tender scene sees the two sisters drinking on a top exterior of a campus building at night, with Alex attempting to teach Justine to wee in an upright position. Alex's efforts to guide her younger sister into adulthood include the offering of a botched Brazilian wax (a hair-raising episode that sees Alex's finger accidentally severed, and gives Justine her first taste of human flesh). Justine spends a significant amount of time in Alex's dorm room and soon realizes that her sister suffers from the same carnivorous compulsion that she is experiencing. Later, Alex reveals her tactic of causing car accidents on a deserted road nearby the campus, a strategy that is whole heartedly rejected by the shocked Justine. This is one of several clashes between the two sisters, but ultimately their emotional connection is not broken by the terms of their cannibalistic affliction.

Justine's relationship with her openly gay roommate Adrien is one that develops both in and out of the classroom as they join forces to survive their initiation to the school. Their friendship is at first platonic; however, as the virginal Justine's desire to consume flesh escalates, so too is a powerful sexual desire born. Adrien becomes the object of her lust and he reluctantly gives in to her advances in their dorm room one evening, engaging in an act of heterosexual sex. This intimate scene is aggressive and violent, in keeping with the earlier tendency of the *cinéma du corps*, as a frenzied Justine attempts to bite and claw at the intimidated Adrien's body. While this carnal awakening represents a coming of age for Justine, Adrien quickly expresses regret and Justine is left to re-evaluate herself in the wake of this emotionally disturbing but transformative episode. Whereas Esther in *Dans ma peau* seeks to enact personal change by withdrawal from society and acts of self-mutilation, Grave's protagonist is concerned with a negotiation of physical and emotional adult relationships, a journey that is fraught with confusion and physical pain.

Writing on Justine's character journey, Harkins-Cross observes that 'the good girl becomes a whore, making out with her new-found image in the mirror, libidinous on the dance floor, and seducing her gay roommate' (2017, p. 6). Certainly, as the 'good girl' that 'turns bad', Justine is a character with traits often seen in the conventional horror film. An obvious comparison can be made with the female protagonist of *Carrie*, who is also a model student and virgin who becomes a destructive force. Further to these stereotypical character traits, imagery of the blood-drenched Justine recalls that of *Carrie*, when the protagonist is similarly drenched in animal blood, an act that in this this earlier film, represents a personalized act of bullying by her vindictive classmates. Carrie responds by destroying her entire community in the film's climactic prom scene, whereas in *Grave*, Justine ultimately seeks acceptance in her new surroundings.

Creed's discussion of the monstrous-feminine sheds further light on a comparison of these two films' female characters. In *Carrie*, we see a teenage protagonist who develops telekinetic powers in parallel with the onset of menstruation. Meanwhile, Justine's coming of age sees her cannibalistic urges build at the same time as she experiences a carnal awakening. Creed observes that 'in the horror genre [...] menstrual blood is constructed as a source of abjection: its powers are so great it can transform woman into any one of a number of fearful creatures: possessed child, killer and vengeful witch' (1993, p. 83). In this sense, the association of maternal and reproductive functions with the abject is 'a construct of patriarchal ideology' (Creed, 1986, p. 83). Blood is a continual motif in both *Carrie* and *Grave*, and while menstrual blood is not directly referenced in the latter film, links to Justine's coming of age are evidenced through various moments of bodily dysfunction, such as her skin rash, and various sexual episodes. For example, a second intimate encounter at a party, in which veteran students lock her in a room with a fellow novice, results in bloody injury when Justine bites off part of the unsuspecting male's lip, 'an act of both dissent and desire (Harkins-Cross, 2017, p. 7). In both films, the female body can be read as a site of difference, as man's sexual other, with the representation of woman as monstrous-feminine reinforcing the ideological project of the conventional horror film (Creed, 1986, p. 83).

However, Justine's negotiation of her cannibalistic tendencies is a journey punctuated by moments of self-discovery and empowerment, such as when she seduces her roommate Adrien. In this moment, her status as pursuer, rather than pursued, allows her to take control and temporarily disrupt the patriarchal gaze. Contrary to the reading of the film offered above, one could view Justine's cannibalism as an act of rebellion against established gender norms, for which she goes unpunished. Whereas Carrie's journey ends with her death at the hands of her mother, Justine is not reprimanded for her actions.

The final scenes of *Grave* see Justine make the shocking discovery of Adrien's murdered and partially eaten body in her dorm room. While she initially fears her own involvement in the crime, it is revealed that her dazed sister Alex, who has been overcome by murderous urges, is the culprit. Alex is jailed for the murder but Justine walks free. In the film's final scene, she lunches with her father, who reveals that the girls' mother also suffers from the cannibalistic disease. Justine recoils as her father opens his shirt, revealing a naked torso that is heavily scarred with old and new bite wounds. His offering of his body to his wife is the solution to their problem, and he expresses confidence in Justine's ability to find her own way of dealing with the affliction. With this ending, Ducournau subverts generic horror film expectations by suggesting hope for the protagonist. This final conversation suggests Justine's ability to control her impulses and manage her condition in the long term. The director comments that 'my movie is very dark, but I wanted it to be clear at the end that there is a solution, and that the solution is in (Justine) [...] when you open your eyes to who you are and your humanity, then there is a solution, and the solution is in you' (Ducournau quoted in Heller-Nicholas, 2017, p. 33). This ending sits in contrast with those of *Trouble Every Day* and *Dans ma peau*, as it sees the protagonist find a place in her community and society in general, rather than withdrawal into a state of complete alienation. Doucournau also provides the viewer with a sense of closure, which is missing from the two earlier films.

4.5.   Conclusion

In this chapter, I have argued that the concept of a mind/body divide is central to the thematic and stylistic concerns of the three French films that are explored. For Denis, de Van and Ducournau, dark and graphic stories place a focus on dangerous encounters with the self and/ or others, occurrences of irreversible bodily transgression and the reforming of identities. All three films feature protagonists who, as cannibals, are unstable and at times, uncontrollable, and who inhabit mutating and dangerous worlds.

It is clear that like *Trouble Every Day* and *Dans ma peau*, *Grave* shares some features of the *cinéma du corps* in terms of setting, graphic imagery and central themes. As is seen in the two earlier films, Ducournau positions the camera so as to capture close-up and extreme close-up shots of distressed skin, placing the viewer close to the gory action that infolds on screen. Furthermore, for all of the works explored in this chapter, mise-en-scène highlights the limits of the body and the corporate/consumer environment in which it exists. However, *Grave* breaks away from the stark tone of these earlier films, in its focus on tender relationships and a positive sense of underlying humanity. Whereas *Trouble Every Day* and *Dans ma peau* follow the journeys of protagonists who are on a path towards self-destruction, *Grave* presents an adolescent coming of age tale, in which cannibalism is a condition that can ultimately be controlled and overcome.

The films examined here draw upon horror tropes such as the monstrous-feminine to address sexual difference; however, by subverting generic conventions, all three interrogate the gender politics of horror. The ambiguous endings of *Trouble Every day* and *Dans ma peau*, deny the viewer a sure resolution and therefore leave existing bodily anxieties standing. Shane's final action as killer in Denis' film, like Esther's hotel room withdrawal in de Van's offering, offers little hope for the return to moral and symbolic order, as the urges to mutilate and consume is not re-repressed. As such, core values such as family and fertility are denied rather than re-established, as is typical of the generic horror film.

Grave's more optimistic ending, by contrast, returns Justine to a world where traditional values are restored. Her father's final reveal creates hope for the upholding of the family unit, despite the onset of Justine's condition. In this sense *Grave* differs from the *cinéma du corps* offerings by offering a more conventional, less ambiguous ending, and one that resolves the protagonist's central problem. Despite this end point, however, Justine's journey is one that subverts generic horror expectations, through her ultimate mastery of her condition. As monstrous-feminine figure, she is rewarded with freedom, rather than punished, signalling a successful coming of age. In this sense, like the two earlier films, the body horror *Grave* both draws upon and exposes horror conventions, displaying the influence of art cinema aesthetics in doing so. While the character ambiguities and lack of narrative cause and effect observed in *Trouble Every Day* and *Dans ma peau* are less evident in Ducournau's film, *Grave* nonetheless moves away from a generic depiction of the female cannibal, and in doing so, asks the viewer to reconsider the gendered tropes of the horror film.

References

Barton-Fumo, M. (2017). Pleasures of the flesh. *Film Comment, 53*(2), 42.

Beugnet, M. (2007). *Cinema and sensation: French film and the art of transgression.* Carbondale, IL: Southern Illinois University Press.

Clover, C. J. (1992). *Men, women and chainsaws: Gender in the modern horror film.* Princeton, NJ: Princeton University Press.

Coulthard, L., & Birks, C. (2016). Desublimating monstrous desire: The horror of gender in new extremist cinema. *Journal of Gender Studies, 25*(4), 461–476, doi:10.1080/09589236.2015.1011100

Creed, B. (1986). Horror and the monstrous-feminine: An imaginary abjection. *Screen, 27*(1) 44–70.

Creed, B. (1993). *The monstrous-feminine: Film, feminism, psychoanalysis.* London: Routledge.

Dooley, K. (2015). Haptic visions of unstable bodies in the work of Claire Denis. *Continuum, 29*(3), 434–444.

Hainge, G. (2012). A full face bright red money shot: Incision, wounding and film spectatorship in Marina de Van's Dans ma peau. *Continuum, 26*(4), 565–577.

Harkins-Cross, R. (2017). Only women bleed. *The Lifted Brow, (Nick Henderson Zine Collection), 34*(Jun), 5–8.

Heller-Nicholas, A. (2017). Fine young cannibals. *Big Issue Australia,* (534), 32–33.

Kawin, B. F. (2012). *Horror and the horror film.* New York, NY: Anthem Press.

Met, P. (2003). Looking for trouble: The dialectics of lack and excess. *Kinoeye.* Retrieved from http://www.kinoeye.org/03/07/met07.php. Accessed on 26 August 2017.

Morrey, D. (2008). Open wounds: Body and image in Jean-Luc Nancy and Claire Denis. *Film Philosophy, 12*(1), i–vi.

Palmer, T. (2006). Style and sensation in the contemporary french cinema of the body. *Journal of Film and Video, 58*(3), 22–32.

Palmer, T. (2007). Under your skin: Marina de Van and the contemporary French cinéma du corps. *Studies in French Cinema, 6*(3), 171–181.

Peranson, M. (2001). CANNES 2001: Every day, trouble; a week into the Cannes Can. *IndieWIRE.* Retrieved from http://www.indiewire.com/article/cannes_2001_every_day_trouble_a_week_into_the_cannes_can/#. Accessed on 26 August 2017.

Quandt, J. (2004). Flesh & blood: Sex and violence in recent French cinema. *Artforum, 42*(6), 126–132.

Tudor, A. (1989). *Monsters and mad scientists: A cultural history of the horror film.* Oxford: Blackwell.

Williams, L. (1984). When the woman looks. In B. K. Grant (Ed.), *The dread of difference* (pp. 15–34). Austin, TX: University of Texas Press.

Wood, R. (1979). Introduction to the American horror film. In R. Wood & R. Lippe (Eds.), *American nightmare: Essays on the horror film* (pp. 6–28). Toronto: Festival of Festivals.

Chapter 5

Gendering the Cannibal in the Postfeminist Era

Louise Flockhart

5.1.   Gendering the Cannibal in the Postfeminist Era

This chapter takes as its starting point Jennifer Brown's (2013, p. 7) argument that the cannibal in literature and film is a mutable figure who 'reappears in various guises at times when popular culture needs to express real fears and anxieties'. I will argue that the female cannibal has emerged as a manifestation of the cannibal from the mid-1990s in films from Europe, South-East Asia and North America. This appearance coincides with the emergence of a postfeminist media culture and I will argue that the cannibal in these texts is used to express fears, desires and anxieties relating to gender in the postfeminist age. The female cannibal raises questions about the limits of the human, especially how gender complicates the relationships between objectification and subjectivity, and representations of women as humans, animals and monsters.

In this introduction I will briefly discuss how the cannibal figure can be used to question binaries. I will then introduce the idea that there are tensions within postfeminist culture between the success of feminism and a backlash against it which are not easily negotiated. These tensions create ambiguity about women's subjectivity and personhood, and the meaning of femininity and monstrosity. I will then discuss how the films use incest, objectification and dehumanization as well as cannibalism to explore the ambiguities of subjecthood. Although the horror genre is not the only one to use the cannibal to communicate fears and anxieties, the films I will discuss utilize gothic conventions and horror tropes in order to de-familiarize and challenge hegemonic conceptions of the human. I will discuss *301/302* (Park, 1995), *The Woman* (Tonino, Van Den Houten, & McKee, 2011) and *Raw* (De Forêts & Ducournau, 2016) in order to demonstrate the fears and anxieties that the female cannibal represents. I will offer a close analysis of certain scenes from the films to support my argument.

When talking about cannibals, I am discussing living human beings — not zombies, werewolves or vampires. The humanity of the cannibal is where the

Gender and Contemporary Horror in Film, 67—81
doi:10.1108/978-1-78769-897-020191006

ambiguities in meaning begin. By eating human flesh, cannibals are marked as different, monstrous, but by being identified as the same as their victims, their humanity is confirmed. As Kristen Guest (2001) has argued, the cannibal is a figure of alterity but is most productive as a symbol for the permeability of boundaries between human and monster. Guest goes on to claim that because cannibalism draws attention to the sameness of the victim and perpetrator it challenges ideas of absolute difference. Furthermore, she argues that this instability is so central to the function of the cannibal that 'Even when it seems to reinforce dominant ideologies or mainstream discourses, [...] cannibalism also reveals the catch twenty-two of oppositional logic by drawing our attention to the relatedness of bodies that lie beneath the ideas they express' (Guest, 2001, p. 3). Even where the cannibalism seems to reinforce a conservative or hege-monic idea — for example, the idea in eighteenth-century texts that cannibals were black and savage — the very evocation of cannibalism, of the relationship between eater and eaten, undermines any certainty about the absolute difference. This is further complicated by the ways women have often been figured as sub-human within patriarchal cultures. While the question of women's humanity within patriarchal cultures is not a new one, it is a central tension of the post-feminist era in which women's roles in society can be interpreted both within a feminist framework and within the context of a postfeminist backlash.

There is an ambivalence in many late-capitalist societies between traditional femininities in which women's primary roles were as mothers and wives and postmodern femininities which reflect both the economic requirements as well as the feminist victories which encourage women to work outside the home. As Heywood and Drake (2004) have pointed out, while the gender wage gap had decreased for younger generations of Americans, this is undermined by the high-est debt-to-income ratio, and economic conditions which have contributed to the rise in delayed marriage and childbirth, dual income households, job insecurity, credit card and loan borrowing — all of which have an impact on gender roles, especially women's position as wage-earners, mothers and domestic labourers. Diana Negra (2009) claims that certain middle-class women are 'retreating' back to traditional feminine roles in the face of harsh capitalist conditions and disillu-sionment about the results of feminism. As one heavily pregnant comedian (ironically) put it:

> I don't want to lean in, okay? I want to lie down. I want to lie the
> fuck down. I think feminism is the worst thing that ever hap-
> pened to women—our job used to be no job! We had it so good!
> (Volk Weiss & Karas, 2016)

Negra (2009) points out that feminism is often a scapegoat for the economic conditions which mean women must work harder for less money with less time to enjoy family life and the benefits of feminism. However, this is complicated because the return to feminine domestic roles can also be seen as the successful feminist renegotiation of the meaning of success and the value of domestic labour and the family. As Joanne Hollows (2006, p. 114) states:

> The domestic can't simply be celebrated as a site of feminine virtue or as a site of pre-feminist subordination. Instead, the meanings of the domestic, and domestic femininities, are contextual and historical and what operates as a site of subordination for some women may operate as the object of fantasy for others.

Asian contexts also have these ambivalences. Kim (2011) describes how the Korean new femininity, *Missy*, which describes young, married women who focus on their own development and appearance instead of their husband's and children's, is ambivalently embraced, negotiated and resisted by Korean women. This identity emerged from a 'marketing campaign but was also [...] influenced by globalized images of femininity and by changing economic conditions' (Kim, 2011, p. 148). Despite the transnational influences, Kim argues that *Missy* also relates to traditional Korean feminine identities. Many of Kim's interviewees suggested that they wanted to be seen as *Missy* but did not embrace the identity fully because they were aware of its commercial origins and felt it was too selfish.

These ambivalences are encouraged by a mediascape in which feminism is both accepted and rejected. Rosalind Gill (2007, p. 40) claims that 'feminist discourses are part of the media' and that for most people feminism is 'entirely mediated'. Similarly, Angela McRobbie (2009, p. 14) argues that in the media, law, education and other institutions, feminism is 'taken into account' but it is an 'equal opportunities' feminism which does not challenge the structures of society, while more radical feminism which critiques social order is negatively invoked. In other words, the media pays lip-service to feminist ideology but does not fundamentally disturb the structures of patriarchal heteronormativity. Thus, by taking feminism into account the media sells an image of empowered femininity and the success of feminism. Negra and Tasker (2007) describe how postfeminist culture incorporates feminism and commodifies it in the image of the empowered female consumer. It ignores economic disparities and emphasizes work as a 'choice' for women. This is, as Negra and Tasker (2007, p. 2) say, 'anchored in consumption as a strategy (and leisure as a site) for the production of the self. It is also the strategy by which other kinds of social difference are glossed over.' In other words, systemic equality is replaced by personal empowerment based on the highly flawed notion of 'choice'. Consumption is so key to postfeminist culture because it is through consumption that subjectivity is expressed. For Negra and Tasker (2007, p. 8, emphasis added):

> The construction of women as both subjects and consumers, *or perhaps as subjects only to the extent that we are willing and able to consume*, is one of the contradictions at the core of postfeminist culture.

The idea that women can be subjects through consumption ties into the late-capitalist ideal of individual power and responsibility. While consumer choices can have a cultural impact there is also a danger that taking the adage 'the personal is political' too literally can create the impression that power lies with the individual despite any systemic oppression based on identities such as gender, class or race. Postfeminist culture questions the oppressiveness of beauty regimes and sexualization and denies women's vulnerability as victims, partly by encouraging women to be consumers. Rebecca Munford (2004, pp. 148–149) claims that while 'girlie' culture can be a site for exercising female agency, confidence and even resistance to patriarchy, it can simultaneously be a site of 'slippage between feminist agency and patriarchal recuperation'. Thus, postfeminist culture is full of contradictions and oscillations between feminine empowerment and choice – to work, to stay at home, to look traditionally feminine and to 'have it all' – and insidious but systemic oppression which limits women's choices.

By making oppression personal rather than institutional, and celebrating feminine empowerment and choice, the postfeminist mediascape misrepresents the gender-based violence and abuses that women do still experience every day. Whitney (2016) argues that the postfeminist gothic responds to this. In this case, the 'postfeminist' in the postfeminist gothic refers to the periodization of texts which respond to postfeminist media cultures. Whitney argues that where postfeminist media culture denies inequality and celebrates feminine empowerment, the gothic reveals the fears and anxieties underlying this ideology. Thus, the postfeminist gothic, like all gothic, 'drag[s] women's ongoing experiences of spectacular violence up from the basement, forcing our postfeminist culture to confront the monsters it denies' (Whitney, 2016, p. 22). Although the postfeminist gothic demonstrates how women are still victimized – and thus, how our culture is not postfeminist – it is nevertheless part of a media culture which refuses to position women as (simply) victims. The complex and ambiguous position this creates demonstrates women's empowerment and victimization simultaneously.

The postfeminist gothic does not only refuse to position women as victims, but also explores the link between femininity and monstrosity. This challenges the meaning of femininity itself, as Stephanie Genz (2007) argues. Genz (2007) discusses how, following from a shift in postmodern gothic towards more humane monsters, monstrosity is often placed onto feminine bodies. Genz argues (2007, p. 69) that the postfeminist monster is sexy, confident and emphatically not a victim. Rather she 'inhabits femininity' in order to access power. Genz (2007, p. 73) is well aware that this plays on a tension in postfeminist media culture between femininity and feminism/power and admits that:

> In postfeminist Gothic, the resignifications of femininity cannot rid themselves of the threat of phallocentricity, the spectre of heterosexism, as they still function within the same cultural imagery that transfers onto women the labels of inferiority and powerlessness.

Nevertheless, Genz argues that employing traditional femininity in this way destabilizes and resignifies femininity as the ambiguity challenges any absolutes. Genz (2007, p. 74) claims that 'Oscillating between subject and object, victim and perpetrator, the postfeminist Gothic monster is the embodiment of these battles of signification, a site of meaning in question.'

The female cannibal, then, as a female monster, challenges the meaning of femininity, and as a cannibal, challenges the meaning of the human. These texts play with the oscillations of power, subjectivity and femininity. The female cannibal allows us to explore the limits of subjectivity and humanity, and expresses a central tension of the postfeminist era — that perhaps, despite feminism's many gains, nothing has really changed. The texts I will discuss employ features such as incest and objectification to question whether women are still victims of patriarchy, still sexual objects, still perceived as subhuman. They present postfeminist empowerment through monstrous consumption and explore to what extent these strategies actually facilitate power and whether women's access to power necessarily makes them monstrous. These texts work on two levels: on one level, these texts show how individual women can access power through femininity and consumption. Although this creates a kind of catharsis and empowerment, the women are often monstrous. On another level, they demonstrate the continuation of patriarchy, institutional misogyny and the limits of postfeminist empowerment. Ambiguity is built into these texts, and no resolution is offered. Indeed, to offer any resolution would defeat their efficacy in challenging absolutes.

5.2. Incest, Objectification and the Limits of Subjectivity

In the majority of female cannibal texts I have studied, incestuous abuse is featured.[1] In most cases, this is a step/father's rape or sexual abuse of his step/daughter. Jones (2013, p. 141) argues that because rape often stands as a metaphor for all misogyny and patriarchal dominance any revenge taken by the victim — such as the brutal murders or castration in many torture porn films — can never have the same 'symbolic weight' as the rape, thus justifying women's violence against men. I will argue that rape/abuse by a family member (what

---

[1]My research has focused mainly on novels and films from the 1990s to the present. In texts I have found before this date, female cannibals have been either part of a cannibal tribe in which case their gender is not particularly significant, or multiple women are changed physically through chemical or magical intervention. This implies undermines the idea of individual choice and implies all women have a shared nature. For example, *Papaya, Love Goddess of the Cannibals* (Maietto & D'Amato, 1978) features implied cannibalism as part of a tribal ritual, or *Flesh-Eating Mothers* (Martin, Ilich, & Martin, 1988) features a cannibalistic disease metaphor for AIDS in which adulterous wives are physically transformed en masse. The more recent *Doghouse* (Loveday & West, 2009) also plays on this idea of all women being contaminated by a biological weapon and turned into zombie-cannibals.

I will call incestuous abuse) is the more specific metaphor in these texts, standing for all misogyny and dominance, and emphasizing that the patriarchal system of oppression begins in the family and often well before sexual maturity. This type of victimization provides a justification for cannibalism as a mode of revenge. However, I will go on to argue that the cannibalism is not merely revenge but a proactive way of (re-)creating an identity and family.

The patriarchal family is based on the fundamental idea that women need protection from some men by other men. Iris Marion Young (2003, p. 4) describes how men in a family offer protection and in exchange the woman 'concedes critical distance from decision-making autonomy'. In other words, she cannot argue with the steps deemed necessary to protect her. The woman essentially becomes property for her father or husband. However, as Herman and Hirschman (1981) describe, when women are the property of men the incest taboo governs their exchange. This is part of what Rich (1983) described as compulsory heterosexuality which (re)produces heterosexual relationships as the basis for the structure of society. A daughter is protected by her father (in theory)[2] until he gives her in marriage to another man who will protect her (in theory). However, because the father has rights over the daughter, he can choose to disregard the incest taboo and rape his daughter as long as he ultimately does give her away. Thus, incestuous (child) sexual abuse can stand for the system of patriarchy as a whole in which women are treated as objects to be given, used or taken even by the men who are supposed to protect them. As Christine Grogan (2016, p. 18) points out 'incest reflects and maintains the status quo: the order of the patriarchy. Perhaps an exaggeration, it is not a departure from patriarchal family norms but its inevitable by-product.' Thus, incestuous abuse can be used to illustrate and illuminate patriarchal oppression through hyperbole. Haaken (1999, p. 37) argues:

> Since the more subtle or ambiguous forms of bad treatment that girls and women endure so readily fall below the threshold of cultural awareness — indeed, they hardly register — dramatizing abuse may be the strategy of resistance most readily available.

Avril Horner and Sue Zlosnik (2009) suggest that incest is a frequently recurring motif in the gothic. The gothic focuses on the family and home as a site of danger, and female sexuality as a point of exploitation and control. Incest is a family secret which reveals the fractures in the normative structures of the family. If we understand that incestuous abuse is based on the idea that women are property, and that it represents the 'more subtle and ambiguous forms of bad

---

[2]This can mean a father-figure such as a stepfather, grandfather or uncle. However, as Herman and Hirschman claim, a man's rights become more diluted the more other men have claims on the same woman — a grandfather might be head of a household but if the father of the girl returns he could challenge the grandfather's authority/ownership.

treatment' directed at women and girls it becomes clear that objectification/ dehumanization is the underlying problem and is represented more widely in these texts. Indeed, the incestuous abuse is not always overt or always a central feature but is a frequently recurring feature in female cannibal texts which serves to reveal other abuses through its excessiveness.

Furthermore, incest in these texts is a form of sexual cannibalism in that it is an act of sexual consumption which takes place within groups of people who are the same. Levi-Strauss (1990, p. 141) claimed that cannibalism is 'the alimentary form of incest'. This constructs an opposition between incestuous abuse performed by men against women, and cannibalism which, in these texts, is most often an act of destruction (and creation of a new identity) performed by women against men.

Gill (2007) argues that within the postfeminist culture, women have gone from being sexual objects to sexual subjects who can 'choose' to objectify themselves to display/exercise power. The emphasis has changed from male judgment to self-policing through the invitation to be a subject on the condition that she matches the male sexual fantasy. Becoming a subject only on the condition one becomes an object is a precarious position which the female cannibal texts explore. On the one hand, these films show how men still objectify women through incestuous abuse and other acts of dehumanization. On the other hand, they show how women can become subjects by objectifying and consuming others as meat. The excessive horror involved in cannibalism shows how monstrous the act of objectification is. However, cannibalism implies that victim and perpetrator are both human subjects. Consequently, they call into question the construction of subjectivity and the limits of the human. Lynda Hart (1994) theorized that the desiring woman is identified both as a violent woman and as a lesbian[3] – the very identity which compulsory heterosexuality renders invisible. The female cannibal, then, as a violent subject whose relationships with women are based on the cannibalism of men, offers one way to explore how violence and consumption expresses feminine subjectivity.

5.3. Monstrous Femininity in *301/302*

Park Chul-soo's *301/302* (1995), a Korean film, examines the lives of two women living across the hall from each other. 302 (Sin-Hye Hwang) has suffered childhood sexual abuse at the hands of her stepfather, a butcher. This has caused her to become anorexic in an attempt to disappear. The woman in 301 (Eun-Jin Bang), however, consumes excessively. Her husband, Kang (Cheol-ho Park), has divorced her because of her obsession with food and, on moving into her new apartment, she quickly tries to feed her anorexic neighbour. When 301 fails to find food that 302 can digest, 302 offers herself to 301 so that 301 can

---

[3]Lesbian here refers not only to lesbian sexuality but to women whose primary relationships are with other women rather than within a heteronormative structure.

cannibalize her. The women are identified by their apartment numbers, anonymizing them and showing their similarities to each other, casting them as doppelgangers and 'everywoman' figures. We see their lives in flashback as a detective investigates 302's disappearance. Their narrative arcs reflect two sides of the patriarchal family – 302's abuse shows the ways that the system can be exploited by step/fathers, while 301's failed marriage reveals the flaws after the marriage exchange. The film uses claustrophobic indoor settings, canted camera angles, and fish-eye lenses to create a sense of dis-ease and entrapment within the domestic space, and uses flashbacks within flashbacks to generate a disorienting narrative structure which challenges any degree of reliability in the narrative.

301 has been disappointed by the promise of heteronormative relationships. As a newlywed, 301 occupies herself at home in a traditional feminine role. She is isolated both physically – only appearing at home or alone in a shop – and socially as she only talks to Kang and mother on the phone. Although she is never encouraged to get a job, the value of her choice to be a housewife is contested. As a modern consumer, Kang would rather eat fast food and does not appreciate her domestic skills. When he asserts his desire to eat out in future, 301 asks if he uses prostitutes too, implying that if a man can purchase food and sex then a wife is superfluous. Angered by his infidelity and disillusioned with the patriarchal family, 301 cooks and feeds her husband his dog before demanding a divorce. The dog is his baby and by making him eat it, 301 destroys the patriarchal family for him as he has destroyed it for her. Without a wife, there can be no legitimate children and 301's proto-cannibalism asserts her subjectivity as a wife and potential mother while simultaneously positioning her as monstrous. The dog is prepared off-screen, rendering the violence invisible. Although 301 later describes the process of plucking, skinning and dismembering the body to 302, the lack of on-screen violence illustrates how 301 hides her monstrosity through her feminine domestic skills. As with many domestic tasks, the audience, like Kang, only sees the result not the process as he whips the lid off the pot and we are given a close-up of a cooked dog's head floating in a bloody liquid.

When 301 first meets 302, she thinks of her as a 'mannequin' demonstrating how 302 has failed to escape objectification through her anorexia. 301 fantasizes about feeding her up, and gives her plates of gourmet food. 301 is obsessed with feeding others in order to create a family. When she discovers 302 throwing the food away, 301 feels rejected again, pushes 302 into her apartment and tries to force-feed her from the bin. She first stuffs some meat into her own mouth as if showing 302 how to eat like a mother shows a young toddler. She then attempts to feed 302. This monstrous act is intercut by a flashback of 302's stepfather coercing her to eat meat which positions 301 as a monstrous parent, at once performing oral rape on 302 even while attempting to mother her. As Genz (2007) stated, by inhabiting femininity 301 accesses monstrous power, but at the same time, 301 feels like a victim as her cooking (and therefore her love) has been rejected again.

Cannibalism expresses both women's subjectivity when 302 offers herself as a human sacrifice. The women become closer as 301 keeps attempting to mother 302 by feeding her. Although 302's body will not absorb the food, she becomes less resistant to 301's mothering, letting 301 bathe her after throwing up. When 301 finally realizes that there is nothing, she can feed to 302 she pours herself a glass of wine and sits at her table facing the camera in a medium shot. She says 'There is no food Yun-Hee can eat.' This is one of the two times 302 is named in the film as 301 finally acknowledges her subjectivity directly to the audience. 302 walks behind her in a robe, touching 301's shoulders to comfort her. At this point, 302 offers herself, standing naked with her head out of shot and her thighs cut by the table, by asking if she looks tasty. The framing of her torso in this way objectifies her visually in synecdoche but her voiceover shows her active participation in her own objectification. The dialogue in this film is sparse with much of 301's and 302's interactions being implied through the flashbacks within flashbacks making this piece of dialogue distinctive.

301 runs to hug her and dark chiaroscuro lighting with a soft focus on the background hint at a lesbian eroticism but this is left ambiguous as they do not kiss before they part. 302 sinks to her knees out of shot which is, again, suggestively pornographic, hinting at oral sex, but also saintly as if kneeling to pray, and we see 301's face in close-up straining as she strangles her. Flashes of hands around 302's neck are cut with shots of her face as she looks up, the white-blue light in the background reflecting on her face and glasses. There is a suggestion of martyrdom in this shot, reminding one of Dreyer's *The Passion of Joan of Arc* (Unknown producer, 1928) in the close-ups of her face with wide eyes. Even as 301 is performing a murder and planned cannibalism, the film plays with the idea that this is actually a loving act, more angelic than monstrous. Indeed, when 301 eventually eats her cannibal meal at the table with her silver-wear, the ghost of 302 sits opposite. Finally eating and smiling, 302 nods at 301. The cannibalism, then, creates a shared identity between these women which is both familiar and potentially erotic, but definitely outside the patriarchal structures of the family.

The film *301/302* emphasizes how women can be objectified and sexually consumed by showing scenes of incestuous abuse and maternal neglect. The film then uses female cannibalism to explore how female desire is consuming and monstrous but can also create alternative female-oriented relationships outside of patriarchal structures. 301's excessive desire to love others oscillates between monstrosity and femininity. Within a patriarchal family, her desire cannot be tolerated as it produces unwanted subjectivity but in a female-oriented relationship, both 301 and 302 can choose to exercise their subjectivity through consumption.

5.4. Consuming Subjectivities in *The Woman*

The Woman (2011) is a film centred on the Cleeks, a middle-class, white family in contemporary northern USA. The father, Chris (Sean Bridgers), captures a wild woman (Pollyanna McIntosh) while hunting. He coerces his family into helping him torture her, and we discover that he has impregnated his eldest daughter, Peggy (Lauren Ashley Carter), and has raised another daughter, Socket (Alexia Marcigliano), like a dog. When Peggy's teacher, Ms Raton (Carlee Baker), confronts him about the pregnancy Chris feeds her to the dogs while Peggy frees the Woman from the cellar. The Woman then kills and eats Chris's wife, Belle (Angela Bettis), Chris and their son, Brian (Zach Rand), and walks off to start a new family with their youngest daughter, Darleen (Shyla Molhusen), Socket and Peggy.

The narrative focuses on the tensions between subject and object as Chris's numerous dehumanizing acts against women are revealed. While Chris objectifies and dehumanizes women, the Woman uses cannibalism to show defiance and subjectivity. However, dehumanization is not straightforward in this film. Chris positions women as animals, denying them human subjectivity, however, he often forgets that animals do not all end up as meat. Chris's incestuous abuse, his capture and torture of the Woman, and his treatment of Socket might be exaggerations but, as Grogan (2016, p. 18) suggests, they are not departures from patriarchal norms. The film draws equivalences between the female characters that alternately position them as human subjects, monsters, animals and meat, destabilizing Chris's oppression and emphasizing empowerment through consumption. The film shows these tensions through frequent close-ups which objectify the body, and eyeline matches, using eye contact to indicate identification between characters.

When Chris ties the Woman up in his cellar he checks her body, eyes and teeth like an animal while she is apparently unconscious. The camera cuts between extreme close-ups of her body where Chris is looking and feeling, and close-ups of his face, gazing off-camera, showing his reactions to her smell and appearance. Chris's gaze does not invite identification or aesthetic pleasure. His lack of direct eye contact, and the lack of a wider frame of reference, is disconcerting and creates an impression of short-sightedness and claustrophobia. As Chris checks her teeth with his ring finger, the Woman's head snaps up and bites down on his finger. We are given a medium shot from the side showing both characters in a single frame for the first time. Despite her being tied up, Chris cannot make the Woman open her mouth and can only rip his hand away, losing his finger. The camera cuts to a medium shot of the Woman, looking directly into the camera and at Chris as she chews his finger and spits out his wedding ring. It is the Woman's ability to look Chris in the eyes as she cannibalizes him that invites the audience to view her cannibalism as empowering. Her direct gaze invites identification and illustrates her power and confidence. Chris denies her any subjectivity but forgets that animals can bite too. The Woman's gaze, however, suggests she recognizes Chris's subjectivity. She smiles as she chews, as if gloating or laughing at his mistake. Gloating can only occur if there is a shared recognition or understanding of the victory/defeat.

When the Woman kills Belle and Chris, the film emphasizes the eye contact that the Woman gives them. Belle ignores the Woman's pleas for help throughout the film despite their shared identity as Chris's victims. Once free, the camera cuts between the Woman and Belle both gazing directly into the camera and at each other before the attack. This illustrates that they share identities as women, victims and subjects and thus the Woman punishes Belle for her passivity – although Belle is a victim she arguably had the power to help. This reflects the individual blame within postfeminist media culture for structural problems. Similarly, when the Woman rips Chris's heart out and eats it she looks him in the eye as he dies. Their eye contact along with the cannibalism shows their shared subjectivity even while the Woman objectifies him as meat.

Not only does the Woman's cannibalism gain revenge, or empower her, it produces a new female-oriented family. After ripping out Chris's heart, the Woman feeds the rest of it to Socket, and then encourages Chris's youngest daughter, Darleen, to lick her father's blood from the Woman's finger which she does with gusto. Peggy refuses to join in the cannibalism but the Woman acknowledges their shared identity as mothers through eye contact and caressing her bump. Peggy then follows as the others walk off into the sunshine. The women (re)assert their subjectivity through cannibal consumption and lesbian-family identity but they are still animalistic, monstrous and nonetheless feminine. Socket, in particular, demonstrates the tensions between being animalistic and a subject. Unlike Ms Raton and Belle who are turned to meat, Socket gains power through (mindless) consumption but she is still not a human subject. However, the Woman's consumption positions her as a monster in the cellar, the cuts between her and the dogs suggest she is animalistic, but she can also choose who and when to consume and when to share her consumption with others to create a family. The cannibalism places them outside the patriarchal family and positions them as monstrous, but it also allows them to choose a family based on a shared consumption instead of incest.

5.5. The Fight for Subjectivity in *Raw*

Julia Ducournau's *Raw* (2016) focuses on the relationship between two sisters attending the same veterinary college. Justine, perhaps named after De Sade's Justine, is an innocent, intelligent young woman one year below her sister, Alex. As part of the freshman class, Justine is pressured into participating in humiliating rituals which encourage the objectification and sexualization of everyone but particularly the young women and Justine's gay roommate, Adrien. After tasting animal flesh for the first time, Justine gets cannibalistic cravings which cause her pain if she ignores. Alex shares these cravings and tries to teach Justine how to kill to get meat but Justine rejects this help. Although the sisters fight, their love conquers all when Justine forgives Alex for killing and eating Adrien. After a prison visit to Alex, their father reveals that their mother has the same cannibalistic desires. The film explores how objectification justifies the abuse of others by those in power. There are two sides to the cannibalism; on the one hand, it is animalistic and uncontrollable and makes them sick, on the other hand, it does allow the girls to assert their subjectivity but only at the expense of others.

In one scene, the new veterinary students discuss the rape of animals. Justine is appalled and argues that animals have rights but Adrien claims that 'the monkey won't turn anorexic and see a therapist'. Justine continues to argue that a monkey is self-aware and would suffer until other young women look at her with disgust when she claims that a raped woman is the same as a raped monkey. The students do not see the act of rape as the same but as contingent upon the subjectivity of the victim which is problematic if women are consistently dehumanized. Furthermore, Adrien's comments reflect the idea that a woman must show visible signs of suffering to prove that she has been raped, effectively performing a victim role. This is the identity that postfeminist media culture tries to deny through encouraging empowerment through consumption and self-objectification.

Very few adults in positions of authority are shown in the film. One of the teachers who is shown is an old, white, male professor. He insists that either Justine or Adrien have cheated on a paper and interviews Justine in his office, pressuring her to admit that Adrien cheated. The camera cuts between the two with Justine shot from above making her look small, chewing her hair and looking visibly upset, and the professor shot from Justine's perspective below him which frames him as powerful. He rants at her telling her that her intelligence scares away good doctors as many would rather leave than compare themselves to her. The misogynistic disdain for her intelligence shows that there are still institutional barriers for young women that may encourage women to return to the home, disillusioned, as Negra (2009) claims, with the results of feminism.

Justine throws up a surreal amount of hair after reluctantly admitting that Adrien cheated not her. The camera is fixed in a nauseating close-up of her regurgitation. Not only does this evoke a comparison with cats throwing up furballs but it hints towards bulimia, a sign of victimhood according to Adrien's earlier glib remarks. Indeed, at the sinks afterwards, a girl informs Justine that 'two fingers make it come up quicker'. Justine's victimization positions her as animalistic, rejecting her own body. However, acts of cannibalism reassert her humanity and subjectivity.

Alex pressures Justine into a bikini wax after making infantilizing comments about Justine's appearance. When some wax gets stuck and Alex threatens to cut it off with kitchen scissors, Justine kicks out and Alex's finger is accidentally cut off. By eating her sister's finger, Justine satisfies her cravings for flesh and reasserts herself as a subject in the face of Alex's objectification of her. Although upset about her finger, Alex tries to teach Justine how to cause car crashes to get people to eat. Justine rejects the idea of treating people as meat; instead, she objectifies herself by dressing up 'slutty' and practising kissing in the mirror. When Alex sees her she comments that Justine is getting thinner and better not be anorexic — in other words, better not be a victim.

The next day Justine is the object of her classmates' disgust in lectures. Adrien shows her a video of herself at a party in the college morgue acting like a dog as Alex tempts her with a dead man's arm. Alex reduces her to animal for rejecting the consumption that she deems necessary for survival. Justine's attempts to self-objectify instead, to get drunk and kiss strangers, backfires as she loses her subjectivity. She attacks Alex and they fight until they bite into one another's arms and look into each other's eyes. The camera circles them tightly in close-up as they are forced to recognize each other's subjectivity. Their fight is broken up when their classmates start choking them with scarves. At the moment, they both embrace their subjectivity and are forced to recognize the subjectivity of the other; they simultaneously become animalistic objects their classmates feel justified in choking. They are consuming subjects that are also read by others as animalistic objects. Justine has been victimized throughout but is nevertheless a subject struggling with the power dynamics of those around her. As with postfeminist media culture, the narrative of empowered consumption glosses over the continued victimization of women through institutional structures.

At the conclusion of the film, Justine's father sits at the dinner table and unbuttons his shirt as he explains that their mother has the same cannibalistic cravings. His scarred chest horrifies Justine as he hopes that she will find a solution. This reflects the generational tensions in postfeminist media culture as women reject second wave feminism for not changing patriarchal systems enough. The retreat home and the rise of 'girlie' culture are a re-embracing of feminine pleasures which were rejected as a strategy to gain an equality that has never come.

Raw uses female cannibalism to explore how objectification can excuse abuse. It shows how women are encouraged to reject a victim position through consumption and self-objectification. This is in opposition to second wave ideas about rejecting feminine beauty regimes and sexualization. Consumption allows Justine and Alex to access power but this is at the cost of being seen as animalistic and monstrous. The women oscillate between being victims of objectification, and embracing objectification and monstrous subjectivity as they consume themselves and those around them.

5.6. Conclusion

The female cannibal has emerged in the late twentieth century alongside the rise of postfeminist media culture. While feminism is taken into account, patriarchal structures still underpin societal norms, especially the family. The incestuous abuses in these films highlight objectification more generally which positions women as property, sexualized objects and animals. By performing acts of cannibalism, the women in these films gain subjectivity by objectifying others but also by recognizing their victims' subjectivities. As cannibals, they are the same as their victims. The cannibalism also offers a chance for these women to create female-oriented families and lesbian identities by sharing consumption with others. This reflects the desire for femininity within postfeminist media culture, and a reclaiming of traditional feminine roles despite the lack of structural change that often characterizes these roles as objectified. The female-oriented cannibal family is then, a fantasy of the destruction of the patriarchal family but not necessarily of traditional femininity. This tension reproduces femininity as monstrous and caring which is enabled by the cannibal as a figure of alterity and sameness.

References

Brown, J. (2013). *Cannibalism in literature and film*. Basingstoke: Palgrave Macmillan.

De Forêts, J. (Producer), & Ducournau, J. (Director). (2016). *Raw* [Motion Picture]. France: Petit Film, Rouge International.

Genz, S. (2007). (Re)making the body beautiful: Postfeminist Cinderella's and gothic tales of transformation. In B. Brabon & S. Genz (Eds.), *Postfeminist gothic* (pp. 68–84). Basingstoke: Palgrave Macmillan.

Gill, R. (2007). *Gender and the media*. Cambridge: Polity.

Grogan, C. (2016). *Father-daughter incest in twentieth-century American literature*. Madison, NJ: Fairleigh Dickinson University Press.

Guest, K. (2001). Introduction: Cannibalism and the boundaries of identity. In K. Guest (Ed.), *Eating their words: Cannibalism and the boundaries of cultural identity* (pp. 1–9). Albany, NY: SUNY.

Haaken, J. (1999). Heretical texts: The courage to heal and the incest survivor movement. In S. Lamb (Ed.), *New versions of victims: Feminism's struggle with the concept* (pp. 13–41). London: New York University Press.

Hart, L. (1994). *Fatal women: Lesbian sexuality and the mark of aggression*. Princeton, NJ: Princeton University Press.

Herman, J. L., & Hirschman, L. (1981). *Father-daughter incest*. London: Harvard University Press.

Heywood, L., & Drake, J. (2004). "It's all about the Benjamins": Economic determinants of third wave feminism in the United States. In S. Gillis, G. Howie, & R. Munford (Eds.), *Third wave feminism: A critical exploration* (pp. 13–23). Basingstoke: Palgrave Macmillan.

Hollows, J. (2006). Can I go home yet? Feminism, post-feminism and domesticity. In J. Hollows & R. Moseley (Eds.), *Feminism and popular culture* (pp. 97–118). Oxford: Berg.

Horner, A., & Zlosnik, S. (2009). Keeping it in the family: Incest and the female gothic plot in Du Maurier and Murdoch. In D. Wallace & A. Smith (Eds.), *The female gothic* (pp. 115–132). Basingstoke: Palgrave Macmillan.

Jones, S. (2013). *Torture porn: Popular horror after Saw.*. Basingstoke: Palgrave Macmillan.

Kim, J. M. (2011). Is 'the missy' a new femininity? In R. Gill & C. Scharff (Eds.), *New femininities: Postfeminism, neoliberalism and subjectivity* (pp.147–158). Basingstoke: Palgrave Macmillan.

Levi-Strauss, C. (1990). *The naked man: Introduction to mythologies, volume 4* (trans. J. Cape). Chicago, IL: University of Chicago Press (Original work published in French, 1971).

Loveday, M. (Producer) & West, J. (Director). (2009). *Doghouse* [Motion Picture]. London, UK: Carnaby International.

Maietto, C. (Producer) & D'Amato, J. (Director). (1978). *Papaya: Love goddess of the cannibals* [Motion Picture]. Italy: Mercury Cinematografica.

Martin, J. A. & Ilich, M. P. (Producers) & J. A. Martin (Director). (1988). *Flesh-eating mothers* [Motion Picture]. USA: Unknown.

McRobbie, A. (2009). *The aftermath of feminism: Gender, culture and social change.* London: Sage.

Munford, R. (2004). "Wake up and smell the lipgloss": Gender, generation and the (a)politics of girl power. In S. Gillis, G. Howie, & R. Munford (Eds.), *Third wave feminism: A critical exploration* (pp.142–153). Basingstoke: Palgrave Macmillan.

Negra, D. (2009). *What a girl wants? Fantasizing the reclamation of self in post-feminism.* London: Routledge.

Negra, D., & Tasker, Y. (2007). Introduction: Feminist politics and postfeminist culture. In D. Negra & Y. Tasker (Eds.), *Interrogating postfeminism: Gender and the politics of popular culture* (pp. 1–25). London: Duke University Press.

Park, C. (Producer & Director). (1995). *301/302* [Motion Picture]. South Korea: Park Chul-Soo Films.

Rich, A. (1983). Compulsory heterosexuality and the lesbian experience. In A. Snitow, C. Stansell, & S. Thompson (Eds.), *Powers of desire: The politics of sexuality.* New York, NY: Monthly Review Press.

Tonino, R., & Van Den Houten, A. (Producers), & McKee (Director). (2011). *The woman* [Motion Picture]. USA: Moderncinè.

Unknown (Producer) & Dreyer, C. T. (Director). (1928). *The Passion of Joan of Arc.* [Motion Picture]. France: Boulogne-Billancourt.

Volk Weiss, B. (Executive Producer), & Karas, J. (Director). (2016). *Ali Wong: Baby cobra* [Live recording]. USA: Netflix.

Whitney, S. E. (2016). *Splattered ink: Postfeminist gothic fiction and gendered violence.* Urbana, IL: University of Illinois Press.

Young, I. M. (2003). The logic of masculinist protection: Reflections on the current security state. *Signs: Journal of Women in Culture and Society, 29*(1), 1–25. Retrieved from http://www.signs.rutgers.edu/content/Young,%20Logic%20of% 20Masculinist%20Protection.pdf.

PART II
BOUNDARIES

Chapter 6

#Selfveillance: Horror's Slut Shaming through Social Media, Sur- and Selfveillance

Hannah Bonner

6.1. Introduction

Social media misuse is the new virtual house of horrors. Whether utilizing social media platforms such as Instagram, SnapChat, Facebook, Twitter and so on, social media can be a rabbit hole of online harassment, slut shaming and bullying that sends teenagers and young adults tumbling down its computer-mediated corridors again and again.[1] The US Department of Health and Human Services reports, 'High school teens spend an average of 2.3 hours on these types of activities on a weekday and 4.3 hours per day on weekends (US Department of Health and Human Services, 2016).' 'Media and communications activities' are broad terms meant to encapsulate not just social media, but television, movies, music, email, etc.; this ancillary online media can be useful not just in connecting or communicating, but for entertainment purposes as well.

---

[1]Additionally, Haley Tsukayama's article 'Teens spend nearly nine hours every day consuming media' in *The Washington Post* states that, 'Teens are spending more than one-third of their days using media such as online video or music — nearly nine hours on average, according to a new study from the family technology education non-profit group, Common Sense Media. For tweens, those between the ages of 8 and 12, the average is nearly six hours per day.' Their reference to the Kaiser Family Foundation's 2010 study further suggests that the numbers could be more like 'an average of five-and-a-half hours of media use for those ages 8-10, 8 hours and 40 minutes for those aged 11-14, and just under 8 hours for 15-18 year-olds' (Tsukayama, 2015, pp. 1, 4).

Gender and Contemporary Horror in Film, 85—99

© **Hannah Bonner**

All rights of reproduction in any form reserved

doi:10.1108/978-1-78769-897-020191007

While people lay bare their interior lives at the ease of a click of a button on sites such as Yik Yak or After School, often such candid confessionals or comments can rapidly escalate toward more incendiary claims or conflicts. Yik Yak was a mostly student-based app where users anonymously posted anything, from complaining about one's homework to directly soliciting sex or cybersex. According to Biz Carson's article 'The Yik Yak app is officially dead' in *Business Insider*, Yik Yak, founded in 2013, constantly, 'faced problems with harassment and bullying in the app and never quite found a good way to combat it' (Carson, 2017, p. 6), eventually leading to the site's shut down in 2017.[2] Though After School, created in 2014, is an anonymous web forum meant for high school students to ask innocuous questions, share embarrassing stories, or reveal crushes, one student stated in Moriah Balingit's *The Washington Post* article: 'with the shield of anonymity, users have zero accountability for their posts, and can openly spread rumors, call classmates hurtful names, send threats, or even tell someone to kill themselves' (Balingit, 2015, p. 16). While the rumour mill has been part and parcel of middle school, high school, and college life for decades, on social media the veil of anonymity adds a nefarious bite due to the 'zero accountability'. In her study *Sexting: Gender and Teens*, Judith Davidson writes about how social media raises questions about public versus private space and how 'society [is] gravitating toward a new relationship to privacy and exposure' (Davidson, 2014, p. 4). The lines between our private and public spheres increasingly blur.

The social media landscape, and its proclivity toward humiliation and harassment, seems to increasingly effect young girls and women, who are often the targets for social media misuse or punished for sharing pictures of their bodies and/or faces, punishment that replicates the patriarchal status quo. Judith Davidson writes, '[...] girls were blamed in regard to sexting incidents, while boys were often seen as hapless victims' (2014, p. 7), illuminating the sexual double standard existent between young women and men. Furthermore, Nancy Jo Sales's sweeping study *American Girls: Social Media and the Secret Lives of Teenagers* examines how social media is making girls more submissive to boys (2017, p. 188).[3] And not only can social media use be gendered, but also many of these sites actively encourage the sexualization and categorization of women such as James Hong and Jim Young's Hot or Not, a site 'Hong and Young create[d] [as] a way for strangers to look at a picture of a woman's face and vote on how she measured up' (Sales, 2017, p. 12). While just a digital upgrade away from, say, a beauty pageant, these social media sites foreground the existent

---

[2]The site did not shut down solely because of bullying.
[3]Sales writes, 'The numbers of girls on social media on a daily basis run high regardless of race, education, and household income, or whether they are living in urban, rural, or suburban areas. In 2015, Facebook, Instagram, Snapchat, Twitter, and online pinboards such as Pinterest were the most popular sites for girls. Girls in 2015 were sending anywhere from 30 to more than 100 texts per day, according to studies' (2016, p. 10).

patriarchal structures and attitudes so deeply ingratiated within our social, cultural and political fabric.[4]

Body-shaming is not new, its lineage is much older. In Liz Lane's essay 'Feminist Rhetoric in the Digital Sphere', she writes that in 2013, 'conservative commentator Erik Erikson called [Wendy] Davis "abortion Barbie"' (Lane, 2015, p. 4) during Davis's 13-hour filibuster to delay a restrictive abortion bill. Erikson's dismissive rhetoric wed Davis's politics to her appearance. Additionally, the 2000s have seen an uptick in plastic surgery with *BuzzFeed* reporting in 2015 that 'patients cit[ed] selfies as a reason for plastic surgery'; and before Instagram, even 'Aristotle called the female form "a deformed male"' (Lee Yang, Celestino, & Koeppel, 2015, pp. 3, 16).

This tendency to judge, overly assess or punish women for their bodies, their sexuality, or their 'sluttiness', appears in the horror genre as well: we might consider internet shaming as the afterlife of our horror education when someone (typically, though not always, female) suffers punishment for eliciting an illicit look, who bares her body, or who delights in her hedonistic (i.e. healthy) sexuality. In Alfred Hitchcock's *Psycho* (1960), Norman Bates stabs Marion Crane in the shower after the audience has admired her in the opening sequence donning just a slip and bra, as if, as David Thomson writes in his book *The Moment of Psycho*, 'there's something in the air that makes sex itself seem illicit' (2009, p. 23); in Steven Spielberg's *Jaws* (1975), the shark attacks Chrissie Watkins for skinny dipping at dawn (and provocatively encouraging her drunk male companion to join her); and in Brian De Palma's *Dressed to Kill* (1980), Robert Elliott slashes Kate Miller with a razor after her infidelity: an unabashed tryst with a stranger, including cunnilingus in the back of a cab while the driver adjusts his mirror so he can watch. Now, in horror films of the twenty-first century, this desire to *torture the woman*, as touted by Alfred Hitchcock, seems increasingly inextricably linked to social media, the Internet and digital technology – to platforms in which the female characters are constantly under watch.[5]

---

[4]In 2016, CNN reported that in an interview with Howard Stern, Donald J. Trump eagerly responded to Stern's suggestion that he would do a show where he just rates women: 'That may be the best idea of all I would say I'm the all-time judge, don't forget, I own the Miss Universe pageant' (Kaczynski, Massie, & McDermott, 2016).

[5]The gaze in film theory is germane to gender. Laura Mulvey's influential essay 'Visual Pleasure and Narrative Cinema' (1975) analyses how the look disproportionately freezes the woman as pure spectacle, rather than rendering her as active agent in the plot. The scopophilic, desiring, if controlling, gaze revolves around women's 'to-be-looked-at-ness'; yet, in horror the gaze gesticulates towards the promise of a woman's torture, punishment and death. In her classic essay 'When the Woman Looks', Linda Williams writes, '[the woman] is often asked to bear witness to her own powerlessness in the face of rape, mutilation, and murder' (1984, p. 17). To be seen and to see is an invariable power struggle in horror films. In the twenty-first century, this genre's modus operandi increasingly depicts the slut shaming and cyberbullying of young women as well.

The screen's ever-present eye evokes a Foucauldian Panopticon cell in which the prisoner is permanently on display, but unaware as to when she is being watched. The possibility of perpetual surveillance is meant to create an obedient prisoner, with Foucault crediting the Panopticon's effectiveness as "the fact of being constantly seen, of being able always to be seen, that maintains the disciplined individual in his subjection" (1995, p. 187). In this essay I equate surveillance with the Panopticon's casual relationship: if one lives under the threat of constant surveillance, one will comport him or herself in a specific way. One's image becomes the central concern. Surveillance is closely akin to what I refer to as *selfveillance*, a form of surveillance that arises out of social media culture. Both sur- and selfveillance proliferate in the social media age due to the ubiquity and prevalence of screens. Selfveillance, digitally documenting one's self, is a term I refer to elsewhere (Bonner, 2018): The morpheme of the −ie suffix added at the end of the word "self" forms a derivative − the selfie is a product of the self, and, herein, an image product, made from the self. The selfie, therefore, is the constructed image of *le corps propre*: the body proper. The selfie puts one's best face forward. Thus, I refer to selfveillance as the internalized impulse to construct the body proper on social media, as the user anticipates the gaze of others and constructs an image that meets the tacit approval of this ubiquitous gaze. In creating one's proper body image, the selfie's construction relies on the position of the hand *sur-*, from above, intimating social media's ubiquitous gaze that routinely surveys one's image. Once a selfie is posted online, the image is susceptible to being viewed by anyone − a 21st century form of surveillance.

Yet, the surveillance and selfveillance in *The Cabin in the Woods* (2012), *Unfriended* (2015) and *#Horror* (2015) underscore how this technology punishes or (slut) shames young women in the horror genre by specifically targeting the social trespasses and mishaps of their young female characters. Digitally documenting oneself, via Instagram or Facebook, or engaging in the ephemeral livestream transmission of Skype, results in lethal consequences for these girls and women, both figuratively (social suicide) and literally (death). It is particularly fitting that this gendered punishment correlate to the horror genre and technology, as both are predicated on the importance of the gaze and women.[6] These films keep within that horror genre's tradition by punishing these women, albeit

---

[6]In Carol J. Clover's seminal text *Men, Women, and Chainsaws: Gender in the Modern Horror Film,* she writes, 'there is something about the victim function that wants manifestation in a female' (1992, p. 13). While I wholeheartedly agree with Clover's claim, I would further venture that in each of these films the victim manifests as female precisely because she is a victim of self- or surveillance.

not just with a rabid slasher or rape, but with the threat of social media bullying, harassment and slut shaming, achieved by means of ceaseless sur- or selfveillance. Thus, I seek to argue how sur- and selfveillance in horror films post-2010 has become a narrative and visual trope that updates the anachronistic killer in the social media age, de-subjectifying and dispersing the lethal gaze across social media and digital platforms. Women in these films lack control, not just over their bodies, but also over their self-image, thus damning the 'slut' or 'final girl' with this digital gaze, and exhuming narratives of the final girl, slut or woman held hostage in horror films in the twenty-first technologically savvy (and culpable) century.

6.2. When a Woman Is Looked At

Films such as Drew Goddard's *The Cabin in the Woods* depict how technology, specifically surveillance, is much more insidious than any vampire or werewolf. *The Cabin in the Woods* satirizes the horror genre's key tropes and motifs as it follows five friends traveling to the titular woods for a relaxing weekend getaway and the monsters they unintentionally invoke. These monsters, housed in a vast mechanical vault known as 'The Facility', annually sacrifice a group of individuals[7] in order to placate the 'ancient ones below', controlled by a mass team of Intel and computer technicians, including the chief organizers (and voyeurs) Gary Sitterson (Richard Jenkins) and Steve Hadley (Bradley Whitford). The zombie, redneck torture family (innocuously dubbed 'the Buckners') in *The Cabin in the Woods* is not the product of chemical spillage or possession, but, rather, released by the press of a button from that endless mechanical 'archive' of 'what nightmares are from'.[8] *The Cabin in the Woods*, through screens, relies on ubiquitous surveillance as a means of instigating terror. It is the 'fact of being constantly seen', whether by high key government surveillance systems or by judgmental peers, that throws these characters into disarray or death.

The scene immediately following the title sequence achieves an atmosphere of ocular omnipresence. The free-ranging camera starts on the street with a long shot of people driving or skateboarding, then rises like a spectre to peer in through Dana's (Kristen Connolly) second story bedroom window with a steady zoom.[9] Dana is initially framed in a long shot, allowing the audience to admire her dancing

---

[7]'[The sacrifice] has always required youth', Sigourney Weaver's character, The Director, says. 'There must be at least five: the whore, she's corrupted, she dies first; the athlete, the scholar, the fool, all suffer and die at the hands of whatever horror they have raised, leaving the last to live or die as fate decides: the virgin.'

[8]An archive whose grid somewhat resembles the endless scroll of an Instagram feed.

[9]Perhaps a cinematographic nod to the opening scene in *Psycho* where the camera tracks in through the blinds of a hotel room in Phoenix, Arizona at precisely 2.43 p.m. The camera pans laterally in Hitchcock's film like a surveillance camera as it scans the city landscape, before finally tracking in through the blinds (intimating other lateral slashes to come, albeit on the body of Marion Crane); similarly, in *The Cabin in the Woods* the camera pans across the neighbourhood street before moving into a crane shot as the camera tracks in toward Dana dancing half-clothed before the open window.

and packing in underwear and a shirt. Goddard then cuts to a medium shot of Dana collecting books and clothes to pack for her weekend getaway. The third shot again shows Dana in a medium shot, but this time with the camera tilted up as something on her desk stops her in her tracks. The tilt underscores a predatory gaze, like someone (or something) is peering up at Dana from beneath the desk. As Dana lifts a notebook from the desk and flips through its pages, the camera angle changes to an over-the-shoulder shot providing the audience with a glimpse as to why she has paused her packing: a drawing of a man. The over-the-shoulder shot is similarly suggestive of surveillance or spying, as if the audience is peering in on Dana during this private moment. And Goddard cements this reading by cutting to another medium shot of the camera tilted up at Dana as her friend, Jules, approaches her from behind, just as the audience did voyeuristically moments earlier. The friends playfully banter about what to pack (school books, no; red bikini, yes) and the scene soon cuts to them on the street entering their RV. As the RV drives away, the camera chronicles their departure, rising again in a crane shot, but this time to the roof of Dana's apartment building where a man clad in black speaks in his headset that, 'the nest is empty. We're right on time.' Thus, the free-ranging camera becomes less a specter (a traditional horror film motif) and more akin to a surveillance drone. The cinematography alerts the audience to themes and apparatuses of surveillance that will plague the remainder of the film as well as the gendered way of looking at women. Dana is the film's 'final girl'. This opening scene is a liminal moment that not only implicitly points to Dana as our protagonist (the scholarly, serious girl in the group of the five friends), but also to the narrative and formal function of surveillance within the film, evidenced with the crane shot that alludes to the aerial dexterity of a drone, always watching our doomed group.

Traditionally, according to Carol J. Clover's *Men, Women, and Chainsaws*, the final girl is 'the distressed female [...] is the image of the one who did not die: the survivor [...] abject terror personified' (1992, p. 35). She is also 'the main character [...] not sexually active' (p. 39) and 'intelligent, watchful, and level headed' (p. 44). While Dana is not overtly sexualized in this sequence (the camera does not track up her body, fetishistically fragment parts of her body in close-up, or show her in slow motion), Goddard's framing allows the audience to blatantly see Dana's half-clothed body. Furthermore, the audience of *The Cabin in the Woods* is not the only audience watching Dana. Within the diegesis, there is a whole audience in The Facility watching these five friends' every move. This extra layer of mediation highlights surveillance's ubiquity, especially when women are under watch (and echoes the panoply of interfaces and screen windows in *Unfriended* as well). The voyeur is no longer just the audience, squirming in their seats from Michael Meyers's point of view as he tracks down his naked sister and her boyfriend in *Halloween* (Carpenter, 1978); now the audience as voyeur watches the voyeurs watch the surveyed.[10]

---

[10]This configuration is similar to Alfred Hitchcock's *Rear Window* (1954), but without the ubiquity of screens and digital interfaces. Whereas Jeffries is housebound in *Rear Window*, only able to piece together the mystery from afar, in *The Cabin in the Woods*, there are microphones and cameras in every room and outdoor area.

On their first evening at the Cabin, Jules and Curt escape their friends' company for a sexual escapade in the woods. Curt chides Jules to take off her shirt, coaxing, 'come on baby, we're all alone'. The shot cuts from them in the woods to a long shot of every intel member at The Facility silently staring up at the surveillance screen of Curt and Jules, as if in rapture. Three gigantic screens of the couple provide three different angles of them. Goddard then cuts to the reaction shot of The Facility members (a swath of men) smiling smugly in anticipation of Jules's strip tease. When Jules defers, saying 'I'm chilly', the men collectively groan. Jules, as an archetype, is later described as 'the whore: she's corrupted, she dies first'. But it is not just Jules's sexual relationship with Curt that renders her a 'whore'; it is also the way she is visually framed within the diegesis. Jules satisfies not just her boyfriend's visual pleasure, but the Facility's audience and the Audience. Jules's desire for her partner, and her willingness to finally bare her breasts for him, is the ultimate transgression that leads to her death, confirming Linda Williams's (1984, p. 32) theory: 'the desiring look of the female victim becomes a direct cause of the sexual crisis that precipitates her own death.' In this network of gazes and diegetic surveillance footage, 'to be on the object side of the camera is to be hurt' (Clover, 1992, p. 171). The mediation of Jules's image is conveyed through a seemingly objective perspective, which is simultaneously a camera and a screen. The surveillance of Jules, just as with Dana, is predacious and the gaze on the sexual female body is an assaultive one; indeed, if the woman acquiesces and delights in the gaze, the look is not just assaultive, but deadly.[11] Jules is slut shamed, and slayed, for her corporeal display and for serving as an optical delight, not just for The Facility members, but also for audience members, both eagerly and anxiously awaiting her to fulfil her function as a prurient trope.

Leo Gabriadze's *Unfriended* (2015) is filmed on a Mac desktop where the cinema screen is the laptop screen, made up of OS-X Maverick display programs and interfaces. It follows six friends during a Skype session on the anniversary of their classmate's, Laura Barnes (Heather Sossaman), suicide. An unknown member of their chat, 'billie227', causes consternation and commotion, only to be revealed as the ghost of Laura who wants to play a game that punishes this group for posting an unflattering video of her that ultimately led to online bullying, and, eventually, her suicide. Her best friend Blaire (Shelley Henning) serves as the key that unlocks the cyberbullying mystery. As Pedro Noel Doreste writes in his dissertation 'Death and the Diagonal Display: Cinema's Planned Obsolescence in the Screen-captured Image', *Unfriended* provides us with, 'a snapshot of present anxieties stemming from the need to stay alive (or current) within online environments' (Doreste, 2016, p. 7). Instead of director Jean-Luc Godard's adage, 'the cinema is truth twenty-four times per second', our lives online are now our social truth 24 hours a day.

---

[11]Susan Sontag makes a similar point in her book *On Photography*, stating: 'to photograph people is to violate them [...] to photograph someone is a sublimated murder [...] the act of taking pictures is a semblance of rape' (1977, p. 177).

Blaire, Jess and Laura in *Unfriended* similarly showcase the way in which surveillance punishes women for eliciting the gaze, as well as selfveillance, and the ramifications of online bullying upon being seen in socially precarious circumstances. *Unfriended*, all about looking and optics, adheres to Carol J. Clover's (1992, p. 167) notion that 'horror privileges eyes because, more crucially than any other kind of cinema, it is about eyes. More particularly, it is about eyes watching horror'. Part of the gimmick in *Unfriended* clearly confirms Clover's theory as each member of the group must watch their peers perish one by one until only Blaire, our final girl, is left. The film begins with a (as-yet-unknown) laptop user clicking from one page featuring a video of Laura's suicide to another that states 'the video that forced [Laura] to kill herself', before a Skype call from 'Mitch' interrupts his or her online surfing. The user is our protagonist Blaire and Mitch is her loyal boyfriend. As Mitch's Skype window pops on screen, the image freezes for several seconds though the audio does not. The delay in the image is a liminal moment underscoring anxieties regarding self-presentation, image of the self and visibility: all pertinent themes in the film. Waiting for the visual introduction of both Blaire and Mitch produces unease as we nervously anticipate who (or what) will be revealed when the signal finally connects. Just as in horror films from the twentieth century when we waited with averted eyes as a character turned a corner in a deserted house, unsure of what they might stumble upon, in *Unfriended* the anxiety arises from delays in media: what could surprise us when the glitch ceases, when the connection clicks.

The audience first hears Blaire whisper tantalizingly to Mitch, 'I got something to show you!' Blaire focuses the laptop on her painted toes and repeats the phrase, albeit this time in a deep-throated accent like one might expect of a monster, an accent Mitch dubs her 'demon voice'. As Mitch's window pops on screen he admits, 'there's other things I want to see more of'. 'I think I know what you want', Blaire replies, adjusting the laptop screen so it captures her legs and, then, her torso. Blaire's ludic fragmentation fetishizes her body for Mitch (and the audience's) scopic pleasure. Since everything the audience sees is from Blaire's laptop screen, she controls how she is visually portrayed; yet, like Audre Lorde proclaims in *Sister Outsider*, 'the master's tools will never dismantle the master's house' (1984, p. 110). Despite Blaire's supposed autonomy over her self-presentation, she still adheres to patriarchal ways of seeing (and showcasing) the female body. Much like a classical Hollywood film might pan up a woman's body from her toes to her head, Blaire readjusts her laptop, so we see her limb by limb, before finally revealing her face when Mitch, bearing a knife, jokingly states, 'take that shirt off or I'll cut it off.' 'Hey that worked!' Blaire laughs as she unbuttons her shirt and suggestively touches her stomach and the top of her underwear. 'You're really sexy when you're violent,' Blaire says offhandedly before revealing to Mitch that she wants to make 'prom night the night', intimating they will finally sexually consummate their relationship. The interchange is then interrupted by their friends Skyping in for a group chat; as Blaire scrambles to button her shirt again, her buddy Jess loudly declares, 'Blaire you're a dirty girl and you're going to hell now.' The audience surveys Blaire and Mitch's relationship through the interface of their laptops, as well as their friends, and, as the audience learns all too quickly, Laura's malignant, murdering ghost, too.

Laura exploits Blaire and Mitch's social status as a couple when she reveals to the group that Laura cheated on Mitch with their mutual friend Adam. Not only did she cheat, she slept with Adam, an action Mitch has been eagerly awaiting, as evidenced by the opening exchange between the couple. However, the photographs and video footage of Blaire and Adam are a product of Laura's surveillance. In what seems like an impossible form of espionage surveillance, Laura takes multiple photographs and videos of Blaire and Adam's tryst. Due to Laura's omnipresence as a vengeful ghost, she can go places and capture images that others cannot. What should have been an intensely private moment is recorded for all these friends to see. The surprise of the surveillance footage's ubiquity is as equally disturbing as Blaire's infidelity. Laura's 'eyes' see everything.

Yet, Laura's surveillance is a particular kind of karmic retribution. At the beginning of *Unfriended* the audience sees a YouTube clip of Laura shoot herself and then another video link entitled 'Laura Barns Kill Urself' of Laura drunk at a party. The YouTube video ends with someone creeping up behind a passed-out Laura, videotaping her with their phone, revealing her white daisy duke shorts that are covered in faeces. Like Brian De Palma's menstruating Carrie (1976) or Regan vomiting in *The Exorcist* (1973), the abject female body is considered especially monstrous in horror films, as evidenced by Barbara Creed's book *The Monstrous-Feminine* (1993). Like Carrie, Laura, too, is relentlessly bullied, albeit online, urged to kill herself for such a bodily affront to female decorum.[12] Subsequently, Laura punishes the purveyor of the surveillance footage (Blaire) by utilizing surveillance footage to achieve her own ends. Unlike the all-male surveillance team in *The Cabin in the Woods* with their scopophillic gaze that simultaneously desires and destroys Jules, Laura wields her now all-seeing and recording eye to let Blaire, and others, get a taste of their own medicine. Furthermore, Laura as an online ghost adheres to a female lineage that Jeffrey Sconce explores in his book *Haunted Media: Electronic Presence from Telegraphy to Television* of 'the spiritualist movement [that] provided one of the first and most important forums for women's voices to enter the public sphere' (Sconce, 2000, p. 13). Just as surveilling technologies and online forums led to Laura's humiliation, so too do they empower her revenge as 'spiritualism empowered women to speak out in public, often about very controversial issues facing the nation, but only because all understood

---

[12]Additionally, Laura lying prone on the ground, intoxicated and half conscious, evokes the notorious descriptions of Syracusesnap, a Snapchat story from 2015 that featured multiple stories of girls having sex. Nancy Jo Sales writes, 'There were pictures of girls' breasts and girls' behinds, many where girls were lying prone on a bed or on the floor, their faces hidden' (2016, p. 5), spotlighting the total sexualization, submissiveness and erasure of girls in these Snapchats, often lying in the lateral position in which we find Laura.

that the women were not the ones actually speaking, at least not women who were still alive' (Sconce, 2000, p. 49). Similar to Dana unleashing the store-house of monsters to murder all the employees of The Facility, (and, thus, leading to the world's total destruction) in *The Cabin in the Woods*, Laura flips surveilling technologies on the five friends that humiliated her. Her voice is mediated by the computer screen, her powers contingent on using the media that led to both her social and actual suicide. Like director Leo Gabriadze, Laura weaponizes the gaze.

6.3.   When a Woman Looks at Her Self

Tara Subkoff's *#Horror* (2015) also explores how social media's sur- and self-veillance does not lead to autonomy or control of the self, but to violence and death. *#Horror* encapsulates this recurrent compulsion to document one's self and the ramifications of this perpetual presence online, as well as cyberbullying. The film follows a group of middle school girls at a sleepover who incessantly post selfies to Instagram and Facebook. As the evening progresses, all hell breaks loose as one by one are killed by their peer: 12-year-old Cat. The girls' social media use links them to the series of murders, as videos and pictures of the murders are then posted on a social media site for visual consumption and entertainment.

The film, much like *Psycho* and *The Cabin in the Woods*, begins with the camera panning laterally across a silent, snowy landscape and slowly tracking toward a red car in which a couple is having sex. Once they consummate their copulation, the woman departs, and the man, Harry, drives away. A phone call moments later from his bereft wife, Alex (Chloë Sevigny), signals that this is an illicit affair. As Alex berates her husband, the camera stealthily approaches the car, handheld. Upon hanging up, the camera suddenly zooms in to the car as Harry's neck is slit, the intensified continuity exaggerated by multiple cuts in quick succession. Subkoff then cuts to Harry, but seen as if from a camcorder, the red recording button in the right-hand corner counting the minutes of footage filmed. The text '#' appears on screen as it is slashed through by a silver streak and then splattered with animated, cartoonish blood.

Director Subkoff satirically renders violence, murder, and death as inher-ent to the social media realm, something worthy of garnering 'likes'. The montage then cuts to the mistress running through the snow, seen through the point of view of the camcorder's lens. Before Subkoff cuts to a close-up of the mistress's screaming mouth, a smiling emoji pops on screen, indicating that we, the audience, are not the only audience witnessing this crime. There is an anonymous forum of observers not just voyeuristically watching this scene but *delighting* in the female's death. As the tagline on the DVD case states, 'Death is trending.' Subkoff details this death as just one of many click-bait moments on social media when Subkoff freezes on the woman's open mouth in a snapshot. The frame then pulls back to reveal a myriad of other snapshots in a grid[13]: lights above a vanity table, blood splattered on an arm, two friends making 'duck face' at the camera. The animated images then flip over, like playing cards, to reveal cartoon candies and jewels with numbers ('230', '125', '315') popping up, as if to suggest that these are the images that have garnered the most likes or points. The recurrent sound of a cash register's trill sonically suggests that these images are bankable, commodified, and entertainment. The 'like' holds its own value and social capital.

While many of these snapshots are selfies, others, such as the mistress's death, are surveillance footage, intimating that both self- and surveillance can lead to social and literal death, while simultaneously boosting one's popularity. When Laura reveals online, at the end of *Unfriended*, that Blaire was the one who betrayed her, Facebook users instantly begin to berate Blaire in the same way they did Laura: encouraging her to kill herself. The ceaseless caustic commentary is as rapid as the plethora of pictures on *#Horror*'s online game that the murderer, Cat, plays, accruing thousands of likes and points for each murder she commits and documents. 'I'll have the most likes, and the top score, and I'll be the top player, and I'll be remembered forever', she says in a self-recorded video at the end of the film. In a 2018 interview with *Marginalia*, poet and essayist Ocean Vuong reflects on the role social media plays in mediating our understanding of the self:

> The premise of the avatar invites, or even pressures, a fabrication and upkeep of an edited and curated self that is put up to all the social pressures and scrutiny of one's actual self. One is perpetually in a room being seen, being judged. And I think that despair is a kind of exhaustion. The ego is replicated and stretched beyond its reach and once breached, leaves us voided. We create so many versions of ourselves that we end up losing ourselves all together, or rather, have nothing left to give to ourselves. (Barylski, 2018)

Cat wants 'the best avatar' in this game, but her 'edited and curated self [...] [manifests] a kind of exhaustion' leaving her crying by the end of the film proclaiming, 'I want it to be over,' before shooting herself. Furthermore, Vuong's description: 'We create so many versions of ourselves that we end up losing ourselves all together, or rather, have nothing left to give ourselves' evokes the image of a spectre, just like Laura's ghost in *Unfriended* — Laura, too, is left

---

[13]A similar narrative and visual configuration appears at the end of Olivier Assayas's *Demonlover* (2002) when protagonist Diane de Monx (Connie Nielsen) is forced to become a part of an online website, Hellfire Club, where users 'play' by deciding how she will be tortured. A chain of images (lateral and squared as if a reel of celluloid film) scrolls across the screen until the user clicks on the image whose storyline he or she would like to pursue.

'voided' by the endless online assaults she suffers and, thus, 'loses [herself] all together'.

Additionally, in #*Horror* the medium of the online game interface pixelates and zooms out to provide the overwhelming scope of all the users online. So, too, does the identity (even as avatars) of these players and users 'replicate and stretch [the ego] beyond its reach' thus 'void[ing]' the individual self: he or she simply becomes one 'like' or avatar out of thousands of users. Subkoff effaces the control or autonomy of one user by amalgamating hundreds of screen shots into the frame. Yet, Cat's video clip multiplies across the screen until Subkoff cuts out all the other visual and sonic 'noise' to just a single frame of Cat against a black screen, delivering her final, chilling monologue. Subkoff lets Cat have the last word, but the pixilation, distortion, and glitch visually confirm that this moment of seeming control is not as self-assured as Cat might want us to think. The medium intimates a level of danger or destruction within Cat's selfveillant video. Similarly, Doreste writes that the opening of *Unfriended*:

> Foreshadow[s] the sinister role that digital technologies will assume later in the film. As the familiar brass section of the Universal Studios title sequence begins to blare, the viewer expects the word 'UNIVERSAL' to smoothly come to a halt horizontally across the illuminated globe of the production company's logo. However, as one waits for the sounds and images to coalesce into the famous emblem, something strange happens: the words jump and glitch, becoming distorted and blurred. (Doreste, 2016, p. 8)

Self- and surveillance in these horror films are unforgiving to its female victims, pillorying them for encouraging the gaze of others; the screens themselves convey the digital unease of being constantly under self- and surveillance by their recurrent glitches and distortion. It is the technology that is omnipotent, able to digitally mutilate (via a glitch) just as the killer literally does.

But some of these girls and women actively chase the gaze, addicted to social media's ubiquitous eye. When Cat's father drops her off at the sleepover he attempts to wrench her phone away, unsuccessfully, multiple times. As Cat gazes up at the house where she will spend her (last) night, she snaps a picture of the house, and the words 'Submit' flash across the screen as the left-hand corner of the frame tallies the number of 'likes' the picture garners. Upon arrival, the girls dress up in an array of designer clothing, creating their own provocative fashion show before a floor length mirror and snapping selfie after selfie for the approval of their anonymous social media audience.[14] Just as the 'whore' or 'slut' is killed

---

[14]As Nancy Jo Sales writes, 'With smartphones and social media, girls had the means of producing the male gaze themselves, and it was as if they turned it on themselves willingly in order to compete in a marketplace in which sex was the main selling point' (2016, p. 198).

first in the horror genre, here the girls sign their death warrant by flaunting their visibility. But whereas the 'whore' or 'slut' is typically tortured by the monster or slasher, in *#Horror* Cat bullies her friends by encouraging them to kill themselves, just as Laura's 'friends' encourage her suicide in *Unfriended* after the drunken images of her circulate online. The horror in these films is the medium itself and the social media culture that these devices cultivate.[15]

6.4. Conclusion

Selfveillance in contemporary horror belies the notion of a selfie or selfveillance as solely decorative or narcissistic. These narratives are deeply entrenched in notions of control or one's lack of control, optics and the assaultive gaze directed at these girls and women. In *Unfriended,* Jess dies via a phallic curling iron lodged down her throat. The death is slowly revealed by a downloaded document on Blaire's computer with text heading the image that reads: 'Looks like she finally STFU.' The shot of Jess is from above, the camera tilted down at her kneeling with her eyes rolled back in her head, recalling images of women from pornography, thus conflating violence, sex and surveillance in a disturbingly graphic image. Just as Jules in *The Cabin in the Woods* loses her head only moments after disrobing (not only for her boyfriend, but various sets of audiences watching her every seductive move), characters like Blaire and Jess cannot escape the surveillance, or internalized selfveillance, of their bodies that calls attention to their sexuality and intimate, private moments in public and condemning ways. As Duncan notes in Todd Strauss-Schulson's satirical horror spoof *The Final Girls* (2015), 'everyone who has sex in this movie dies. It's awesome!' This genre is well aware, as Marc Blake and Sara Bailey discuss in their how-to book *Writing the Horror Movie*, 'that old saw — the threat of female sexuality' (2013, p. 30) is doubly threatening under the ubiquity of a panoply of screens.

In her book *I Am Not a Slut*, author Leora Tanenbaum writes that when young girls are now 'branded "sluts" via social media, each girl determined that she would rather die than live with her reputation' (2015, p. 273). While Laura and Cat confirm Tanenbaum's claim by taking their lives when they no longer 'truly control [their] digital personas [...] [thus putting their] reputations at risk' (2015, p. 22), characters such as Jules, Dana and Blaire are also killed and

---

[15]In a 2015 interview with *Elle* magazine, Subkoff says that this film is about 'cultural narcissism, and how it affects these young women who are killing themselves over being cyberbullied. And it started because I asked my friend's daughter, "what is horror, to you?"' The interviewer than, rather sardonically, asks, 'And she was like, "Horror is a bad Instagram post?"' Subkoff replies, 'So much worse. This girl was cyberbullied very badly. So she decided to go away to boarding school in another country [...] And the cyber bullying *followed* her there [...] when bullying follows you home, and there's no escape and no end, to me, that's horror' (Krentcil, 2015).

punished for simply existing under the gaze: of men, of the audience, of government surveillance and of a digital interfaces whose periodic glitches and frozen screens are harbingers of more trouble to come. The lethal gaze disperses across various media platforms, but always results in female's social and physical death. If 'death is trending' in #*Horror*, so is the myriad of media that young adults recurrently use in order to put their best self forward, their *le corps propre*, endlessly constructing a perfect image for the gaze's approval. But to look and be looked at courts brutality in this genre predicated on horror, terror and steadfast sexualized tropes. It is a brave new world where surveillance of the self-connotes, but does not denote, a semblance of control over our self(ies). Teenage trauma is truly trenchant and trending.

Acknowledgements

I am grateful to Matthew Hipps and Thomas Jackson for their generous feedback and friendship. For her careful eye and ear, I have nothing but boundless gratitude for my sister, Isabel, when it comes to finding the right word in the right place. Chang-Min Yu is a constant source of constructive criticism – I am thankful for his patience, time and support.

References

Assayas, O. (2002). *Demonlover*. Citizen Films.
Balingit, M. (2015). Millions of teens are using a new app to post anonymous thoughts, and most parents have no idea. *The Washington Post*. Retrieved from https://www.washingtonpost.com/local/education/millions-of-teens-are-using-a-new-app-to-post-anonymous-thoughts-and-most-parents-have-no-idea/2015/12/08/1532a98c-9907-11e5-8917-653b65c809eb_story.html?utm_term=.344ca1c35ffb
Barylski, A. (2018). Ocean Vuong: Poetry, bodies, and stillness. *Marginalia*. Retrieved from http://marginalia.lareviewofbooks.org/ocean-vuong-poetry-bodies-and-stillness/
Blake, M., & Bailey, S. (2013). *Writing the horror movie*. London: Bloomsbury Academic.
Bonner, H. (2018). Our bodies, our self(ies): Mediating and mitigating social media selfveillance in girls. *HBO's Original Voices: Race, Gender, Sexuality and Power*. New York, NY: Routledge.
Carpenter, J. (1978). *Halloween*. Compass International Pictures.
Carson, B. (2017). The Yik Yak app is officially dead. *Business Insider*. Retrieved from http://www.businessinsider.com/yik-yak-shuts-down-2017-4
Clover, C. J. (1992). *Men, women, and chainsaws*. Princeton, NJ: Princeton University Press.
Creed, B. (1993). *The monstrous-feminine: Film, feminism, psychoanalysis*. New York, NY: Routledge.
Davidson, J. (2014). *Sexting: Gender and teens*. AW Rotterdam: Sense Publishers.
De Palma, B. (1976). *Carrie*. United Artists.
De Palma, B. (1980). *Dressed to kill*. Filmways Pictures.

Doreste, P. N. (2016). *Death and the diagonal display: Cinema's planned obsolescence in the screen-captured image.* Atlanta, GA: Emory University.

Foucault, M. (1995). *Discipline & punishment: The birth of the prison.* New York, NY: Vintage Books.

Friedkin, W. (1973). *The Exorcist.* Warner Bros.

Gabriadze, L. (2015). *Unfriended.* Universal Pictures.

Goddard, D. (2012). *The cabin in the woods.* Lionsgate.

Hitchcock, A. (1954). *Rear window.* Paramount Pictures.

Hitchcock, A. (1960). *Psycho.* Paramount Pictures.

Kaczynski, A., Massie, C., & McDermott, N. (2016). Donald Trump to Howard Stern: It's okay to call my daughter a 'piece of ass'. *CNN.* Retrieved from https://www.cnn.com/2016/10/08/politics/trump-on-howardstern/index.html

Krentcil, F. (2015). Exclusive: A first look at Tara Subkoff's Millennial Horror Flick Starring Chloë Sevigny. *Elle.* Retrieved from http://www.elle.com/culture/movies-tv/interviews/a28601/tara-subkoff-horrorinterview/

Lane, L. (2015). Feminist rhetoric in the digital sphere: Digital interventions & the subversion of gendered cultural scripts. *Ada: A Journal of Gender, New Media, and Technology* (8). Retrieved from doi:10.7264/N3CC0XZW http://adanewmedia.org/blog/2015/11/01/issue8-lane/

Lorde, A. (1984). *Sister outsider: Essays and speeches.* New York: Crossing Press.

Mulvey, L. (1975). Visual pleasure and narrative cinema. *Screen, 16*(3), 6–18.

Sales, N. S. (2017). *American girls: Social media and the secret lives of teenagers.* New York, NY: Vintage.

Sconce, J. (2000). *Haunted media: Electronic presence from telegraphy totelevision.* Durham, NC: Duke University Press.

Sontag, S. (1977). *On photography.* New York, NY: Picador.

Spielberg, S. (1975). *Jaws.* Universal Pictures.

Strauss-Schulson, T. (2015). *The final girls.* Stage 6 Films and VerticalEntertainment.

Subkoff, T. (2015). *#Horror.* IFC Midnight.

Tanenbaum, L. (2015). *I am not a slut: Slut-shaming in the age of the internet.* New York, NY: Harper Perennial.

Thomson, D. (2009). *The moment of Psycho: How Alfred Hitchcock taught America to love murder.* New York, NY: Basic Books.

Tsukayama, H. (2015). Teens spend nearly nine hours every day consuming media. *The Washington Post.* Retrieved from https://www.washingtonpost.com/news/the-switch/wp/2015/11/03/teens-spendnearly-nine-hours-every-day-consuming-media/?utm_term=.85b3fdb7ba5f

US Department of Health and Human Services. (2016). *Office of adolescent health.* Retrieved from https://www.hhs.gov/ash/oah/facts-and-stats/day-in-thelife/index.html

Williams, L. (1984). When the woman looks. *The dread of difference: Gender and the horror film* (pp. 17–36). Austin, TX: University of Texas Press.

Yang, E. L., Celestino, M., & Koeppel, K. (2015). Women's ideal body types throughout history. *BuzzFeed.* Retrieved from https://www.buzzfeed.com/eugeneyang/womens-ideal-body-types-throughouthistory?utm_term=.rwea7D87V#.hpGzdqjd7

Chapter 7

Gay Porn (Horror) Parodies

Joseph Brennan

This chapter considers the influence of horror on the production of commercial gay pornography. I see this influence reflected especially in the production and popularity of gay pornographic films inspired by horror franchises that have been remade in recent decades. A notable example is Wash West's 2003 *The Hole*, which is a parody of Gore Verbinski's 2002 *The Ring*, an American remake of Hideo Nakata's 1998 Japanese classic *Ringu*. *The Hole* 'gives a sense of the overall concept of the movie and the cultural scenarios invoked', yet repositions this narrative into a gay pornographic, 'comic framework' (Escoffier, 2007, p. 74). The feature also proved to be commercially and critically popular, taking out a number of honours at gay porn industry awards, such as the 2004 Grabby Awards and 2004 GAYVN Video Awards, winning Best Video and Best Director, among other accolades. 'Gay porn parodies' have already attracted interest from scholars, namely as examples of a 'productive mix of parodic comedy and dead-serious eroticism' (Herring, 2016, p. 6) and for their transgressive qualities, given that, as I argue elsewhere (see Brennan, 2014), 'texts parodied in gay porn are almost exclusively texts with little or no gay representation in the original' (2014, p. 256). This point on transgression applies to the horror genre particularly, where certain scholars (i.e. Benshoff, 1997) have argued that 'queerness' in the genre has tended to function as 'monstrous' sexuality. In the present chapter, I take as my focus gay porn parodies of horror films from the slasher and 'torture porn' cycles. The specificity of the horror genre is addressed, as is the importance of gender. But particular focus is directed toward the structural aspects of gay porn parodies and the degree to which horror parodies in particular have the *potential* to blend pornographic homosex with graphic violence, perhaps most extreme in the slasher and torture porn horror variants. Other potentialities are also explored, such as for the easing of narrative/sex porn tensions.

7.1. Parody and Gay Porn (with Horror as Case Study)

In making sense of the self-reflexive elements of gay porn — which, for some, might be thought to be at odds with certain received wisdoms, such as of sex as

Gender and Contemporary Horror in Film, 101–115
© **Joseph Brennan**
All rights of reproduction in any form reserved
doi:10.1108/978-1-78769-897-020191008

event and porn as *show* (see Williams, 1989, p. 147) – Richard Dyer (1994) makes the point that 'being meta is rather everyday for queers' (1994, p. 60). By this, Dyer is suggesting that 'elements of parody and pastiche and the deliberate foregrounding of artifice in much gay porn' are in line with other aspects of gay culture, including 'modes like camp, irony, derision, theatricality and flamboyance', all of which 'hold together an awareness of something's style with a readiness to be moved by it' (1994, pp. 60–61). In other words, he is saying that in much of gay porn there is not necessarily a divide between sex and porn, event and show, real and artifice – a position, it is worth noting, not shared by all theorizing the form (i.e. Morris's view on the 'limited and strict set of "elements"' in contemporary gay porn (in a study by Morris & Paasonen, 2014, p. 222)). Instead, Dyer argues for a more fluid understanding, as gay porn is often knowing of the conditions and structures of its own construction, a degree of self-awareness that is also characteristic of gay culture, and therefore, the show of porn *is* the event (1994, p. 60). No more is this true than in the tradition of porn parodies.

Parody is of course ubiquitous in the heteroporn context also. Yet gay porn is somewhat distinct, affording itself an extra level of subversion by virtue of its necessary 'queering' of routinely heteronormative texts (Brennan, 2014, p. 256), together with the meta-discursive tradition of gay culture that Dyer outlines. Noting the 'extremely common device' of parodying a mainstream media title in gay porn, Jeffrey Escoffier (2007) observes that such a device sometimes goes no further than 'a sexually explicit joke on the original title' (as in Miami Studios's 2006 *I Know Who You Did Last Summer*, a play on words of the 1997 slasher *I Know What You Did Last Summer*), yet in 'most cases' constitutes 'a full-fledged erotic adaptation of the original' (2007, p. 73). I am more inclined to invert Escoffier here, not convinced that 'most cases' of parodic titling in gay porn manifest in a full-fledged adaptation; after all, popular cultural referencing is endemic in gay porn as it is in gay culture, and as such, referencing of the popular often extends well beyond mere titling, yet without the staging of an erotic re-imagining – such referencing that is constitutive of the mantle of the popular and the on-going 'pornification' of gay culture. (See, for instance, Mercer's (2006) discussion of commonality and difference between the gay porn and Hollywood film star, which points to the wider cultural referencing that takes place within gay porn.)

Also, it should be noted, not all texts that go beyond title-only parody result in adaptations as fully-fledged as the example Escoffier chooses: Wash West's multi-award winning *The Hole* (2002). Escoffier's (2007) extant reading of the feature (see pp. 74–75) explains already the characteristics of *The Hole* that render it full-fledged, which are inclusive of *mise-en-scène* and a narrative that functions on multiple levels as a queer re-imagining; in the feature, the death-in-seven-days premise of the original is transformed into gay-in-seven-days, a transformation that allows *The Hole* to function at one level as a comedic coming-out story, and at another, as 'a horror movie for those "straight" homophobic viewers who believe that merely seeing a gay porn movie will help make them gay' (Escoffier, 2007, p. 74). Such layering effectively bridges the horrific

tape of the original and its serious characteristics with the comedic and homoerotic aspects that gay porn parody necessitates. In short, the feature successfully
captures and subverts the spirit of the original. These are characteristics that
make the text interesting – and suitably polysemic – from the perspective of the
horror genre and gay porn form alike, while also marking-as-productive (see
Herring, 2016) exploration of such texts from a scholarly perspective. In fact, a
search for examples that aspire either *in part* or *fully* to an erotic adaptation of a
mainstream slasher or torture porn title was the condition of inclusion in the
present chapter and is what results in a list that is rather short – especially considering gay porn's tendency towards over-production.

Scott Herring's (2016) recent thought piece on gay porn parodies has been a
key influence in formulating the present argument. In much the same way that
Dyer compared camp with gay porn to argue for the potential for self-reflection
and a distinction – between event and show – presented in Linda Williams's
(1989) classic text, *Hard Core*; writing more than two decades later, Herring
rethinks a line from Leo Bersani's (1987) equally influential, 'Is the Rectum a
Grave?' The line from Bersani was as follows: 'Parody is an erotic turn-off, and
all gay men know this' (1987, p. 208). And Herring's means of counter-point is
gay porn parodies. The 'treasure trove' of titles in the genre convinces Herring
that parodic camp is not necessarily incompatible with sexualization; quite the
contrary: the campy formulae that is 'repeatedly incorporated into this visual
media of hardcore eroticism' convinced him that for many, 'camp provides gay
men with an entry into sexual desire rather than an exit' (2016, pp. 5–6). Yet
Herring does not engage in a depth reading of any of the gay porn titles he
mentions – *Surelick Holmes* (2007) and *21 Hump Street* (2013) among them –
favouring instead a retrospective consideration of 'modernist' examples from the
early part of the twentieth century, which is where my chapter will take his position further through consideration in depth of more recent examples.

To draw out another line from Bersani, he does pinpoint a potential in parody when he observes that male gay camp is 'largely a parody of women [...]
[and] of a certain femininity', which provides a point of connection with this collection's consideration of horror *and* gender, as well as a segue into the significance of using horror as a case study for gay porn parodies (1987, p. 208). The
slasher and torture porn cinematic genres, together with gay pornography, lend
themselves uniquely to productive critique, especially concerning gender. This is
in part due to the queering aspect of gay porn parody, which carries the benefit
of immediately avoiding straightforward (often overly-simplistic) associations
between, for instance, slasher films and (hetero)pornography as both embodi-
ments of violence against women, and as sharing certain structural conventions
(see Erens, 1987, for such a reading; also see Kendall, 2004, who conceives of
gay porn in much the same way, namely as violence against feminized men).
The opportunity to *do* (or *perform*, see Butler, 1990) gender differently, and to
invert certain heteronormative and heterosexist conventions of mainstream
cinema is part of the utopian potential of gay porn as parody. I acknowledge the
queer traces already present in horror cinema – torture and body horror
variants especially, for example, *Hostel* (2005) and *Tusk* (2014) being recent

examples. Admittedly such queer traces often occur subtextually, though textual examples are present too, for example, the twist endings of Terror Train (1980) and Sleepaway Camp (1983). I also acknowledge the 'connection of the monstrous with sexual difference, especially homosexuality' trope in slasher films, whereby one does not need to look far to find examples of the rise of the spectre of homosexuality (Ognjanović, 2012, p. 227; also see Benshoff, 1997; Humphrey, 2014).

It is from this tradition for queerness that more manifestly queer examples have emerged, inclusive of the homoerotic tradition of prolific filmmaker David DeCoteau as well as Paul Etheredge-Ouzts's *Hellbent* (2004), billed as the first all-gay slasher film. Yet, it is the transgressive qualities of gay porn parodies that render them most interesting. *Hellbent*, for example, constructs an original, all-gay narrative instead of subverting the heteronormative narratives of the series that the texts I discuss here parody. Claire Sisco King (2010) adds credence to this position in her analysis of *Hellbent* and her disappointment at the text's 'ambivalence toward queerness, undercutting the film's subversive potential' and disciplining 'queer reading strategies' by advocating 'a version of homosexuality that complies with heteronormative expectations' (2010, p. 250). The same of which cannot be said for gay porn parodies. By virtue of the necessity that such texts achieve intertextual resonance within the viewer in order to be meaningful, gay porn parodies rely on a level of textual literary in the viewer, with certain cues in the text that tie it to the heavyweights of mainstream slasher and torture porn franchises – such mainstream recognition of narrative and character convention that is then queered via a pornographic re-imagining. This returns us to self-reflexivity, present in both porn text and the interpretations of those *reading* it (see Fiske & Hartley, 1978, for more on the active reading practices of media audiences).

7.2. Close Readings

Adopting a self-reflexive stance on gay porn myself, the texts selected for analysis are all texts that, via parody and to varying degrees, reflect both on gay porn and the horror genre, reconstituting (and at times, critiquing) the conventions of both. I acknowledge a certain tendency to preference examples engaged in 'meta-activity' here in service of my own meta-analysis (Dyer, 1994, p. 60); a preference that is in line with textual analysis as a method of strategic selection and presentation of aspects of a text as evidence for an overall argument (Fürsich, 2009). But also, such selection was informed by the need to compare those that merely go beyond the title reference with those that constitute a fully fledged parody, so as to better understand the genres (both of porn and cinema). In other words, the readings seek to explore the ability to not only make reference to a mainstream slasher or torture porn text, but to adopt elements of this text that serve as key signifieds in the meaning of the erotic adaptation. To draw on an example I used elsewhere, Afton Nills's 2010 *Twinklight* is a parody of the *Twilight* franchise, which originated with Catherine Hardwicke's 2008 *Twilight*.

My previous reading demonstrates how *Twinklight* functions as a parody of the original through an examination of marketing materials and individual scenes, demonstrating that *Twinklight* 'is clearly advertised as not only about sex [...] [where] iconic scenes from the canon [original film] (including the restaurant scene and the first kiss) are replicated with attention to lighting, props and positioning, converting the romance for gay consumption' (2014, p. 256).

I identified nine texts for analysis – from the slasher genre: Bryan Kenny's 2010 *A Nightmare on Twink Street* (inspired by the *Nightmare on Elm Street* series, which commenced with Wes Craven's 1983 original, and was remade in 2010 by Samuel Bayer), Andy Kay's 2012 *Black XXXmas* (inspired by Bob Clark's 1974 *Black Christmas*, remade in 2006 by Glen Morgan), Frank Fuder and Angel Skye's 2009 *Halloweiner: Friday the Fuckteenth* and Chi Chi LaRue's 2016 *Scared Stiff* (both inspired by the *Friday the 13th* series, commencing with Sean S. Cunningham's 1980 original, remade in 2009 by Marcus Nispel), Bromo's 2017 *Cream for Me* (*Scream* series, commencing with Wes Craven's 1996 original); and from the torture porn genre: Jett Blakk's 2006 *Bonesaw*, John Bruno's 2006 *Rammer* and Bryan Kenny's 2010 *Raw I* and 2011 (with Andy Kay) *Raw II* (inspired by James Wan and Leigh Whannell's 2004 *Saw*, which spawned a franchise). Notice a tendency in the above for the release of parodies to coincide with the introduction to a new audience of now-classic films from the 1970s and 1980s, which is suggestive of the influence of horror remakes, reboots and reimaginings on the production of commercial gay pornography.

Close reading revealed that the foregoing texts are best organized into two categories, those that *riff off* aspects of another text and those that *spoof* another text entirely, the latter of which constitutes parody in a more meaningful sense and is generally the more elusive of the two, which adds credence to my earlier point around inverting Escoffier's (2007, p. 73) observation on gay porn parodies. Such a typology of gay porn parodies is not clear-cut, with the riff-to-spoof categories forming a continuum rather than distinct subgenres. *Scared Stiff*, for instance, is an abstract riff, so loosely based on the formula of 1980s masked-killer-stalking-cabin-in-the-woods-teenage-archetypes horror – typified by *Friday the 13th* – that it could equally be understood as an entirely original text; a text, it is interesting to note, that the director describes as 'mixing porn and camp' (LaRue in Sweetbriar, 2016). Each text will be addressed individually, with particular emphasis placed on select examples that have something important to say. It is worthwhile to first consider narrative.

7.2.1. Narrative (vs Sex)

Notoriously poor acting-accruement aside (lending these texts a distinctly *pornish* quality that some like, i.e. LaBruce in Hays, 2005, p. 24), together with meniscal budgets for any effects above and beyond the progression to a 'money shot' – described by Emily Shelton (2002) as porn's '"amateurish" production style, technical ineptitude, and bad acting' (2002, p. 135) – it is worth reflecting first on narrative in gay porn parody. For such reflection also invites a note on

narrative in contemporary gay porn more broadly, which is complicated somewhat by the affordances of non-linear, domestic consumption (see Bolton, 2004)
and ejaculation-driven viewing structures – in which case, as Todd G. Morrison
(in Nielsen & Kiss, 2015) observes, disruption to viewing occurs on occasion, if
the viewer might, 'ahem, "finish" prior to that seminal scene' (2015, p. 132).
Additionally, pay-per-scene revenue streams, even for features, have an impact
on narrative in porn. In the internet age, narratives in commercial gay porn now
more commonly unfold within a single scene, and are often housed on a single
site devoted to a particular niche (*Bait Bus*, baitbus.com, for instance, is an early
example in which straight-identified men are tricked into gay sex in a bait 'n'
switch scenario). Transformation of the structure of porn brought about by technology brings to mind Dyer's (1985) reminder in his classic essay on gay porn
that narrative is present even in the simplest pornographic loops, such as
quarter-in-the-slot machines. Yet for our purposes here, and in the context of
the exposition of narrative in a cinematic sense, I believe more strongly that the
factors set out above serve to weigh in favour of sex over narrative dominance
in contemporary porn features.

Porn parodies are significant, therefore, as they carry the banner for a certain
level of requisite investment in narrative on porn's behalf, which has the potential to enhance the sex – a view that arises in Clarissa Smith, Martin Barker,
and Feona Attwood's (2015) study into why audiences enjoy porn, namely
because it 'challenges us to introduce narrative into sex' (2015, p. 276). The
most full-fledged of porn parodies are of interest, therefore, for the way in which
they redress the sex-narrative imbalance, strengthening the 'webbing' (see
Mercer, 2017, p. 53) between sexual vignettes with a coherent narrative that
encourages greater investment in more linear viewing practices. In fact, adherence to a well-defined narrative is one of the reasons for my avoidance of the
icons of horror. As a specific franchise (e.g. *Friday the 13th*), or even specific
film (e.g. *Black Christmas*), requires a more pronounced and singular engagement in contrast with figures such as Dracula and Frankenstein, who have been
subject to reinvention countless times over the last century, including as
figures of parody. Measuring such adherence to a well-defined text or set of texts
permits us to consider the points at which porn parodying retells, brushes with
via mere reference, or reworks entirely texts of reference. Such considerations
that all assist in developing a typology of gay porn parodies, and in making
observations on the connective points between gay porn and slasher/torture porn
texts especially. Other key components will be addressed as well (sound, for
instance), but in a more integrated fashion in the close readings. We begin with
discussion of four parodies, all of which straddle parody of specific horror franchises with a commitment to the gay porn 'twink' subgenre.

7.2.2.   *Twink Porn with a Side of Parody*

A Nightmare on Twink Street, *Black XXXmas* and *Raw I* and *II* all occupy a
middle ground between riff and spoof, containing a number of references in their
narratives to the horror texts to which their titles refer, yet not entirely attaining

the level of narrative recognition to be classified as a full spoof. This, I suggest, can be explained by these four texts' connection with the 'twink' porn genre (see Mercer, 2017, pp. 81–82), and an age 18–23 boyish look, which takes preference over the retelling of the narratives to which their titles refer. All four titles appear to be affiliated with Boy Crush's (boycrush.com) now-defunct dark twink-themed venture, Boy Lair. Mercer's (2017) recent discussion – aptly titled 'The Problem with Twinks' (2017, pp. 81–83) – of the subgenre provides the necessary context for understanding these texts. The 'problem', as Mercer sees it, is that the term 'twink' has become so overused that it is at risk of becoming meaningless. Yet, among the most dominant connotations of the term remains a range of largely pejorative, feminine signifieds. Twink, therefore, most commonly stands for a young, slender and (sometimes) virginal (femme-) masculinity. In the words of Zeb J. Tortorici (2008), the twink performs 'a consumable and visually/anally receptive masculinity' (2008, p. 206). Such characteristics permeate the parodies.

In *A Nightmare on Twink Street*, Freddy Krueger – the slasher film and pop culture icon – is reconstituted as a twink, 'a crazy hot guy' who 'died a virgin' and fucks other virgin twinks in their dreams as revenge. With dreams that are described by the 'victims' as 'kind of creepy, and kind of sexy at the same time' (scene one), the spirit of Krueger is reinvented. In the place of 'that most feared and hated of suburban bogeymen: the murderous child molester' (Murphy, 2013, p. 85) invading the dreams of the children of those who killed him, we have a twink Kruger who was lynched for being gay during a time of widespread homophobia, and died before he could fuck his boyfriend. So now he fucks young boys in their dreams, taking their virginity. While there is a clear reinvention – and perhaps subversion – of the original, the horrific narrative and visual elements of the original have all been softened to such an extent that they lose much of their meaning. In contrast to the horribly burned original, twink Kruger has no disfigurement. While he has 'the glove' – and therefore knives for fingers – he removes this glove so as to service you sexually, preventing any potential for violent penetration. The most violating act he performs is to piss on you as the ultimate punishment (scene two), and that is only if you are not 'into' erotic urine play – a fairly standard twink kink (e.g. Piss Twinks, pisstwinks.com; Boys Pissing, boys-pissing.com). There is little evidence of a horror component. First, all 'victims' are real-life gay men, making Freddy's revenge on the homophobic faction that put him to death, not exactly the punishment-by-fucking-spree that it could be. In fact, despite the premise, the sex is coded as consensual, with victims putting up little resistance. While penetrating a victim, for instance, twink Freddy exclaims: 'You like Freddy's dick?' To which his victim replies, 'Yeah, I like Freddy's dick.' And later, 'Yeah, fuck me', and at climax, 'Fuck me some more Freddy' (scene four). And when twink Freddy is dragged out of the dream world, he is 'punished' too, engaging in group sex. 'Now it's time I planted seed in your virgin hole', one of his former victims tells him. That the production is condomless and has the tagline 'One, two, Freddy's coming in you', seems like a missed opportunity to add to the horror aspects, especially given later entrants in the franchise such as Stephen

Hopkins's 1989 *A Nightmare on Elm Street 5: The Dream Child*. In the feature's final scene, a jump scare sees Freddy claim an actual victim (via penetration of his glove into a twink's chest, rather than his penis into a twink's anus). Notably, this scene of (presumably) fatal action is not connected directly with any of the feature's sex, thus acting as 'webbing' only.

The same can be said for *Raw I* and *II*, which at their centre detail a twink bondage narrative, whereby *Saw*'s infamous (and deadly) traps are reduced to kinky displays that are only mildly 'extreme' – hand restraints, anus expanders, electric shock sticks, etc. For the purpose of discussion, we will focus on *Raw II*. *II* opens with an introductory video from the Jigsaw character that makes clear that those captured were chosen for their interest in kinky sex. Resembling the opening of the first *Saw* film, two boys are chained at either side of a room that is only mildly 'grimy'. A key to the other's restraints is hidden inside one of the kinky twink performers, who needs to retrieve it via the anus with his fingers. The scene includes an X-ray image, a device that connects it with the staging of a number of traps from the original series. Yet, the seriousness of the situation the boys find themselves in is relieved before even penetration can begin: as soon as the instruction to fuck is given via video link, both boys smile and proceed with enthusiasm. The narrative of the piece – much the same as the Freddy twink feature – is certainly missing the morality tale of the original. In fact, it is precisely the selected twinks' proclivity for kink play that has landed them in the fetishist's lair in the first place, that is, in the company of a fellow twink with similar, though perhaps slightly kinkier, inclinations. Even the capturing component can be understood in line with the BDSM leanings of the twink porn genre. In fact, the capture and sexual torture of 'straight' men is a common gay porn trope – and would have in fact been a better fit as parody, that is, as a subversion of the twisted morality storytelling of *Saw*. The feature's bondage connections do allow slight blending of webbing and sex scene narratives, but only slight. For example, 'tests' that those captured face include challenging a twink's resolve not to move while a large spider crawls over his naked body. But there is no death, and the potential for death is only ever suggested, which prevents the feature from a full-fledged parody. The feature ends, for instance, with the lights being switched off, and two twinks left in the room. Though there is no suggestion that they have been left to die, as is the case with the protagonist from the original. Instead, these boys are more likely being kept for play another time. This is supported by a twist of the feature, which is that Miles Pride, who was one of the original two from *Raw I*, is in fact in on the game, and speaks highly of the generosity of their host (a key plot device from *Saw II*). There is no sexualized gore resistant from play, nor any suggestion of it. Though there is the occasional plea for the play to stop, it is not in any manner that is suggestive of actual damage to the anus – a point that is perhaps in keeping with certain pornography regulation restricting such suggestion, in the UK, for instance (see Brennan, 2017, p. 425). There is not character death in the feature.

In *Black XXXmas,* there is death of characters, which comes as a welcome connection with the source material. And the feature is set in a fraternity (an inversion of the sorority setting of the original). Also, certain aspects of the feature — that is, the Christmas setting, the house's troublesome history, the gift-giving house ritual, the incessant and menacing calls to the house, a mysterious gift (a black dildo in this case) — offer enough resemblance to the parodied text to suggest reference to *Black Christmas* even without the titular pun (the remake of which was styled as *Black X-Mas* in promotional materials). Yet there are also aspects that depart from the original and prevent the parody being realized fully. No information is provided on the killer himself, and defining features such as the killer's propensity for suffocation and eye-gouging, and the complicated, incest-fuelled family history is also absent. References to the twink trope are plentiful, and inclusive of 'first-time' sexual initiation rituals (complete with paddling), with the killer being revealed to be himself a twink, who then proceeds to fuck the 'final boy' (Jasper Robinson), who requires little convincing to submit sexually before being locked away in a chest once they have both climaxed. With death playing a more explicit role in the narrative, we start to gain appreciation for the applicability of the twink/slasher combination, given that the twink is coded as feminine and slashers have traditionally been concerned with a trope of the female victim, such as the final girl (see Clover, 1987). While death is presented on screen, it never intrudes on the sex scenes, which without the violent interludes, stand as pure porn, without any overt horror references. The inability, or unwillingness, of these parody texts to integrate the sex with violence is important to consider in the context of horror.

7.2.3. *Uneasy Connections between Explicit (Homo)Sex and Violence*

Understanding the significance of gay porn horror parodies lies in recognition of what is left out, what is *not* explicit in the combination of two media genres (porn and, in this case, slasher/torture porn) notorious for their unapologetic explicitness. There is something to be said around the reticence in porn parody of combining explicitness with explicitness, explicit porno-sex with explicit bodily gore, whereby the 'physical effects' of each — that is, the graphic (multi-angled) penetrations, and the (admittedly, much less) graphic violence — exist only ever side-by-side, never as one integrated spectacle. Sexual action followed by violent action followed by sexual action, or sex webbed with violence on repeat until the end. It is curious because sex with violent death is routine in the slasher genre (see, for instance, Clover, 1987), and yet, of course, the sex is only simulated in this case, and the believability of the gore often hangs on the skills of make-up effects or computer-generated imagery in depicting penetration of flesh from instruments of violence. When the impossibility of the penis becoming that instrument is observed, as has been the case here, the uncomfortable courtship between anal eroticism and death is revealed. A courtship that perhaps conjures up uneasy — and especially *unsexy* — connotations, such as the anus as a 'grave', to return to Bersani (1987), and the spectre of death that has haunted gay sex ever since the AIDS crisis of the 1980s, which was when slasher films were at their height of popularity; a connection between the bodily invasion of AIDS and the fetishistic components of blood and gore in slasher films of which has been made by others (i.e. Aguado, 2002, p. 167).

The risk, perhaps, in combining the two lies in parody becoming something else, something beyond camp. Something frightening, or de-sexualized, or even 'arty'? Such as with the 'gut-fuck' scene in Bruce LaBruce's 2008 zombie film *Otto; or Up with Dead People*, where male-to-male penetration of a stomach wound opens up 'an entirely new erotic entry point' (Elliott-Smith, 2014, p. 152). Yet this is not the same. Zombie and vampire homosex does not typically result in death, but instead an *un*dead or *living*-dead state, a definitionally in-between position that is supported because it connects with a more familiar eroticism: violent, life-endangering sex as passage to eternal living. This explains why vampire sex in gay porn parody *Twinklight* is frequently inclusive of actual anal penetration with a penis, together with simulated teeth penetration with the aid of artificial blood. So sex *with* violence, yet violence that is itself sexy. The disconnection of sex with death scenes in slasher and torture porn parodies continues a tradition of discomfort with correlations such as sex as violence, violence as sex; often also connected with gender as violence coded as male, and sex as coded as female. It is a discomfort that some texts progress more than others, *Cream for Me, Halloweiner: Friday the Fuckteenth, Rammer* and *Bonesaw* for instance, which will be our final examples.

Cream for Me is the most recent and also the clearest illustration of a riff off an original (*Scream*). While reference is made to particular kills from the first film – including the opening kill (scene one) and the infamous 'garage door' scene (scene three) – and it comes complete with zingy one-liners like 'You chase me around and that's all you got?' (scene one), the feature does not venture beyond the comedic. In re-imagining *Scream*, it creates gay porn obsessed perpetrators – 'What's your favorite vintage porno?' (scene one) – that wear the costume, but wield dildos in place of knifes. And following a surprise introduction, engage in consensual sex with the men they visit, who willingly partake in what 'looks like fun' (scene one). The final scene comes close to non-consensual performance, yet is so removed from the original – featuring three costumed fuckers, inclusive of former 'victims' – that it functions more as 'Halloween costume themed' content than parody. In short, in re-imagining *Scream* from knowledge and performance of vintage slasher films to knowledge and performance of vintage gay porn, the parody does not in fact effectively adopt horror elements (beyond the occasional menacing score during scene interludes).

The next example goes further in connecting with horror. It may have been titled to reference two slasher goliaths – John Carpenter's 1978 *Halloween* and *Friday the 13th* – yet *Halloweiner: Friday the Fuckteenth* is really only a parody of one of these (*Friday the 13th*), a point that highlights the 'in name only' tradition of much parodic porn titling – (Jerry Jensen's 2000 *Hunks on Haunted Hill*, to give yet another example). *Friday the Fuckteenth* has a familiar narrative. A group of (all-gay) teens travel to a cabin beside 'Crystal Lake'. Yet while there is an awareness of the formula – with one teen observing, 'I think he will kill us while we're having sex' – key misunderstandings of the nature of the original suggest a low level of familiarity overall, or more likely, that the need for the parody to be 'full-fledged' was not a high priority. For instance, there is description of a dead man running around with a chainsaw (rather than Jason Voorhees's iconic machete) and Crystal Lake is described as the place where 'all those horror movies are from', which is confusing given that it is in fact a fictional location that exists only in the filmic universe.

Of interest in this parody is a sense of bleed between the sex and violence. There are four sex scenes in the feature. A single death follows three of these (scenes two to four), then a mass of deaths in quick succession at the end (beginning with the anally receptive partner from scene one). While scenes two through four feature a fucking pair, only one dies, and it is the anally receptive ('bottom') each time. And although the death scenes still function more as brief interludes, that each time it is the bottom who is murdered (while the penetrating 'top' survives) seems suggestive of a connective point with the sex act: where penetration doubles as penetration, and the top as the penetrator (phallic killer). There is also overlap with the original in the creativity of death scenes. In scene three (Luke Riley and Roland Haye), Haye flexes his biceps in the mirror while face-fucking Riley, an especially 'cocky' action that is similar to a sex scene from the remake featuring the characters Trent and Bree, released that same year. Riley is then murdered following sex by way of a large dildo down the throat. Then, in scene four (Angel Skye and Kurt Wild), Skye starts the scene by telling Wild, 'I have a boyfriend you know', which also resembles the Trent-as-cheating-boyfriend narrative of the 2009 remake. Skye (the top) turns out to be the killer, and is also the one from the introduction to the feature that suggests the group will be killed 'while we're having sex', connecting sex with death in the killer's view. Skye is also one of the feature's directors, knowledge of which lends the text a layered meaning similar to Escoffier's reading of *The Hole*.

Skye as director, performer in-text, and (it is revealed) the murderer as well creates a position unique to porn and its all-hands-on-deck approach, and is one that makes for much meta-textual significance (think *Scream* and its killers-as-documentarians aspect) in terms of the function of sex and death in the piece. In this regard, music (dissonant piano chords) and poor production values come to carry new meaning in *Friday the Fuckteenth*; the shaky camera work and documentary-style shots lending the feature a certain stalker-aesthetic (filmed in the bushes) that also connects with Voorhees as a voyeuristic killer. In scene two, for example, certain camera angles (from behind and operated by a hand-held and with generally poor vocal differentiation) and a by-the-lake location give the impression of the models being 'watched'. In another scene, set in a wood cabin (scene four), low production values (i.e. shadows and footsteps of crew) actually double as a potential killer, stalking the boys in the act. I am perhaps edging towards 'reparative readings' (Sedgwick, 2003, pp. 123–151) here in my search for meaning, yet do so knowingly, in particular of the potential such readings bring to texts as culturally de-valued as porn parodies. While sex is never *interrupted* by death, as is routine in *Friday the 13th*'s formula, this parody does successfully *imply* an impending death interlude through its narrative choices and – whether intentional or not – amateur execution, resulting in a bleeding of sex with narrative.

Rammer achieves this in a more meaningful way. Not only are its scenes more connected with the narrative of *Saw*, but the feature takes the morality tale aspect of the original to the point of episodic seriality, where each scene has a contained narrative arc and 'victims' include, to quote from the studio's (Falcon Studios) description, 'a very nasty boss', 'a hateful racist', 'a selfish lover' and finally, the *pièce de résistance*: 'four notorious homophobes'. Each captive is schooled in tolerance and sexual servitude, with many of the hallmarks of the original, including distinctive surveillance set pieces (see Tziallas, 2010, for an excellent visual essay on *Saw*'s distinctive surveillance aesthetic). The feature is noteworthy because the narrative of forceful conversion of the captive party to the joys of diverse homosex forms part of the language exchanged while fucking – for example, when a man receiving fellatio describes the man captive as a 'mean, fucking racist bastard' then instructs a third party to 'slam that big fat black fucking cock inside that fucking white ass'. The result being a blending of narrative with sex that means, even when extracted, the sex scenes still carry a narrative that references the original. Yet there is no death, and victims succumb quickly to the pleasure of homosex, in much the same way that the straight-to-gay narrative plays out in gay porn (e.g. Str8 to Gay, str8togay.com).

Bonesaw, another *Saw* parody, is more notable still as it both features death as part of the narrative and also integrates the *threat* of death into the sex. The feature functions more as a film, with the scenes connected to a singular narrative of morality and revenge, complete with narrative twists, puzzles and traps that are so suggestive of the original. There is a single victim protagonist (Lee) who is confronted with a three-trap challenge, each which requires from him escalating feats of sexual endurance. Test one is to be an observer only, to witness but not engage two 'fine specimens of manhood' that 'if you were out cruising, either one would make their way to your bedroom'; test two is to bring a caged man to orgasm in fifteen minutes under the threat of poisonous gas (a test Lee fails); while test three requires Lee to bring two men to orgasm within 20 minutes, providing the kind of service Lee 'so often provide[s]' yet with the threat of an electric saw should the sex extend beyond a restrictive radius. During this final scene, the electric saw is running and wielded by the masked killer who swipes at the performers when they come near the circle's edge, the threat of bodily pain co-existing with the exhibition of bodily pleasure. Lee is saved at the end by an ex-boyfriend, who, it is revealed, is also the orchestrator of his grisly ordeal. Though there are comedic elements – such as in the establishing scene when the killer's voice is first heard through a speaker: 'Morning, Lee. Hardly stereo surround, I know.' – comedy does not play a central role.

Lessons on the dangers of gay promiscuity read as much more primary. 'You always made the wrong decisions in your life, Lee', the Jigsaw character informs him, with the competitive sexual games that follow registering both as recompense from a lover scorned, and as a perverse moralistic commentary on the consequences of gay male casual sex. Even the presence of condoms throughout the piece has meaning. On one level, these are a practicality, a mandate of the studio (and pornography of the time), yet other layers of meaning cannot be ignored, such as of safety in gay casual sex, important still in the face of life or death encounters – whereby gay sex *is* a matter of life or death and such decisions have consequences (i.e. Bersani, 1987). The presence of condoms also reads as a marker for the reality of the sex (as not-staged). Gay sex as punishing is connoted elsewhere also. The lead investigator, for instance, misses capturing the killer and preventing the final killings because he is having sex with a colleague, functioning as an interesting narrative use of sex in porn as considerable screen time that impacts on the in-real-time length of the 'torture sequences' (a lingering gaze on the spectacle that is much longer than that achieved in the original).

Bonesaw is a suitable final example as it ventures further than most in blending porn with horror. The text receives a mention in Steve Jones and Sharif Mowlabocus's (2009) article on 'shock' pornographies, for instance, when they nominate it as an example of a text that moves 'beyond parody and generic "borrowing" to a point where the audience may become uncertain as to exactly what genre of film they are watching – the film being at once "too horrific" to be porn, and too sexually focused to be horror' (2009, p. 616). A key moment of horrific intensity in the text being when, following the third test and sexual climax of each of the performers, the killer thrusts the spinning electric saw into the chest of one of the men. In the words of a reviewer of the parody, 'to get away with this kind of carnage in gay adult video, more wit is required than perpetrator Jett Blakk is able to inject' (Tramontagna, 2006). It is a comment that points to the discomfort of a parody with elements that take it beyond that 'productive mix of parodic comedy and dead-serious eroticism' (Herring, 2016, p. 6), transgressing even the structural expectations of the hybrid genre by taking its viewers beyond camp.

7.3. Conclusion

Williams (1999) makes the following distinction between pornography and horror films: the former, she writes, are 'more often deemed excessive for its violence than for its sex', while the latter are often deemed 'excessive in their displacement of sex onto violence' (1999, p. 268). It is an observation that points to the potential of gay porn horror parodies as a bridge, as a 'connective thread' (see Tziallas, 2010) between the making visible of pleasure *and* pain on the body. In effect melting the viewing and sounds of bodily pleasure (porn) with the viewing and sounds of bodily pain (horror) within a single text. As this chapter has explored by way of example and close reading, it is a potentiality that is not often fully realized, nor is it a realization that is easy to digest (as *Bonesaw*'s departure from camp illustrates). Yet it is a potentiality that remains all the same. Such potential serves as illustration of the value and uniqueness of gay porn horror parody as constitutive of certain resistive possibilities – such as of narrative structure, gender binary and sexuality norms – that come through the combination of two of the most historically reviled, and routinely dismissed, media forms.

References

Aguado, V. L. (2002). Film genre and its vicissitudes: The case of the psychothriller. *Atlantis, 24*(2), 163–172.

Benshoff, H. M. (1997). *Monsters in the closet: Homosexuality and the horror film.* Manchester: Manchester University Press.

Bersani, L. (1987). Is the rectum a grave? *October, 43,* 197–222.

Bolton, M. C. (2004). Cumming to an end: The male orgasm and domestic consumption of gay pornography. *M/C Journal, 7*(4). Retrieved from http://www.journal.media-culture.org.au/0410/08_cumming.php

Brennan, J. (2014). Not 'from my hot little ovaries': How slash manips pierce reductive assumptions. *Continuum, 28*(2), 247–264.

Brennan, J. (2017). Abuse porn: Reading reactions to Boys Halfway House. *Sexuality & Culture, 21*(2), 423–440.

Butler, J. (1990). *Gender trouble: Feminism and the subversion of identity.* London: Routledge.

Clover, C. J. (1987). Her body, himself: Gender in the slasher film. *Representations, 20,* 187–228.

Dyer, R. (1985). Male gay porn: Coming to terms. *Jump Cut, 30,* 27–29.

Dyer, R. (1994). Idol thoughts: Orgasm and self-reflexivity in gay pornography. *Critical Quarterly, 36*(1), 49–62.

Elliott-Smith, D. (2014). Gay zombies: Consuming masculinity and community in Bruce LaBruce's *Otto; or, Up with Dead People* and *L.A. Zombie*. In S. McGlotten & S. Jones (Eds.), *Zombies and sexuality: Essays on desire and the living dead* (pp. 140–158). Jefferson, NC: McFarland.

Erens, P. (1987). *The seduction*: The pornographic impulse in slasher films. *Jump Cut, 32,* 53–55.

Escoffier, J. (2007). Scripting the sex: Fantasy, narrative, and sexual scripts in pornographic films. In M. Kimmel (Ed.), *The sexual self: The construction of sexual scripts* (pp. 61–79). Nashville, TN: Vanderbilt University Press.

Fiske, J., & Hartley, J. (1978). *Reading television.* London: Methuen.

Fürsich, E. (2009). In defense of textual analysis: Restoring a challenged method for journalism and media studies. *Journalism Studies, 10*(2), 238–252.

Hays, M. (2005). Gay guerrilla filmmaking and terrorist chic: Toronto filmmaker Bruce LaBruce discusses his latest art/porn feature. *The Raspberry Reich. CineAction, 65,* 20–24.

Herring, S. (2016). The sexual objects of "parodistic" camp. *Modernism/Modernity, 23*(1), 5–8.

Humphrey, D. (2014). Gender and sexuality haunts the horror film. In H. M. Benshoff (Ed.), *A companion to the horror film* (pp. 38–55). Malden, MA: Wiley.

Jones, S., & Mowlabocus, S. (2009). Hard times and rough rides: The legal and ethical impossibilities of researching 'shock' pornographies. *Sexualities, 12*(5), 613–628.

Kendall, C. N. (2004). *Gay male pornography: An issue of sex discrimination.* Vancouver: University of British Columbia Press.

King, C. S. (2010). Un-queering horror: *Hellbent* and the policing of the "gay slasher". *Western Journal of Communication, 74*(3), 249–268.

Mercer, J. (2006). Seeing is believing: Constructions of stardom and the gay porn star in US gay video pornography. In S. Holmes & S. Redmond (Eds.), *Framing celebrity: New directions in celebrity culture* (pp. 145–160). Abingdon: Routledge.

Mercer, J. (2017). *Gay pornography: Representations of sexuality and masculinity*. London: I.B.Tauris.

Morris, P., & Paasonen, S. (2014). Risk and utopia: A dialogue on pornography. *GLQ, 20*(3), 215–239.

Murphy, B. M. (2013). 'Children misbehaving in the walls!' or, Wes Craven's suburban family values. In A. Andeweg & S. Zlosnik (Eds.), *Gothic kinship* (pp. 81–96). Manchester: Manchester University Press.

Nielsen, E-J., & Kiss, M. (2015). Sexercising our opinion on porn: A virtual discussion. *Psychology & Sexuality, 6*(1), 118–139.

Ognjanović, D. (2012). Why is the *tension* so *high*? The monstrous feminine in (post) modern slasher films. In C. J. S. Picart & J. E. Browning (Eds.), *Speaking of monsters: A teratological anthology* (pp. 227–238). New York, NY: Palgrave Macmillan.

Sedgwick, E. K. (2003). *Touching feeling: Affect, pedagogy, performativity*. Durham, NC: Duke University Press.

Shelton, E. (2002). A star is porn: Corpulence, comedy, and the homosocial cult of adult film star Ron Jeremy. *Camera Obscura, 51*(17), 115–146.

Smith, C., Barker, M., & Attwood, F. (2015). Why do people watch porn? Results from pornresearch.org. In L. Comella & S. Tarrant (Eds.), *New views on pornography: Sexuality, politics, and the law* (pp. 267–285). Santa Barbara, CA: Praeger.

Sweetbriar, B. (2016). Naked sword − *Scared stiff! Gloss Magazine*, 28 October. Retrieved from http://www.glossmagazine.net/2016/10/naked-sword-scared-stiff/

Tortorici, Z. J. (2008). Queering pornography: Desiring youth, race, and fantasy in gay porn. In S. Driver (Ed.), *Queer youth cultures* (pp. 199–220). Albany, NY: State University of New York Press.

Tramontagna, G. (2006). *Bonesaw. The Guide*, September. Retrieved from http://archive.guidemag.com/magcontent/invokemagcontent.cfm?ID=E97FA437-A62C-48E3–98A7FBAF8E63C671

Tziallas, E. (2010). Torture porn and surveillance culture. *Jump Cut, 52*. Retrieved from https://www.ejumpcut.org/archive/jc52.2010/evangelosTorturePorn/index.html

Williams, L. (1989). *Hard core: Power, pleasure and the 'frenzy of the visible'*. Berkeley, CA: University of California Press.

Williams, L. (1999). Film bodies: Gender, genre and excess. In S. Thornham (Ed.), *Feminist film theory: A reader* (pp. 267–281). New York, NY: New York University Press.

Chapter 8

'In Celebration of Her Wickedness?': Critical Intertextuality and the Female Vampire in *Byzantium*

Matthew Denny

This chapter seeks to explore the ways in which *Byzantium* (Dir. Neil Jordan, 2012) exploits the intertextual qualities of vampire fiction in order to critique and rework the generic conventions associated with the representation of the female vampire. While any genre film might be dubbed intertextual in a very loose sense, I contend that *Byzantium* merits special consideration because of the ways in which it engages critically with a history of representation and for the partial, trace-like quality of its allusions. Analysing this critical intertextuality through the lens of (feminist) postmodern theory, I will demonstrate the ways in which *Byzantium* points to the possibility of alternative representations by taking up and critically reworking existing images and stories.

Byzantium focuses on the relationship between mother and daughter vampires Clara (Gemma Arterton) and Eleanor (Saoirse Ronan). The pair lives an itinerant existence, pursued by a patriarchal sect of vampires seeking to destroy them. The titular Byzantium is a dilapidated hotel in the seaside town in which Clara and Eleanor take refuge. Beyond the primacy the film grants to the female voice through Eleanor's confessional writing (Abbott, 2017, p. 153), *Byzantium* is a fairly conventional example of vampire fiction, and my identification of the film as postmodern likely requires some further justification.[1]

Outlining the stylistic features of postmodernism, Christina Degli-Eposti lists qualities such as self-reflexivity, intertextuality, bricolage and multiplicity as well as parody and pastiche (1998, p. 18). Degli-Eposti describes these techniques as 'strategies of disruption' (1998, p. 18). Referring specifically to Hollywood film, Catherine Constable additionally identifies 'self-conscious

---

[1] Abbott also notes that the voice of the female vampire has been 'comparatively silent' in recent years.

Gender and Contemporary Horror in Film, 117–132
doi:10.1108/978-1-78769-897-020191009

narration', 'self-reflexive spectacle' and 'abbreviated, artificial characterization' as key postmodern aesthetic strategies (2015, p. 36). Reading this catalogue of features, *Byzantium* is likely not the first film that comes to mind – particularly in comparison to more ostentatiously postmodern works such as *The Cabin in the Woods* (Dir. Drew Goddard, 2012) and the films of the *Scream* (Dir. Wes Craven, 1996, 1997, 2000, 2001) franchise. Rather than the overt parody and pastiche of these films, the intertextuality of *Byzantium* is more fleeting and oblique – an intertextuality in passing. Nevertheless, I maintain that if we examine *Byzantium* through the lens of feminist postmodern theory we are able to appreciate the ways in which the film uses the strategies of intertextuality and a self-reflexive foregrounding of storytelling and the act of writing in order to rework and rewrite the conventionally misogynistic representation of the female vampire in more feminist terms.

The trace-like intertextuality of *Byzantium* is most readily apparent in the ways in which Byzantium employs names from foundational works of vampire fiction (see Abbott, 2017, p. 155). The character of Ruthven (Jonny Lee Miller) is named for the Byronic vampire in John Pollidori's *The Vampyre* while Darvell (Sam Riley) is the namesake of the protagonist of Byron's own 'The Burial: A Fragment/Fragment of a Novel'.[2] A yet more elusive example of this trace-like intertextuality is Clara's adoption of the moniker 'Camila', tantalizingly close to Carmilla and yet not an exact match. Clara also goes by Claire, perhaps recalling Carmilla's use of aliases such as Marcilla and Mircalla.[3] This 'imperfect' intertextuality points to a history of vampire fiction, opening a dialogue with these earlier texts – although *Byzantium* is arguably more engaged with later adaptions of *Carmilla* that Sheridan Le Fanu's original.

While these names gesture towards a history of vampire fiction, the characters of Ruthven and Darvell bear scant resemblance to the original bearers of their names. Ruthven is notable, however, as while the character is human rather than vampiric, he is perhaps the most 'monstrous' character in the film. While not a vampire, there is nevertheless something vampiric in Ruthven's very human monstrosity. Ruthven is a sexual predator who uses his good looks and social rank to prey on young women. His entrapment of these women, forcing them into a life of prostitution can be read as an analogue for the transformation from human to vampire. This reading is supported by the later misreading of Eleanor's biography as allegorical, with the sex workers employed by her mother identified as the vampires of Eleanor's tale. Ruthven's later deterioration and disfigurement by venereal disease also replicate the unveiling of the vampire's true, monstrous form.

Rather than a direct reference, the allusions built around Ruthven are more an echo or suggestion of resemblance; causing meaning to shift and realign in

[2]Miller had previously played the title role in the BBC's Byron (2003), adding further intertextual resonance to the character.
[3]Abbott also notes that Clara and Claire echo Clara Byron and Claire Clairmont, reinforcing the allusions to Byron.

new patterns. This realignment serves to shift the qualities and associations of the monstrous away from the female vampire and on to Ruthven. The category of the monstrous is thus no longer aligned with a 'deviant' feminine identity that transgresses the norms of a patriarchal society but with a human male character who embodies these norms (see Christopher Craft, 1984, pp. 19–21). The identification of Ruthven as a representative of patriarchal power is confirmed by Darvell's intention to recruit Ruthven to the patriarchal sect of vampires known as 'The Pointed Nails of Justice'. Savella (Uri Graviel), the apparent leader of the group, reminds Darvell that he was he was charged with finding 'a man of good blood' to join their fraternity, suggesting that Darvell believes Ruthven meets this description. From this, we can confirm that far from being aberrant, Ruthven's behaviour is in keeping with the attitudes of the patriarchal power. Through its shifting and oblique intertextuality, *Byzantium* realigns monstrosity with patriarchal dominance rather the female vampire's transgression of patriarchal norms.

Setting aside intertextuality for the moment, we can move on to briefly consider the other major postmodern strategy of the film – its self-reflexive attention to storytelling and the act of writing. The female voice and female storytelling are of central importance to *Byzantium*. This is most obviously signalled through Eleanor's compulsively autobiographical writing; but is also apparent in the way Clara weaves narratives around herself through her equally compulsive lying. This foregrounding of storytelling can be understood in terms of the postmodern concern with self-conscious narration identified by Constable. The identification of Eleanor as a writer and of the story of the film as her narrative serves to both suggest a connection between writing and identity and the role narratives play in shaping and determining experience. If intertextuality is the key strategy whereby *Byzantium* realigns existing meanings, it is through self-reflexive attention to writing and particularly rewriting that the film addresses the possibility of creating new meaning.

The foregrounding of writing is evident from the beginning of the film, which opens with a slow track to reveal Eleanor in the act of writing, accompanied by her voiceover narration: 'My story can never be told. I write it over and over, wherever we find shelter. I write of what I cannot speak: the truth.' This opening immediately frames Eleanor's story as one that remains untold and unspoken, despite her constant rewritings. It is a narrative that exists, but goes unheeded. Eleanor's words may reflect the secrecy in which she and Clara must live, concealing their true identities from the human world, but it also speaks to Clara and Eleanor's status in vampire society. The only other vampires encountered in the film are male. The group regards vampirism as a purely male privilege, deeming Clara a usurper of male power whose very existence is abhorrent. Indeed, Clara is doubly transgressive. Not only does she gain access to this all-male realm, she further deviates from the conventions of male legitimacy by passing on her vampiric inheritance to a female heir. To be a woman is to be illegitimate, outside of the law. Conversely, the legitimacy of the male vampires' claim to power is reinforced through associations with the conventions of onscreen depictions of detectives and law enforcement. When Darvell (Sam Riley) inspects the burned out remains of Clara's and Eleanor's flat, his usual dark suit and long coat are supplemented by a face mask and blue latex gloves, drawing on a visual vocabulary of forensic investigation. The apparent head of the order, Savella (Uri Graviel), wears a similar if more old-fashioned combination of suit and coat, complete with a Marlowe-esque broad brimmed hat. These associations are also borne out in the ways the male vampires interacting with humans. Attempting to track down Clara, Werner (Thure Lindhadrt) conducts himself as if carrying out a missing person or murder investigation. The ability of the male vampires to 'pass' as police while Clara is forced into the role of outlaw further confirms their legitimacy within both vampire and human society.

Eleanor's story remains unspoken because her voice is not considered valid and both she and Clara remain trapped in the roles assigned to them by the dominant male narrative.[4] From this, it becomes clear that writing is of central importance to both the postmodern and feminist impulses of the film. Indeed, I would argue that the two go hand in hand and that it is by deploying the techniques associated with postmodern film that *Byzantium* is able to mount its feminist critique.

According to Catherine Constable (2015), the dominant model of postmodern aesthetics in film studies is based on Fredric Jameson's conceptualization of postmodernism. Jameson's postmodernism is an example of what Constable has described as nihilistic postmodernism (2015, p. 45). Nihilistic conceptualizations of postmodernism frame the postmodern turn in terms of a series of losses or deaths – for example, the death of the author, the end of history and the replacement of reality with hyperreality. However, as Constable observes elsewhere, such a definition of postmodernism 'is a self-fulfilling prophecy', effectively limiting 'what the viewer is prepared to see in any given postmodern film' (2014, p. 381) Constable proposes an alternative to this 'rhetoric of nihilism', favouring an approach that draws upon 'affirmative postmodernisms' such as those of Linda Hutcheon (Constable, 2009, pp. 53–54). Hutcheon's postmodernism, I will argue, is far more compatible with the concerns of feminist theory that Jameson, and thus serves as a suitable framework through which to analyse the ways in which *Byzantium* deploys postmodern intertextuality in the pursuit of feminist critique. It is, however, necessary to first outline some of the salient points of Jameson's postmodernism in order to better appreciate Hutcheon's (feminist) response to Jameson's nihilistic model.

Summaries of Jameson's work frequently emphasize his equation of postmodernism with the death of history. This is, however, only one of a series of conceptual deaths he associates with postmodernism and the post-structuralist turn. Most relevant to the concerns of this chapters are Jameson's identification of postmodern intertextuality as pastiche and his thoughts regarding the 'death of the subject' (Jameson, 1983, pp. 113–114).

---

[4]Crucially, Eleanor's writing is also an act of rewriting. This has significant bearing on the film's critical intertextuality and will be discussed in this context later in the chapter.

According to Jameson, the intertextual references of postmodern texts are examples of pastiche. Like parody, pastiche involves the imitation or 'mimicry' of other styles, particularly their 'mannerisms and stylistic twitches' (Jameson, 1983, p. 113) While both parody and pastiche are imitative, Jameson defines pastiche as the 'neutral' practice of such mimicry (1983, p. 114). Parody and Pastiche can therefore be distinguished in terms of purpose. Where parody mimics a style in order to ridicule its deviations from the norm, pastiche merely uncritically copies that style.[5]

Jameson's distinction between critical parody and uncritical pastiche echoes a similar distinction he makes between modernist and postmodern practices of quotation. Modernist works remain distinct from the commercial forms and mass cultural texts from which they quote. In postmodern works, these mass cultural texts are incorporated in the work in a way that blurs the distinctions between high art and mass culture (Jameson, 1983, p. 112). This sheds further light on Jameson's concerns regarding the replacement of (modernist) parody with (postmodern) pastiche. For Jameson, parody is a form of quotation that maintains a critical distance from the original. Pastiche on the other hand lacks the distance of proper modernist quotation, and as such a postmodern text is incapable of critique, resigned instead to 'imitate dead styles' (1983, p. 115). Jameson's denial of the critical potential of postmodern works would preclude any identification of *Byzantium* as *both* postmodern *and* critical. Indeed, to identify a text as postmodern in the sense suggested by Jameson would serve to stamp the work as always already a failed critique. Jameson's conceptualization of postmodernism cannot account for the ways in which *Byzantium* critically realigns the category of the monstrous through the incorporation of names from early examples of vampire fiction and is therefore blind to one of the key ways in which *Byzantium* mounts its postmodern feminist critique.

Perhaps more pressing from a feminist perspective is Jameson's stance on the death of the subject. Jameson observes a consensus across disciplines acknowledging the death of the 'individualist subject'. Jameson identifies two theoretical positions regarding the death of the subject, an orthodox position that treats the death of the subject as the loss of a once viable category, and a more 'radical' post-structuralist position that asserts the subject never existed in the first place. Jameson is less concerned with the fine distinctions between these positions than he is with the threat the death of the Subject poses to definitions of art as self-expressive. From the perspective of feminist theory, there is much more at stake. On the one hand, the unsettling of a definition of the (Enlightenment) Subject as White, male and European is useful to feminist theory, while, on the other hand, it also results in the de-valuing and destruction of the category just at the point that previously excluded groups might gain access. This speaks to the concerns identified by Christine Di Stefano (1990, p. 75) regarding the incompatibility of

---

[5]An additional, unmentioned, function of parody is that it proclaims its status as copy and therefore reinforces the status of the unique style it mimics as original.

feminism and postmodern theory: the death of the Subject merely perpetuates the exclusion of women from the category of Subject.[6]

We can identify an echo of these concerns in the different attitudes Eleanor and Clara adopt regarding their own status as subject, or rather the differing types of Subjectivity each seeks to attain. Eleanor's autobiographical writing represents a repeated attempt to assert her status as Subject that goes consistently unrecognized. Eleanor's constant reiteration of her past experiences can be seen as an attempt to construct the sort of coherent Humanist Subject envisioned in Wordsworth's *Prelude*, her writing 'a dark/Inscrutable workmanship that reconciles/Discordant elements' (Wordsworth, 1995, p. 55). Clara, however, delights in a constantly contradictory identity, where not even her name remains stable. If Eleanor seeks recognition as an Enlightenment Subject, then Clara can be seen as embracing the death of that very category. However, both of these approaches result in the exclusion of Eleanor and Clara from the category of subject – Eleanor because her status as Subject is not recognized and Clara because she actively denies the category. *Byzantium* does point to ways in which a postmodern female subjectivity that is not simply a rejection of the category subject can be attained, but in ways that are not accounted for in Jameson's conceptualization of postmodernism. As Constable asserts, following a nihilistic conceptualization of postmodernism such as Jameson's imposes a limit on the ways in which a text may read. For this reason, Constable advises taking up Hutcheon's conceptualization of the postmodern rather than the more familiar Jamesonian model we are able to avoid such self-limiting readings.

Like Jameson, Hutcheon conceptualize postmodernism in relation to the series of critical 'deaths' enacted by poststructuralism. Unlike Jameson, Hutcheon approaches postmodernism from a perspective informed by post-structuralist theory and thus with a very different set of critical preferences. Whereas Jameson laments the confusion of boundaries brought about by postmodernism; a post-structuralist perspective strives to challenge oppositions, revelling in the collapse and confusion of boundaries. For Hutcheon, postmodernism is closely associated with the critical practice of deconstruction.

Hutcheon aligns postmodernism with deconstruction through the identification of what she describes as the 'de-doxifying' impulse of postmodern art and culture (1989, p. 4). In coining the term de-doxifying, Hutcheon plays on Barthes's notions of *doxa* and *para-doxa* from *The Pleasure of the Text*.[7] Elsewhere

---

[6]Contrary to Jameson's assertion, there are significant conceptual differences between suggesting there was a category of Subject, but that this no longer exists and the post-structuralist deconstruction of the concept.
[7]In *The Pleasure of the Text* (Barthes, 1994), *doxa* is referred to as both 'opinion' (p. 18) and as 'nature' (p. 28), paradoxa is 'dispute' (p. 18) while '*paradoxical* formulae' are 'those which proceed literally against the *doxa*' (p. 54); in 'Change the Object Itself: Myth Today' Barthes aligns *doxa* with his concept of myth and the 'overturning of culture into nature' and the rendering of the purely contingent as 'Common Sense, Right Reason, the Norm, General Opinion' (Barthes, 1977, p. 165).

Hutcheon describes this de-doxifying impulse more straightforwardly as a 'de-naturalizing critique' (1989, p. 3). The de-naturalizing impulse of postmodernism is apparent in its concern with pointing out that what we consider natural is in fact cultural: 'made by us, not given to us' (Hutcheon, 1989, p. 2). In particular, the self-reflexive and parodic art of postmodernism underlines the realization that all cultural forms of representation, high or low, are 'ideologically grounded' (Hutcheon, 1989, p. 3). The de-naturalizing impulse of postmodernism therefore echoes deconstruction's demonstration of the violently hierarchical properties of binary oppositions, in that both are concerned with challenging the perceived neutrality of representation and (philosophical) language (Derrida, 2010, pp. 38–39).

By identifying the de-naturalizing impulse of postmodernism and aligning it with deconstruction, Hutcheon is able to counter the claim that postmodernism is 'disqualified' from political involvement because of its appropriation of existing stories and images (1989, p. 3). Contrary to Jameson, Hutcheon argues that postmodernism *is* capable of critique, albeit a 'strange kind of critique' (1989, p. 4). Postmodern critique is strange because it is unavoidably complicit, bound up with the object of its criticism (Hutcheon, 1989, p. 4). The complicitous critique of postmodernism recognizes the impossibility of escaping implication in what it nevertheless seeks to analyse and undermine (Hutcheon, 1989, p. 4). In light of this, Hutcheon offers a general definition of postmodernism as 'the name given to cultural practices which acknowledge their inevitable implication in capitalism, without relinquishing the power or will to intervene critically in it' (Hutcheon, 1989, p. 26).

Hutcheon's conceptualization of postmodern intertextuality as complicitous critique challenges the criticisms of postmodern works as offering nothing more than 'a value-free, decorative, de-historicized, quotation of past forms', suggesting instead that through irony postmodern works offer a de-naturalizing form of acknowledging the history and politics of representation (Hutcheon, 1989, p. 90).

The political potential of postmodern parody emerges from the ironic and paradoxical nature of postmodern art. According to Hutcheon, postmodern parody performs 'a paradoxical installing as well as subverting of conventions' (1989, p. 14). Hutcheon's identification of postmodernism as paradoxically installing and subverting, as de-naturalizing problematizes the straightforward association of postmodernism with a series of critical deaths evident in Jameson.[8] Hutcheon asserts that, contrary to the 'standard negative evaluation', postmodernism does not claim that everything is 'empty' at the centre but rather interrogates and calls in to question the politics and power of that centre (1989,

---

[8]Although Hutcheon rescues postmodern parody from 'the ahistorical and empty realm of pastiche', she nonetheless sets up a distinction between postmodern works and other 'nostalgic' practices evident in contemporary culture that lack the deconstructive and critical irony of postmodern parody. For example, Hutcheon describes television as 'pure commodified complicity, without the critique needed to define the postmodern paradox' (Hutcheon, *The Politics of Postmodernism*, 1989, p. 10).

p. 38). Put another way, acknowledging that something, such as the subject, is constructed and cultural is not the same as declaring that such a thing does not exist. According to Hutcheon, postmodernism makes representation 'into an issue' and so questions our assumptions about the supposed transparency and naturalness of representation (1989, p. 32). In postmodern texts, 'the representation of history becomes the history of representation' (Hutcheon, 1989, p. 58). Hutcheon once again draws on the notion of postmodernism as complicitous critique, noting that while it is impossible to escape the history of representation, it is possible to critique it through parody and irony (1989, p. 58). Taking up Hutcheon's affirmative conceptualization allows us to move outside the self-fulfilling prophecy of nihilistic postmodernism and engage with the critical impulse of *Byzantium*'s intertextuality. The usefulness of taking up Hutcheon also goes beyond opening up the potential to consider Byzantium as both critical and postmodern. Hutcheon's framing of postmodernism in terms of de-naturalization and a critical attitude to the history of representation also aligns with the feminist project of *Byzantium* and in particular its concern with the representation of the female vampire. Moreover, Hutcheon's postmodernism also allows for the retention of the Subject as a viable category, albeit with the recognition that the very concept 'Subject' is constructed, contingent, 'historically conditioned and historically Constructed' (Hutcheon, 1989, p. 38).

For Hutcheon, a postmodern notion of the subject brings with it 'an awareness of both the nature and historicity of our discursive representations of the self' (1989, p. 39). Hutcheon identifies such an awareness with poststructuralism, but also foregrounds the separate influence of feminist theory. Specifically, feminist theory is seen to problematize the 'apocalyptic' figuring of the Subject in terms of loss and dispersal by keeping the 'question of identity' open 'in the name of the (different) history of women (Hutcheon, 1989, p. 39). For feminist postmodern art, subjectivity is not something fixed but rather something 'in process' (Hutcheon, 1989, p. 39). Nor is it conceived of as autonomous or outside of history. Rather postmodern subjectivity 'is always a gendered subjectivity, rooted also in class, race, ethnicity, and sexual orientation' (Hutcheon, 1989, p. 39).

Hutcheon's retention of an always already gendered category of postmodern subjectivity provides us with an alternative to the choice between striving towards an unattainable and exclusionary Enlightenment Subjectivity and the rejection of Subjectivity. Looked at from this perspective, both Eleanor's writing and Clara's duplicity can be reinterpreted as creative acts of subjectivity 'in process'. Clara and Eleanor are able to redefine what it means to be a subject on their own terms. Taking this view, the separation of mother and daughter group in favour of heterosexual pairings at the film's close is not (only) acquiescence to heterosexual normativity but represents Eleanor's and Clara's recognition of *each other* as autonomous subjects. In other words, rather than striving for recognition as a subject in the terms dictated by the patriarchal Pointed Nails of Justice, Eleanor and Clara are able to define subjectivity on their own terms.

Of further relevance to *Byzantium* is Hutcheon's claim for the close relationship between the practice of feminist theory and her own concept of postmodern

complicitous critique. For Hutcheon, postmodern complicitous critique simultaneously 'inscribes and subverts the conventions and ideologies of the dominant
cultural and social forces' (1989, p. 11). According to Hutcheon, this paradoxical double process of installing and subverting is influenced by 'the feminist
need to inscribe first – and only then subvert' (1989, p. 39). Understanding postmodern quotation as a paradoxical installing and subverting acknowledges that
the critique of a particular code or convention will also unavoidably involve
appropriation of that code or convention.

Hutcheon's appeal to the metaphor of inscription returns us to motif of writing and rewriting in *Byzantium*. For Eleanor, by writing her story, she performs
the process of Subjectivity. This is initially a fruitless endeavour; her story
remains unspoken and her selfhood unrealized. Worse, when Eleanor's story is
shared, it is misinterpreted as allegorical and as a result, her subjectivity is
pathologized, her writing characterized as 'dark, passionate, violent, *sick*, bril-
liant'. Eleanor's writing is doomed to be either unspoken or interpreted according to conventions that prove an unsuitable framework for understanding. It is
only at the film's conclusion that Eleanor discards her old story, to begin the telling of a new one. The focus on Eleanor's storytelling aligns the inscription/sub-
version dynamic Hutcheon identifies in feminism and postmodernism with the
process of rewriting. Following this, it would be appropriate to consider the
intertextual quotation of Byzantium in terms of *rewriting* existing representation
in order to produce new stories from old.

Having argued for the close fit between *Byzantium*'s dynamic of writing and
rewriting and Hutcheon's conceptualization of postmodernism in terms of complicitous critique, it is important to recognize that all genre cinema engages with
a similar dynamic of repetition in difference. For example, in Catherine
Hardwicke's adaptation of *Twilight*, the protagonist Bella (Kristen Stewart)
confronts the attractive but mysterious Edward (Robert Pattinson). Having confirmed her earlier suspicions with a period of frenzied searching of vampire lore
on the internet, Bella makes the following accusations:

> You're impossibly fast. And strong. Your skin is pale white, and
> ice cold. Your eyes change colour and sometimes you speak like -
> like you're from a different time. You never eat or drink any-
> thing; you don't go into the sunlight [...] I know what you are.

In this exchange, *Twilight* plays out a familiar trope of vampire fiction – the
listing of various rules and characteristics that serve to identify the vampire.
Such listing serves a double function. Firstly, echoing elements familiar from
other texts ensures the vampires of this film are recognizable *as* vampires in
accordance with established conventions. Secondly, by abandoning, reworking
or inventing conventions, the vampires of this text are made to appear novel, if
not entirely unique. Such negotiation between convention and novelty in vampire fiction represents a rather overt manifestation of the dynamic of repetition
and difference that shapes genre filmmaking (Neale, 1980, p. 48).

There is no equivalent scene in *Byzantium*, indeed the film exhibits very few examples of the usual play with repetition and difference typical of the vampire film. Setting aside the novel replacement of fangs with a singular claw-like nail, *Byzantium* is almost perversely unconcerned with either repeating or reinventing the iconographic conventions of the vampire genre. There are notable exceptions of course, the aforementioned nail, the spectacular waterfalls of blood and the meeting of the Nameless Saint which echoes Anne Rice's God of the Grove (Rice, 2003, p. 376). Furthermore, an absence of the typical trappings of garlic and Christian cross can be understood as a reworking of iconographic convention in its own right.

What marks the intertextuality of *Byzantium* as postmodern is not the extent to which it engages or does not engage with the conventions of genre, but rather the extent to which its reworking of genre conventions is also a reworking of conventions of representation. Take, for example, the exchange between Clara and Werner (Thure Lindhart) before she decapitates him. The conversation plays out before a large mirror in which Clara's reflection is in focus but Clara is not. Rather than simply reworking the convention of the disparity between the vampire and its reflection, this scene engages with the themes of essence/appearance associated with the trope. In particular, it provides a visual prompt to considering how Clara is positioned in relation to this binary. However, this play with convention can be understand in relation to Clara's duplicity. Like Eleanor, Clara is a storyteller. Where Eleanor suffers from an almost pathological truthfulness, Clara easily moves from one lie to the next, adopting new identities as is appropriate. The solidity of Clara's reflection in comparison with the diffuseness of her body attests to the convincingness of these assumed personas, but also suggests the unknowability or absence of a 'true' self.

This reconfiguration of the relationship between appearance and essence can also be understand in terms of the external perceptions of Clara taking primacy over any outward projection of internal self. Clara's essence is unknowable and ultimately unimportant in determining how she is treated by those in power. The personas that Clara adopts are those thrust upon her by men — she behaves according to the expectations of men.[9] This is borne out in the subservient attitude Clara adopts in her interaction with Werner in the above sequence, but also more broadly across the film. Where the Pointed Nails of Justice see Clara as a threat to the power of men, she lives out the most extreme version of this fear — preying on abusive men and usurping their power. Clara is trapped within a framework that sees powerful women as monstrous and so embraces her monstrosity as the only route to power available to her.

Returning to the interaction with Werner, it is through the adoption of appropriate and expected behaviour that she is able to overcome him. This

---

[9]It is interesting to note that the role of mother is the one role Clara is unable to perform to the satisfaction of the person who projects it upon her: Eleanor. Much of the conflict between Eleanor and Clara arises from Clara's failure to meet Eleanor's expectations regarding appropriate behaviour.

points to the necessity of Clara's deceptions, as defensive mechanism and camouflage that allow her pass through the world of men in (relative) safety. This play with reflections can therefore be understood in terms of the simultaneous installing and subverting of complicitous critique. Through Clara, the trope of the deceptive woman whose appearance masks her true, unknowable intentions is interrogated to reveal the necessity of such behaviours. However, in order to examine this trope, the film must first assert it. Clara remains duplicitous, but duplicity as a characteristic is revalued – we are invited to celebrate her wickedness.

For the most part, the intertextuality of *Byzantium* is of a different, more elusive sort, as seen through the film's play with names. Rather than a reworking of the generic conventions of the vampire film, this more elusive intertextuality represents an engagement with a history of vampire fiction. Moreover, and in keeping with Hutcheon's understanding of postmodern texts as engaged with the history and politic of representation, the intertextuality of *Byzantium* is primarily concerned with deconstructing the historical representation of the female vampire as a sexually deviant transgressor of patriarchal norms Specifically, *Byzantium* seems to be positioning itself in relation to a cycle of erotic vampire films produced in Britain and mainland Europe throughout the 1970s. Most prominently, the film calls to mind *Daughters of Darkness* (Dir. Harry Kümel, 1971) and Hammer's Karnstein films.[10] The erotic vampire films of French director Jean Rollin also belong to this cycle, but the influence of these films seems less apparent in *Byzantium*. Hammer in particular serves as a key point of reference for the film, with a sequence from *Dracula, Prince of Darkness* (Dir. Terrence Fisher, 1966) shown on television within the film. I will investigate the implications of this quotation in more detail later in this chapter.

Such concrete examples of quotation are, however, rare in Byzantium. The intertextuality of *Byzantium* is more often expressed through a similarity of tone, or a suggestion of similarity than it is through direct quotation. The intertextuality of *Byzantium* is one of hints and traces, rather than quotations – an intertextuality in passing that rarely announces itself. More prosaically, *Byzantium* also recalls these films through a similarity in character type, situation and location, if not execution. This is most clear if we briefly consider *Byzantium* alongside *Daughters of Darkness*.

Both films centre on a pair of vampires, one older woman and one younger, seeking refuge in a rundown seaside town and occupying a largely empty hotel. While positioned on opposite sides of the North Sea, the coastal towns of Hastings in Sussex and Ostend in Flanders share a windswept bleakness

---

[10]Beginning with *The Vampire Lovers* (Dir. Roy Ward Baker, 1970), an adaptation of *Carmilla*, and followed by *Lust for a Vampire* (Dir. Jimmy Sangster, 1971) and *Twins of Evil* (Dir. Jon Hough, 1971). Although not related to the Karnstein films, *Countess Dracula* (Dir. Peter Sasdy, 1971) similarly focuses on the female vampire as antagonist rather than merely as victim or bride as is more common in Hammer's Dracula films.

exploited by both *Byzantium* and *Daughters of Darkness*. The hotel locations central to both films are suggestive of faded grandeur, and much is made of the bleak juxtaposition of concrete and grey ocean swell. There are of course important differences. In *Daughters of Darkness,* the relationship between the vampires is romantic, or at least sexual, whereas Clara and Eleanor are a mother and daughter masquerading as sisters. The other key difference is that where Clara and Eleanor ultimately achieve freedom by the end of the film, the vampires of *Daughters of Darkness* are gruesomely dealt with, indicative of a narrative logic whereby the vampire, the woman, the lesbian must be punished for her transgressions. This logic also informs *The Vampire Lovers*, Hammer's adaptation of *Carmilla*. As with *Daughters of Darkness*, vampirism is closely associated with queer sexuality and 'unnatural' female sexual appetite. While Ingrid Pitt's performance as Carmilla is highly sympathetic and suggestive of a complex relationship between love and vampiric appetite, the film ultimately reasserts the heteronormative and patriarchal *status quo*. After her death, Carmilla's portrait transforms to reveal a fanged skull, revealing and reaffirming her status as monstrous predator rather than the conflicted, tragic lover suggested by Pitt's performance.

Byzantium also takes up the theme of the reassertion of patriarchal power, but with crucial departures. Unlike Carmilla, Clara and Eleanor escape. They are not punished for their transgressions, indeed it is key to the postmodern feminist project of the film that they are not. Just as Clara's duplicity is revalued as necessary defence, the apparent transgressions of Clara and Eleanor are reframed not as a transgression, but justified and essential rebellion. It is in this respect that I see *Byzantium* as engaged in a critical intertextual dialogue with this 1970s cycle. The partial and imperfect quotations suggest a similarity, or a kinship between Byzantium and *Daughters of Darkness* or *The Vampire Lovers*, and yet in its difference from these films *Byzantium* opens up the possibility for both critique and the creation of new meaning.

A more concrete example of this process can be found in *Byzantium*'s engagement with *Dracula, Prince of Darkness*. In an unusually overt referential moment in the film, Eleanor is shown watching *Dracula, Prince of Darkness* on television. The scene she is watching centres around the staking of Helen (Barbara Shelley) by a group of monks lead by Father Sandor (Andrew Keir). As is so often the case, prior to becoming a vampire Helen is the epitome of upstanding Victorian morals, but after her encounter with Dracula becomes a threatening, sexualized presence. In the staking sequence, Helen is held down by a group of clerics while Father Sandor stakes her. The writhing screaming Helen is returned to silence and peace in death. Following the pattern established in the analysis of *Daughters of Darkness* and *The Vampire Lovers*, it seems reasonable to also read this sequence as a reassertion of patriarchal order on a rebellious woman. It is interesting (although perhaps not surprising) that this scene, of all the examples that could have been chosen from the Hammer back catalogue, should feature in *Byzantium*.

More interesting than this moment of overt quotation, however, is the way in which Helen's death is then played out within film's climatic moments, with

Clara taking the place of Helen. While there is no attempt to slavishly recreate the composition or choreography of the scene, and the method chosen for Clara's execution is decapitation rather than staking, there is a sufficient trace or echo of the earlier scene for it to be read as a reference to and reworking of the *Dracula, Prince of Darkness* sequence. The inclusion of the sequence playing on the television earlier primes the viewer to read the later scene in relation to it, encouraging the drawing of comparisons between the two moments. Where Helen is returned to an acceptably passive and demure state – indeed rendered ultimately passive and obedient through death – Clara's rebellion and worth is recognized, the previous power overthrown.

It is perhaps unsatisfying that in this moment Clara must be 'rescued' by Darvell, her rebellion against patriarchy legitimized and realized by a man. Here, Hutcheon's concept of complicitous critique is useful once again. Rather than dismissing this moment as a failure of critique due to its complicity in the system it purports to critique, it can be recognized as both critical and complicit.[11]

In addition to reworking the narrative trajectory of transgression and punishment seen in the earlier films, *Byzantium* also reworks the visual representation of the female vampire. Where earlier films present the female vampire as eroticized spectacle, *Byzantium* reworks this erotic imagery in terms of the sensual. In opposing the erotic and the sensual in this way, I hope to draw a distinction between a presentation of the female body and female sexuality for the voyeuristic gaze of the viewer and an alternative mode of representation that celebrates the pleasure and power experience by an embodied female subject.

Clara's rebirth as a vampire is a standout moment in this respect. The sequence draws on the erotic combination of blood and the female body, a convention particularly prevalent in Hammer films, but transforms this imagery through excess and exaggeration. Mary Ellmann's work on stereotypes indicates how exaggeration might be employed as a critical strategy. Ellmann identifies the 'explosive tendency' of stereotypes, noting that every stereotype has a limit, and that when 'swelled' to that limit, the stereotype will explode. For Ellmann, this explosion results in either the 'total vulgarization' of the stereotype or 'a reorginization of the advantage, now in fragments, around a new center of disadvantage' (Ellmann, 1968, p. 131). Ellmann's language echoes that of Hutcheon, who sees the critique of postmodernism not as the emptying of the centre of meaning, but as a reorganization of meaning around a new centre.

Clara's ecstatic bathing in the torrents of blood that cascade over her following her transformation can therefore be read as an excessive amplification of the delicate splatters of blood that adorn the bodies of Carmilla (Yutte Stensgaard) in *Lust for a Vampire* or Countess Bathory (Ingrid Pitt) in *Countess Dracula*. It is productive, then, to consider this sequence in dialogue with the earlier films,

---

[11]As Abbott notes, Darvell intervenes because he has been inspired by Eleanor's code of mercy (rather than justice) and seeks to join with Clara in hunting the powerful and protecting the weak (Abbott, *Undead Apocalypse*, 2017).

where similarity is used to emphasize and articulate the differences. All three of these sequences foreground the revivifying effects of blood, but where the two Hammer films frame this in terms of the desirability of the female body for a male onlooker present in the scene, *Byzantium* instead focuses on the awakened sensual appreciation of Clara, presenting her alone in nature. There is a stark contrast to the sequence in *Countess* Dracula, where countess Bathory is discovered bathing in blood by her suitor Imre Toth (Sandor Elès). The sequence in *Countess Dracula* operates according to a dynamic of revelation – both the Countess' secret and her body – the result of Toth breaching the privacy of the Countess. The sequence is voyeuristic and, when the countess becomes aware of Toth's presence, she attempts to conceal herself from his gaze. In *Byzantium*, however, Clara is untroubled by onlookers and able to relish the experience provided by her newly heightened senses.[12]

The shift from object of a voyeuristic gaze to subject positioned in the landscape echoes Mulvey's 'Visual Pleasure and Narrative Cinema' in interesting ways. The presence of male onlookers in both *Countess Dracula* and *Lust for a Vampire* resonates with Mulvey's remarks regarding the alignment of the viewer's gaze with than of male protagonists onscreen, while the absence of any such character in the waterfall sequence resists this. Indeed, the sequence from *Byzantium* recalls Mulvey's characterization of the typical representation of male subjectivity in classical Hollywood cinema in terms of the figure in the landscape (1989, p. 20). While Mulvey uses landscape more figuratively to describe the different treatments of space evident in the representation of women through close-up and soft focus compared to deep focus and wider framing associated with the depiction of male characters, the term nevertheless echoes the a Romantic tradition of Subjectivity formed through encounters with sublime landscapes.

This sequence therefore draws together multiple threads. It deconstructs previous representations of the female vampire as erotic spectacle, and constructs Clara as Subject. However, it represents Subjectivity in notably Romantic terms, and therefore relies upon a certain history of representation – one that is traditionally exclusively male. *Byzantium* thus negotiates the tensions between postmodernism and feminism outlined earlier in this chapter. Feminism cannot afford to do away with the subject. However, by moving subjectivity into the realm of writing and representation, *Byzantium* is able to retain it as a viable postmodern category.

In this chapter, my aim has been to demonstrate how adopting Hutcheon's conceptualization of postmodernism as a critical engagement with the history of representation might allow us to better understand *Byzantium* as a critically feminist work and to appreciate the film's strategies of intertextuality and self-reflexivity. Throughout, I have made reference to the 'trace-like' quality of

---

[12]Stacy Abbot explores the concept of the sensuous in relation to *Byzantium* more fully in *Undead Apocalypse.*

Byzantium's intertextuality. While I feel that Hutcheon's notion of complicitous critique is invaluable for beginning an interrogation of the ways in which *Byzantium* uses intertextuality, it doesn't quite capture the elusiveness of the film's intertextuality. This leaves us caught between a language of traces that isn't concrete enough, and a postmodern vocabulary that's insufficiently subtle. We might instead consider a vocabulary of inheritance which, neatly captures the sense of 'family resemblance' that I identify between Byzantium and these texts from the 1960s and 1970s. A daughter may resemble her mother, but there will also be differences. Traits are inherited across generations, but they are also transformed. Inheritance also encapsulates the theme of legacy – or rather the policing of legacy – that runs through *Byzantium*.

References

Abbott, S. (2017). *Undead apocalypse: Vampires and zombies in the 21st century.* Edinburgh: Edinburgh University Press.

Barthes, R. (1977). *Image music text* (trans. Stephen Heath). London: Fontana.

Barthes, R. (1994). *The pleasure of the text* (trans. Richard Miller). Oxford: Blackwell.

Constable, C. (2009). Postmodernism and film. In S. Connor (Ed.), *The Cambridge companion to postmodernism* (pp. 43–61). Cambridge: Cambridge University Press.

Constable, C. (2014). Postmodern cinema. In Branigan & Buckland (Eds.), *The Routledge encyclopaedia of film theory* (pp. 376–382). London: Routledge.

Constable, C. (2015). *Postmodernism and film: Rethinking hollywood's aesthetics.* New York, NY: Wallflower Press.

Craft, C. (1984). "Kiss me with those red lips": Gender and inversion in Bram Stoker's *Dracula. Representations, 8*(Autumn), 107–133.

Degli-Esposti, C. (1998). Postmodernism(s). In C. Degli-Eposti (Ed.), *Postmodernism in the cinema* (pp. 3–18). Oxford: Berghahn Books.

Derrida, J. (2010). *Positions* (trans. Alan Bass). London: Continuum.

Di Stefano, C. (1990). Dilemmas of difference: Feminism, modernity, and postmodernism. In L. J. Nicholson (Ed.), *Feminism/postmodernism* (pp. 63–82). London: Routledge.

Ellmann, M. (1968). *Thinking about women.* New York, NY: Harcourt.

Hutcheon, L. (1989). *The politics of postmodernism.* London: Routledge.

Jameson, F. (1983). Postmodernism and consumer society. In H. Foster (Ed.), *Postmodern culture* (pp. 111–125). London: Pluto.

Mulvey, L. (1989). *Visual and other pleasures.* Indianapolis, IN: Indiana University Press.

Neale, S. (1980). *Genre.* Wiltshire: BFI Publishing.

Rice, A. (2003). *The Vampire Lestat.* New York, NY: Richard Knopf.

Filmography

Byron (Julian Farino, 2003).

Byzantium (Neil Jordan, 2012).

The Cabin in the Woods (Drew Goddard, 2012).
Countess Dracula (Peter Sasdy, 1971).
Daughters of Darkness (Harry Kümel, 1971).
Dracula: Prince of Darkness (Terrence Fisher, 1966).
Lust for a Vampire (Jimmy Sangster, 1971).
Scream (Wes Craven, 1996).
Scream 2 (Wes Craven, 1997).
Scream 3 (Wes Craven, 2000).
Scream 4 (Wes Craven, 2010).
Twilight (Catherine Hardwicke, 2008).
Twins of Evil (Jon Hough, 1971).
The Vampire Lovers (Roy Ward Baker, 1970).

Chapter 9

'There's a Ghost in My House': The Female Gothic and the Supernatural in *What Lies Beneath* (2000)

Frances A. Kamm

The so-called Female Gothic — a much-explored category which refers to women writers working in this mode, or Gothic stories which focus on female protagonists — can be defined by its relationship to the supernatural. With a convention which can be traced back to the novels of Ann Radcliffe, the Female Gothic usually denies the possibility of the supernatural and this trend is maintained for the majority of the Hollywood 1940s Gothic films; the latter of which *What Lies Beneath* (2000) overtly evokes. And yet *What Lies Beneath* signals as much a deviation from these traditions as it is a continuation: the film confirms that there *is* a ghost in Claire's house, thereby inflecting the Female Gothic story with the supernatural. By incorporating ghosts into a mode of storytelling which has previously been defined by its rejection of such, *What Lies Beneath* becomes an intriguing case study in the history of the Female Gothic. There are two scenes in the film which succinctly demonstrate the significance of this change:

> 'I heard noises. I-I-I didn't want to disturb you [...]'
>
> 'What kind of noises? Where?'
>
> 'At the house. I was scared.'
>
> 'Did you call the police?'
>
> 'No.'
>
> 'I'm going to have the police check on the house while I'm gone.'
>
> 'Oh great. "Could you check in on my wife: she's hearing voices." Wait until that gets around.' (Claire and Norman, *What Lies Beneath*)

Gender and Contemporary Horror in Film, 133–149
© Frances A. Kamm
doi:10.1108/978-1-78769-897-020191010

> There's a ghost in my house. I saw her in the water beside me, in
> the bathtub. (Claire to therapist, *What Lies Beneath*)

These two conversations, which take place approximately 24 minutes and 41 minutes into *What Lies Beneath*, respectively, aptly illuminate the complex relationship between the film's heroine – Claire – and her experiences of the supernatural; experiences which are complicated further by contextualizing the film as the Female Gothic. In the first scene, a dishevelled Claire goes to her husband Norman's workplace to tell him about the strange occurrences taking place in their house. The conversation continues when they return home, and Norman's plan to have the authorities protect Claire inspires her self-deprecating comments which imply her fears are the result of her own imagination or possible insanity. The second statement is made later by Claire during her therapy session. Here, Claire's resolve is clear: the supernatural exists and a ghostly presence explains the phenomena she has witnessed thus far. She trusts what her senses tell her ('I saw her') and this revelation is no longer a damning indictment on Claire's perception of events; rather this realization functions to reaffirm Claire's confidence in her own judgements and relocates the fears she faces away from herself and onto another, external force.

The two scenes are representative of the two broadly defined approaches Gothic stories – in general – have traditionally taken in relation to the supernatural: either spectres are rationally attributed to an over-wrought imagination – the supernatural explained – or ghosts are real. Ultimately *What Lies Beneath* confirms the latter and it is this affirmation within an otherwise conventional Female Gothic text which challenges interpretation. What happens when the supernatural is combined with – and becomes an integral part of – a Female Gothic narrative? What impact does this have upon Claire as a Gothic heroine and representations of gender? This chapter will explore these questions and argue that, whilst the inclusion of the supernatural can be said to break with previous definitions of the Female Gothic, *What Lies Beneath*'s depiction of a ghost actually re-imagines and re-emphasizes the concerns at the centre of this tradition. The film uses the supernatural to explore Claire's relationship with the domestic space and the status of her marriage within it. The paranormal events thus function less as a commentary on life after death – as other supernatural tales might – and more as a ghostly reminder of the perils of real-life, living relationships. The fear and suspense evoked by Claire's experience with a ghost acts as a misdirection away from a more terrifying truth: the reality of male violence against women. *What Lies Beneath* therefore establishes a dialectic relationship between the supernatural and Female Gothic traditions, blurring the boundaries between external threats and a subjective paranoia; the validation of the heroine's experiences and a denial of her perception.

The Female Gothic was coined by Ellen Moers who defines the idea as 'the work that women writers have done in the literary mode that, since the eighteenth century, we have called the Gothic' (Moers, 1976, p. 90). Moers argues that Ann Radcliffe 'firmly set' the conventions of this genre which concerns 'a young woman who is simultaneously persecuted victim and courageous heroine' (p. 91). The term has since been extensively debated. For example, this literary tradition has been explored as 'gothic feminism' (Hoeveler, 1998); as a critique of 'patriarchal control' (Milbank, 1992); as centring on family structures (Williams, 1995); and as emphasizing the mother figure specifically (Kahane, 1985). This array of interpretative possibilities is testament to the fact 'There is not just one Gothic but Gothics' (Fleenor, 1983, p. 4). These 'Gothics' are summarized by Diane Wallace and Andrew Smith in their overview of the extensive scholarship on this topic (Wallace & Smith, 2009), and the continued currency of the Female Gothic as a term is highlighted again in the more recently published *Women and the Gothic* (Horner & Zlosnik, 2016). Although the Female Gothic can, therefore, be said to challenge classification, the genre has been distinguished from its opposite: the so-called Male Gothic. Bruce F. Kawin demonstrates this point albeit within a different context. Kawin writes there are two 'types' of ghost story: those that permit the existence of ghosts and those which 'use a bait-and-switch technique' (Kawin, 2012, p. 112). The latter Kawin associates with the 'Gothic novel' although this summation needs qualification: his first category is associated with the Male Gothic, whilst the latter is the Female Gothic where the 'presence of the supernatural is often suggested, but all mysterious events tend ultimately to be rationalized and explained' (Punter & Byron, 2004, p. 279). This 'bait-and-switch' is most commonly attributed to Radcliffe's work: '[no] one was more notorious for dashing the cold water of reason on ghostly thrills than Ann Radcliffe' (Tibbetts, 2002, p. 101). E. J. Clery describes the effect of this convention: Radcliffe 'milks the supernatural situations for all they're worth […] and then in the end tosses them away like worthless husks' (Clery, 2000, p. 67). This denial of the supernatural signals an emphatic (and, perhaps, clumsy) return to the world of logic and reason, exorcizing spectres to 'the provenance of imaginative and emotional excess' (Smith, 2007, p. 147).

The Gothic films released in Hollywood in the 1940s are direct descendants of the Radcliffean Female Gothic in their utilization of the 'supernatural explained' trope. These films include *Rebecca* (1940), *Gaslight* (1944), *The Spiral Staircase* (1946), *Secret Beyond the Door* (1948) and *Sleep, My Love* (1948). In a manner analogous to the literary Female Gothic, the 1940s Gothic films have similarly been subject to different categorizations and interpretations. Mary Ann Doane analyses the cycle as the 'paranoid woman's film' (Doane, 1987), whilst Thomas Elsaesser employs the phrase 'Freudian feminist melodrama' (Elsaesser, 1987, p. 59). Elsewhere Mark Jancovich analyses the films as contemporaneously perceived horror films (Jancovich, 2013), and Maria Tatar re-frames the cycle in light of the Bluebeard fairy tale (Tatar, 2004). Helen Hanson highlights the connection between the Gothic's literary heritage and the 1940s films explicitly by calling the latter the 'Female Gothic film' (Hanson, 2007). Whichever phrase is privileged, the films possess a similar plot structure and centralize the Gothic heroine, as Diane Waldman summarizes:

[A] young inexperienced woman meets a handsome older man to whom she is alternately attracted and repelled. After a whirlwind courtship [...] she marries him. After returning to the ancestral mansion of one of the pair, the heroine experiences a series of bizarre and uncanny incidents, open to ambiguous interpretation, revolving around the question of whether or not the Gothic male really loves her. She begins to suspect that he may be a murderer. (Waldman, 1984, pp. 29–30)

Like the Radcliffe novels before them, the 1940s Gothic films also deny the possibility of the supernatural. The 'bizarre and uncanny incidents' which do occur are usually explained and/or are connected to the heroine's love interest or husband. In *Gaslight* Paula is plagued by strange noises and dimming lights in her house and, when she attempts to alert her maid, the older woman assures her mistress that she just 'imagines things'. Similarly, Alison's interaction with a mysterious man she mistakes for a therapist is used as further evidence by her husband of her fractured mental state in *Sleep, My Love*. In both cases these experiences could be attributed to paranormal or unexplained phenomena – at least from the heroines' perspective – and yet the events are instead relegated by other characters to the imagination, thereby casting aspersions on the heroine's sanity; a judgement she begins to accept herself. This internalized threat may be alleviated at the film's conclusion – it is revealed the husbands of both Paula and Alison are responsible for their wives' 'madness' and are trying to murder their spouses – but such a resolution functions to emphasize how the proven danger is real, tangible and very much living.

This trend is sustained for the majority of the films within the cycle with remarkable consistency although, as with all rules, there are exceptions. Out of the 27 films Hanson lists as belonging the 'Female Gothic cycle of the 1940s' (Hanson, 2007, p. 225), four films do contain, or could be interpreted as alluding to, supernatural occurrences. However, it should be noted that even when a 1940s Gothic film does permit the existence of the paranormal, interactions with the spectre usually functions outside of the Gothic heroine's experiences or central concerns. For example, in *Dragonwyck* (1946), Miranda marries Nicholas, the owner of the titular manor. Amongst the many subplots, Miranda learns of Nicholas's deceased great-grandmother whose ghost plays her harpsichord whenever a tragic event occurs but the music can only be heard by those with the family blood. In this instance, the supernatural is not 'explained' (the film does not reveal, for example, the noises heard by Nicholas and his daughter to be the result of living person's trick) and yet this ghostly encounter does not involve Miranda or directly concern her relationship to Nicholas: the usual focus of the Female Gothic narrative. *The Uninvited* is a more complicated example. Brother and sister Rick and Pamela move into Windward House which, they discover, is haunted by a ghost named Mary, the (assumed) dead mother of a young woman named Stella. Stella becomes the archetypal Gothic heroine and, whilst she interacts with the supernatural entities (even going into a trance during a séance), the main investigation into the house's paranormal secrets do not involve her. The climactic confrontation with the malign Mary occurs *without* Stella's on-screen presence and, in fact, centres upon Rick's interaction with the haunted space. In this way, both *Dragonwyck* and *The Uninvited* introduce the supernatural into a Female Gothic story but do so in a way which separates or segments the presence of ghosts *away* from the experiences of the Gothic heroine.

Robert Zemeckis's *What Lies Beneath* evokes the intriguing question of what happens to a Female Gothic narrative when the supernatural is not only confirmed but − importantly − becomes an integral part of the heroine's investigation and the film's resolution. The film begins as Claire bids farewell to her daughter, Caitlin, as she leaves home to attend college. Claire is left at home with her husband (and Caitlin's stepfather) Norman who is a successful academic; Claire abandoned her career as a musician many years before. Soon Claire begins to experience strange occurrences in the house: a door that does not stay shut; the bathtub that fills itself with water; the written message on the mirror; her computer continuously typing 'MEF'. Claire believes the house is haunted and that the ghost belongs to her neighbour, Mary, who she had previously observed having marital problems. When this theory is disproven − Mary is alive and well − Claire's attention focuses on Madison Frank who is described as a missing person in a newspaper clipping Claire finds inside a broken picture frame. Madison is the spirit haunting Claire: the latter eventually remembers how Norman had an affair with one of his students, and it is revealed Madison was that former lover. Norman confesses to murdering the postgraduate when she threatened to reveal their relationship. Norman then attempts to murder Claire by paralysing her within a filling bathtub but Madison's spirit helps her escape. Eventually, Norman's pursuit of Claire ends with the couple plummeting into the lake within their truck. Madison's body is disturbed from its watery grave and her reanimated corpse seizes Norman so that he drowns too, liberating Claire from both a premature death and a murderous husband.

As this plot synopsis illustrates, *What Lies Beneath* incorporates the Female Gothic tradition of a woman imperilled within the home who doubts her own experiences before her investigation reveals the source of fear is located in her romantic relationship: in this case within an established marriage. Hanson argues the film is part of the 'neo-Gothic': films from the 1990s onwards which 'revive, revisit and rework elements of the female gothic film of the 1940s' (Hanson, 2007, p. 173). In particular, Hanson notes the affinity *What Lies Beneath* shares with Alfred Hitchcock's *Rebecca* (1940). In the story, the unnamed heroine marries Maxim de Winter and returns to live at his ancestral home Manderley. The new Mrs de Winter feels intimated by the memory of Maxim's late first wife − the eponymous Rebecca − believing her husband to still be in love with his former spouse. The new mistress of the manor eventually discovers the opposite to be true: Maxim hated Rebecca and hid her body after she accidentally died (in a change from the novel). Rebecca's body washes ashore, launching a police investigation although Maxim is absolved. The couple is free from Rebecca's shadow but Manderley is burned down by Rebecca's faithful maid Mrs Danvers. Claire in *What Lies Beneath* and the new Mrs de Winter are haunted – literally in the former, figuratively in the latter – by a past lover/wife of the male character who is also in some way involved in the woman's death. It is this secret he keeps from his current wife and Gothic heroine. The association between water and death – both Madison and Rebecca are hidden in watery graves from which their bodies return – underlines the connection between the films further (Hanson, p. 195).

What Lies Beneath may owe its 'greatest debt' (Hanson, p. 195) to *Rebecca* but these similarities neglect to mention the major difference: the twenty-first century film gives the dead woman an on-screen embodiment and confirms the existence of her ghost which was only hinted towards within the mise-en-scène of its predecessor 60 years prior. Where Hitchcock implies a 'presence from Rebecca's absence' (Tatar, 2004, p. 83), Zemeckis creates a spectacle of Madison's spectral hauntings and gruesome appearance. In one scene, Claire returns into the house after conducting an unsuccessful séance with her friend Jody. On screen right Claire walks away from the camera and up the staircase at the very back of the space; on the left the frame captures the reflection of the hallway mirror showing the computer in another room which mysteriously switches itself on: this signals the beginning of Madison's haunting. The camera cuts to a medium shot of Claire clearing away the items used for the séance, including the Ouija board. The tense string music, which has previously accompanied Claire's frightening experiences within the house, continues to build on the soundtrack. The camera moves and tracks Claire's movement through the space, mimicking her walking, crouching and stretching, without any edits: the viewer's experience of the house is kept closely aligned to Claire. This patterning is altered when Claire moves from the bedroom and the camera continues to track backwards, pausing to reveal the frame of the bathroom door on screen left – echoing the framing of the computer earlier – with pockets of steam rising into the air. The camera follows Claire as she enters the foggy bathroom, with the bathtub full of water again. As she pauses in fear, the camera circles Claire to capture her reflection in a bathroom mirror: a shadowy face moves across its surface. Claire approaches the bathtub and, as she leans over, the camera captures a woman's reflection on the surface of the water retreating on the right. This is revealed *not* to belong to Claire: as the mysterious figure disappears, Claire's reflection is depicted on the left. Exasperated and frightened, Claire calls out 'what do you want?' and the response appears on the mirror, written in the steam: 'you know'. As the music crescendos, the camera moves towards the haunting words, Claire's terrified reaction visible in the reflection permitted by the letters' streaks in the steam.

The new Mrs de Winter has a comparably scary experience in Manderley, which also depicts the vulnerability of the heroine within the private spaces of a house (the bedroom and bathroom). When the heroine prepares to enter Rebecca's room in the West Wing, a similar emphasis is placed on deep focus framing: the camera remains as a long shot as she hesitantly ascends the staircase, the framing again emphasizing the intricate design of the mise-en-scène. The heroine's movement again dictates the viewer's exploration of the space, as the camera tracks backwards in conjunction with the new Mrs de Winter's approach. *What Lies Beneath*'s moving one shot conveys a convoluted geography of the domestic space, and this uncertainty and suspense is created here albeit, conversely, through editing: the new Mrs de Winter is seen entering the room in a static long shot from screen right; as she approaches a translucent curtain, the camera cuts to a face-on medium shot from the other side of this veil. As the heroine moves forward, another edit frames her left side as she moves further into the room. The edits are jarring, framing the heroine from unexpected angles as the room reveals other unseen spaces. These transitions contrast to, and are held in tension with, the heroine's active exploration of the area suggesting – like the mobile framing in *What Lies Beneath* – that an unseen force is present. *Rebecca* even uses mirrors to emblematize the existence of the supernatural: full-length mirrors adorn Rebecca's wardrobe, and other mirrors are glimpsed in the bathroom, on the dressing room's wall, and on the dressing table. When Mrs Danvers enters the room and recounts Rebecca's daily routine, she manipulates the new Mrs de Winter into retracing these past footsteps and, when the heroine is glimpsed within these reflective surfaces, the implication is clear: the timid and awkward heroine is present in a space belonging to – and still dominated by – the confidence and beauty of (an absent) Rebecca. The scene climaxes with an emotionally distraught Mrs de Winter trapped by the housekeeper: framed together in a medium shot dominated by shadow, Mrs Danvers reflects on how she still hears Rebecca's 'quick light step' in the house, whilst the new Mrs de Winter cowers in fright against the door. As Mrs Danvers increases the intensity of her arresting dialogue on the afterlife – she posits that Rebecca has returned to watch Manderley's new couple – the camera moves into a close-up, emphasizing the heroine's distress and tears.

Despite the similarities in framing, music and mise-en-scène, the question Mrs Danvers taunts the new Mrs de Winter with – 'Do you think the dead come back and watch the living?' – is given very different responses in each film. In *What Lies Beneath,* the answer is an emphatic yes: Claire experiences paranormal events some of which – such as the computer and the woman's reflection in the water – occur without her knowledge, emphasizing further the confirmed status of these activities as supernatural. *Rebecca* does not draw the same conclusion as no actual spirit appears. Rebecca's memory is reincarnated through her possessions and Mrs Danvers's soliloquy, whereas Madison is literally reanimated and her physical manipulation of spaces – the water, steam and the computer – provide a visual index for her dead/undead existence. This has implications for what Diane Waldman calls the 'central feature' of Gothic stories, namely 'ambiguity, the hesitation between two possible interpretation of events' (Waldman, 1984, p. 31). In *Rebecca,* this ambiguity mainly centres on the new Mrs de Winter's belief that Maxim is still in love with Rebecca but the scene in the West Wing provides a sinister catalyst for this suspicion, with inflections of the supernatural. When Mrs Danvers insists that Rebecca has returned to haunt Manderley, the heroine sobs 'I don't believe it' and yet her emotional reaction betrays her. The new Mrs de Winter's susceptibility to such a notion becomes synonymous with, and a reinforcement of, her interpretation of

Maxim's feelings. Both are incorrect: despite the effective terror of the scene, Rebecca is not a ghost, and Maxim loathes his late wife. Yet the ambiguity of the film, and this scene specifically, is created by the narrative's 'paranoid mechanism of projection' (Doane, 1987, p. 127). Mary Ann Doane later explains:

> The camera movements in [scenes from *Rebecca* and *Caught*] can be described as hysterical − frantically searching for, retracing the path of, the lost object, attempting to articulate what is, precisely, not there. As such the camera movements have the status of symptoms. (p. 155)

The 'symptoms' here are of the new Mrs de Winter's emotional excessiveness, exposing a misguided obsession with her former counterpart. Maxim's love for Rebecca is as much 'not there' as the latter's ghost. Waldman notes that 'resolution' to the previously mentioned hesitation and ambiguity provides the 'validation or invalidation of feminine experience' (Waldman, 1984, p. 31). When the new Mrs de Winter later learns that Maxim hated Rebecca, 'the heroine's happiness is purchased at the price of the invalidation of her independent judgment' (p. 31). When one considers the West Wing scene and Mrs Danvers's evocation of the supernatural, the new Mrs de Winter is, in effect, invalidated twice: Rebecca does not haunt the house either figuratively in Maxim's affections or literally as a ghost. The unease experienced in the scene is rather the result the heroine's own personally felt inadequacies. The confirmation of the supernatural in *What Lies Beneath* has the opposite effect. The film's camera movements are, to borrow Doane's terminology, also searching for 'the lost object' and articulating what is 'not there' except, ironically, this investigative gaze does find visual confirmation of this presence. The exploration of space, and Claire, are not 'hysterical': Madison *is* a ghost and this spirit is responsible for the uncanny transformation of the domestic. Madison's appearance to viewers outside of Claire's perception only emphasizes the point, lending further sympathy to Claire when she attempts to share her experience with Norman only to be told she is 'overreacting'. *What Lies Beneath* and *Rebecca* may therefore tell similar stories, use comparable motifs and even echo each other in their depiction of the heroine imperilled within her home, but their respective treatment of the supernatural − as either explained or confirmed − is intimately related to the invalidation or validation of the heroine's perception. *What Lies Beneath*'s validation of Claire's feminine experience of the (significantly supernatural) events, problematizes the label of the 'paranoid woman's film' (Doane, 1987).

Waldman notes that '[within] a patriarchal culture' the resolution of the Gothic's ambiguity or hesitation − the heroine's eventual validation or invalidation within the plot − possesses an 'ideological function' (Waldman, 1984, p. 31). In a narrative like *Rebecca*, which Waldman identifies as symptomatic of Gothic films made earlier in the 1940s cycle, the heroine's invalidation operates to equate 'feminine subjectivity with some kind of false consciousness' (p. 33). In many ways, this is reflective of how the 'bait-and-switch' or explained supernatural in Radcliffe's work can be interpreted. Drawing on the work of Todorov, Margaret L. Carter calls this resolution of 'the fantastic-uncanny' a necessary ploy for Radcliffe in the Age of Enlightenment: 'The challenge facing Radcliffe's heroes and heroines is to find a way of eschewing materialism while also shunning the hazardous vice of superstition' (Carter, 1987, p. 25). Robert Miles concurs, noting that the explained supernatural trope provides a way for characters to 'return to the "daylight", rational world' but only after 'the mind was allowed to wander, to believe, and conjecture' (Miles, 1995, p. 132). The explained supernatural should then be seen less as a lack or criticism in Radcliffe's work (as Walter Scott famously argued[1]) particularly because, despite the story's rational conclusion, these ventures into the supernatural are still an integral part of the novel (Miles, 1995, p. 133). Terry Castle similarly argues for this significance, arguing that Radcliffe's paranormal episodes – and their resolution – point towards a larger eighteenth-century historical movement towards 'the supernaturalization of everyday life' (Castle, 1995, p. 123). Radcliffean ghosts are not so much dispelled as internalized, indicating a 'growing sense of the ghostliness of other people' (p. 125). This 'haunted consciousness' (p. 137) is extended by Rebecca Munford in her reading of the novel *Rebecca* (1938) as depicting a 'spectral femininity' where Rebecca's 'phantasmal status' is not just as an implied ghost but could also 'be read as a symptom of the narrator's self-spectralization' (Munford, 2016, p. 124).

This 'spectral femininity' is arguably emphasized by the film adaptation of du Maurier's text. In the film, the spectator is not just told of the heroine's feelings of inferiority but is *shown* the causes and effects of such an atmosphere, as demonstrated in the West Wing scene. Here, one could argue that the new Mrs de Winter is 'spectralised' by being forced to embody Rebecca's movements; the supernatural is not present in the literal sense evoked by Mrs Danvers but this still remains a relevant metaphor. Therefore the scene may well be a symptom of a 'false consciousness' (Waldman, 1984) but this is not an insignificant experience: indeed, like the Radcliffean predecessors, the scene still evokes a powerfully uncanny and haunting atmosphere which may aid in the evocation of 'wishes and fears' (Miles, 1995) relevant to the Gothic's depiction of gender relations, and the film's historical contexts specifically.[2] *What Lies Beneath* adds other layers of complexity to these readings. The film could be said to remove the possibility of reading the film as a 'haunted consciousness' or suggesting a 'spectral femininity' like *Rebecca* precisely because the haunted and spectral are not metaphoric but real. This marks a radical difference from the Female Gothic tradition – both Radcliffean and in 1940s Hollywood – but it also arguably distances *What Lies Beneath* from its main Gothic reference point in Hitchcock. As Robert Ebert muses in his review of the film:

---

[1] See Miles (1995).
[2] Waldman historically situates the Hollywood Gothic films within the 1940s and the wartime and post-war contexts.

Hitchcock would not, however, have done this film in his day or any other day, because Hitchcock would have insisted on rewrites to remove the supernatural and explain the action in terms of human psychology, however abnormal. (Ebert, 2000)

I argue that the film's interpretative possibilities extend beyond this simplistic evaluation. Just as the line between the explained and the evoked supernatural could be said to have been deliberately blurred in Radcliffe's work, so too does *What Lies Beneath* complicate its use of the supernatural which provides three other avenues for analysis. First Madison's ghostly presence does not completely remove the Gothic ambiguity of events, or the significance of the invalidation/validation of the heroine articulated by Waldman. When Claire confronts Norman after the events in the bathroom, she passionately exclaims: 'He killed her and I'm not crazy!' The intense scene above validates Claire – she is not 'crazy' – but she is not completely correct either; Claire accuses the wrong 'he' and is frightened by the ghost of the wrong 'her'. This invalidation is made painfully clear when Claire confronts her male neighbour Warren only for Mary to immediately appear alive and well. This public humiliation is underlined with Warren's question for Claire – 'are you alright?' – a concern echoed again by Claire's therapist in the following scene; the terror of Claire's experience with Madison in the bathroom, whilst not invalidated, is subverted back towards the realm of 'false consciousness'. Claire's incorrect assumptions for nearly half the film fulfil a function beyond being a MacGuffin-nod to Hitchcockian conventions; rather the ghost's identity is still a spectral mystery. In *The Mysteries of Uldopho* (1794), Emily is anxiously drawn to a veiled picture and a curtain hiding what she thinks is a body. The motif of the veil is utilized again in the West Wing scene from *Rebecca*: the thin veil partitions the entrance to Rebecca's room and it is behind this curtain that Mrs Danvers eerily appears as a silhouetted figure. In these cases, the veil becomes emblematic of the permeable barrier between the living and the dead, the animate and the inanimate, the present and the absent. Questions of identity and the truth are symbolically represented: the veil allows light to pass through yet also obscures vision. The steam in the bathroom scene of *What Lies Beneath* functions in a similar way. The fog signals Madison's arrival and provides her with an ethereal canvas upon which she can communicate with Claire. Claire perceives these messages but her judgment has been literally and figuratively clouded: the heroine cannot yet see clearly through the mist to view the truth. Madison's association with water is given added poignancy: much like the lake where Madison was discarded, water is transparent but it also conceals. Claire's invalidation at this point in the film only confirms how the Gothic's ambiguity still remains.

Mark Jancovich disagrees with Doane's and Waldman's assessment of the Gothic heroine's investigation in the 1940s film, highlighting how the protagonist's perception is 'rarely invalidated' (Jancovich, 2014, p. 249). For films such as *Gaslight* and *Sleep, My Love* this is true: the distressing episodes Paula and Alison experience may not be symptoms of their madness – as they are led to believe – but they *do* experience these events and they are correct to challenge them as they *are* in danger. Similarly, Claire *does* encounter supernatural activities and she is right to attribute this danger to a living source: a murderous husband; Claire just initially fails to identify the correct male threat. By aligning the spectator's experience so closely with Claire's, the film makes the viewer complicit in this mistake, particularly when one considers how evidence of the truth is present throughout the film. Near the beginning of *What Lies Beneath* Claire stands in the hallway and the audience can see through a window behind her a woman in a bathrobe run from a house. The sounds outside draw Claire's attention and, as she watches her neighbours argue, a reverse shot frames Claire's face in a medium close-up just as a hand reaches around her neck. Claire is shocked and then relieved as the camera re-positions to reveal Norman caressing her. Claire's perception is not so much invalidated as misdirected: she looks outside for evidence of marital dangers when she should be looking behind her, and Norman's introduction subtly alerts the viewer to this truth too. Norman is also constantly juxtaposed with Claire's terror and fear: she interacts with Norman just after Madison's appearance above and in an earlier scene when Madison first haunts the bathroom. When Claire is trying to retrieve her dog's ball from the lake, Claire stares enthralled at the water's surface and sees a barely visible face. Claire's meditation is abruptly disrupted with a jump scare – for protagonist and viewer – of Norman's phone call. This alignment of Norman with Claire's unsettling experiences within the house further validate Claire's fear as justified, even prophetic: like her experience of the supernatural, it is simply that Claire does not consciously understand or acknowledge the significance of her perception.

This predicament points to the second way the supernatural further complicates the border between validation and invalidation, and the complexities of the heroine's experiences. The film still evokes the notion of a feminine 'false consciousness' which is aligned with the appearance of a ghost but, crucially, Claire is not invalidated like a Radcliffean heroine or the new Mrs de Winter *because* of this. However, the supernatural is still framed within the subjective. *What Lies Beneath* is not just about the revelation that the ghost is Madison, or that Norman is responsible for her death, but it is also a 'hesitation' or ambiguity caused by the mysteries of Claire's mind: Claire *does* actually know an integral piece of the investigation's puzzle – Norman's affair – but she has repressed this memory. When Claire is seemingly possessed by Madison, she passionately begins to undress Norman on the study desk. She suddenly sees an image of herself drenched in rain reflected in the hallway mirror – the same mirror already associated with supernatural events in the earlier haunting scene. This ethereal encounter appears to be entirely subjective: Norman raises his head to follow her gaze and sees only the normal surroundings reflected. And yet the supernatural is not explained in this way, or simply invalidated: Claire looks back to Norman and, as she cryptically suggests 'his wife' is suspicious, her face morphs into Madison's and Norman throws her to floor in fright. This scene dramatizes Claire's remembrance of Norman's affair when, as she recovers from the possession, she immediately states: 'You know. I know. I was there.'

For the first time in the narrative, Claire's knowledge exceeds the viewer's as she reveals this part of the mystery. The supernatural, in this instance, does not cloud her perception but brings this clarity. By channelling Madison, Claire embodies not just an uncanny trope – the double – but she emblematizes the uncanny process: as Freud argues, the uncanny is that 'which leads back to what is known of old and long familiar' (Freud, 1919, p. 340); memories or traumas previously forgotten through repression. The return of this repressed knowledge causes a self-spectralization where Claire from the past becomes a ghost to herself. Claire's mind being allowed 'to wander' (Miles) reveals – in a twist on Castle's argument – a haunted *un*conscious. The supernatural of the film thus still functions to pathologize Claire in a manner akin to the Radcliffean Female Gothic tradition but, in doing so, *What Lies Beneath* intimately links ghosts to the uncanniness of Claire's memories. This complicates the implicit opposition between the supernatural and 'human psychology' Ebert characterizes in his review above. Claire's investigation into the house, Madison, and Norman equally becomes an investigation into herself, marking a paradoxical collapsing of borders between the existence of the supernatural as a validated, external threat, *and* as an uncanny, subjective and deeply personal experience.

Claire's transformation into both a double of herself and Madison's doppelgänger brings a new visual meaning to Munford's idea of 'spectral femininity'. The concept takes on additional significance when one considers the 'ideological function' (Waldman, 1984) of these events and this highlights the third way *What Lies Beneath* complexly engages with the supernatural and the Female Gothic form. Claire's repression of Norman's affair allegorically speaks to the invisibility of male transgressions, however hard Claire otherwise works to bring such injustices to light: her willingness to believe Mary was murdered by her husband signals her awareness of the dangers that can exist within relationships, particularly from the male figure. Indeed, even her suspicions around Mary are not completely invalidated: Mary later confesses to Claire that she feels overwhelmed in her marriage and had considered leaving her husband. The story's engagement with gender relations illuminates a larger question which looms over the Female Gothic tradition, namely whether these stories 'should be seen as radical or conservative' (Punter & Bryon, 2004, p. 280). As Fred Botting notes the genre 'straddles contradiction and challenge, persecution and pleasure' (Botting, 2008, p. 153). Waldman demonstrates the conflict: she argues that *Gaslight* and *Sleep, My Love* validate their heroines' fears and 'dramatize the attempts of a patriarchal order to achieve hegemony over feminine perception' but the films ultimately only '[come] close to voicing a critique' of these inequalities' (Waldman, 1984, pp. 34–35). Tatar contextualizes this crisis of interpretation within the challenges posed by Bluebeard as an origin text. The 1940s films, Tatar argues, 'stage a double movement between agency and victimization' in which marriage 'functions as a kind of trap' which, even after the mystery is solved, does not release its female victim:

When the secrets beyond the door to marriage are solved, there is real closure. The woman who has passed beyond the door is now permanently encased behind it, with nothing left to investigate, analyse, and interpret once she has figured out what is behind her husband's threatening behaviour. (Tatar, 2004, p. 107)

The supernatural in *What Lies Beneath* does not function to distract away from these feminist questions, nor does it exist at an adjunct from them: rather Madison's ghost operates to re-emphasize, in a radical way, how it is the relationship between living women and men which resides at the heart of the Female Gothic. This is highlighted by the film's depiction of female solidarity. In *What Lies Beneath,* women are shown to be frank and honest with each other about their lived experiences within the domestic sphere, as with Jody and Mary, and it is Madison — who is, after all, the victim of what can happen within relationships behind closed doors — who saves Claire from a similar fate. Madison's actions in the film's finale could also be for revenge although a debate over Madison's motivations ignores the film's subversive intervention in the Female Gothic mode: the fact that Madison appears at all. Madison and the supernatural exist to validate the danger of a male threat and violence within the home; a threat which is still an unacceptable reality.[3] Madison is the archetypal Bluebeardian victim which Claire, as the tyrant's wife, traumatically discovers (the secret chamber is replaced by the lake; blood is substituted by water as the motif of crime, investigation and trauma) except here, in the film's twist on tradition, Madison is afforded her own visual presence and agency through the supernatural.

This representation of a dead woman is part of another lineage in art and visual culture beyond the Female Gothic but just as controversial. Elisabeth Bronfen highlights this tradition in her analysis of the female corpse which she sees as a recurring trope in literature and art since the eighteenth century (Bronfen, 1992). Brian Norman highlights this convention in literature, arguing that in this medium dead women are able to 'speak for themselves' and thus raise pertinent socio-political questions (Norman, 2013, p. 2). Jane O'Sullivan moves the discussion into film where she identifies 'a recent spate of films in which the dead female body is a persistent presence' which requires a 're-articulation' of the body through investigation to solve the mystery and ultimately remove the corpse 'from view' (O'Sullivan, 1996, p. 237). A tension, then, can exist between the dead woman's visual presence or narrative voice as a symbol of agency and the disturbing sight of the corpse which needs to be narratively and physically laid to rest. Deborah Jermyn and Joanne Clarke Dilman offer

---

[3]The murder of Madison in *What Lies Beneath* is symptomatic of what Marilee Strong calls an 'eraser killing: a form of intimate partner or domestic homicide that is committed almost exclusively by men, done in a carefully planned manner, often through bloodless means' (Strong & Powelson, 2008, p. 9). Her book explores the long history of this kind of real-life killings.

contrasting ways of interpreting this contradiction. For Jermyn, the female corpse is a direct descendant of the Gothic tradition, including the 1940s films, except now the deceased woman who was formerly absent or implied through her possessions is given form by her returning (dead) body. She argues that 'the site/sight of the female victim's body can become a troubling and disruptive presence' creating a space for an important subtext 'beneath the surface of the dominant text' (Jermyn, 2004, pp. 156–157). For Clarke Dilman, this 'dead-but-not-gone-convention' undermines its own feminist claims, arguing that:

> [...] the visualisation and narrativization of a dead woman with agency in the 2000s is a way to accommodate a feminist logic while negating it at the same time and to assuage societal guilt over women's death through scenarios that convey their stories from beyond the grave. (Clarke Dilman, 2014, p. 11)

What Lies Beneath does not offer an easy reading in light of these debates. Madison is given a visual presence denied to an 'Other Woman' (Russ, 1973) like Rebecca and yet such agency is inevitably limited − or removed − by the fact she is dead. This is emphasized in the way Madison is not able to tell her own story: her life is to be inferred by the fragments Claire collects during the course of her investigation and, more sinisterly, how and why Madison died − from her own point of view − remains unknown: it is Norman who narratives the story of her life and death twice, changing his account from her suicide to murder. Madison seems to have as little control as a ghost as she had when she died. And yet the film does not shy away from the causes of her death: during his confession Norman defends his murderous acts − both of the past and those he is about to commit on Claire − by arguing, 'She gave me no choice − and neither have you.' Norman represents a misogynistic masculinity which derives strength from keeping women in roles defined by the patriarchy − the home-maker versus the lover − which inevitably depend upon his social and economic power for definition. Norman therefore sees his attack on Madison and Claire less as an unexpected reaction and more as a justified, logical action to maintain this *status quo*. The film exposes this thinking for the oppressive and sexist big-otry that it is, and the Female Gothic form provides a framework for this power-ful message: the film maintains viewer alignment with Claire narratively, stylistically *and* morally, and the addition of the supernatural reinforces the hor-ror and injustice of this male violence against women, making visible what may otherwise remain a 'secret beyond the door'.

What Lies Beneath represents a return to the Female Gothic and indicates how questions about female identity and gender equality, which infused Radcliffe's stories and the 1940s films, have 'come back to haunt the contempor-ary moment' (Hanson, 2007, p. 198). Indeed, the spirit of the Female Gothic genre continues to possess many recent reincarnations of the Gothic on-screen, within films such as *The Others* (2001), *The Orphanage* (2007), *Crimson Peak* (2015) and *Under the Shadow* (2016). As illuminated in this chapter, the main difference between these contemporary examples and their eighteenth- and twentieth-century forebears is the status of the supernatural. Hanson does not highlight this in her analysis on the neo-Gothic film and yet *What Lies Beneath* evidently signals a turning point for this tradition: ghosts exist, and they inspire, influence and imperil the Gothic heroines in these narratives. *What Lies Beneath* depicts a particularly complex combination of the Female Gothic with the supernatural. The film does signal a change in the Female Gothic tradition by seemingly placing less emphasis on female paranoia and complicating the invalidation/validation dynamic Waldman identifies in the 1940s films. Yet these differences work, paradoxically, to reinforce the Female Gothic's central concern: the relationship between women and men. *What Lies Beneath* introduces one new, radical element: the Bluebeardian victim or Other Women is now, through the supernatural, released from the bloody chamber or from beyond the veil to become an embodied presence on-screen. If Madison has the potential to emblematize the injustices of, and give a fictional voice to, the women murdered at the hands of men, then the film suggests this is a message which cannot and should not be silenced: in the very last scene of the film, Claire lays a single red rose on Madison's grave and, as the image fades to black, an outline of Madison's face eerily appears in the snow. This final supernatural flourish symbolizes how Madison refuses to be silenced or contained, her façade breaking through the borders of the narrative and the frame. She, like the Female Gothic genre, makes a promise to again return from the dead.

References

Botting, F. (2008). *Gothic romanced: Consumption, gender and technology in contemporary fictions*. New York, NY: Routledge.

Bronfen, E. (1992). *Over her dead body: Death femininity and the aesthetic*. Manchester: Manchester University Press.

Carter, M. L. (1987). *Specter or delusion? The supernatural in Gothic fiction*. London: UMI Research Press.

Castle, T. (1995). *The female thermometer: 18th century culture and the invention of the uncanny*. Oxford: Oxford University Press.

Clarke Dillman, J. (2014). *Women and death in film, television, and news*. New York, NY: Palgrave Macmillian.

Clery, E. J. (2000). *Women's Gothic: From Clara Reeve to Mary Shelley*. Tavistock: Northcote House Publishers Ltd.

Doane, M. A. (1987). *The desire to desire: The woman's film of the 1940s*. London: Palgrave Macmillan.

Ebert, R. (2000). *What lies beneath*. Retrieved from https://www.rogerebert.com/reviews/what-lies-beneath-2000. Accessed on December 2017.

Elsaesser, T. (1987). Tales of sound and fury: Observations on the family melodrama. In C. Gledhill (Ed.), *Home is where the heart is: Studies in melodrama and the woman's film* (pp. 43–69). London: BFI Publishing.

Fleenor, J. E. (Ed.) (1983). *The female Gothic*. Montreal: Eden Press.

Freud, S. [1919] (2003). 'The uncanny.' Reprinted in: *The uncanny*. London: Penguin Books.

Hanson, H. (2007). *Hollywood heroines: Women in film Noir and the female Gothic film*. London: I.B.Tauris.

Hoeveler, D. (1998). *Gothic feminism: The professionalization of gender from Charlotte Smith to the Brontes*. Philadelphia, PA: Pennsylvania State University Press.

Horner, A., & Zlosnik, S. (2016). *Women and the Gothic: An Edinburgh companion*. Edinburgh: Edinburgh University Press.

Jancovich, M. (2013). Bluebeard's wives: Horror, quality and the paranoid woman's film in the 1940s. *The Irish Journal of Gothic and Horror Studies, 12*(Summer), 20−43.

Jancovich, M. (2014). Horror in the 1940s. In H. M. Benshoff (Ed.), *A companion to the horror film* (pp. 237−254). West Sussex: John Wiley & Sons Inc.

Jermyn, D. (2004). You can't keep a dead woman down: The Female corpse and textual disruption in contemporary hollywood. In E. Klaver (Ed.), *Images of the corpse: From the renaissance to cyberspace* (pp. 153−168). Madison, WI: University of Wisconsin Press.

Kahane, C. (1985). The Gothic mirror. In S. N. Garner, C. Kahane, & M. Sprengnether (Eds.), *The (M)other tongue: Essays in feminist psychoanalytical interpretation* (pp. 334−351). Ithaca, NY: Cornell University Press.

Kawin, B. F. (2012). *Horror and the horror film*. London: Anthem Press.

Milbank, A. (1992). *Daughters of the house: Modes of the Gothic in Victorian fiction*. London: Palgrave Macmillan.

Miles, R. (1995). *The great enchantress*. Manchester: Manchester University Press.

Moers, E. (1976). *Literary women: The great writers*. New York, NY: Oxford University Press.

Munford, R. (2016). Spectral femininity. In A. Horner & S. Zlosnik (Eds.), *Women and the Gothic: An Edinburgh companion* (pp. 120−134). Edinburgh: Edinburgh University Press.

Norman, B. (2013). *Dead women talking: Figures of injustice in American literature*. Baltimore, MD: John Hopkins University Press.

O'Sullivan, J. (1996). Gals on the slab: Fetishism, re-animation and the female dead body. *Social Semiotics, 6*(2), 231−244.

Punter, D., & Byron, G. (2004). *The Gothic*. Hoboken, NJ: Wiley Blackwell.

Russ, J. [1973] (1995). 'Somebody's trying to kill me and I think it's my husband': The Modern Gothic. Reprinted in *To Write Like A Woman: Essays in Feminism and Science Fiction* (pp. 94−119). Bloomington, IA: Indiana University Press.

Smith, A. (2007). Hauntings. In C. Spooner & E. McEvoy (Eds.), *The Routledge companion to Gothic* (pp. 147−154). London: Routledge.

Strong, M., & Powelson, M. (2008). *Erased: Missing women, murdered wives*. San Francisco, CA: Wiley Imprint.

Tatar, M. (2004). *Secrets beyond the door: The story of bluebeard and his wives*. Princeton, NJ: Princeton University Press.

Tibbetts, J. C. (2002). The old dark house: The architecture of ambiguity in the turn of the screw and the innocents. In S. Chibnall & J. Petley (Eds.), *British horror cinema* (pp. 99−116). London: Routledge.

Waldman, D. (1984). 'At last I can tell it to someone!': Feminine point of view and subjectivity in the Gothic romance film of the 1940s. *Cinema Journal, 23*(2) (Winter), 29−40.

Wallace, D., & Smith, A. (2009). *The female Gothic: New directions*. London: Palgrave Macmillan.

Williams, A. (1995). *Art of darkness: A poetics of Gothic*. Chicago, IL: University of Chicago Press.

Filmography

Crimson Peak. (Dir. Guillermo del Toro, 2015, USA).

Dragonwyck. (Dir. Joseph L. Mankiewicz, 1946, USA).

Gaslight. (Dir. George Cukor, 1944, USA).

Rebecca. (Dir. Alfred Hitchcock, 1940, USA).

Secret Beyond the Door. (Dir. Fritz Lang, 1948, USA).

Sleep, My Love. (Dir. Douglas Sirk, 1948, USA).

The Orphanage. (Dir. J. A. Bayona, 2007, Spain).

The Others. (Dir. Alejandro Amenábar, 2001, France, Italy, Spain, USA).

The Spiral Staircase. (Dir. Robert Siodmak, 1946, USA).

The Uninvited. (Dir. Lewis Allen, 1944, USA).

Under the Shadow. (Dir. Babak Anvari, 2016, Jordan, Qatar, UK).

What Lies Beneath. (Dir. Robert Zemeckis, 2000, USA).

Chapter 10

The Monstrous-feminine and Masculinity as Abjection in Turkish Horror Cinema: An Analysis of *Haunted* (*Musallat*, Alper Mestçi, 2007)

Zeynep Koçer

Cinema has a century-long history in Turkey. Directors from many generations have produced examples of different cinematic styles, movements, and genres from socio-realism and melodramas to historical epics and the fantastic (Dönmez-Colin, 2008; Suner, 2006). The period between the 1950s and the 1980s is called the 'Yeşilçam era' (Kırel, 2005; Maktav, 2001). The 1960s were the golden years of Yeşilçam as film became major mass entertainment with almost 300 films produced annually. Yeşilçam experimented with historical epics, science fiction and horror, but the most popular and profitable genres were comedy and melodrama (Güçhan, 1992; Kılıçbay & Onaran İncirlioğlu, 2003). With a total of four horror films during this time period, horror was perhaps the most neglected of the genres. With this in mind, I will first explore the reasons horror has been neglected in Turkish cinema.

The presence of monsters in film represents certain anxieties, and their death or transformation provides much-needed closure. The 'monstrous body' in this sense is 'an embodiment of a certain cultural moment' (Cohen, 1996, p. 4) and should be read within its socio-economic and political contexts. Therefore, I will move on to highlighting the socio-economic, cultural and political contexts that were catalysts for the horror genre's emergence at the beginning of the 2000s.

Finally, I will discuss gender representations in the film *Haunted* (2007). For over eight decades, cinema in Turkey has been discussing male and female anxieties that were closely related to rapid urbanization, industrialization, the emergence of a bourgeois and working class culture with melodramas and comedies. These numerous films have become the locus of dense scholarly work (Akbulut, 2008; Arslan, 2005; Erdoğan, 2011; Güçhan, 1992; İri, 2016; Oktan, 2008; Sancar, 2013; Suner, 2006; Ulusay, 2004; Yılmazkol, 2011) on gender representations that

Gender and Contemporary Horror in Film, 151–165
© Zeynep Koçer
All rights of reproduction in any form reserved
doi:10.1108/978-1-78769-897-020191011

discuss the ways in which these films communicate female and male anxieties of humiliation, alienation, exploitation and oppression. In addition the films of the 1980s have been labelled as the 'women's films' due to the influence of the debates on feminism in Turkish culture and politics in the 1980s. Issues such as female labour, abortion, homosexuality, prostitution that have been widely discussed in cinema have also been the topic of scholarly work. Therefore, gender has been a fruitful area of scholarly work in films studies in Turkey. Yet, because horror is a newly flourishing genre, not much academic work on horror cinema in general and gender in horror in particular have been produced. My aim is to explore masculinity as abjection in Turkish horror cinema, as well as the ways in which femininity becomes monstrous.

My theoretical framework is based on Julia Kristeva's notion of the abject and Barbara Creed and Carol J. Clover's canonical critical analyses of gender in American horror cinema.

10.1. From 'Isolated Cases' to the Emergence of Horror as Genre in Turkey

Technical inadequacies in terms of special effects, make-up, sound and production design are widely given as an explanation for the limited number of Turkish horror productions (Scognamillo & Demirhan, 2005). It is a fact that such expertise is vital, particularly for a genre that derives its power from these technical assets as much as, if not more than, from its narrative. The audiovisual components of filmmaking were certainly not among Yeşilçam's strongest assets, even in its golden years, and producers were more interested in investing in the risk-free genres of melodrama and comedy and obtaining well-written scripts than in planning the visual language of their films. Özkaracalar (2012) suggests that this particular lack 'might have acted as a deterrent to indulging in a genre where they [directors] felt such elements were necessary and they would not take risks' (p. 250).

Özgüç (2005) highlights another aspect of Yeşilçam that prevented the production of horror films, arguing, 'Our famous stars do not want to play these types [killers, cutthroats, perverts, and monsters] because they are against the conditions of our cinema. For this reason, in Turkish cinema [these characters] often take their places as side characters' (p. 353). What Özgüç means when he talks about 'the conditions' are the star system and audience expectations in Turkey. In Yeşilçam, producers stereotyped stars, and the audience embraced them according to those stereotypes (e.g. the poor but dignified Anatolian peasant or the good-hearted upper-class bourgeois). The audience even embraced antagonists such as vicious feudal lords or mean upper-class urbanites as long as they fit neatly within their stereotypes. What is more, the criminals of Yeşilçam according to Özgüç were perceived as 'innocent since the crimes they committed were derived from the prejudices and injustices they faced' (2005, p. 353). Oran (2001) points to another possible reason when he suggests, 'Turkish audiences like to identify with the characters on the screen and [...] horror movies do not offer grounds for such a strong level of identification' (as cited in Özkaracalar, 2012, pp. 249). This argument, however, falls short because 'foreign horror films had always existed in the Turkish market' (Özkaracalar, 2012, p. 249–250), and they 'constituted an important part of the video, VCD, and DVD market' (Danacı, 2015, para. 8).

Another argument to explain the lack of horror cinema is the dearth of horror literature in Turkey. It is a fact that the Turkish literary tradition then relied on social realism rather than the use of the horror or science fiction genres to discuss the anxieties of their times. In other words, until the 1970s, there were no figures like Edgar Allan Poe, Mary Shelley, or H.P. Lovecraft in Turkey who imagined monsters mirroring certain socio-economic, political, historical, or sexual anxieties. Ali Riza Seyfi's novel *Kazıklı Voyvoda* (*The Voivode with the Stakes*, 1928), an adaptation of *Dracula* (Bram Stoker, 1897) and *The Frankenstein Book Series*,[1] which was published in the 1940s, are among the few examples. In addition to technical inadequacies and producer and audience expectations, the horror genre may not have existed because of 'the absence of certain motifs frequently utilized in conventional Western horror movies in the Turkish cultural setting, such as vampires, werewolves, gothic castles, or serial killers' (Özkaracalar, 2012, p. 250). Özkaracalar (2012) finds this argument essentialist and maintains that 'the folk belief in vampires originated in Orthodox lands and was originally pretty much alien to, for instance, Western and Protestant populations—until being appropriated by popular cultures there' (p. 250). Moreover, although cowboys were also absent from Turkish history, 'enterprising Turkish filmmakers clearly did not care at all and, in the wake of the "spaghetti western" boom abroad, turned out dozens of homemade westerns set in the American Wild West' (Özkaracalar, 2003, p. 205).

There are only four[2] horror films that were produced in the Yeşilçam film industry. *Çığlık* (*Scream*, dir. Aydın Köseoğlu, Duru, & Arakon, 1949) is the first Turkish horror film however because no copy of this film exists today, little is known about it other than its plot and its poster. According to Scognamillo and Demirhan (2005), 'the film is set in a single location and fails to provide a sense of fear or anxiety' (p. 63). Due to the fact that *Scream* is not available to watch, many sources consider *Dracula in Istanbul* (*Drakula İstanbul'da*, dir. Mehmet Muhtar, 1953) as the first Turkish horror film instead. This film is an adaptation of the novel entitled *The Voivode with the Stakes* (*Kazıklı Voyvoda*, 1928). The object of horror, the Voivode with the Stakes, aka Vlad the Impaler, was not a stranger to the Turkish audience due to the history of the Ottoman

---

[1]According to Ilgın (2015), it is unclear if they were original stories inspired by Shelley or translations from other texts (para. 4).
[2]There is a fifth film called *Dark Waters* (*Karanlık Sular*, Kutluğ Ataman, 1994). However, the film was made after the Yeşilçam film industry (mid-1950s–late 1980s) collapsed. Because I have been discussing the Yeşilçam era, the list of horror films does not include *Dark Waters*.

Empire.[3] The film is also famous for presenting the character of the Count with fangs for the first time on the big screen (Özkaracalar, 2012, p. 251). Common Christian iconography utilized in Western vampire films, such as the use of holy water or crosses, are missing in the Turkish version: 'it is only garlic that repels the vampires' (Özkaracalar, 2003, p. 208). The film does not replace common Christian iconography with Islamic imagery; indeed, it is quite secular in its approach to religion. According to Özkaracalar (2012), the reason for the omission of Islamic imagery can be understood 'in the light of the fact that *Dracula* was translated into Turkish at a time when Turkey was undergoing a full-swing secularisation drive at the hands of the new Republican regime' (p. 251).

Almost two decades after *Dracula in Istanbul* came the next horror movie. *The Dead Don't Talk* (*Ölüler Konuşmaz Ki*, dir. Yavuz Yalınkılıç, 1970) tells the story of a couple haunted by an undead creature much like a zombie at a strange mansion. The difference between *The Dead Don't Talk* and *Dracula in Istanbul* is the use of Islamic imagery. The character of the *hoca*, an Islamic religious figure and the male saviour of the newly emerging genre, is first utilized here. He is the elderly wise man who recites from the Qur'an, makes charms, defeats evil, and saves the victims.

The final film is *Satan* (*Şeytan*, Metin Erksan, 1974). Very much like *The Exorcist* (dir. Friedkin, 1973), *Satan* is about a possessed girl who lives in a broken home and suffers for her mother's sins. As in *The Dead Don't Talk*, *Satan* deploys the character of the *hoca* and replaces Christian imagery and motifs with Islamic imagery, such as reciting the Qur'an instead of the Bible and using rose water instead of holy water. What is more, in the final scene of the film, Gül (Canan Perver) visits the *hoca* who saved her and kisses his hand in gratitude. The use of Islamic imagery does not necessarily mean that these alterations will enable Turkish audience to embrace horror as a genre. Rather, the decision is ideological. It is about 'the reconfirmation of Islam's power and validity' (Özkaracalar, 2003, p. 214) and falls 'within the conflict between modernization and tradition in general and materialism and religion in particular' (Özkaracalar, 2012, p. 252).

These four films, scattered as they are over four decades, failed to establish a certain set of codes and conventions. As Özkaracalar (2012) puts it, they are 'isolated cases' (p. 250) and imitations and/or adaptations of Euro-American horror films. However, the horror genre that emerged with the beginning of the new millennium can definitively be categorized as a genre that 'created its own rules by 2014 and made great strides towards becoming an industry on its own' (Danacı, 2015, para. 1).

---

[3]Vlad Tepes, a real historical figüre provided one of the inspirations for Stoker. Tepes was a Walachian ruler (voivode) nicknamed Dracula, which means 'Son of Dragon' or ('Son of Satan', according to an alternative translation), who was notorious for impaling his enemies – including the Turks. 'The Voivode with the Stakes' was an integral part of Turkish history as taught in every high school level Introduction to History course in Turkey (Özkaracalar, 2003, p. 207).

10.2. The Emergence of Horror Cinema in the 2000s

Horror film production in Turkey started at the beginning of the 2000s. Among the socio-economic and cultural reasons for this surge was the boost in horror literature that started in the 1970s (Dural, 2016, para. 15), the influence of major figures such as Giovanni Scognamillo and Galip Tekin in the 1980s and 1990s, and 'the rapid increase in fandom practices,[4] the academic interest, and the addition of horror into the university curriculums' (Özkaracalar, 2012, p. 254). In addition, the move from film to digital, the use of computer technology and the return of audiences to local productions[5] in the 2000s made it less risky in terms of investment than in an age of expensive film and producers reluctant to experiment with genre. However, there was still a need for what Özkaracalar (2012) calls 'a chance event', a horror film produced with a limited budget that to everyone's surprise makes it so big in the box office that the producers are encouraged to make another one. That chance event came in 2004 with the release of *Dark Spells* (*Büyü*, dir. Orhan Oğuz), a film about a team of archaeologists who go to a cursed village for an excavation.[6] In addition to the many small unfortunate events that took place during the shooting of the film, a large fire broke out in the theatre where the film's premiere was being held. This particular incident encouraged rumors that the film was cursed, which brought the film significant commercial attention.

The release of *Dark Spells* and the four[7] other horror films that followed in 2006 marks the real beginning of the Turkish horror genre, now dominated by narratives of possession that rely on Islamic cosmology and the character of the jinn as their choice of monster.[8] Jinn are believed to be God's creation in the

---

[4]Fandom practices play an important part in the fascination of particular genres such as sci-fi, fantasy and horror and internet is among the most signicant tools that help disseminate fandom practices towards horror films through blogs, fanzines, magazines and games.

[5]Local films have been attracting larger audiences than foreign films in the domestic market since 2005.

[6]*Okul* (*The School*, Yağmur & Durul Çetin, Taylan, & Taylan, 2004) was released before *Dark Spells*. However, it is a hybrid genre that juxtaposes comedy and horror. In some cases it is even categorized under the 'youth' and 'comedy' genres (see https://boxofficeturkiye.com/film/okul-2004006) with no mention of horror. This is why I chose to start the discussion on Turkish horror cinema with *Dark Spells*.

[7]*Gen* (*Gen*, Togan Gökbakar, 2006), *Araf* (*The Abortion*, Biray Dalkıran, 2006), *Küçük Kıyamet* (*The Little Apocalypse*, Durul & Yağmur Taylan, 2006), and *Dabbe* (*Dabbe*, Hasan Karacadağ, 2006).

[8]Among the total 89 films, 59 of them directly place jinn as the antagonists of the film. In addition to those 59 films, 12 more were produced that used another sort of demon as the protagonist. Ghosts, the fear of the impending apocalypse, as well as hauntings with no direct reference to jinn or demons constitute only 14 films, leaving us with four films that cannot be categorized under the main theme of pre-Islamic and/or Islamic horror. I would like to highlight again that this total does not include films that mix comedy with horror.

framework of Islam (Gingrich, 1995; Padwick, 1924). According to the Qur'an, human beings are made of earth (Gingrich, 1995) or clay (Peterson, 2007), and jinn are made of the fire of hot wind or smokeless fire. They are mortal like human beings, and they eat and procreate (El-Aswad, 2002). They also have free will (Peterson, 2007) and have a spirit like human beings; as a result, like humans, they will either go to Heaven or Hell. There are different kinds of jinn with different names, intentions and powers. Jinn who possess great power are called *ifrit* or *marid* (Peterson, 2007, p. 95). Consequently, the choice of names for the films are mostly derived from names of particular jinn such as *Dabbe, Marid, Azazil, Ammar, Deccal, Mihrez* and *Sinsiran* or from other Qur'anic references, such as *Semum, Siccin, Ceberrut, Bezm-i Ezel* and *Şeytan-ı Racim.* Due to this influence of Islam, the genre is often referred to as 'Islamic horror'. However, myths and folktales about malevolent spirits possessing human beings or causing illness and miscarriage or about disfigured creatures stealing newly born children were passed down from generation to generation in Anatolia long before Islam reached the land. Therefore, even though this new genre is commonly referred to as Islamic horror, it is rather a synthesis of Islamic cosmology and pre-Islamic oral culture.

The political climate of the 1990s also witnessed the rise of political Islam in Turkish politics and culture when the pro-Islamist Welfare Party (RP) won the local elections in 1994 and the national elections a year later. In 1997, the Turkish Constitutional Court closed down RP due to activities in violation of the Turkish constitution's secularism article. Its successor, the Virtue Party, was also disbanded for the same reasons in 2001. The Justice and Development Party was founded in August 2001 in an attempt to reclaim the territory of the centre right in Turkish politics. In the 2002 elections, it came out as the winning party and has been ruling Turkey ever since. It can be argued that since the late 1990s, Turkey has been witnessing a 'rapid development of the conservative/ Islamist media' (Kaya & Çakmur, 2010, p. 529). Özkaracalar (2016, para 4) suggests that the genre has now produced enough films to 'examine how and where Islamic horror films are integrated with current Islamist hegemony building processes'. However, the preference for using jinn and Islamic texts does not necessarily mean that all of these films are produced according to a certain Islamist political agenda due to the fact that 'western horror motifs neither fit the folkloric horror tales nor the religious beliefs of people in Turkey' (Özkaracalar, 2016, para. 5). After all, horror films are made up of our 'collective nightmares' (Wood, 2004), and both Islamic and pre-Islamic cultures have produced enough monsters to scare all of us.

Today, the horror genre is flooded with stories of malevolent jinn that terrorize their victims. The first possession story comes with the film *Dark Spells*, however, it is *Haunted* (*Musallat*, Alper Mestçi, 2007), which presented the audience the main antagonist, the jinn, as a transgressive, volatile figure of abjection, to use Julia Kristeva's term, for the first time in Turkish cinema. Moreover, *Haunted* holds a unique place among its contemporaries because it challenges the codes and conventions of the horror genre in terms of gender representations. It not only narrates a story of male possession instead of relying on the well-established trope of female possession and victimization, it also does not fetishize or punish the female gaze, which is another common element in mainstream cinema in general, and horror cinema in particular. In my analysis of *Haunted*, I will use the theoretical framework of Barbara Creed, Carol J. Clover and Julia Kristeva to discuss the monstrous-feminine and masculinity as abjection.

10.2.1. *Haunted*

Haunted tells the story of a young couple, Suat (Burak Özçivit) and Nurcan (Biğkem Karavus) whose lives are terrorized by evil jinn. Leaving Nurcan behind in a small village in Anatolia, Suat migrates to Germany as a *Gastarbeiter* to make money so he can marry his beloved, a girl with what the village folk call a 'condition'. The film is divided into two parts that take place over a period of nine months. The first part is set in Berlin and Istanbul, where we see Suat suffering from homesickness and loneliness as he fails to adapt to his new life. Within the course of six months, Suat is haunted by dark visions involving his mother, married life to Nurcan, and her pregnancy. The last three months shows how Suat's mental and physical health deteriorate and Western medicine fails to provide a diagnosis. That is when his childhood friend Metin (İbrahim Can) takes Suat to Istanbul to seek the help of Hacı Burhan Kasavi (Kurtuluş Şakirağaoğlu), a very famous religious figure who tells Metin that powerful jinn possessed Suat. On the ninth month, jinn kill Suat, Metin and Burhan's entire family, leaving only Burhan's granddaughter behind. This is where the first part of the film ends and the second part begins. The second part follows the same nine-month period and portrays Suat's life in the village with his mother and Nurcan, his wedding, her pregnancy and the birth of their offspring. At the end of the film, these two parts come together. It is revealed that jinn that had been in love with Nurcan since she was a child, took the shape of Suat, married Nurcan and impregnated her while Suat was in Germany. It is also revealed that Nurcan's 'condition' was a result of being raped by jinn since she was a child.

10.3. The Monstrous-feminine and Its Abject Womb in *Haunted*

When we explore the representations of femininity throughout the history of horror cinema, we see that women have been chased, hacked to pieces and killed by all sorts of human and non-human monsters. This gender-specific trope of victimization has been canonically theorized about in academic work by scholars such as Linda Williams (1996), Carol J. Clover (1987), Barbara Creed (1993) and Robin Wood (2004), to name a few. The case in horror films in Turkey in general, and *Haunted* in particular, is not much different.

Islam strictly forbids human beings from interacting with spirits of the unseen world. It teaches that this sort of interaction may provoke jinn and cause dangerous results. In Turkish horror films, this disturbance always comes from a woman, who through unholy rituals summons jinn to ask for favours related to lust, greed and wrath (such as seeking help to kill the wife, lover, or mother of the man she loves). Accordingly, at the end, the women who summon jinn are punished. It can be argued that by immediately establishing these female characters as 'sinners', these films not only lay the groundwork for the punishment of women but also present femininity as monstrous – as much so as the monsters that answer the women's calls. However, the real monstrous-feminine in these films is by tradition the possessed woman, who is placed on the side of the abject with her filthy appearance, unnatural voice, impure soul and – to make matters worse – her abject womb, bearing the monster's offspring.

Haunted breaks this particular convention in the sense that there is no female perpetrator, and the main female protagonist, Nurcan, is not possessed. She shows no signs of possession; her mind and body are intact with no scars or wounds. Moreover, the storyline and the film neither fetishize Nurcan nor punish her gaze. Yet the film still manages to create a monstrous-feminine out of her and, accordingly, treats femininity according to the sexist values of patriarchal ideology by having jinn torment Suat by taking on her appearance. When jinn possess Suat's mind, they become omnipotent in his subconscious and are able to show him whatever they want. When the jinn appear to Suat in Nurcan's image, she is depicted as pale and red-eyed with an abnormally huge pregnant belly, and she speaks in a devilish male voice in a different language – presumably Arabic. She directs her monstrous gaze towards Suat, terrifying and castrating him to the point that he cannot have sex with the prostitute, his close friend Metin brings to his house 'to cheer him up'. In these visions, her doubling is uncanny rather than abject because she 'arouses dread and horror' (Freud, 1919, p. 1) and 'in reality [is] nothing new or foreign, but something familiar and old' (Freud, 1919, p. 13).

After years of being a victim of rape, Nurcan is finally impregnated by jinn. This non-consensual act not only victimizes her but also sets the grounds for her punishment, as she becomes monstrous for bearing the offspring of her inhuman rapist. As Creed (1993, pp. 53, 56) suggests, 'the women who give birth to aliens or possess mutated wombs are not all active monsters like the witch or the vampire', but 'they are all defined as monstrous in relation to their wombs, their reproductive capacity'. They are also associated with the abject as a 'construct of patriarchal ideology' (Creed, 1993, p. 7). Hence, when Nurcan becomes monstrous, her womb is placed on the side of the abject. Together they signify the loss of boundaries and threaten the 'identity, system, order' (Kristeva, 1982, p. 4). Together, they represent the defilement and transgression of patriarchal laws in general and exogamy in particular.

In *Haunted*, the birthing scene holds particular importance. The two parts of the film span a nine-month period and are divided into four subparts with the help of the intertitles: 'one month', 'three months', 'six months' and 'nine months'. In other words, these three-month periods are Nurcan's three trimesters, and the film therefore becomes the story of Nurcan's pregnancy and the birth of the offspring. The scene in which Nurcan gives birth takes place in a small room inside the house. The white sheets of the bed are already covered in blood. Nurcan is depicted as being in agony, with midwives milling around her. The jinn disguised as Suat waits outside the house with the other men, representing the gendered nature of the separation of public and private spheres. After several minutes of torment, their offspring is born with pitch-black eyes, its body covered in blood and filth, its feet and hands twisted and inverted.

Longmore (1985, p. 33) points to the association with images of disability malevolently depicted in popular entertainment and literature. According to Longmore (1985), 'these physical disabilities typically involve disfigurement of the face and head and gross deformity of the body'. He also argues that 'the criminal and "monster" characterizations show that disability deprives its victims of an essential part of their humanity, separates them from the community, and ultimately requires that they be put to death' (p. 34). As support for Longmore's argument is the scene when the midwives see the deformed, grotesque appearance of the − abject − offspring, their reaction is disgust, fear and horror.

Barbara Creed (1993) suggests that the confrontation with the abject in horror films occurs 'in order to eject the abject and redraw the boundaries between the human and the non-human' (p. 14). Consequently, the midwives start screaming, 'It is not human', labelling it as 'monster', 'devil's seed' and 'filth' and killing it with the scissors they used to cut the umbilical cord. In other words, they first define and then destroy the thing that would disturb their self-definition, their 'other', the thing that 'does not respect boundaries, positions, rules, the in-between, the ambiguous, the composite' (Kristeva, 1982, p. 4). How ironic that it is women who are often represented in similar ways uses a phallic object to destroy the very thing that disrupts the patriarchal ideology.

10.4. The Male Saviours and the Rational Bystanders

Clover (2005, p. 66) suggests that occult films provide 'two competing systems of explanation, [...] the White Science and Black Magic'. While a rational male bystander represents White Science, priests, sorcerers or other practitioners of magic represent Black Magic. After the female character starts to show the symptoms of possession, such as vomiting, moving objects, cursing and so on, the rational male faces the quandary 'between clinging to the rational, scientific understanding of human behavior or yielding to the irrational' (Clover, 2005, p. 85). The inevitable lesson of the modern occult film according to Clover (2005) is that 'White Science has its limits, and that if it does not yield, in the extremity, to the wisdom of Black Magic, all is lost' (p. 66).

The horror genre in Turkey parallels Clover's arguments and presents an apparent conflict between Western medicine and unorthodox[9] Islamic practices.

---

[9]While the existence of jinn and the act of possession is within the Islamic cosmology, the act of exorcising the spirits is still an unorthodox practice in the sense that, though they may be performed for purely benevolent reasons, they are still acts that meddle with the unseen world. Islam strictly bans any sort of meddling or interference with the unseen.

The character of the *hoca* is the male saviour. He is a well-respected, devout old man who makes charms, performs the ritual by reciting the Qur'an and holds the power to cleanse and save the female victims by casting away jinn. He is the equivalent of the priest who undertakes the exorcism in occult films. The rational bystander, however, is usually the husband or a friend of the possession victim. It is important to point out that this male character does not experience a crisis in faith and is not a non-believer. He is a believer whose faith in religion is dwindling. Through these two male characters, Turkish horror films communicate an anxiety that has been the topic of literature and other arts since the Ottoman Empire: the opposition between Westernization/modernization and tradition/religion. Since the Ottoman Empire, the perception towards Westernization/modernization has been about drawing and managing boundaries rather than opposing them (Koçer, 2012, pp. 18, 58). In other words, it has always been a matter of how much society is supposed to modernize/Westernize without breaking its bonds with tradition. Horror films in Turkey satisfy this particular anxiety when the *hoca* casts away jinn and saves the victim, and the rational bystander yields and reaffirms his faith. I would argue that this is also the core example of 'how Islamic horror films are integrated with current Islamist hegemony building processes' (Özkaracalar, 2016, para. 4), with their strong underlying premise that positions tradition/religion over Westernization/modernization.

Haunted presents an interesting case; the rational male bystander is not only Westernized/modernized but is already living in Germany, a Western country that is coded as modern. Metin is a hardworking, German-speaking, law-abiding, Westernized male, yet when Western medicine cannot diagnose Suat, he yields without hesitation and takes Suat to Istanbul to see Burhan to seek a cure in accordance with Islamic beliefs. I argue, therefore, that the anxiety in *Haunted* does not stem from the opposition between Westernization/modernization and tradition/religion but rather from a more familiar anxiety that resides within the horror genre: the erasure of the patriarchal authority. Suat has been suffering from unexplainable night terrors, shortness of breath and constant fainting since the beginning of the film. Metin witnesses his friend's gradual deterioration of mental and physical health. However, it takes him six months to acknowledge that there is something wrong with Suat, and it happens right after Suat fails to have sex with a prostitute. It can be argued that the possibility of his best friend being impotent is what really terrifies Metin, not the night terrors, fainting, hallucinations, addiction to painkillers or lack of appetite. In other words, *Haunted* does not burden its male character with a crisis of faith; it rather induces a crisis of masculinity by laying bare the anxiety and the possibility of the erasure of male authority through impotence.

10.5.   Masculinity as Abjection

Haunted portrays a male possession, which is rare because traditionally 'the portals of occult horror are almost always invariably women' (Clover, 2005, pp. 70–71). As a possessed being, Suat is a figure of abjection 'in that the boundary between self and other has been transgressed' (Creed, 1993, p. 32). Moreover, jinn that possess Suat in *Haunted* are coded as masculine, which brings forth a threat to the patriarchal ideology's compulsory heteronormativity. How does the film subdue the anxieties raised by the possession of a male character – conventionally impenetrable – by a creature that performs the same sex?

First, the film keeps Suat's body intact; his physical appearance does not change. He has no scars or wounds on his body, on the outside or internally. It is only his mind that jinn possess. In other words, by limiting possession to the mind, the film keeps the body impenetrable. However, even mental possession does not come cheap. When jinn penetrate Suat's mind, they subjugate it and show him flashes of terrible images of his mother, Nurcan and his life in the village. Suat's mind hence becomes 'the terrible place' (Clover, 1987, p. 192). No matter how much medication Suat takes, he cannot banish these nightmarish images. Moreover, as Clover (1987) suggests, 'occult film codes emotional openness as feminine, and figure those who indulge it, male and female, as physically opened, penetrated' (p. 101). I argue that *Haunted* depicts this "emotional openness" by assigning Suat the role of the hysteric, an illness associated with femininity. In the film, Suat displays symptoms of hysteria fluctuating between completely mute states to complete frenzy. He either shakes, screams and faints as a result of flashes of horrific images or remains completely mute, watching television, working at the factory and wandering in the streets alone. Jinn's presence in Suat's mind also becomes a threat to the construction of his whole self. As the borders that confine and defend the subject from psychosis disintegrate, his whole sense of self disintegrates; Suat becomes hysterical and psychotic. He can no longer 'reject or repress all forms of behaviour, speech and modes of being regarded as unacceptable, improper, or unclean as a condition to enter the symbolic order' (Clover, 1993, p. 37). In the absence of borders that "deny us our desired return to a lost imaginary plenitude" (Plain, 2008, p. 3), Suat lingers, in an eternal limbo, longing to go back to his mother, her womb, back to the Imaginary. The film depicts this desire for regression with the obsessive phone calls from Suat to his mother. In the scene where Suat calls his mother, no matter what he tells her and how much he yells, screams and cries, he fails to communicate with her because she replies with the same sentences. It is as if she neither hears him nor speaks his language. Naturally, the mother who remains in the Imaginary can no longer 'hear' him; she can no longer 'speak' to him. Because Suat will never be allowed back 'in', his only option is to find the cure that will expel the abject so he can go back to functioning within the laws of the symbolic order. However, Suat dies, and his death is among the reasons the film stands out from its contemporaries. Even though Burhan is assigned the role of the devout male saviour, he fails to save Suat. After the midwives kill the offspring, the jinn go on a killing spree. First, they kill Suat when he takes off the charm Burhan gave him. Later, jinn kill Metin. Finally, they pay a visit to Burhan's house. The room starts to shake, and hundreds of cockroaches invade the house through the gap under the door, signalling the arrival of jinn. Finally, we see the high-angle shot constructed as the subjective gaze of jinn looking down at Burhan's family as their bones break. When Burhan comes back home, he first sees the corpses of his family, hands and feet inverted and twisted, eyes and mouths wide open. He then sees his granddaughter Büşra (Cansu Aktay), who is sitting across the corpses of her parents unable to speak and in complete shock. In tears and with blood dripping from his nose, Burhan starts to scribble the whole event in his diary on the floor. Cockroaches appear again. The high-angle shot shows Burhan as he lies on the floor; the jinn have not left. This is a rare shot; it renders Burhan, the male saviour, small and vulnerable and, perhaps most importantly, defeated.

10.6. Conclusion

Looking at the body of work in Turkish horror films that have been produced since 2004, it is possible to categorize them as a genre for various reasons. First, they derive their objects of horror from Islamic cosmology and horrific pre-Islamic Anatolian legends and folktales. Second, like comedy, melodrama or any other genre, horror is culturally gendered and thus provides many opportunities to investigate the internal mechanisms and power dynamics of patriarchal ideology through its depictions of gender.

Horror films in Turkey are almost always possession stories, and, as traditional portals of evil, female characters are usually the ones who are possessed. Through possession, the films place femininity on the side of the abject. *Haunted* is unique in that it tells the story of a male possession. To contain the anxiety raised by the transgressive nature of the possession of a male character by a creature that performs masculinity, the film limits possession to the mind of its male protagonist; his body remains impenetrable. This way the film sidesteps a possible reading of its male protagonist as homosexual.

Pregnancy holds another significant place within the Turkish horror genre. Jinn impregnate the female character, Nurcan, in *Haunted*. With pregnancy, Nurcan begins to be depicted as monstrous in relation to her maternal capacity as her womb has also become abject. Male characters in Turkish horror films, on the contrary, fall into two main categories. With slight variations, they are either depicted as the devout elderly male *hoca* who save victims of possession or constructed as the rational male bystander who yields to Islamic belief and reaffirms his faith. In all these films, including *Haunted*, however, the main conflict is more about the anxieties that stem from the opposition between Westernization/modernization and tradition/religion and women's place in both, rather than opposition between religion and science. This tension, which 'remains not only at the forefront of the Turkish political scene, but deeply embedded within the Turkish socio-cultural psyche' (Özkaracalar, 2003, p. 215), has been the central topic in literature and the arts since the modernization movement began in the late nineteenth-century Ottoman Empire. Modernization/Westernization has always been encouraged as long as it does not threaten the patriarchal ideology and remains within the lines drawn by the dominant political structure, be it the Ottoman Empire or the Turkish Republic. Hence, while Western education, literature, arts, science and technology were appreciated, women were constantly reminded of their role as the 'mothers of the nation', even in the reform era right after the Empire fell and modern Turkey was founded. As a result, the stories of the victimization and the punishment of excessively Westernized, promiscuous women along with the stories of the mockery and downfall of excessively Westernized men have been retold in literature and cinema as cautionary tales. This mainly male crisis of reconstructing and sustaining patriarchal ideology still manifests itself in the politics, culture and collective consciousness of Turkish society. The gender-specific trope of victimization in Turkish horror films reveals male anxieties about the loss of male authority via its stories of female possession. After all, in the horror genre, 'behind the female "cover," there is always the story of a man in crisis' (Clover, 2005, p. 65).

References

Akbulut, H. (2008). *Kadına Melodram Yakışır: Türk Melodram Sinemasında Kadın İmgeleri*. Istanbul: Bağlam Yayınları.

Aksoy, F. (Producer), & Oğuz, O. (Director). (2004). *Dark Spells/Büyü* (Motion picture). Turkey: UFP.

Arslan, U. T. (2005). *Bu Kabuslar Neden Cemil? Yeşilçamda Erkeklik ve Mazlumluk*. Istanbul: Metis.

Aslan, H. (Producer), Taylan, D., & Taylan, Y. (Directors). (2006). *The Little Apocalypse/Küçük Kıyamet* (Motion picture). Turkey: Limon Yapım.

Ataman, K. (Producer), & Ataman, K. (Director). (1994). *The Serpent's Tale/Karanlık Sular* (Motion picture). Turkey: Onar Film.

Clover, J. C. (1987). Her body, himself: Gender in the slasher film. *Representations Special Issue: Misogyny, Misandry, and Misanthropy* (Autumn, 1987), *20*, 187–228.

Clover, J. C. (2015). *Men, women and chain saws: Gender in the modern horror film* (Princeton Classics ed.). Princeton, NJ: Princeton University Press.

Cohen, J. J. (1996). Monster culture (seven theses). Retrieved from https://www.englishwithtuttle.com/uploads/3/0/2/6/30266519/cohen_monster_culture__seven_theses__3–20.pdf, pp. 3–25.

Creed, B. (1993). *The monstrous-feminine: Film, feminism, psychoanalysis*. London: Routledge.

Çetin, S. (Producer), Taylan, Y., & Taylan, D. (Directors). (2004). *The school/okul* (Motion picture). Turkey: Plato Film Production.

Dalkıran, B. (Producer), & Dalkıran, B. (Director). (2006). *The abortion/Araf* (Motion picture). Turkey: DFGS Yapım.

Danacı, F. (2015, March 26). Onuncu yılında Türk korku sineması. *Öteki Sinema*. Retrieved from http://www.otekisinema.com/onuncu-yilinda-turk-korku-sinemasi/

Demirağ, T. (Producer), & Muhtar, M. (Director). (1953). *Dracula in Istanbul/Drakula İstanbul'da* (Motion picture). Turkey: And Film.

Dönmez-Colin, G. (2008). *Turkish cinema: Identity, distance and belonging*. London: Reaktion Books.

Dural, S. M. (2016, June 22). Yerli edebiyatta ve sinemada korku öğesi. *Rotka*. Retrieved from http://www.rotka.org/yerli-edebiyatta-ve-sinemada-korku-ogesi/

El-Aswad, E. (2002). *Religion and folk cosmology: Scenarios of the visible and invisible in rural Egypt*. Westport, CT: Praeger Publishers.

Erdoğan, İ. (2011). *Medyada Hegemonik Erkek(lik) ve Temsil*. Istanbul: Kalkedon.

Erksan, M. (Producer), & Erksan, M. (Director). (1974). *Satan/Şeytan* (Motion picture). Turkey: Saner Film.

Freud, S. (1919). *The uncanny*. Retrieved from http://web.mit.edu/allanmc/www/freud1.pdf

Friedkin, W. (Director). (1973). *The Exorcist* [Motion picture]. California, CA: Warner Bros and Hoya Productions.

Gingrich, A. (1995). Spirits of the border: Some remarks on the connotation of jinn in North-western Yemen. *Quaderni di Studi Arabi*, *13*, 199−212. Retrieved from http://www.jstor.org/stable/25802775

Güçhan, G. (1992). *Toplumsal Değişme ve Türk Sineması: Kente Göç Eden İnsanın Türk Sinemasında Değişen Rolleri*. İstanbul: İmge.

Ilgın, Ö. (2015, September 7). Türk sinemasında korku filmleri. *Açık Günlük*. Retrieved from https://ozgurilgin.wordpress.com/2015/09/07/turk-sinemasinda-korku-filmleri/

İri, M. (2016). *Türk Sineması'nda Erkeklik Performansları*. Derin.

Karacadağ, H. (Producer), & Karacadağ, H. (Director). (2006). *Dbbe/Dbbe* (Motion picture). Turkey: J-Plan.

Kaya, R., & Çakmur, B. (2010). Politics and the mass media in Turkey. *Turkish Studies*, *11*(4), 521−537.

Kılıçbay, B., & Onaran-İncirlioğlu, E. (2003). Interrupted happiness: Class boundaries and the 'impossible love' in Turkish melodrama. *Ephemera*, *3*(3), 236 49.

Kırel, S. (2005). *Yeşilçam Öykü Sineması*. İstanbul: Babil Yayıncılık.

Koçer, Z. (2012). *Masculinities in Yılmaz Güney's star image in the 1960s and 1970s* (Unpublished doctoral dissertation). I.D. Bilkent University, Ankara, Turkey.

Köseoğlu, M., Duru, N. (Producers), & Arakon, A. (Director). (1949). *Scream/Çığlık* (Motion picture). Turkey: Atlas Film.

Kristeva, J. (1982). *Powers of horror: An essay on abjection*. (L. S. Roudiez, Trans.). New York, NY: Columbia University Press (Original work published in 1980).

Longmore, K. P. (1985). Screening stereotypes. *Social Policy*, Summer, *16*, 31−37.

Maktav, H. (2001). Türk Sinemasında Yoksulluk ve Yoksul Kahramanlar. *Toplum Bilim*, Yaz, *89*, 161−189.

Oktan, A. (2008). Türk Sinemasında Hegemonik Erkeklikten Erkeklik Krizine: *Yazı-Tura* ve Erkeklik Bunalımının Sınırları. *Selçuk İletişim*, *5*(2), 152−166.

Özgüç, A. (2005). *Türlerle Türk Sineması*. İstanbul: Dünya Yayıncılık.

Özkaracalar, K. (2003). Between appropriation and innovation: Turkish horror cinema. In S. J. Schneider (Ed.), *Fear without frontiers: Horror cinema across the globe* (pp. 205−217). Godalming: FAB Press.

Özkaracalar, K. (2012). *Horror films in Turkish cinema: To use or not to use local cultural motifs, that is not the question*. In P. Allmer, E. Brick, & D. Huxley (Eds.), *European Nightmares: Horror Cinema in Europe since 1945*. (pp. 249−260). London: Wallflower Press.

Özkaracalar, K. (2016, February 13). İslami korku filmlerinin ideolojik/siyasi topoğrafası. *İleri Haber*. Retrieved from http://ilerihaber.org/yazar/islami-korku-filmlerinin-ideolojiksiyasi-topografyasi-50243.html

Padwick, C. E. (1924). Notes on the jinn and the ghoul in the peasant mind of lower Egypt. *Bulletin of the School of Oriental Studies, 3*(3), 421–446. Retrieved from http://www.jstor.org/stable/607434?seq=1#page_scan_tab_contents

Peterson, M. A. (2007). From jinn to genies: Intertextuality, media, and the making of global folklore. *Folklore/Cinema: Popular Film as Vernacular Culture*, 93–122. Retrieved from http://www.jstor.org/stable/j.ctt4cgnbm.8?seq=1#page_scan_tab_contents

Plain, G. (2008). From 'the purest literature we have' to 'a spirit grown corrupt': Embracing contamination in twentieth-century crime fiction. *Contemporary Fiction, 20*(1), 3–16.

Sancar, S. (2013).*Erkeklik: İmkânsız İktidar. Ailede, Piyasada ve Sokakta Erkekler.* İstanbul: Metis.

Scognamillo, G., & Demirhan, M. (2005). *Fantastik Türk sineması.* İstanbul: Kabalcı.

Stoker, B. (2000). *Dracula.* New York, NY: Dover Publications.

Suner, A. (2006). *Hayalet Ev: Yeni Türk sinemasında aidiyet, kimlik ve bellek.* İstanbul: Metis.

Toktamışoğlu, M. (Producer), Akdeniz, B. (Producer), & Mestçi, A. (Director). (2007). *The Haunted/Musallat* [Motion picture]. Turkey: Dada Film & Mia Yapım.

Toktamışoğlu, M., Kaplanoğlu, K. (Producers), & Gökbakar, T. (Director). (2006). Gen/Gen (Motion picture). Turkey: Dada Film & Tiglon.

Ulusay, N. (2004). Erkek Filmleri'nin Yükselişi ve Erkeklik Krizi. *Toplum ve Bilim,* Güz, *101,* 144.

Williams, L. (1996). When the woman looks. In B. K. Grant (Ed.), *The dread of difference: Gender and the horror film* (pp. 17–36). Austin, TX: University of Texas Press.

Wood, R. (2004). An introduction to the American horror film. In B. K. Grant & C. Sharrett (Eds.), *Planks of reason: Essays on the horror film* (pp. 107–141). Lanham, MD: Scarecrow Press Inc.

Yalınkılıç, Y. (Producer), & Yalınkılıç, Y. (Director). (1970). *The dead don't Talk/ Ölüler Konuşmaz Ki* (Motion picture). Turkey: Onar Films.

Yılmazkol, Ö. (2011). *2000 Sonrası Türk Sineması'na Eleştirel Bakış.* Istanbul: Okur Yayınları.

PART III
CAPTIVITY

Chapter 11

Gender Ideologies, Social Realities and New Technologies in Recent Latin American 'Abduction' Horror

Niall Brennan

11.1. Introduction

Horror film is hardly new to Latin America. Largely, film scholars have emphasized paradigms of socially engaged, 'serious cinema' over exploring how genre, cult or other transgressive film-making modes have developed in and reflected the region (Tierney, 2014). To characterize Latin American horror, it is typified by the supernatural, which indeed contradicts serious cinema. Since 2010, Latin American film-makers have revisited horror's 'abduction' subgenre. This chapter analyses three such films — *Scherzo Diabolico* (García Bogliano, 2015), *Luna de Miel* (Cohen, 2015) and *Sudor Frío* (García Bogliano, 2010) — to suggest how their depictions of gender and class complicate assumptions about everyday life in the region, and how this mode of horror reconfigures gender ideologies to challenge Latin American social–political structures such as *machismo* and patriarchy. By integrating concepts of hybridity with Freeland's (1996) reworked feminist strategy for analysing horror, this chapter argues that, in tandem with new means of accessing and viewing Latin American horror globally, we should rethink how the abduction subgenre reflects new realities of Latin American society.

11.2. Gender Roles in US Horror

In a recent volume devoted to Latin American genre film, Dapena (2017) observes: 'The new respectability of the horror genre and its concurrent recognition in institutional circles [...] is one example of how attitudes towards genre films have drastically changed in Latin America' (2017, p. 159). Tierney (2002,

Gender and Contemporary Horror in Film, 169–185
doi:10.1108/978-1-78769-897-020191012

2014; Ruetalo & Tierney, 2009; Syder & Tierney, 2005) has attempted to extricate Latin American horror from its status of 'cult cinema' so that research can continue to 'determine how this work may progress without reifying the problematic clichés of a peripheral cinema and a peripheral continent' (2014, pp. 134–135). With the respect of Latin American horror established and research into its significance underway, crucial to the aims of this chapter is recognizing a 'move away from the masochistic/empathetic or sadistic/voyeuristic identification on the part of spectators' to engage in how 'horror cinema in Latin America provides new avenues to map out the changes in the politics of gender and sexual identity' (Subero, 2016, pp. viii–ix). Tudor (1997) also notes that 'it is a mistake to seek an explanation of horror's appeal which aspires to universality and [...] has no recourse to [...] the diversity of horror audiences both within and across cultures' (1997, p. 53). Moreover, we should not ask 'why horror?' in assuming its universal popular appeal, but rather, 'why do *these* people like *this* horror in *this* place at *this* particular time?' (Tudor, 1997, p. 54; original emphases). Given these arguments, it is worth exploring how gender has been deployed in horror more broadly before returning to Latin American horror specifically.

North American horror is a clear place to start, both because of the number of films made and because the nature of gender roles in US horror has provided scholars with analytical models and points of difference. Welsh's (2010) analysis of gender differences in relation to characters' sexual activity and survival rates in slasher films, or 'movies that contain scenes of explicit violence primarily directed toward women' which occur 'during or immediately following mildly erotic scenes' (Cowan & O'Brien, 1990, p. 187), reveals that 'while sexual behavior may generally be a perilous moral transgression', there is 'greater risk inherent for female characters' (1990, p. 770). Moreover, death scenes are prolonged for sexually engaged female characters, and 'female characters who were not engaged in sexual activity were depicted more positively' (Cowan & O'Brien, 1990, p.187). In an influential study, Clover (1987) observes that underlying slasher films 'is the assumption that the sexes are what they seem [...] that this identification along gender lines authorizes impulses toward sexual violence in males and encourages impulses towards victimization in females' (1987, p. 206). Additionally, the role of abject terror 'is gendered feminine, and the more concerned a given film with that condition [...] the more likely the femaleness of the victim' (Clover, 1987, p. 212). However, while abject terror may be gendered feminine, horror's tendency 'to re-represent the hero as [...] female would seem to suggest that at least one of the traditional marks of heroism, triumphant self-rescue, is no longer strictly gendered masculine' (1987, p. 219).

Cowan and O'Brien (1990) find that gender roles in US slasher films do not necessarily predict female characters' demise, namely sexually active female characters. Rather, 'patterning and therefore meaning varied with gender' when comparisons were made between films (Cowan & O'Brien, 1990, p. 195). New patterns therefore enable deriving 'some positive elements' from the films' messages about women, such as that survival 'depends on competence and instrumentality, but not at the expense of the feminine-valued traits', while 'unmitigated masculinity ends in death, an historically modern message' (Cowan & O'Brien, 1990). These studies offer challenges to slasher films' predictable demise of (sexually active) female characters, which becomes even more crucial in considering the moral implications of such predictions. Moreover, they suggest that female characters' survival is a matter of resourcefulness rather than of virtuousness.

Beyond predictable or unexpected patterns of how gender informs characters' survival, Williams (1991) considers the temporal dimensions of horror, and therefore how timing provides added ways of interpreting gender roles and relations:

> Some of the most violent and terrifying moments of the horror film genre occur in moments when the female victim meets the psycho-killer monster unexpectedly [...] This surprise encounter, too early, often takes place at a moment of sexual anticipation when the female victim thinks she is about to meet her boyfriend or lover [...] Again the key to the fantasy is timing – the way the knowledge of sexual difference too suddenly overtakes both characters and viewers, offering a knowledge for which we are never prepared. (p. 11)

Inscribing gender onto characters and the temporal dimensions by which gender is articulated in horror are key aspects of this study. However, we need to consider hybridity in tandem with Freeland's reconfigured feminist approach to reading horror texts before arriving at the films analysed here.

11.3. Hybridity and Horror in Latin America

The above discussion anticipates considering relations between US and Latin American film-making not as wholly characterized by 'Hollywood's self-appointed mission as goodwill imperialist ethnographer of the Americas' (López, 1993, p. 71). Indeed, the US underwrote early Latin American film-making in its 'Good Neighbor' policy, and Hollywood exported scores of films that consolidated clichés of 'tropical island retreats, banana republics, quaint Argentine gauchos, pistol-wielding Mexicans, sexy señoritas, and Brazilians dancing at carnival' (Barrenechea, 2009, pp. 227–228). However, rather than reviving critique of US imperialism as it unquestionably informed early Latin American film-making, a more nuanced look at inter-American histories which do not 'run the risk of dismissing the Hispanic ingenuity that was generated by US imperial hegemony' is needed (Barrenechea, 2009, p. 235). The latter perspective reveals that through 'deployment of cultural networks of uneven exchange, Hollywood reconfigures our understanding of US and Latin American film history' to uncover the 'multidirectional ways in which Latin American cinemas are linked to Hollywood' (Barrenechea, 2009, p. 235).

Transnational perspectives on Latin American film-making complement this thinking, in that it is 'too reductive to say that the Latin American industry is merely modeling itself after larger capitalistic audio-visual enterprises, and thus becoming ideologically congruous with them' (Alvaray, 2013, p. 81). Still, Latin

American partnerships with Columbia, Warner and Sony have 'contributed to the accelerated visibility of Latin American products' globally (Alvaray, 2013, p.81). Therefore, a useful perspective from which to assess political—historical and socio-economic exchange between North American and Latin American 'versions' of horror is that of hybridity. As such, Latin American horror offers 'unstable contact zones of a wide variety of national, regional and transnational determinants' (Alvaray, 2013, p. 69) in which hybridity serves as a key analytical strategy.

García Canclini (1995, 2000, 2006), a prominent theorist of Latin American hybridity, writes: 'Neither the "paradigm" of imitation, nor that of originality, nor the "theory" that attributes everything to dependency [...] are able to account for our hybrid cultures' (1995, p. 6). He departs from 'conventional categories and pairs of oppositions [...] employed for talking about the popular' (1995, p. 206) to focus on urban culture as a site in which such polarities converge to give popular culture new meaning. Furthermore, hybrid texts and their location in urban culture can be viewed through three signifying processes: decollection, deterritorialization and impure genres (García Canclini, 2006). The first addresses the 'problem of whether the organization of culture can be explained by reference to *collections* of symbolic goods', while the second 'puts into doubt the possibility of cultural systems finding their key in the relations of the population with a certain type of *territory*' (García Canclini, 2006, p. 428; original emphases). Impure genres, with 'intersection between the visual and the literary, the cultured and the popular', bring the 'artisanal nearer to industrial production and mass circulation' (García Canclini, 1995, p. 249). Thus, the 'impurity' by which Latin American horror has grown can be conjoined with decollected influences on Latin American productions and deterritorialized global regard of the genre, this analysis included.

For Martín-Barbero (1993, 2001), hybridity reaches beyond Euro-indigenous miscegenation, or *mestizaje*, to provide a strategy for interpreting the region's cultural production. This requires acknowledging how, following colonization and independence, Latin America realized new dependencies on a global market, thereby creating 'unequal development' within 'the basic inequality on which capitalist development rests' (Martín-Barbero, 2001, p. 626). This discontinuity contextualizes 'gaps' between Euro/North American and Latin American 'versions' of modernity, enabling identification of the uneven ways in which culture has been produced and experience has unfolded in Latin America. Thus, discontinuity points to the 'made—remade' contradictions in Latin American experience as a 'modernity which is not contemporary' thereby 'free[ing] the concept from misunderstandings that [...] limit its usefulness' (1993, p. 151). In reclaiming the idea of discontinuity, Martín-Barbero ultimately asks questions of originality, or Latin America's 'problem' of imitating Euro/North American ideals of modernity and the means by which the latter has been achieved. Thus, *mestizaje* reflects an amalgam of the experiential/representational dimensions of Latin American life, or its 'hybrid of foreign and national, of popular informality and bourgeois concern for upward mobility' (Martín-Barbero, 2001, p. 633).

While indebted to García Canclini and Martín-Barbero, Kraidy (2005) seeks to examine 'the space in which several objects and ideas related to hybridity emerge' rather than 'attempting to understand a unique and permanent discourse' (2005, p. 14). Kraidy employs a 'critical transcultural' approach to hybridity: critical in that discursive and political—economic analyses underpin studying hybrid texts, and transcultural in that '"trans-" suggests moving through spaces and across borders, not merely between points' (2005, p. 14). Kraidy invokes Said's (1994) notion of the contrapuntal, in which 'various themes play off one another', yet there is 'an organized interplay that derives from the themes' (1994, pp. 59–60). The contrapuntal underpins four ways in which Kraidy uses a critical transcultural approach to analyse hybrid texts. First, the 'open trope of hybridity' unifies focus on relations between not only texts and experience but between *institutions*, texts and experience; second, it enables identifying the 'integration of material forces and discursive processes' rather than viewing them independently; third, the contrapuntal allows 'Situating media processes in their broader social context', thus circumventing the 'mediacentrism that has bedeviled much media research'; and fourth, the contrapuntal allows moving beyond 'bipolar models' such as global/local, foreign/national, to focus instead on the 'complex processes at play' within and between each of these constitutive forces (Kraidy, 2005, p. 13).

Conceptions of hybridity are reflected in several Latin American horror films that invoke gender ideologies in their creation and reception. In Brazilian horror, many scholars (Anselmo-Sequeira, 2013; Dunn, 2001; Fernandes, 2002; Stephenson, 2011; Tierney, 2004) have researched José Mojica Marins' acting and film-making roles. As director of and actor in a trilogy of films, Marins and his character Zé de Caixão depict the abduction, rape, torture and murder of scores of female victims. The aims of this trilogy are to criticize the 'reactionary, conservative underpinnings of a society that allowed itself to be dominated by a 21-year-long military dictatorship' and 'affirm the same heteronormative "eternal truth" that served as the rhetorical backbone for that same dictatorship' (St-Georges, 2016, p. 567). Through a hybrid lens that sees interplay in texts, contexts, institutions and experience, Marins films thus can be interpreted as working alongside, and against, 'institutional accomplices, justified [in a] reign of terror in a perceived need to preserve traditional philosophies of order' (St-Georges, 2016, p. 567).

Given the political commentary of Marins' first two films and their release during the dictatorship's early years, unsurprising is that his third film was made well after the regime's demise. Still, there is consistency between Brazil's 1960s oppressiveness and its present-day neoliberal impetus, in that in his lattermost film, Zé reemerges:

> surprised to see a similarly uncanny coexistence of divergent temporalities, with some parts of São Paulo appearing to have achieved 'modernity' [...] while other sections of the city [...] appear to be mired in unpaved, third-world underdevelopment. This visual strategy highlights the [...] uneven chronological progress the country has made since the last time he made contact with the city during [...] the dictatorship. (St-Georges, 2016, p. 564)

Draper (2016) analyses two contemporary Brazilian films that mobilize discourses of gender and class in revealing ways. *Neighbouring Sounds* (Mendonça Filho, 2012) and *Adrift* (Dhalia, 2009) represent what Draper calls 'materialist horror' (2006, p. 119) to reshape Latin American horror's fantastical traditions into commentary on present-day violence and inequality. *Adrift* assumes the view of an adolescent girl who sees domestic violence enacted in her middle-class community and becomes aware of its presence in her home, amplifying her fear of men. *Neighbouring Sounds* combines universal horror tropes with every-day middle-class experience to evoke a collective fear of Brazil's racial economic divides. Echoing Tierney's concern for how Latin American films are granted 'paradigms of a realist and engaged "[third] world cinema"' (2014, p. 130), Draper notes how these films 'depart from the dominant strand of Brazilian cinematic social realism' to uncover the 'paranoia and belligerence of [...] the Brazilian middle/upper classes' (2016, p. 133). Through hybridity's lens, again, these films conjoin historical and contemporary Latin American realities with global cinematic qualities to provide new ways of viewing horror and its socio-political implications.

Hybridity is also key in interpreting *Planet Terror* (Rodriguez, 2007), a film which also invokes the geo-ethnic dimensions of *mestizaje*. *Planet Terror* is an American film but is set at the Mexico/US border. According to García (2014), the film's setting plays into the apocalypse that occurs from local authorities' attempts to gain control of a deadly biochemical agent, and the apocalypse represents post-9/11 US, its economic turmoil and role in Middle East conflicts. Thus, for the characters fleeing the apocalypse, Mexico symbolizes refuge and promise. Additionally, the film's heroes, bisexual and physically abused bio-chemist Dakota Block and sexually exploited stripper Cherry Darling, symbolize masculinity's demise and female body empowerment (García, 2014). Hybridity also assumes geo-ethnic dimensions through *Planet Terror*'s characters. 'Miscegenation in *Planet Terror* is transgressive since the fusion of races [...]' occurs between working-class characters' who 'become the main authority figures among the survivors in the face of the Apocalypse' (García, 2014). Although one could argue that any text incorporating diverse agents, contexts, temporalities and institutions constitutes a hybrid text (Kraidy, 2002), a key difference in Latin American horror is that by depicting distinct aspects of Latin American life using transnational elements, the former is intensified through familiar, even universal, mechanisms.

11.4.   Reconfiguring Feminist Readings of Horror

Freeland's (1996) reconfigured feminist reading of horror challenges much of the work discussed above, in that it leaves even less assumed about and probes to an even greater extent how gender is naturally encoded into the genre. Additionally, Freeland critiques dominant views on horror to integrate both institutional and experiential perspectives in ways that expand on conceptualizing hybridity.

Critiquing Lacanian precepts of castration anxiety and visual fetishism invoked by Mulvey (1975), Creed (1993), Kristeva (1982) and Williams (1991), Freeland makes two salient points about the psychoanalytic premises on which these readings of horror rest. First, 'psychodynamic film theories that depend upon [...] basic distinctions between males and females [...] rely upon certain notions of gender that are themselves problematic and under question by feminists' (Freeland, 1996, p. 201). Second, although 'psychoanalytic feminists construct genderized accounts of the tensions in horror between key features of spectacle and plot', it is nonetheless 'possible to construct a theory of horror that emphasizes these same tensions without genderizing them' (Freeland, 1996, p. 202). In sum, feminist readings that deploy psychoanalysis to seek 'meaning' in horror texts only solidify the gender differences they wish to disrupt.

Freeland therefore offers strategies for 'constructing feminist readings of horror films' that 'place special weight on their gender ideologies' (1993, p. 204). Most usefully, she poses questions that extricate reading horror from psychoanalytic contradictions: they consider narrative/representational and technical/formal features of films; they situate films in larger historical/generic trajectories; and they interrogate adherence to, and departure from, predictable gender encodings:

> How do the film's structures of narrative, point of view, and plot construction operate in effecting a depiction of gender roles and relations? Does the film offer a 'heroic modernist' narrative of mastery, centered upon a male character [...] Or, is there a non-standard narrative centered upon female characters, offering [...] a more open-ended and ambiguous conclusion? Does the film reference historical or genre precedents [...] and if so, how does it comment upon, replicate, parody, or revise the gender thematics of its predecessors? What are the film's implicit rhetorical presuppositions about natural gender roles and relations? Does the film present possibilities of questioning or challenging these presumptions? (1993, p. 206)

Freeland's strategy solidifies this study's conceptual framework. It also provides ways of identifying how the films analysed here depart from US paradigms, especially in terms of the latter's predicable gender encodings, and therefore, their 'natural' depictions of how gender roles and relations should be mapped onto reading Latin American society.

11.5.   Recent Latin American Abduction Horror and Gender Ideologies

As Freeland notes, an overlooked component of critiquing gender ideology in horror is its historical/genre precedents. Crucially, this chapter argues that the films examined here are important because of their foray into unexplored historical/genre territory. Still, Euro/North American precedents inform the films. Several film fan/aficionado websites provide lists of 'the best' Latin American horror films,[1] and approximately 30 films qualify, due to 'fright effects', narrative, cinematography and popularity, with overlap between lists. Setting aside nebulous criteria of the 'best' horror, the lists are consistent in terms of the most appealing Latin American horror subgenres, which, from the 1960s onward, qualify as hauntings, possessions and psychoses, and vampirism and witchcraft, or the supernatural. Additionally, only two 'abduction' films appear of these lists, Marins' *This Night I'll Possess Your Corpse* and *Sudor Frío*. It seems, therefore, that abduction horror has few precedents in Latin America, and that Marins' films of 50 years ago serve as the closest.

Precedents are different where US horror film-making is concerned. The *Saw* (2004–2017) franchise is influential when considering Jigsaw's proclivity to hold captive his victims and subject them to torture as tests of their survival, instead of killing them. The *Hostel* (2005, 2007, 2011) trilogy offers class links to the films examined here, in that both monster and victims are middle class rather than redneck psychopaths stalking middle-class victims, for which *The Texas Chainsaw Massacre* (1974) sets a precedent. There are also clear 'surgical horror' links between *Saw*, *Hostel* and the films considered here.

Canonical American horror films suggest other precedents. *The Silence of the Lambs* (1991) epitomizes a psychopath both smarter than his victims and their rescuers, and able to surveil his victims' rescue attempts. In *Misery* (1990), the victim's abduction/torture is far from arbitrary; instead, it results from an obsession that drives the depths of his torture further. *I Spit on Your Grave* (1978; 2010) sees the depravities to which the victim is subject ultimately met with methodical revenge. In this rape-and-revenge tradition, *The Virgin Spring* (1960) and *The Last House on the Left* (1972; 2009) also serve as precedents. *Carrie* (1976), too, is influential. Carrie is captive to her mother's zealotry and to her classmates' ridicule, which send Carrie into a vindictive tailspin. In these films, depicted gender ideologies follow a known pattern: women are victims; their survival hinges on sexual acts; men are not immune from elimination, but their masculinity is liable; and female characters' resourcefulness equates with survival. The significance of *Scherzo Diabolico*, *Luna de Miel* and *Sudor Frío*, however, lies in how they consciously adhere to, and knowingly depart from, the abduction tradition's 'known' traits to offer revealing commentary on everyday Latin American life, social codes and institutions.

11.5.1. *Scherzo Diabolico*

Scherzo Diabolico is initially structured from the view of Aram, a straight-laced, middle-class accountant. Ironically, Aram is hostage to the figures and

---

[1]See *Complex* (www.complex.com), *Fandango* (www.fandango.lat), *Inverse* (www.inverse.com), *Latin Times* (www.latintimes.com), *Remezcla* (www.remezcla.com), *Taste of Cinema* (www.tasteofcinema.com) and *Vix* (www.vix.com).

circumstances around him. His boss, Licenciado, promises the firm will be Aram's upon Licenciado's retirement. As revenues dry up, this promise rings hollow, and Aram increasingly puts in unpaid overtime. At home, Aram's wife, Macarena, harangues him about his lack of promotion and voluntary work, also refusing Aram sex. Leon, Aram's son, wears a superhero costume constantly and interacts with Aram only to use him as target practice. Aram is also beholden to Mendez, a gangster who avoided prison time thanks to Aram, but who insists on repaying his debt in unseemly ways. Ultimately, Aram is hostage to the firm's Partners, two men whose ashen faces and dirty fingernails cast them as archetypical vampires. Aram realizes that his situation is eroding and takes action, and his plan to abduct someone becomes clear. Aram's victim is Anabela, Licenciado's daughter, which is revealed only after Aram begins precisely tracking her routine. Wearing a *dia de los muertos* mask to conceal his identity, Aram abducts Anabella and holds her captive in an abandoned warehouse outside of Mexico City, chaining her by the neck to a column.

Anabela offers an alternative perspective. She walks from home to school, stopping occasionally to turn around, half-aware that she is being followed. She converses with a girlfriend, recounting online exchanges with older preying men. Upon Anabela's abduction, her fear is palpable as she both anticipates and dreads Aram's return to the warehouse. Anabela is also hostage to a rat that gnaws on her toes as she sleeps. Other female roles provide key perspectives in constructing *Scherzo Diabolico*'s gender ideologies. Macarena, while cold and shrewish, reveals intense maternalism when Leon becomes involved in Aram's scheme. Aram also meets regularly with a prostitute, who proves instrumental in teaching him to tie someone up, which Aram later uses on Anabela. Perla, a new hire and with whom Aram has a torrid sexual affair, self-interestedly backs Aram's promotion. These characters' roles are revealing in how they unwittingly support Aram's plans to acquire what he 'sees as coming to him' and serve as foils to his middle-class conventional façade.

Scherzo Diabolico's construction of gender ideologies seems typical of horror's abduction subgenre: Aram wields power over the women surrounding him; they in turn are supplicant. This paradigm shifts drastically when Aram's goal is realized and he gains control of the firm. Following Anabela's abduction, Licenciado unravels. Licenciado's unhinging coincides with Perla's self-interested support of Aram and the Partners' promotion of him. With his goal achieved, Aram releases Anabela into the wilderness. At home, Anabela is sullen and uncommunicative. On the street, Licenciado encounters Aram and tells him he is a 'free man', but how strange it is that as soon as he resigned, Anabela returned. Moreover, Licenciado just purchased a CD of classical music favourites, including Chopin's 'Scherzo', which Aram had suggested to him. Exiting from the shop behind her father, Anabela is introduced to Aram, but darkly retreats.

'Scherzo' is catalytic in Anabela's transformation into vigilante from victim. In order to desensitize her during her abduction, Aram plugs Anabela's ears with a recording of the piece and plays it while dragging her into the warehouse. Released, Anabela gloomily sits at the table with her parents. Licenciado attempts to lighten the mood by playing the CD he just purchased. Yet upon hearing 'Scherzo', Anabela runs into her bedroom to retrieve a baseball bat from her closet. Concerned, Licenciado follows. Anabela turns on him and batters him to death. She then goes to the kitchen, where she seizes a carving knife and kills her bewildered mother. At this moment, we recognize that Anabela has been victimized not only by Aram, but also by the many institutions that should have looked after her.

Crucially, Anabela's slaughter of Aram and his significant others is reduced to the last 20 minutes of the film. Aram receives calls from Licenciado, who he knows is dead. He encounters decals of a rat on the boot of his car, a table in his apartment and in his wallet. The firm's files disappear overnight, leaving Aram in peril with the Partners. Macarena receives videos Aram recorded of Perla during sex, and both learn that a 'secretary' met with Leon at his school, advising him, 'The next time we play baseball, I'll be the batter, and you'll be the ball'. Frantic, Aram contracts Mendez and his simpleton lover, Wheels, to kill Anabela at the firm's offices that night. Soon after they arrive, Aram finds Wheels' disembowelled body, then Mendez, with his throat slit. Turning around, Aram encounters Anabela, who strikes him with her bat. Impaired, Aram rushes home, begging Macarena and Leon to depart. He receives an urgent call from Perla, telling him that she will be killed if he does not return to the office. There again, Aram finds Perla bound and gagged with Anabela before her. Anabela knocks Aram out and, ironically, attaches a harness to his neck. Awakening, Aram watches Anabela bind Perla's head with cling-wrap, then knock her dead. Anabela tells Aram that the place where he took her will be where she tortures Leon for the next six months. Aram scoffs, but the office doorbell rings: Macarena and Leon are below, looking for him. Anabela smiles before blowing Aram's head off with a shotgun. *Scherzo Diabolico* closes with an aerial shot of a familiar road to a remote warehouse; swooping in, a superhero cape appears hanging out the boot of Aram's travelling car.

11.5.2. Luna de Miel

Luna de Miel's gender encodings rely heavily on the torture porn tradition. Yet the film offers views of everyday Latin American life and how the latter is shaped by entrenched gendered positions. The film's viewpoint is also evenly split between captor and captive. Jorge, a physician, lives in an upscale Mexico City neighbourhood. His parents died a while ago, but Jorge, who remains in their rambling house, continues to reckon with their deaths, having left the place unaltered. Isabel, a neighbour, is young, pretty and fitness-driven. She runs past Jorge's house daily, of which Jorge takes fastidious note. As this pattern unfolds, it becomes clear that Jorge is obsessed with Isabel and has made a strange promise to his parents. *Luna de Miel* thus invokes gender roles in psychoanalytically typical fashion, and with clear nods to *Psycho*. Jorge is psychologically repressed, and by his parents' appearance in their photos, they were pivotal in this. His relationship with his parents has thus been displaced by a psychosexual obsession with Isabel. *Luna de Miel* is also filmed in a duochromatic scheme, again invoking *Psycho*. Its muted coloration further contributes to *Luna de Miel*'s grittiness and conspicuous ways in which the torture porn tradition is invoked.

Jorge buys a new shower fixture and writes himself prescriptions. He also reconfigures the wiring at his door and receives an electrified dog collar by delivery. These errands seem arbitrary, yet significant is the protracted eye contact made between Jorge and Pablo, Isabel's boyfriend, when Jorge attempts to follow Isabel on one of her runs. These plot elements coalesce when Jorge abducts Isabel while she is running past his house. Jorge, feigning car trouble, stops Isabel to help him. As Isabel leans into the car to examine his 'problem', Jorge plunges sedatives into her neck, Isabel passes out, and he drags her to the dungeon he has outfitted. Until this point, *Luna de Miel*'s viewpoint was that of Jorge's. Upon her abduction, the film's view shifts diametrically to that of Isabel, reflecting most how gender ideologies are encoded into the film.

Jorge imprisons Isabel and subjects her to abuse in torture porn mode. To stop Isabel's struggles to free herself, Jorge injects her with more sedatives, she again loses consciousness and dreams of lovemaking with Pablo. Isabel awakens to find Jorge sitting by her bed and, desperately struggling, vows, 'I will kill you.' The crux of Jorge's plans for Isabel comes to fruition when, acting as groom and priest, he 'marries' Isabel who, wearing a wedding gown, weeps, chained to a bed. Still wearing the gown, Isabel makes her first escape attempt, rushing at Jorge, but is knocked unconscious by the electrified collar around her neck. *Luna de Miel* differs from the other films considered here in that, still unconscious and in the gown, Isabel is raped by Jorge. Key here is that Isabel's rape is offered as a natural outcome of their 'marriage'. More so, Isabel is unconscious while raped by Jorge, depriving her of agency and compounding her victimization.

Isabel, naked and strapped to the bathroom ceiling, is sprayed down by Jorge, but then makes her second escape attempt, seizing a pair of stockings and lunging at Jorge to strangle him. He shocks her again, and she falls atop him as if in consensual embrace. In retaliation, Jorge straps Isabel into a wheelchair, pries her mouth open with a dental dam and sprays acid and salt into it. He looks on with empirical interest as blood drips down her chest. Isabel, unconscious, dreams again of lovemaking with Pablo. This time, Pablo seems distracted; he has 'something going on' with which he cannot contend. 'We will be alright', Isabel assures him, 'we always will be'. Isabel is raped a second time by Jorge, who afterwards caresses her hand as if in a mutual display. Isabel's rape raises questions about *Luna de Miel*'s narrative motive against invocations of the torture porn/rape-and-revenge traditions: does they specifically adhere to the film's plot, or are they gratuitously offered to solidify gender-encoded violence as it expectedly fits within a transnational mode?

These questions are answered as *Luna de Miel* concludes. Jorge subjects Isabel to 'procedures' that follow the surgical horror tradition, first removing the flesh of Isabel's left-hand fingers, leaving them bloody stumps. In a surprising 'connection', Isabel and Jorge smoke marijuana together, Jorge discloses that his parents were murdered during Mexico's dictatorship, and that it has been difficult for him to reckon with their deaths. After drinking wine with Isabel, Jorge becomes drunk and they begin to undress in apparent consensual sex. But Isabel pulls Jorge's shirt over his head and strangles him with the chain attached to her neck. In a third escape attempt, Isabel unchains herself and races to the front door, only to be shocked into unconsciousness upon touching the knob. Revived, as the monster is never so easily killed, Jorge lashes out by hitching Isabel to the ceiling. Hoisting her upwards, Jorge tells Isabel, 'I won't kill you, but you'll wish I did' until her arms give. Surprisingly, Pablo appears at Jorge's door and Jorge lets him in. Pablo's calm demeanour over Isabel's disappearance is suspect; additionally, when Jorge offers Pablo coffee, he already knows that Pablo takes it 'without sugar'. Goaded by Pablo's presence upstairs, Jorge goes to the dungeon and, in his most diabolical moment, produces a scalpel to pierce Isabel's eye. In returning to the questions above, it seems incongruous that if Jorge loves Isabel as much as he claims to, he would subject her to such abuse. The gratuitous nature of Isabel's torture instead appeals to a larger, expected transnational narrative.

Jorge hesitates to pierce Isabel's eye. Instead, upstairs again, he stabs the unwary Pablo with sedatives and confesses to him, 'I couldn't kill her!' before Pablo loses consciousness. *Luna de Miel*'s gender-encoded plot construct is thus revealed. Jorge binds Pablo and stands him before Isabel, a ball gag strapped into his mouth and a winch attached to it. Jorge tells Isabel that Pablo asked him to kill her so that he could collect insurance money upon her death. Forcing Pablo to confess as Isabel watches, Jorge tightens the winch until the ball gag explodes his head. Isabel's abduction has not been the work of a sole psychopath. Rather, two monsters used Isabel for material purposes, and her torture, more simply, was a gratuitous side effect. In the last minutes of the film, Jorge disposes of Pablo's body in an acid vat, and Isabel finally escapes. Striking him with a metal pole, Isabel plunges Jorge's face into the acid with her mutilated hand until his face is a blackened wreck. In an epilogue, Isabel appears in running gear at the same shop where Jorge stalked her, a black glove covering her disfigured hand. Encountering a friend who wonders where she has been, Isabel nonchalantly replies, 'I've been busy.' Isabel returns to the dungeon where she was tortured, dressed in a loose blouse and tight shorts, her hair comely tousled. She approaches a bloody, mutilated figure chained to the ceiling. Smiling, Isabel circles around Jorge's body while caressing it.

11.5.3. Sudor Frío

Sudor Frío's invocations of torture porn offer revealing statements about Argentinian political history and its attempts to reconcile the latter through the film's gender ideologies, also introducing telling elements of technology to the film. The film's viewpoint is that of Ramón. Ramón and friend Ali go in search of his ex-girlfriend, Jackie, who disappeared after meeting another man. But Jackie left traces of her location through social media and mentioned a 'blonde guy' she intended to meet. Jealous, Ramón enlists Ali to find Jackie. Using GPS, they trace her to a derelict house in an undesirable Buenos Aires neighbourhood. Ali enters the house to find Jackie while Ramón sits in his car. Waiting, Ramón spies an elderly man attempting to cross the road and jumps out to help him. The old man thanks Ramón and disappears into the house Ali had just entered. Inside, Ali encounters the 'blonde guy' but, approaching him, sees his arms drop from his body. He is a living corpse, and Ali is attacked from behind.

When Ali does not soon return, Ramón assumes the role of hero. He scales an adjoining fence, cutting his hand and disturbing the derelict neighbours. Inside, Ramón encounters a quintessential haunted house: dark, cluttered and frozen in time. On an old television set, a 1970s comedian disparages women's demands for equal rights, which establishes the film's narrative premise. In classic haunted-house mode again, Ramón unadvisedly climbs the stairs to find a glassed-in chamber in which a young woman, naked and bound, is forced to solve an equation written on a chalkboard by two old men, one of whom Ramón had just helped. Hiding, Ramón spies Ali, their next victim, cowering in the corner. When the woman is unable to solve the equation, as Ramón and Aly watch in dread, she is beheaded. This test is meant to prove the inadequacy of women's intelligence, misuse of Spanish, and the erosion of young people's attentiveness, as one old man explains. Ironically, they have been using social media, with the 'blond guy' as bait, to lure female victims to their torture and death, later revealed by a computer monitor displaying updates to a Facebook-like page.

Sudor Frío's opening sequence provides background to this scenario. It shows historical footage of people tortured by the military during Argentina's 'Dirty War'. Subtitles reveal that a splinter pair absconded with large amounts of nitroglycerine, yet neither the pair nor the explosives were ever found. The old men are this splinter pair, relics of Argentina's unreconciled political history and symbolic of an ideological battle never won. Flashback sequences of two younger men looking for political dissidents confirm that this is the same pair. Ali miraculously solves an equation put to her in a similar test, but the pair leaves her with explosives on her forehead and lap. Ramón emerges from hiding to search the web, learning how to deactivate nitroglycerine. Freeing Ali, Ramón dispatches her to seek help. Seeking Jackie, he finds her strapped to a table in a dungeon, her body bathed in explosives, from which she will detonate at any minute. Yet Ramón cannot help but interrogate Jackie about her unfaithful reasons for coming to the house in the first place.

Looking for escape, Ali finds another part of the dungeon but is attacked by a horde of zombie women, detritus of the old men's 'corrective' project. Heroically again, Ramón bursts through a wall and rescues Ali. Further contributing to *Sudor Frío*'s gender encodings is how Ramón slowly removes Jackie's toxic clothing, revealing her sweat-soaked breasts and pubic hair. Ali watches, satisfied, as Jackie's hair is cut from her head, and Jackie must slither on her back out of the dungeon in order to escape. Freed, the trio must still evade their captors, and Ali does so by scaling the same fence Ramón did to summon the rogue neighbours. The neighbours, snorting cocaine, rally, hacking through the adjoining wall to find Ramón batting one of the old men who is garbed in a

HASMAT suit to fend off the escaped zombie women. Beaten and cornered, Ramón grabs a bottle of nitroglycerine and hurls it at his assailant, exploding him in a shower of blood and guts. Jackie has been cornered by the other psychopath, however. Just before he douses her with nitroglycerine, she dives into a tub of water. Ali, again captive and with nitroglycerine on her forehead, seizes the bottle and hurls it at her own captor, debilitating him, while Jackie spectacularly emerges from the tub. As the old man lies on the floor, groaning, Ali and Jackie appear above him. 'Who are these guys?' Jackie asks. 'Just a couple of old motherfuckers who've gotten away with things for too long', Ali replies, before they both toss him into the dungeon to be devoured by the zombies.

11.6. Conclusion

The thread that ties together *Scherzo Diabolico*, *Luna de Miel* and *Sudor Frío* is their victims' pursuit of retribution for male oppression which, in Latin America, is further symbolized as historically institutionally persistent roles of *machismo* and patriarchy. In this sense, and to return to Freeland's reconfigured reading of horror, these films challenge 'heroic modernist narratives of male character mastery' to provide instead 'nonstandard narratives centered on female characters' through 'more open-ended, ambiguous conclusions'. With Anabela, her pursuit does not rectify the torture she suffered during captivity as much as it overthrows the instrumental role she played in Aram's quest for upward mobility and the ways in which the latter hypocritically belies middle-class Mexican society. Similarly, Isabel's vengeance is not about subjecting Jorge to the same means of torture to which she was exposed; rather, she symbolically redresses injustices women have suffered at men's hands in complicit, systematic ways. Given Ramón's heroism, *Sudor Frío* adheres more to traditional, male-centered narratives. Yet Ali represents a generationally savvy challenge against patriarchal codes crystalized in Argentinian sociopolitical history. However, worth noting again is that these 'nonstandard' narratives are reduced to the films' final minutes, mitigating grand claims of their radically rewriting expected encodings of gendered roles and relations.

Nevertheless, the films challenge horror's links between female victimization and sexual activity, in that this link is absent where otherwise it may have conspicuously present. Anabela and Jackie are certainly sexualized, but sexual activity on their parts never becomes a plot-driving factor, save Ramón's implicit references to Jackie's infidelity. Isabel's rape, however, does not constitute sexual activity, but rather adheres to torture porn/rape-and-revenge traditions in transnationally predictable ways. Again, we should question whether the plot device of Isabel's rape is an 'essential' aspect of *Luna de Miel*, or if it is more gratuitously presented. Williams' temporal observations of horror's gender encodings also reemerge as useful. In these films, we are submitted to protracted depictions of men's rationale for, and deliberations involved in, women's abduction and torture, only to be confronted with the latter events in sudden, if not entirely unexpected, manners.

Hybridity is key to interpreting the films considered here. They decollect tropes otherwise relegated to North American slashers and Latin American supernatural horrors; they deterritorialize themes proximately ties to Latin American life to expose universal middle-class hypocrisy and political–historical injustice; and they combine horror's universal features to reveal the impure nature of Latin American genre film-making. Discontinuity reveals itself through portrayals of male psychopaths not yet 'caught up' to the realities of modern Latin American experience and women's irrevocable place in the latter. Through these films, the concept also reveals how contemporary Latin American life is no longer reduced to disparities between the 'foreign and national' or 'popular informality and bourgeois upward mobility', but rather how women's entrance into hegemonic society presents affronts to Latin America's accepted hegemony. Kraidy's critical transcultural approach to hybridity manifests in contrapuntal exchanges between text, context, experience and institutions in these films as well, in that everyday modes of Latin American experience are heightened through transnational narrative themes, local contexts, international partnerships and global viewerships, including regional box-office and international distribution success. Worth noting, however, are the ways in which these conceptualizations of hybridity evade the encoded gender roles and relations within the hybrid texts they otherwise seek to interrogate.

In this final sense, it is also clear that the abduction subgenre is new to, or has been recently resuscitated in, Latin American horror film-making. Moreover, the channels by which the films considered here have been made available, through streaming services such as Netflix and Amazon, increasingly characterize the ways Latin American horror is released globally and, to invoke Tudor, *which* kinds of films are availed to *which* kinds of audiences and at *which* junctures in our understanding of their reflection of Latin American life. It is therefore worth concluding that as Latin America's supernatural modes of horror recede into the distance, transnationally attractive subgenres such as the 'abduction' will not only mark future Latin American genre film-making but will also inform our social–political understandings of the region.

References

Alvaray, L. (2013). Hybridity and genre in transnational Latin American cinemas. *Transnational Cinemas, 4*(1), 67–87.

Anselmo-Sequeira, D. (2013). The country bleeds with a laugh: Social criticism meets horror genre in José Mojica Marins' 'A Meiia-Noite Levarei Sua Alma'. In D. Och & K. Strayer (Eds.), *Transnational Horror Across Visual Media: Fragmented Bodies*, 141–155. New York & London: Routledge.

Barrenechea, A. (2009). Hemispheric horrors: Celluloid vampires from the 'good neighbor' era. *Comparative American Studies, 7*(3), 225–237.

Clover, C. J. (1987). Her body, himself: Gender in the slasher film. In Representations, 20, Autumn, 1987 (pp. 187–228).

Cowan, G., & O'Brien, M. (1990). Gender and survival vs. death in slasher films: A content analysis. *Sex Roles, 23*(3/4), 187–196.

Cohen, D. (Director). (2015). *Luna de Miel* [Motion picture]. Argentina: Grotesque.

Creed, B. (1993). *The monstrous-feminine: Film, feminism, psychoanalysis.* London: Routledge.

Dapena, G. (2017). Genre films then and now. In M. D'Lugo, A. M. López, & L. Poldalsky (Eds.), *The Routledge companion to Latin American cinema* (pp. 150–162). London: Routledge.

Dhalia, H. (Director). (2009). *Adrift* [Motion picture]. Brazil: O2 Filmes.

Draper, J. A. III (2016). 'Materialist horror' and the portrayal of middle-class fear in recent Brazilian film drama: *Adrift* (2009) and *Neighbouring Sounds* (2012). *Studies in Spanish & Latin American Cinemas, 13*(2), 119–135.

Dunn, C. (2001). *Brutality garden: Tropicália and the emergence of a Brazilian counterculture.* Chapel Hill, NC: University of North Carolina Press.

Fernandes, A. A. (2002). Entre la démence et la transcendance: José Mojica Marins et le cinéma fantastique: José Mojica Marins e o cinema fantastico. *Cinémas d'Amérique Latine, 10*, 117–128.

Freeland, C. A. (1996). Feminist frameworks for horror films. In L. Eubank & M. Cohen (Eds.), *Film Theory and Criticism* (6th edition), (pp. 742–763). New York, NY: Oxford University Press.

García Bogliano, A. (Director). (2010). *Sudor Frío* [Motion picture]. Argentina: Pampa Films & Paura Flics.

García Bogliano, A. (Director). (2015). *Scherzo Diabolico* [Motion picture]. Mexico: F.

García Canclini, N. (1995). *Hybrid cultures: Strategies for entering and leaving modernity.* Minneapolis, MN: University of Minnesota Press.

García Canclini, N. (2000). Contradictory modernities and globalisation in Latin America. In V. Schelling (Ed.), *Through the kaleidoscope: The experience of modernity in Latin America* (pp. 37–52). London: Verso.

García Canclini, N. (2006). Hybrid culture, oblique powers. In M. G. Durham & D. M. Kellner (Eds.), *Media and cultural studies: KeyWorks* (pp. 422–444) (revised edition). Malden, MA: Blackwell.

García, E. (2014). Latino action heroes, strippers, and non-hegemonic miscegenation: Family apocalypse in Robert Rodriguez's Planet Terror. *Post Script—Essays in Film and the Humanities, 33*(3), 59–121.

Kraidy, M. (2002). Globalization of culture through the media. In J. R. Schement (Ed.), *Encyclopedia of communication and information* (Vol. 2, pp. 359–363). New York, NY: Macmillan Reference USA.

Kraidy, M. (2005). *Hybridity, or the cultural logic of globalization* (pp. 1–14). Philadelphia, PA: Temple University Press.

Kristeva, J. (1982). *Powers of horror: An essay on abjection.* New York, NY: Columbia University Press.

López, A. M. (1993). Are all Latins from Manhattan? Hollywood, ethnography and cultural colonialism. In J. King, A. M. López, & M. Alvarado (Eds.), *Mediating two worlds: Cinematic encounters in the Americas* (pp. 67–80). London: BFI Publishing.

Martín-Barbero, J. (1993). *Communication, culture and hegemony: From the media to mediations.* London: Sage.

Martín-Barbero, J. (2001). The process: From nationalisms to transnationals. In *Media and cultural studies: KeyWorks* (1st ed., pp. 626–657). Malden, MA: Blackwell.

Mendonça Filho, K. (Director). (2012). *Neighboring Sounds* [Motion picture]. Brazil: Hubert Bals Fund & CinemaScópio.

Mulvey, L. (1975). Visual pleasure and narrative cinema. *Screen, 16*(3), 6–18.

Rodriguez, R. (Director). (2007). *Planet Terror* [Motion picture]. New York, NY: Dimension Films.

Ruetalo, V., & Tierney, D. (2009). *Latsploitation, exploitation cinema, and Latin America*. New York, NY: Routledge.

Said, E. (1994). *Culture and imperialism*. London: Vintage.

Stephenson, W. (2011). Ritual of the sadists: The subversive horror cinema of José Mojica Marins. *Film Matters, 2*(3), 28–32.

St-Georges, C. (2016). Brazilian horrors past and present: José Mojica Marins and politics as reproductive futurism. *Journal of Latin American Cultural Studies, 25*(4), 555–570.

Subero, G. (2016). *Gender and sexulaity in Latin American horror cinema*. London: Palgrave Macmillan.

Syder, A., & Tierney, D. (2005). Mexploitation/exploitation: Or, how a crime-fighting, vampire-slaying Mexican wrestler almost found himself in an Italian sword-and-sandals epic. In S.J. Schneider & T. Williams (Eds.), *Horror International*, 33–55. Detroit, MI: Wayne State University Press.

Tierney, D. (2002). El terror en Elbesodelamujeraraha. *Revista Iberoamericana, 68*(199), 355–366.

Tierney, D. (2004). José Mojica Marins and the cultural politics of marginality in third world film criticism. *Journal of Latin American Cultural Studies, 13*(1), 63–78.

Tierney, D. (2014). Mapping cult cinema in Latin American film cultures. *Cinema Journal, 54*(1), Fall 2014, 129–135.

Tudor, A. (1997). Why horror? The peculiar pleasures of a popular genre. *Cultural Studies, 11*(3), 47–55.

Welsh, A. (2010). On the perils of living dangerously in the slasher horror film: Gender difference in the association between sexual activity and survial. *Sex Roles, 62*, 762–773.

Williams, L. (1991). Film bodies: Gender, genre, and excess. *Film Quarterly, 44*(4), 2–13.

Chapter 12

Misogyny or Commentary? Gendered Violence Outside and Inside *Captivity*

Shellie McMurdo and Wickham Clayton

Even before its release, *Captivity* (2007) was ostracized by critics and has largely been overlooked in horror scholarship. The film, however, stands as an example of late-phase torture horror, due to its emergence after the peak of popularity torture horror briefly enjoyed. Furthermore, it is a horror film that − unusually for its time of release − centralized a conflict between the sexes, pre-dating films such as *A Girl Walks Home Alone at Night* (2014) and *Raw* (2017), in their more overt feminist narratives. However, the assumption that *Captivity* is a flagrantly misogynistic film is glib, and this speculation on the film's content was due partially to its ill-advised advertisement campaign. This perception can also be linked to the film's alignment to the torture horror subgenre, which is thought to be overtly sexual and misogynistic in nature − an assumption we disagree with.

Captivity centres on Jennifer Tree (Elisha Cuthbert) − a model who is stalked, drugged and abducted, waking in a large underground cell. During her time in confinement, Jennifer is force fed, force-dressed and psychologically tortured. Jennifer discovers another captive, Gary (Daniel Gilles), who is ultimately revealed to be one of Jennifer's two captors, the other being Gary's brother, Ben (Pruitt Taylor Vince). After a violent confrontation, in which Gary proclaims his love for Jennifer, stabs his brother and shoots two police officers, he returns to Jennifer's cell where he 'rescues' her. Jennifer quickly realizes that she is one in a long line of captive females and the film closes with Jennifer killing Gary with a shotgun, before she escapes onto the street outside, finally free, but − as the camera pans up to show the audience − still under the watchful eye of her mediated billboard image.

Beginning by positioning *Captivity* as a continuation of its director, Roland Joffé's, previous work, this chapter will then move to outline the long and complex relationship that the horror genre has had with gender representations. This section will work to link our examination with previous established work on the slasher subgenre, of which torture horror is arguably a descendant. Previous work on the male gaze then allows us to explore the recurrent theme of the

Gender and Contemporary Horror in Film, 187–204
© **Shellie McMurdo and Wickham Clayton**
doi:10.1108/978-1-78769-897-020191013

mediated female form – and idealized female beauty – in *Captivity*, while our positioning of concepts of the 'Final Girl' and the male gaze as absolutely central to horror scholarship enables us to demonstrate how Cuthbert's Jennifer initially functions as a self-aware deconstruction of the final girl, before frustratingly ending the film as an archetypal representation of it.

Joffé, initially a television director,[1] established himself as a significant filmmaker with his first feature, *The Killing Fields* (1984), set amidst Pol Pot's Cambodian genocide. This British film earned recognition at America's prestigious industry awards through the Academy of Motion Picture Arts and Sciences. It earned nominations for Best Picture and Best Director, and won awards for Best Cinematography, Best Film Editing and Best Actor in a Supporting Role. This success was followed by the Anglo-Franco co-production *The Mission* (1986) featuring American mega-star[2] Robert De Niro. This film also went on to earn nominations for Best Director and Best Picture and winning the award for Best Cinematography.

These successes gave Joffé leverage to launch a career in Hollywood, which was met with lukewarm to negative reception. The 1989's *Shadow Makers* about the Manhattan Project was harshly criticized by Desson Howe (1989, n.p.) of *The Washington Post* who stated, 'Its effect is more innocuous than lethal, a cloud of un-drama wafted along by director Roland Joffe (sic).' More notable is Joffé's ill-received *The Scarlet Letter* (1995) adapted from Nathaniel Hawthorne's 1850 novel. According to Bruce Daniels (1999, p. 2), 'The movie lost nearly US$50 million and was considered a bomb from its first weekend of domestic sales through its foreign distribution and video cassette release. The public stayed away in droves.' Joffé never attained the success of his first two films prior to making *Captivity*, however, there is a distinct commonality amongst his films: an effort to redress the representational balance and tell stories that restore agency to traditionally maligned groups.

This is consistent with Joffé's first two pictures. *The Killing Fields*, while initially driven by white actor Sam Waterston, centres primarily and for much of the film on the non-professional actor Dr Haing S. Ngor who had experienced the horrors of the Khmer Rouge regime first-hand. Ngor's character in the film is, not unlike Jennifer in *Captivity*, captured, tortured and orchestrating his own escape. James Park (1984, p. 15) writes, '*The Killing Fields* is even more sharply distinguished from films about Vietnam made by American directors. It does not share the exclusively American orientation of such films as *The Deer Hunter* and *Apocalypse Now*, nor does it ever lose the human message in orgies of hardware or distracting allegory.' *The Mission*, while again centring on white characters played by De Niro and Jeremy Irons, fundamentally asks questions about

---

[1]This includes work on *Coronation Street* (ITV 1960–Present), *Crown Court* (ITV 1972–1984) and a BBC adaptation of Elizabethan playwright John Ford's '*Tis Pity She's a Whore* (1980).
[2]Whose contemporary celebrity status we happily verify via Bananarama's 1984 chart-topping single 'Robert De Niro's Waiting'.

the effect of colonization on indigenous people, and according to Joffé, attempts to answer in a way that gives the indigenous people agency:

> Because you hold the moral high ground, and because part of your moral high ground is to say, 'Modern civilization is bad; therefore, Indians shouldn't have it,' doesn't mean that you can afford to ignore the rights of the Indians. I think that's intensely paternalistic. What the film is arguing, and I think it argues it very clearly, is *they* will choose. They have the right to choose *and* they have the right to go against what you think is in their particular interest.
>
> Dempsey (1987, p. 7, emphasis in the original)

This illuminates a preoccupation with the concerns of minority groups; however, a particularly interesting case here, especially as regards representation and its implications for *Captivity*'s approach to gender, is *The Scarlet Letter*. Daniels' identification of (and outrage at) major historical misrepresentations and changes to Hawthorne's original novel is not entirely unjustified; the film contains a toothless attempt at reframing the focus on native Indians in a manner which Daniels addresses. However, most significant are the changes to the story's main character. Hester Prynne in the novel is subjected to the evils of a patriarchal society as the story builds towards tragedy. Joffé's Hester (Demi Moore), however, is bold, headstrong and overtly seeking her own sexual pleasure. Daniels (1999, pp. 3−4) argues, 'She is a wisecracking, confrontational feminist who injects gender into nearly every scene. Not only is this absurdly ahistorical, it is also unbelievable as propaganda and offensive to modern feminists.' To underline this, Daniels (1999, p. 4) writes, 'Being annoying and chippy to virtually every male or authority figure should not be made the litmus test for women's advocacy − especially when one has an aerobically sculpted body that is shown off at every opportunity. This feisty feminist is naked a lot.' This may have been written almost 20 years ago, but it does beg the question of what, exactly, Daniels thinks a feminist *should* do, and why, indeed, he is an expert here.[3] However, while quality is questionable, these adjustments made through adaptation are notable.

Joffé's decline in success is lamented by Robert Shail (2007, p. 113) who writes, 'Whatever reservations might be voiced about the commercial compromises inherent in his first two films, there was enough cinematic flair and liberal good intentions on show to suggest that Joffé should be capable of more work of real substance.' Cinematic flair remains unquestioned, but it is the liberal good intentions that, while consistent, seem largely forgotten particularly where *Captivity* is concerned. Misguided or not, Joffé's concern with minorities (within

---

[3]Daniels does not suggest, with or without research, what the best behaviour for a feminist is, or why he is qualified to make such an assertion.

the context of the western film industries) does not only extend to indigenous and non-white people, but to women as well as evinced by *The Scarlet Letter*. This concern, and these 'good intentions', is present in *Captivity*, a film within a genre that has its own complex relationship with gender representation.

The phrase 'torture porn' was coined by David Edelstein (2006) in his article detailing the emergence of the subgenre in *New York Magazine*. Edelstein expresses puzzlement at the rise in popularity of more visceral horror and laments the presence of 'viciously nihilistic' films in his local multiplex (rather than where we can assume he believes they belong, in back-alley fleapit cinemas and the sticky back pages of sordid magazines). Although Edelstein does not provide the reader with a definition for what constitutes as a torture porn film, including such disparate films as *The Passion of the Christ* (2004) and *Wolf Creek* (2005) in his assessment, attempts have been made since to define the exact characteristics of the subgenre.

Jeremy Morris (2010, p. 45), for example, notes that torture porn differs from other horror narratives in its lack of supernatural elements and suggests that it has instead a preferential focus on the brutality that human beings are willing to inflict on each other. Meanwhile, Luke Thompson (2008) defines the characteristics of the subgenre more simplistically, as being 'realistic horror about bad people who torture and kill'. Steve Jones's (2013, pp. 15–16) more nuanced definition of torture porn argues that films belonging to the subgenre will generally share two main qualities, '(a) they chiefly belong to the horror genre and (b) the narratives are primarily based around protagonists being imprisoned in confined spaces and subjected to physical and/or psychological suffering.'

If we return to Edelstein's article, we can also discern a curious gendered component to his thoughts on torture porn, such as when he rhetorically asks if watching these films is similar to the way that 'some women cut themselves (they say) to feel something'. In keeping with this interesting use of charged language, the use of the suffix '-porn' implies a latent sexual angle to these films, as does Edelstein's use of the word, due to his argument that the spurting blood in these films is equivalent to the ejaculatory 'money shot' of pornography. The coining of the term 'torture porn' therefore imbues the subgenre with an implied sexually gratifying angle, and this misconception can be seen in later journalistic responses to the subgenre. For example, in his review of *Captivity*, James Berardinelli (2007) warns his readers that in addition to the film being 'morally repugnant', that they should 'make no mistake about it – this is masturbation material for those who enjoy this sort of thing'.

The equation of the horror genre to pornography is not new, and torture porn is one of many horror subgenres to have had this comparison drawn against it. The slasher films of the 1980s for instance were compared to hardcore pornography by Janet Maslin (1982), in an article during which she also criticizes any female that is involved in the production or consumption of horror, as they 'should know better'. Indeed, the apparent inherent misogyny of horror cinema is something of a given in journalism, such as reports by Emine Saner (2007) and Nada Tawfik (2015) show, and as Cochrane (2007) generalizes in her article for *The Guardian* newspaper, the horror genre, and torture porn in particular, is a place where 'sex and extreme violence collide'.

Given this supposedly inescapable misogyny of the horror genre, it comes as no surprise that torture porn, perhaps due to the popularity it enjoyed in the first decade of the new millennium, has been criticized for its preferential focus on the suffering of its female characters (Cochrane, 2007; Griffiths, 2014). The film that is the focus of this chapter, *Captivity*, does indeed feature a young, attractive female as a main character who endures suffering. However, *Captivity* also attempts – not always successfully – to centralize a conflict between the sexes and their attendant characteristics, rather than focus on any sexualized aspects of Jennifer's torture.

Our preference towards the term 'torture horror' (as per Morris, 2010) rather than torture porn therefore is due to our mutual finding that the violence in torture horror is not any more sexual than that of other cinema and is certainly no more misogynistic. To support our argument, we cite a qualitative study carried out by Steve Jones of 45 'torture porn' films. In his sample group, Jones (2013, p. 133) found that the ratio of men killed compared to women was 244–108 (with an additional 293 incidences of serious injury committed on a male body to 144 incidences of comparable injuries to the female form). More interesting still, is Jones's findings relating to the aggressor of these incidents, with 206 incidents of males harming females, 155 incidences of females harming males and a comparatively large 351 incidents of men harming men. In terms of sexual violence, Jones notes that there were, in his sample, 67 acts of sexual violence, with 37 of these incidents happening off-screen. In addition, he notes there were 42 consensual sex acts in these films, with only half of these acts depicted on screen. It is clear that torture horror is inarguably a violent subgenre, and a graphic descendant of slasher films, splatter films, body horror and even further back, the Grand Guignol. But it would be inaccurate to say that torture horror is a particularly sexually charged subgenre.

Torture Horror, as a distinct subgenre of horror cinema, began to emerge in the early 2000s, with its progenitor arguably being *Saw* (2004),[4] a film which climaxes with a character carrying out a self-amputation of his foot with a hacksaw. The success of this film spawned a franchise which, as of 2017, still sees entries released. Writing before the release of *Jigsaw* (2017), the eighth instalment of the saga, Simon Thompson noted that the *Saw* franchise had grossed US$873.3 million worldwide, positioning the saga as one of the most financially successful horror series of all time.

In the wake of *Saw*, films followed such as *Hostel* (2005), *The Devil's Rejects* (2005) and *The Ruins* (2008), all featuring extended scenes of bodily suffering and gore. Reaching a peak in popularity around 2007, torture horror films began to be positioned as limit experiences, and the level of saturation the

---

[4]Though Edelstein among others, as stated, has included the earlier *The Passion of the Christ*.

subgenre achieved lead to its aesthetics entering mainstream consciousness, forming the basis of theme park thrill rides and mazes,[5] and with the term 'torture porn' being used in self-referential horror narratives such as *Scream 4* (2011).[6] The popularity of the subgenre also resulted in elements of its aesthetics appearing in non-horror films, such as a torture scene in *Casino Royale* (2006), or the brutal opening scenes of *Law Abiding Citizen* (2009). With the growth of the subgenre, there came a body of criticism towards it, with torture horror being described as 'morally repellent' (Queenan, 2007, p. 16), 'rancid [...] joyless' (Hornaday, 2008), 'cretinous' (Cashmore, 2010) and 'perverse' (Slotek, 2009). These potent and emotive terms suggested torture horror was something to be avoided, lest an un-cautious audience member become sucked into the depraved pit these films seemed to inhabit.

The phrase 'torture porn' itself has now become a signifier of bad quality, such as in assessments of the season seven premiere of *The Walking Dead* (2010−), where the violence shown was largely derided as 'just torture porn' (Kain, 2016), or in criticism of Darren Aronofsy's divisive film *Mother!* (2017), which was disparaged as a 'biblically infused version of torture porn' (Smith, 2017). Meanwhile, lists such as 'Pure Anguish: 10 Torturous Horror Films You Should Suffer Through' (Watercutter, 2012) suggest that torture horror films are something to be endured rather than enjoyed. More recently still, the release of serial killer drama *Hounds of Love* (2016), and the return of the *Saw* saga after seven years, has been met with numerous articles decrying a return to the popularity of torture porn aesthetics (Lee; 2017; White, 2017a), and although Steve Jones's monograph, *Torture Porn: Popular Horror after Saw* (2013), has gone some way to legitimizing the study of torture horror in film scholarship, it is still a relatively understudied area of film studies.

However, *Captivity* is of interest to us due to not only it's position at the end of the popularity enjoyed by the first wave of torture horror (if indeed, the release of *Hounds of Love* and *Jigsaw* is heralding a renewal of interest in the subgenre), but also as an intriguing forbear to more overly feminist horror texts in its attempt to, often falling frustratingly short, present a feminist torture horror film. An understanding of how *Captivity* accomplishes this can be established through relevant, arguably related, work on the Slasher subgenre.

---

[5]In the United Kingdom, Saw − The Ride is one such rollercoaster at Thorpe Park, which opened to the public in 2008, followed by the now seasonal opening of the Saw − Alive Horror Maze in 2010; in addition to this, there is the Snuffhouse experience in Blackburn. In America, torture porn aesthetics have formed the basis of multiple Halloween Horror Nights, such as the Hostel themed Universal Studios maze in 2011, which sought to 're-imagine the film's dehumanizing torture chambers' (Beard, 2011). A relatively new development is 'extreme experiences' like MacKamey Manor in California, a seven-hour ordeal before which patrons must sign a waiver form (Carroll & Ryan, 2015).

[6]In which the character of Trudie states that she 'hates all that torture porn shit'.

The concept of the 'Final Girl' has been widely disseminated throughout not only scholarship but also popular culture as well.[7] Furthermore, the concept of the male gaze, as introduced by Laura Mulvey, and more broadly the gaze itself, has been widely discussed as a key theoretical model in the reading of horror texts. Considering this is a publication specifically about horror and feminism/gender, we will not reiterate what the Final Girl is, nor 'the gaze' – discussions of which you can find in other chapters – but will instead establish key elements of these concepts, how they link to feminism and, particularly, how that relates to *Captivity*.[8]

In revisiting the idea of the Final Girl, Carol J. Clover, who is credited for having coined the term, feels it necessary to explicate the function of this particular character. Clover (1992/2015, p. xi) writes, 'The point is fear and pain – hers and, by proxy, ours.' Clover goes on to say that 'It is with the Final Girl's suffering that the film leads us to identify, and not only narratively, but cinematically' (Clover, 1992/2015, p. xi). Clover (1992/2015, p. x) clearly frames the position of the Final Girl not exactly as protagonist and closely qualifies the idea that she is the 'hero':

> 'Tortured survivor' might be a better term than 'hero'. Or, given the element of last-minute luck (she happens, in her flailing, on a cup of hot coffee or some other such item, which she throws into her assailant's eyes), 'accidental survivor.' Or, as I call her, 'victim-hero,' with an emphasis on 'victim.'

It is therefore notable that Clover, while finding it unique that slashers create a locus for male viewers to willingly identify with a female character, establishes that the success of that character is less important than the fact that we see her suffer.

This recent overview by Clover is useful to establish not only a clear summary and clarification of this character's position within any narrative, but also to establish that the author maintains this view. Janet Staiger, however, has undertaken an extensive analysis of a large selection of slasher films, including a range of tables establishing statistical support for her arguments. Through this method of data collection and analysis, Staiger finds problems with Clover's arguments, including the figure of the Final Girl. Staiger (2015, p. 222) claims that, while Clover makes much of the fact that the Final Girl is masculine or at least masculine-feminine, 'They may be quite feminine.' Furthermore, Staiger argues that these feminine Final Girls learn from and are supported by the men around them, as well as women and children. Staiger writes, 'They learn from those people so that they do take control of their battle with the killer' (Staiger, 2015,

---

[7]See the 2015 slasher spoof *The Final Girls* (dir. Todd Strauss-Schulson).

[8]Wickham Clayton (2015, p. 11) establishes torture horror as an aesthetic and narrative trend within the development of the slasher film, and we here use theory surrounding slasher films to explore the elements of this particular film.

p. 222). So, while suffering, torture and pain may be the focus, Clover's assertion that the Final Girl is purely extant for victimization and does not have the where-withal to forcefully despatch the killer, or torturer, is contestable. In fact, Staiger (2015, p. 225) argues that the framing of the 'monster' may reverse: 'Yet, I would point out that in becoming these aggressors, the Final Girl also becomes, non-normal, a monster and, while adult, contradictorily also associated with the abject, the other side of "now", a terrible place of loss and death.'

This becomes problematic from a feminist perspective according to Rebecca Stringer. In writing of revenge/vigilante narratives, particularly *The Brave One* (2007) where the avenger has been framed as victim (admittedly of sexual violence in her case studies), Stringer (2011, p. 280) states that such narratives 'distort the political spirit of feminist anti-violence efforts, suggesting that feminists are for the counter-violence of vigilantism when, Valerie Solanis notwithstanding, they generally are not.' This observation is useful here particularly, where *Captivity* does contain elements of sexual violence. Although the response to violence by the Final Girl in this film is one of survival, of making an effort to escape with her life, the viewer is granted the opportunity to indulge in the satisfaction and pleasure of attacking the attackers. However, the violence assumed by the killer(s) as well as the victim(s) is deeply entrenched in the way that the gaze works and functions within these films.

The significance of the gaze is often reduced to the key tenet of the person who controls the gaze has the power. Clover distinguishes between the 'assaultive', or masculine, and the 'reactive' or feminine gaze. Extending psychoanalytic thinking, Clover (1992/2015, p. 182) asserts that 'horror movies are obsessively interested in the thought that the simple act of staring can terrify, maim, or kill its object – that a hard look and a hard penis (chain saw, knife, power drill) amount to one and the same thing' [parenthesis in the original]. This is further explored (and more widely applied) by Barbara Creed (2005, p. 200) who, in considering Jack the Ripper as a phallic monster, and by our inference male slashers, writes that films featuring this figure:

> draw upon the horrified uncanny gaze that was created by the cinema and remained central to the nature of cinematic looking throughout the twentieth century. Deployed in relation to scenarios that traverse moral and bodily boundaries and invoke the threat of the uncanny, this gaze is central to the formation of the horror genre.

Both Clover and Creed acknowledge the male, phallic, assaultive gaze as central to horror broadly, and to slasher killers particularly, with Clover (1992/2015, p. 184) arguing that this gaze may inhabit the woman, but not comfortably.

The reactive gaze, however, is reserved for the woman, and by extension the viewer, in line with Clover's complex thinking about the relationship and identification between audience and horror's 'victim-heroes'. According to Clover (1992/2015, p. 200):

Certainly horror plays repeatedly and overtly on the equation between the plight of the victim and the plight of the audience. Whatever else it may be, the ploy of showing us an about-to-be-attacked woman watching a horror film depicting an about-to-be-attacked woman is also a clear metacinematic declaration of our common spectatorial plight.

In other words, seeing with and as a vulnerable woman foregrounds the viewer's vulnerability as well — as an object for assault, for attack, for penetration, both in the body through identification and in the eyes through viewing.

In *Captivity*, work on the gaze crosses over into an understanding of receiving the gaze in visual culture. Laura Wilson (2015, p. 97) highlights a significant element of the film's narrative, writing that, as Jennifer is forced to watch videos of other women being tortured with the awareness that this will happen to her, 'Torture, therefore, becomes a process of the gaze, suggesting a critical stance towards cinematic spectatorship.' It is therefore useful to highlight Laura Mulvey's (1989/2009, p. 35) assertion that 'for women (from childhood onwards) trans-sex identification is a *habit* that very easily becomes *second nature*. However, this Nature does not sit easily and shifts restlessly in its borrowed transvestite clothes' [emphasis in the original]. Gaylyn Studlar confronts and reworks the way Mulvey and others have theorized how the viewer receives the gaze, especially as regards masochism. Studlar (1984/2000, p. 215) concludes that 'The spectator must comprehend the images, but the images cannot be controlled. On this level of pleasure, the spectator receives, but no object-related demands are made.' Therefore, the process of torture in the film is closely linked to, via Mulvey, the habit of uncomfortably adopting a trans-sex identification, and via Studlar, being an object for forced reception.

This brief overview is important to establish as Clover's work on the Final Girl and the gaze in horror are central to the function of *Captivity* as well as engaging with a reading of gender in the film. While Clover's work has been subjected to some re-evaluation, some of these core ideas are useful in the way that this film is understood, both as a challenge to gender representations in torture horror, as well as a flawed challenge to gender representation. *Captivity*'s approach is complex, and while not wholly successful, useful as a point for discourse to understand the way it challenges long-held tropes of horror, slashers and torture horror.

Mark Kermode (2007), British film critic and horror cinema aficionado, called *Captivity* a 'loathsome car crash of a movie', as well as an example of 'vulgar opportunism', puzzling 'what the hell happened' to Roland Joffé, while Owen Gleiberman (2007) of *Entertainment Weekly* dismissed Capivity as a '*Saw* clone'. Most relevantly for this chapter's discussion, Joe Leydon (2007) of *Variety* magazine predicted that the film was 'destined to be better remembered for its grisly billboard imagery than for its relatively tame torture-porn tropes', before calling it 'a thoroughly nasty piece of work'. The billboard advertising campaign for *Captivity* is of central importance to this chapter, as its use of torture porn aesthetics led to a pre-judgement of the film, and an assumption around its content, much the same as how the term 'torture porn' implies the content of these films with no reference to their actual themes.

After being screened at Sitges Film Festival in 2006, as a thriller, *Captivity* was subjected to extensive reshoots and editing, with scenes of gore added in, perhaps to capitalize on the popularity of torture horror at the time (Floyd, 2007; Miller, 2009; Scheck, 2007). However, the timing of the film's release, with torture horror's popularity waning, resulted in *Captivity* being cited as the film that essentially marked the end of audience's thirst for torture horror. We therefore posit it may have been more a matter of advertising misfires and a missed zeitgeist that lead to the film's lack of success and subsequent ill-repute.

The billboard campaign for *Captivity* features four stages of torture inflicted on a female victim. These stages are abduction, confinement, torture and termination. The 'abduction' poster shows a female face in extreme close-up, with only half her face visible, her eye staring out of the frame, at her audience. A finger, clad in what appears to be a black medical style glove, further obscures her features. The 'confinement' poster shows the same female face, but behind a wire fence. In this poster, the female's tearstained visage looks out imploringly at her audience while her bloodied fingers grip the wire of the fence. In the 'torture' poster, the female's face is again partially obscured, this time by bandages covering the majority of her face and the seemingly blood-filled tubes emerging from her nostrils. Again in this poster, her eyes look pointedly out of the frame at her audience, her mouth agape. The final poster, entitled 'termination', shows what we must assume to be the same female, now deceased, laying with her head lolling off a metal surface. Her mouth and nose are visible, but her eyes, which in the other posters were a central feature, are out of frame.

The public display of these posters was met with controversy, with self-proclaimed feminist Joss Whedon heading a campaign to have the posters removed from public billboards. There was also a mobilization of public outcry in the form of a telephone complaint campaign to Lionsgate, *Captivity*'s distribution company (Grossberg, 2007; Gurwitch, 2007). On his personal website, Whedon (2007) compared the posters' treatment of women to the honour killing of 17-year-old Du'a Khalil Aswad and goes on to note that the advertisements were 'part of a cycle of violence and misogyny that takes something away from the people who have to see it'. Whedon went on to criticize the torture horror subgenre as a whole, stating 'the advent of torture porn and the total dehumanizing not just of women (but they always come first) but of all human beings has made horror a largely unpalatable genre'.[9]

---

[9]These emotive comments and the spearheading of the anti-advertising campaign by Whedon are intriguing when viewed in light of the recent controversy regarding Whedon's own treatment of women, especially with the statements made by his now ex-wife Kai Cole (2017), who notes that 'he used his relationship with me as a shield [...] so no one would question his relationships with other women or scrutinize his writing *as anything other than feminist*' (emphasis added). This later controversy brings a sliver of contradiction to Whedon's crusade against this campaign and his self-proclaimed 'woke bae' (White, 2017b) status.

In spite of its reputation, when compared to other torture horror films such as *Hostel*, or any of the *Saw* films, *Captivity* is relatively tame both in its use of graphic gore and the number of torture scenes featured in the film. If we are to take the term 'torture' as meaning the act of deliberately inflicting psychological or physical pain on a restrained person, then there are seven scenes in the film which come under the bracket of torture. In keeping with Steve Jones's findings regarding gendered violence in torture horror, we can confirm that the worst of the film's violence is from males and inflicted on males. For example, to use the film's own parlance, in terms of 'termination', *Captivity* details the death of one female (off screen) in comparison to five males. And although the film features extended scenes of Jennifer being restrained and an instance of forced feeding – where body parts are put in a blender and the resulting purée is funnelled into her mouth clearly against her wishes – she actually comes to little physical harm during the film. The criticism of the film therefore seems to stem from the assumed brutality and assumed gendered violence of its content based on the billboard campaign images, and its self-aware (and potentially, for the film-maker's, mistaken) positioning as a film belonging to the torture horror sub-genre, and therefore, a misogynistic horror film. In order to explore how *Captivity* considers gender more fully, a close analysis of the content of *Captivity* demonstrates the complexity of representation within the film.

Cuthbert's Jennifer functions in narratively and characterologically similar ways to Clover's – and therefore Staiger's revised – 'Final Girl'. Under Joffé's direction, however, there is a distinctive self-awareness which undercuts many of the inherent problems of misogyny evoked by the archetype. This self-awareness, while providing greater complexity, ultimately begins to re-service the Final Girl trope, but not without some notable restructuring at the outset.

There are two views of Jennifer at the start of the film – as subject and as object, and these views are coded in visually clear ways. As subject, Jennifer herself is part of the mise-en-scène. However, when Jennifer appears as object it is not her, but an image of her which is part of the mise-en-scène. Jennifer, as a subject and narrative agent prior to her capture, is shown 'unfiltered' (conceptually and diegetically – an imperfect concept as the film itself is a reproduced image). The first shots of her without a buffer between herself and the camera are extreme close ups of her putting on make-up prior to a photo shoot. The first shot is of her mouth as red lip paint is applied. The lighting and focus captures the details of her skin: pores, small hairs below the mouth and the strings of tacky paint as the applicator is lifted from her lip. Next, a three-quarter shot of her eye as eyeshadow is brushed on, again, pores and small hairs dot the frame. Finally, her other eye to the camera, with slight wrinkles around the eye as her mascara is applied. While the make-up enhances certain features, the natural contours of the young woman's face, of a person's skin, are not covered or removed, as they are in the photographs taken during her shoot, or in the foot-age filmed by her stalker as he (and the stalker as per Clover's slasher conventions is absolutely a 'he') follows and films her. Jennifer's face is further shown in close-up both during and after the shoot, her natural features, including a small youthful pimple on her chin, again apparent.

Jennifer as object is not herself captured by Joffé's camera. She is instead shown on the cover of a magazine the stalker glances at, on advertisements on the sides of buses, on the instant digital renderings during the modelling shoot and through the viewscreen of the stalker's digital camera. Within these images, she has no agency, she is captured and her image manipulated to fit the needs of those reproducing her image. This she has no control over, and significantly, her natural pores, hairs and lines are removed for, one assumes, increased 'perfection'. Joffé attempts to capture Jennifer (or rather Cuthbert) *as she is*, and juxtaposes this with images of *how others want her*. This appears to be a way of distinguishing between the film's ethos and the ethos of the world of the film.

There is a recurrent theme in the film of mediated images of beauty. For instance, early in the film when Jennifer first awakens in her 'holding room', she is next to what appears to be a window looking towards a beautiful beach, where a lone palm tree moves in the breeze. This image is quickly revealed to be illusory. Jennifer's own mediated image is also shown throughout the narrative as an object of beauty. In addition to a large poster bearing her face near her bed, her image can also be seen in the archival interview footage that is used to mock her, through the CCTV camera in her room, or through the glass behind which she first appears to apparent fellow captive Gary, her beauty untouchable to him. There is a line of commentary constant throughout the film, although often clumsily wrought, around the commodification of not only Jennifer's body, but also of the female form more generally by the male gaze. This is shown in a scene where the audience become aware that Gary is in fact one of Jennifer's captors, as after he has sex with her, he walks out of their confining rooms and speaks to his brother, Ben. The brothers are recording Jennifer's captivity, with Ben having just watched Gary and Jennifer's lovemaking. After a brief conversation about their respective roles in Jennifer's capture, torture, seduction and implied eventual demise, Gary asks his sibling if he has ever wanted to swap roles, in order to experience having sex with the women they capture. Ben responds that he feels he already does experience this vicariously through his brother, because, as he tells Gary 'If you're inside her, I'm inside her.'

It is not only Jennifer's image that sets the film apart from more generic offerings, but her behaviour. The film refuses to overtly give in to what Kim Newman (1988/2011, p. 203) refers to as 'The Idiot Plot'. This is a device which 'demands that, in order to build up suspense and justify the horror sequences, all the characters act like idiots' [10] (Newman, 1988/2011, p. 203). *Captivity* does not succumb to such lazy narration. In fact, Joffé seems to take great pains to avoid making Jennifer appear in any way complicit with either her capture or retention, unlike the films where Newman perceives pleasure is to be derived from an ability to condescendingly de-empathize and ultimately blame the victim for

---

[10]Newman's (1988/2011, p. 203) preferred example is *Friday the 13th* (1980), which 'is full of people wandering off into the darkness on the lookout for a nice, secluded spot where the killer can polish them off'.

their demise. Furthermore, any choices she makes that lead to her capture and after are not only reasonable, but generous and self-valuing. The interview snippets of Jennifer that she is shown are similarly neither presented as being chosen at random nor is an interview ever left to play in full. Each snippet is implied to have been carefully curated by her captors, to place an emphasis on aspects of Jennifer's personality as presented in interviews (much is made of her coldness for example). At one point, Jennifer is shown an interview clip where she notes 'I like the attention', hinting at her captor's belief that his attention towards Jennifer is not unwanted, and that Jennifer was 'asking for it'. Another interview snippet shows Jennifer stating 'beauty opens doors, it always has and always will'. The playing of this particular interview snippet is followed by a threat being made towards Jennifer's beauty.[11] In this scene, Jennifer is made to believe that acid will be showered onto her face after being forced to watch a video where this torture is carried out on an unnamed female. Jennifer faints, and wakes up back in her room, with bandages concealing the presumed damage to her face. This turns out to be a trick, in keeping with the psychological rather than physical torture of Jennifer, when she removes the bandages she finds her beauty untarnished, save for a crude piece of special effects latex make-up — which she peels off.

Leading up to her capture, Joffé establishes empathy with Jennifer. The film shows her on the phone, presumably with an agent, discovering that she expected to get a day off of work (reinforcing that modelling is not her identity, simply a useful source of income), and establishing a tender relationship with 'the only person that loves her' — her pet dog, the latter being used as a form of torture later in the film. Finally, she arrives at a club where she is stalked and kidnapped. Although she arrives alone, she is seen waiting in the club and receives an email which reveals she was expecting to meet someone there who has just cancelled. Her martini is drugged, but not because she leaves it with somebody else, but because the drug is placed in the drink as the waitress's back is turned before she brings it to her table. As Jennifer begins to feel strange, she collects her purse and dog — not leaving either behind with somebody else — to go to the restroom; a reasonable response to the situation. Unfortunately, the restroom is in an isolated corridor where she is knocked out before waking in her cell. Furthermore, upon realizing her predicament, she does everything evident to attempt escape, all of which has unfortunately been identified previous to her captivity. Jennifer is not a passive captive, and her first act of defiance in the film is to throw the beauty products placed on a table in her room on the floor, rejecting the femininity her captor apparently desires from her. She also rejects the tight clothes and high heels her captor wants her to wear, however she does eventually acquiesce to wearing these, due to an extended aural assault from the speakers placed in her room. The climax of the film sees Jennifer finally

---

[11]There is something of a trope of informed attractiveness at play here. Elisha Cuthbert has frequently been ranked highly in annual 'hottest women' lists for men's magazines such as *FHM* and *Maxim*.

being able to change out of these restrictive garments and instead put on a shirt and trousers coded as more masculine, or androgynous, the clothes swamping her small frame and erasing her female silhouette.

As Jennifer realizes that Gary is not who he purports to be, he corners her in the kitchen, where she is shown barefoot next to a dead body and cleaning products. Gary asks Jennifer to show him that she belongs to him, and she begins to clean on her hands and knees, before using a cleaning spray, coded here as a marker of female domesticity – given that Jennifer is quite literally 'barefoot in the kitchen' – to temporarily disable Gary, and return to the site of her suffering, her basement prison. In this final sequence of the film, Gary taunts Jennifer about her ability to wield and use a gun, with him at one point gaining control of the weapon, straddling Jennifer and running the barrel of the gun over her face and mouth. Jennifer does, however, finally shoot Gary in the groin, relieving him of his other 'weapon', before shooting and destroying the poster of herself that the audience first saw near the beginning of the film. It is only when, therefore, Jennifer violently destroys and rejects this image of her commodified beauty that she is able to make a serious attempt to escape. Here, the overt commentary of earlier in the film does ultimately devolve into common tropes of the slasher – weapon/phallus conflation which is made explicit through the literal emasculation of Gary, as well as the masculinization of the feminine in order to defeat the masculine. These tropes sit uncomfortably with the seeming feminist setup of the narrative, but the film's self-awareness presents some refreshing, if incomplete, progress.

It is clear that from the outset, and through the setup, Joffé makes the effort to create a female character, and Final Girl, worthy of empathy (as though characters need earn it), and also one whose only 'crime' is being an attractive and desirable woman. A woman who we later discover is subjected to violence and torture at the hands of men who only value the beauty seen through her objectified image, willing to discard her once their male sexual dominance and superficial desires have been sated. It is clearly the men who are the problem. Not the woman. Not Jennifer.

In conclusion, whether it is agreed that the torture horror subgenre is necessarily linked to the Slasher or not, the Final Girl archetype is still alive and well in *Captivity*. However, this function appears to be initially deconstructed, then ultimately reinforced. This is simultaneously progressive (an awareness of the Final Girl trope allows divergence and commentary upon its problematic elements) and reactionary (ultimately adhering to a traditional depiction of a woman in distress, who succeeds by morphing into a man). Whether or not *Captivity* belongs to the torture horror subgenre, or was placed in that category due to the inserted scenes of gore and the infamous advertising campaign, it is clear that torture horror suffers from the weight of (non) viewers' assumptions. That the subgenre is impenetrably misogynistic, and 'women-hating', appears simply untrue for this film, as could be argued about most of the films falling under the torture horror banner. In these texts made firmly within a culture of patriarchy, there is sometimes some critical awareness and cultural challenge on display of said culture in these, or at least this, film.

References

Beard, L. (2011). 'Hostel' hits Universal Studios. *Entertainment Weekly*, July 28. Retrieved from http://www.ew.com/article/2011/07/28/hostel-univeral-studios-theme-park-maze/. Accessed on December 13, 2017.

Berardinelli, J. (2007). 'Captivity'. *Reel Views*. Retrieved from http://www.reelviews.net/. Accessed on January 06, 2018.

Carroll, R., & Ryan, M. (2015). 'Extreme haunted houses: Inside the real life kingdom of masochists.' *The Guardian*, October 30. Retrieved from https://www.theguardian.com/lifeandstyle/2015/oct/30/extreme-haunted-house-masochists-mckamey-manor. Accessed on January 29, 2018.

Cashmore, P. (2010). 'Will this new movie kill of torture porn for good?' *The Guardian*, August 28. Retrieved from http://www.theguardian.com/film/2010/aug/20/torture-porn-frightfest-quiz. Accessed on January 11, 2018.

Clayton, W. (2015). Introduction: The collection awakens. In W. Clayton (Ed.), *Style and form in the hollywood slasher film* (pp. 1–14). Houndmills: Palgrave Macmillan.

Clover, C. J. (1992/2015). *Men, women, and chain saws: Gender in the modern horror film*. Princeton, NJ: Princeton University Press.

Cochrane, K. (2007). For your entertainment. *The Guardian*, May 1. Retrieved from http://www.theguardian.com/film/2007/may/01/gender.world. Accessed on January 06, 2018.

Cole, K. (2017). Joss Whedon is a "hypocrite preaching feminist ideals": Ex-wife Kai Cole says (guest blog). *The Wrap*, November 22. Retrieved from https://www.thewrap.com/joss-whedon-feminist-hypocrite-infidelity-affairs-ex-wife-kai-cole-says/. Accessed on January 11, 2018.

Creed, B. (2005). *Phallic panic: Film, horror and the primal uncanny*. Carlton: Melbourne University Press.

Daniels, B. (1999). Bad movie/worse history: The 1995 unmaking of *The Scarlet Letter. Journal of Popular Culture, (Spring)*, *32*(4), Arts Premium Collection, 1–11.

Dempsey, M. (1987). Light shining in darkness: Roland Joffe on "The Mission". *Film Quarterly*, (Summer), *40*(4), 2–11.

Edelstein, D. (2006). Now playing at your local multiplex: Torture porn. *New York Magazine online*, January 01. Retrieved from http://nymag.com/movies/features/15622/. Accessed on November 21, 2017.

Floyd, N. (2007). 'Could critics of 'torture porn' at least watch the movies?' *Time Out*, June 20.

Gleiberman, O. (2007). Captivity. *Entertainment Weekly*, July 18. Retrieved from http://www.ew.com/article/2007/07/18/captivity/. Accessed on January 11, 2018.

Griffiths, E. (2014). Tortured, slashed, and raped: Why horror films are completely anti-feminist. *SoFeminine.co.uk*, October 7. Retrieved from https://www.sofeminine.co.uk/news-celebrities-tortured-slashed-raped-why-horror-films-are-completely-anti-feminis1046213.html. Accessed on January 11, 2018.

Grossberg, J. (2007). Controversial Captivity posters pulled. *E News*, March 20. Retrieved from http://www.eonline.com/news/54688/controversial-captivity-posters-pulled. Accessed on January 11, 2018.

Gurwitch, A. (2007). Scary movie: Captivity's ad campaign. *The Nation*, May 9. Retrieved from https://www.thenation.com/article/scary-movie-captivitys-ad-campaign/. Accessed on January 11, 2018.

Hornaday, A. (2008). 'Untraceable': Snared in its own sordid trap. *Washington Post*, January 25. Retrieved from http://www.washingtonpost.com/wp-dyb/content/article/2008/01/24/AR2008012402997.html. Accessed on January 11, 2018.

Howe, D. (1989). '*Fat man and little boy*' (Review). *The Washington Post*, October 20. Retrieved from http://www.washingtonpost.com/wp-srv/style/longterm/movies/videos/fatmanandlittleboypg13howe_a0b238.htm. Accessed on October 25, 2017.

Jones, S. (2013). *Torture porn: Popular horror after saw*. New York, NY: Palgrave MacMillan.

Kain, E. (2016). 'The Walking Dead': Season 7, Episode 1 review: The wrath of Negan. *Forbes*, October 23. Retrieved from https://www.forbes.com/sites/erikkain/2016/10/23/the-walking-dead-season-7-episode-1-review-the-wrath-of-negan/#1d73ef797796. Accessed on January 11, 2018.

Kermode, M. (2007). Captivity. *The Guardian*, June 24. Retrieved from https://www.theguardian.com/film/2007/jun/24/drama.thriller. Accessed on January 11, 2018.

Lee, B. (2017). Saw too much: Why the horror genre doesn't need a torture porn comeback. *The Guardian*, October 24. Retrieved from https://www.theguardian.com/film/2017/oct/24/saw-too-much-why-the-horror-genre-doesnt-need-a-torture-porn-comeback. Accessed on January 11, 2018.

Leydon, J. (2007). Captivity. *Variety*, July 23. Retrieved from http://variety.com/2007/film/markets-festivals/captivity-1200557854/. Accessed on January 12, 2018.

Maslin, J. (1982). Bloodbaths debase movies and audiences. *New York Times*, November 21, p. 13.

Miller, R. (2009). 10 movie events that shaped the decade (for movie fans). *Screen Rant*, December 21. Retrieved from https://www.screenrant.com/10-movies-decade/. Accessed on January 11, 2018.

Morris, J. (2010). The justification of torture horror: Retribution and sadism in saw, hostel, and the devil's rejects. In T. Fahy (Ed.), *The philosophy of horror*. Lexington, KY: University Press of Kentucky.

Mulvey, L. (1989/2009). *Visual and other pleasures (second edition)*. Houndmills: Palgrave Macmillan.

Newman, K. (1988/2011). *Nightmare movies: Horror on screen since the 1960s*. London: Bloomsbury.

Park, J. (1984). Bombs and Pol Pot. *Sight and Sound* (Winter), *54*(1), 14—16.

Queenan, J. (2007). Slash 'n' Burn. *The Guardian*, June 2. Retrieved from https://www.theguardian.com/film/2007/jun/02/features16.theguide4. Accessed on January 11, 2018.

Saner, E. (2007). Everything but the ghoul. *The Guardian*, April 6. Retrieved from https://www.theguardian.com/film/2007/apr/06/2. Accessed on January 12, 2018.

Scheck, F. (2007). Genre cleverness eludes "Captivity". *Reuters*, July 16. Retrieved from http://www.reuters.com/article/film-film-captivity-dc/genre-cleverness-eludes-captivity-idUSN1340593720070716. Accessed on January 11, 2018.

Shail, R. (2007). *British film directors: A critical guide*. Edinburgh: Edinburgh University Press.

Slotek, J. (2009). Collector missing a big piece — The plot. *The Toronto Sun*, May 29.

Smith, K. (2017). Jennifer Lawrence's Grotesque spoof of the nativity. *National Review*, September 14. Retrieved from http://www.nationalreview.com/article/451338/jennifer-lawrence-mother-sickest-movie-ever-made-disgusting-torure-porn. Accessed on January 12, 2018.

Staiger, J. (2015). The slasher, the final girl, and the anti-denouement. In W. Clayton (Ed.), *Style and form in the Hollywood slasher film* (pp. 213–228). Houndmills: Palgrave Macmillan.

Stringer, R. (2011). From victim to vigilante: Gender, violence and revenge in *The Brave One* (2007) and *Hard Candy* (2005). In H. Radner & R. Stringer (Eds.) *Feminism at the movies: Understanding gender in contemporary popular cinema* (pp. 268–282). London: Routledge.

Studlar, G. (1984/2000). Masochism and the perverse pleasures of the cinema. In E. Ann Kaplan (Ed.), *Feminism and film* (pp. 203–225). Oxford: Oxford University Press.

Tawfik, N. (2015). Are horror films inherently sexist? *BBC.com*, August 5. Retrieved from http://www.bbc.com/culture/story/20150805-are-horror-films-inherently-sexist

Thompson, L. (2008). Bad blood. *LA Weekly*, January 3.

Thompson, S. (2017). The 13 highest-grossing horror film franchises of all time at the U.S box office. *Forbes*, October 6. Retrieved from https://www.forbes.com/sites/simonthompson/2017/10/06/the-highest-grossing-horror-film-franchises-of-all-time-at-the-u-s-box-office-2/2/#6b7150b73b77. Accessed on December 13, 2017.

Watercutter, A. (2012). Pure anguish: 10 torturous horror films you should suffer through. *Wired.com*, October 27. Retrieved from https://www.wired.com/2012/10/10-best-torture-films/. Accessed on January 11, 2018.

Whedon, J. (2007). Let's watch a girl get beaten to death. *Whedonesque.com*, May 19. Retrieved from http://www.whedonesque.com/comments/13271

White, A. (2017a). Torture porn? True crime exploitation? Or both? Why Hounds of Love could be the most disturbing film of the year. *The Telegraph*, July 26. Retrieved from http://www.telegraph.co.uk/films/0/torture-porn-true-crime-exploitation-hounds-love-could-disturbing/. Accessed on January 11, 2008.

White, A. (2017b). Five times Joss Whedon, self-proclaimed 'woke bae', blew his feminist credentials. *The Telegraph*, August 21. Retrieved from http://www.telegraph.co.uk/tv/0/joss-whedon-5-times-blew-feminist-credentials/. Accessed on January 15, 2018.

Wilson, L. (2015). *Spectatorship, embodiment and physicality in the contemporary mutilation film*. Houndmills: Palgrave Macmillan.

Music

Bananarama (1984) 'Robert De Niro's Waiting' In: *Bananarama*, London Records, LP.

Filmography

A Girl Walks Home Alone at Night (2014, dir. Amirpour).
The Brave One (2007, dir. Jordan).
Captivity (2007, dir. Joffé).

Casino Royale (2006, dir. Campbell).
The Devil's Rejects (2005, dir. Zombie).
The Final Girls (2015, dir. Straus-Schulson).
Friday the 13th (1980, dir. Cunningham).
Hostel (2005, dir. Roth).
Hounds of Love (2016, dir. Young).
Jigsaw (2017, dir. Speirig and Speirig).
The Killing Fields (1984, dir. Joffé).
Law Abiding Citizen (2009, dir. Gray).
The Mission (1986, dir. Joffé).
Mother! (2017, dir. Aronofsky).
The Passion of the Christ (2004, dir. Gibson).
Raw (2016, dir. Docournau).
The Ruins (2008, dir. Smith).
Saw (2004, dir. Wann).
The Scarlet Letter (1995, dir. Joffé).
Scream 4 (2011, dir. Craven).
Shadow Makers (1989, dir. Joffé).
The Walking Dead (2010–).
Wolf Creek (2005, dir. McLean).

Chapter 13

"My Name Is Alice. And I Remember *Everything*." Project Alice and Milla Jovovich in the *Resident Evil* Films

Steven Gerrard

Up until the turn of the millennium, there had been very little representation of women and women action characters in action movies. That domain belonged, in the main, to muscular, often monosyllabic actors/characters such as Sylvester Stallone, Arnold Schwarzenegger, Chuck Norris, Jean-Claude van Damme, Bruce Willis, Kurt Russell, Steven Seagal and Wesley Snipes. Film franchises like *The Terminator* (1984–date), *Predator* (1987–date) and *Die Hard* (1988–2013), with their spectacular set-pieces, convoluted narratives (in which the hero, his family, countless innocent bystanders, street blocks, whole cities and even the world were threatened) and brutish, violent scenes have almost always been incredibly popular at the box office. Products of their time, they reflected the American policies of then-President Ronald Reagan and George Bush, where America's expansionist aims were clearly in evidence, most notably in the characters themselves. For example, in *Die Hard*, Bruce Willis' character (John McClane) represents the American sheriff fending off the crooked 'outsider' Hans Gruber (played by Alan Rickman), whilst Sylvester Stallone's John Rambo may have run from the law in the superior anti-Vietnam thriller *First Blood* (1982, dir. Ted Kotcheff); he later flexed his Republican-themed muscles in *Rambo: First Blood Part II* (1985, dir. George P. Cosmatos) and *Rambo III* (1988, dir. Peter MacDonald), as Chuck Norris saved America from the communist threat in *Invasion USA* (1985, dir. Joseph Zitto).[1]

The drive of the Hollywood industrial machine, once the action genre really came into its own in the 1980s through movies like the 'Rambo' films, created a

---

[1]See Jeffords (1993); Tasker (1993).

Gender and Contemporary Horror in Film, 205–218
© **Steven Gerrard**
doi:10.1108/978-1-78769-897-020191014

whole genre in its own right. Like the Western before it, the action movie genre celebrated the lone hero fighting injustice in a brutal, capitalist-oriented world. There were no action women in these films. Rather, the female stayed at home, looked after children, cooked, cleaned, sometimes also held down a job and was either left to watch the hero wander 'into a whole world of hate' as one soldier remarks in *Predator*, or became part of that world through being kidnapped by the villain. That the action movie eventually turned towards more horror-like elements seemed a natural step for a genre already set with one foot in the past, whilst trying to look for new avenues for its hero's adventures. For example, John Carpenter's *The Thing* (1982) is not an action movie *per se* but has all the elements of action coupled with science fiction and horror overtones. The same can be said of Central-American-jungle-set *Predator* (1987, dir. John McTiernan) and its Los Angeles-suburbanized *Predator 2* (1990, dir. Stephen Hopkins), in which an alien hunter seeks out human prey. Each film became a hybrid: action/horror/science fiction (which I will refer to as AHS for the rest of the chapter, for the sake of brevity). But for the most part, female leads (or indeed, female characters) were still often pushed to the boundaries of the narrative, rather than to the fore.

When one looks at the history of the AHS film, it becomes apparent that prior to the turn of the millennium, only two notable female roles came to prominence: Ellen Ripley (Sigourney Weaver) in the *Alien* franchise (1979–2017) and Sarah Connor (Linda Hamilton) in the first two films of *The Terminator* series (1984 and 1991). Each character was unexpectedly caught up in extraordinary circumstances and became crucial to events that unfold in their individual narratives. Across four movies, Ripley's character arc radically changes. In *Alien* (1979: Ridley Scott), she blows up a mining vessel to escape from the nightmarish Xenomorph creatures of Planet LV-426; in *Aliens* (1986: James Cameron), she unwillingly leads a commando unit to the same storm-ridden planet to destroy the Xenomorphs, along the way becoming a surrogate mother to Newt, a young female survivor of the colonists; after crash-landing on a prison planet, Fiorina 'Fury' 161, and finding that Newt has died in the crash, Ripley discovers she has a Xenomorph growing inside her in *Alien 3* (1992); by her final appearance in *Alien: Resurrection* (1997), Ripley has been cloned, and this ersatz version of herself has become a hybrid half-human/half-Xenomorph. At the end of that film, Ripley heads back to Earth smiling at the possibilities that await her. Sarah Connor's character arc changes just as much. In *The Terminator*, she is a café waitress who meets up with a time-travelling soldier who tells her that her unborn son will one day lead the Resistance and destroy Skynet, an all-powerful computer system that has taken over the world. In *Terminator 2: Judgement Day* (1991), Sarah, now muscular, weapons-trained and traumatized by all she knows, escapes from a mental asylum with the aid of her son, John and a re-programmed Terminator T-1000 (Arnold Schwarzenegger) to try and stop Skynet once and for all. What is interesting to note at this point is that whilst Ellen fails to reunite with her daughter (who died as an old woman before Ripley could return to Earth in *Aliens*), she is optimistic at Earth's future, despite the fact that she is a hybrid killing machine. For Sarah, the dystopian future cannot be avoided, as both she and her son are inextricably linked to saving it. Whilst there may be hope for

Sarah, it is only through a violent struggle of knowing that she can never win the ultimate battle of an event that is time-locked and will always happen.

By the millennium, the role of women in AHS films was changing. A Washington University survey of undergraduates (2003) found that 74% of male respondents watched female action heroes for their sexual attractiveness, 57% for the storyline, 51% for the violence shown and sfx proved an attraction for 46% of viewers. For females, 73% of female viewers watched to see their own sex in action roles; 63% were interested in the narrative; humour appealed to 58%; and sfx drew 40% of the audience's attention. Interestingly, 41% of females related to female action heroes, whilst 34% found nothing to relate to at all, which could either be an indictment about the action heroine as having no relatable qualities to its audience, or that the narrative does not hold interest.[2] Kathryn Gilpatrick's 2010 survey of women protagonists in action films released between 1991 and 2010 showed that 7% took control of their situation, whilst 58% were submissive to their male counterparts. Interestingly, 30% were dead by the end of the narrative.[3] Whilst they were few and far between, secondary characters began to emerge as narrative-leaders in their own right. Lara Croft (Angelina Jolie) in *Lara Croft: Tomb Raider* (2001, dir. Simon West) and *Lara Croft Tomb Raider – The Cradle of Life* (2003, dir. Jan de Bont) and Beatrix Kiddo/The Bride (Uma Thurman) in *Kill Bill vol. 1 and 2* (2004, dir. Quentin Tarantino) clearly demonstrated that there was an important role for women to play in action films. This became more apparent through such characters as Trinity in *The Matrix* (1999, dir. The Wachowski Brothers); Lisbeth Salander in *The Girl with the Dragon Tattoo* (2009, dir. Niels Arden Oplev); Yu Shu Lien in *Crouching Tiger, Hidden Dragon* (2000, dir. Ang Lee); the three *Charlie's Angels* Natalie, Dylan and Alex (2000, dir. McG); numerous characters in the Marvel and DC universes; Katniss Everdeen of *The Hunger Games* series; and Mindy McReady/Hit-Girl in *Kick-Ass* (2010, dir. Matthew Vaughan).

However, Gilpatric argues that the debate continues as to whether these characters actually break down gender barriers in action films, and in particular AHS films. Her research has provided evidence that female action characters shown in American cinema are not actually images of empowerment. They do not draw upon femininity as a source of power, arguing that they are not 'post-gender women' who operate outside the boundaries of traditional gender restrictions. Rather, she posits the idea that 'they operate inside highly socially constructed gender norms, rely on the strength and guidance of a dominant male action character, and end up re-articulating gender stereotypes.'[4]

This gender stereotyping remains an important and difficult area to navigate in relation to AHS films. Sherrie Inness (1999) argues that women in action films suggest, through a more tough, masculinized image, that there are a variety of gender roles open to women, but that the female's toughness is often mitigated

---

[2]Andrade (2003).
[3]Gilpatric (2010). Please also see Tasker (1998) for a similar approach to the subject.
[4]Tasker (1998).

by her femininity, which is often seen as a sign of weakness.[5] Whilst AHS men such as Thor (with his cape flapping in the breeze), Iron Man (with his shiny, well-kept suit) and Hulk (with his emotional temper tantrums) try to reclaim their masculinity through their actions, female action heroes (and in particular AHS's female characters) are exerting a type of machismo whilst still trying to retain feminine traits. For example, in *The Avengers Assemble* (2012, dir. Joss Whedon), Black Widow/Natasha Romanoff (Scarlett Johansson) wears a short black dress, black stockings and black high-heels as she beats up her assailants by breaking their legs, head butting them, hitting them with a chair, stabbing one through the foot with a chair leg, breaking an assailant's hand and finally roping the lead villain with a chain and tossing him over a drop, and then swaps this outfit for figure-hugging black leather when she joins her Avengers counter-parts. However, for a character like Jane Foster in *Thor* (2011, dir. Kenneth Branagh), it is her brain, not brawn, and expertise in astrophysics that helps her. Perhaps characters like Foster, who are arguably a more attainable role model for young women than the bow-and-arrow-wielding Katniss Everdeen, would for 'female intellectuals [...] prove less of a box-office draw than battling babes'.[6]

This outlook does prove problematic, however, in an area that cannot be avoided. Despite any attempt at providing strong, positive role models for young women through these female action heroes, one thing remains: the women and the characters they have portrayed have often been highly sexualized – as the Black Widow's outfit, described earlier, illustrates. AHS her-oines like Lara Croft are excellent characters, created and then performed with attention to providing positive role models for women. Yet at almost every given opportunity, their female form is displayed for gratification, be that from a male or female perspective and reliant on the viewer, even if they wear figure-hiding outfits or not. Females in AHS-hybrids may re-affirm Laura Mulvey's (1975) idea of 'The Male Gaze' where females are always objectified, looked at, dis-played and all for the male's scopophilic pleasure. In other words, women 'become the images of meaning rather than the maker of meaning'.[7] Mulvey's ground-breaking essay asserted that the cinema of classical Hollywood directed and controlled the look of the filmgoer through the eyes of the male protagonist. As Hollywood was controlled by men, and the majority of films were made by men for a male audience, Mulvey argues that the female is objectified at every given opportunity for the male's gratification. This is problematic as Mulvey assumed that it was only heterosexual males that watched films. However, her argument is important as even in today's multimedia world, the '(Fe)Male Gaze' has not been eradicated at all. Characters are viewed, watched, looked at, scrutinized and sexualized, as countless television adverts, billboard posters and films still testify.

[5]Inness (1999).
[6]Cox (2013).
[7]Mulvey (1975).

Along the same lines as Mulvey's investigations, Annette Kuhn (1982) argued how media representations of women are economically, politically and symbolically oppressed. Kuhn saw women as visual accessories within the narrative. By stressing the importance of how media perpetuate patriarchal ideology, she sees women's representations in cinema as fixed and mediated.[8] This means that females in cinema are unable to reflect the real social world. If this argument is accepted as true, then the role of women in the AHS-genre needs to be scrutinized.

According to Rick Altman (1984), there are two approaches to genre theory: the first is that Hollywood produces films that reflect audiences' preferences and desires; the second approach is that Hollywood manipulates audiences.[9] The first approach is based purely on economic lines, with tried and tested formulas enabling a 'product' to be developed for an engaged audience that has been almost programmed into 'wanting' such products. It is this genre approach that has become the most lucrative element to Hollywood's film-making. The second, more ideological approach, means that stereotypes abound (especially in AHS films) through a set of fixed formula that delivers financially less-risky movies that pander and cater to an audience spoon-fed ideologies about patriarchal philosophies. Audiences have preconceived notions of genre, narrative and characters. Whilst these conventions are seldom broken, each genre has its own construction of male and female characters. Whilst the roles of tough women in AHS films have certainly risen since the millennium, they still fall into the 'trap' of Hollywood representation: female action heroes must not only be resilient but also beautiful. Schubert (2007) argues that:

> The first step to qualify as a female hero in a man's world is to be young and beautiful. If not young then she must be Botoxed to look young. If not beautiful, then she must have silicone breasts, be aided by plastic surgery, wigs, make up and never ever a wrinkle on her pretty face.[10]

This is important because Schubart clearly sees AHS female heroes as having to conform to what is *expected* of them: *physical perfection*. From that standpoint, it could also be argued that the AHS female hero usually exhibits other traditionally feminine traits: nurturing behaviour, kindness, being overly emotional and so on. Whilst some Hollywood female roles of the 1990s moved from stay-at-home moms to business executives, the new millennium saw AHS females emerge as empowered, intelligent, strong, aggressive, sexy and beautiful in their own right. Whilst it could be argued that these traits are part-and-parcel of a male-dominated industry that is paying lip service to mostly male

---

[8]Kuhn (1982).
[9]Altman (1984).
[10]Schubert (2007).

demographics (and it could be suggested that this demographic is for 14- to 35-year-olds), the fact that female role models in AHS films are now composited of intelligence and inner- and outer strength, whilst also demonstrating traditionally more-feminine traits such as beauty, humanity, kindness, warmth and emotions, clearly indicates that characters like Katniss Everdeen and others appeal to a wider audience demographic than before. That the AHS female remains central to the narrative, reliant on genre conventions, character arc and *mise-en-scene*, remains significant. It is with this in mind that this chapter now turns to analyze arguably *the* AHS's most neglected, but powerful female heroine: Project Alice from the *Resident Evil* franchise.

13.1.   *Resident Evil*: The Films

The *Resident Evil* movie franchise comprises of six films (2002–2016) and are very loosely based on the Japanese Capcom video game franchise of the same name.[11] The film rights were bought by Constantin Films in 1997, and in 2001, Sony Pictures Entertainment acquired distribution rights and hired British film director Paul W. S. Anderson to both write and direct the first movie. Anderson continued working in the franchise, writing screenplays for all six films and directing Episodes 1, 4, 5 and 6. He felt that that most video game adaptations always under-performed at the box office and that *Resident Evil* 'deserved a good celluloid representation' and as such wanted no 'tie-ins' with the game series.[12] Anderson changed his view by the second films and included characters such as Jill Valentine, Carlos Olivera, Umbrella Corporation chief Albert Wesker, Chris and Claire Redfield and Ada Wong in later movies.

Despite numerous and usually hostile reviews, all the films performed well at the box office: *Resident Evil* had a production budget of US$35 million, whilst the worldwide box office figure was US$102,984,862; *Apocalypse* – US$45 million/US$129,342,769; *Extinction* – US$45 million/US$148,412, 065; *Afterlife* – US$60 million/US$300,228,084; *Retribution* – US$65 million/US$240, 004,424; *The Final Chapter* – US$40 million/US$312,257,250: US$290 million/US$1.233 billion. These impressive box office returns indicate that the AHS (zombie) genre has appeal to a wide-ranging audience. That audience may consist of the game-related fan base, plus a growing cinematic one. What is important to note here is that the franchise has a *female* lead, and this can only lead to the conclusion that a character like Project Alice (and the actress portraying her) add to the franchise's appeal across both the male and female demographic.

---

[11]The films are as follows: *Resident Evil* (2002, dir. Paul W. S. Anderson); *Resident Evil: Apocalypse* (2004, dir. Alexander Witt); *Resident Evil: Extinction* (2007, dir. Russell Mulcahy); *Resident Evil: Afterlife* (2010, dir. Paul W. S. Anderson); *Resident Evil: Retribution* (2012, dir. Paul W. S. Anderson); *Resident Evil: The Final Chapter* (2016, dir. Paul W. S. Anderson).
[12]Anderson (2001).

13.2.   Overview of the Films

Resident Evil and the ensuing franchise charts the convoluted journey that Alice (Project Alice as she becomes) undergoes in order to not only find out her origins and destiny, but also her attempts to stop the Umbrella Corporation (headed by Dr Isaacs, Chairman Albert Wesker and the AI Red Queen) and its destruction of the world's population through the development of its T-virus, which changes the dead to the undead. Project Alice moves through a variety of locations, including city and suburban landscapes, desert areas and numerous Hive facilities which belong to Umbrella, whilst forming bonds of friendship with a variety of characters. At the end of her narrative, Alice has been revealed to be a clone of Alicia, a young woman suffering from progeria, a progressive, fatal wasting disease, who now looks like an elderly woman. Alicia was the original subject of her father, Professor Marcus' development of the T-virus' ability to regenerate dying (or dead) cells. Alice destroys Umbrella, including all its personnel held in storage, releases the anti-virus into the air and water and rides off into the distance pursued by giant, dragon-like zombified bird hybrids.

13.3.   Project Alice: Character Physical Presence and Character Arc

Project Alice serves as an axis on which the entire franchise is based and which the entire narrative revolves around. The way that she is represented through *mise-en-scene* (including location, props, costumes) and her convoluted character arc will now be analyzed.[13] The importance of *mise-en-scene* in relation to Alice cannot be underestimated. Through a combination of locations, she becomes a part of those locations both belonging and yet not belonging to them. There are two household locations that feature prominently in the franchise: first, the chateau-style Looking Glass House (*Resident Evil*) with its beautiful décor, high mirrors, polished wooden floors and marble pillars, and its counterpart suburban house (*Retribution*) in which Alice becomes a stay-at-home-mom, looks after the household, performs chores and is a wife. The series also sees numerous underground Hive facilities, replete with laboratories, labyrinthine corridors, dark and dank basements and brightly lit torture rooms. Other locations include the cityscape and the desert, through which Alice, her cohorts and Umbrella personnel travel and interrelate.

With such places like The Hive seeming 'real' for the characters, they take on the idea of having a solid 'place' within the world of the film. Despite the fantastical narratives, they seem real to the characters and, by appropriation, the film's audience. When Alice walks through, touches, scales, jumps, runs, drives and interacts with her locations, she *becomes* a part of the location, and as such is

---

[13]See Dapolito (2016) for details of how Dapolito applies this technique to action films.

fetishized within it as part of its overall schema, whilst the audience journeys through those locations as spectators.

In the case of the household, Alice feels lost. When in the Looking Glass House, she is puzzled due to memory loss. Although later episodes see her return to the location, she remains confused. Even though she has personal possessions (clothes in a drawer, jewellery on her dressing table), they mean nothing to her due to this confusion, where Umbrella has created this fictionalized world for her to move through. As she walks through the house, soldiers burst in and truss up her 'husband', Spence. They bundle him and Alice down through trapdoors into The Hive, which is under the property. The chateau has become a place of threat, illusion and danger for Alice – as such, the psychogeographical impact this has upon her brings about only confusion.

In *Retribution,* the suburbanized house remains just as confusing. The audience first see Alice in bed with her husband, Carlos, and then in the kitchen talking to her daughter, Rebecca. At first, Alice looks disoriented, as she has not been married or had children in previous instalments. Therefore, the domestic becomes a threatening non-place, where she feels ill at ease. When zombies crash through the doors, Alice and Rebecca run, hide and escape through the house and out into suburbia. Outside, the street is ablaze with cars overturned and people fleeing. The two run into another house, only to be confronted by the now-zombified Carlos who kills her. Therefore, Alice's entry into the domestic sphere, much like the Looking Glass House, means she cannot function: she may seem like the perfect idealized housewife whilst wearing her red checked shirt and blue jeans, making coffee for Carlos and lunch for Rebeca, but this is all an illusion. Therefore, the ideology of the house as a place of haven impacts upon Alice in negative ways: first, they confuse, then they endanger.

It is only when Alice enters The Hive, in all its various forms that she seems at home – or, at least, at ease. Despite her hesitancy in the first film, by the end of her narrative, Alice moves through these spaces with ease, whether they are dark corridors or brightly lit laboratories. This comes to its fore in the climax to *The Final Chapter.* Alice is confronted by Dr Isaacs, Wesker and her original self, Alicia. Surrounded by a mix of opulent décor and hi-tech equipment, she escapes into the Hive and detonates a series of explosives that destroy the complex, killing everyone within it. As the walls come crashing down, she runs into the open. In the case of 'place', the Hive's destruction reinforces Augé's (1995) ideas that this is never completely erased as it is hinted that Hive facilities still remain. From a psychogeographical viewpoint, this can be taken further: the memory of The Hive will always be a part of Project Alice (who is, after all, a clone of Alicia) who has come to be dominated by its physicality, until the only way to save herself is by its destruction. She has destroyed part of herself.

Even though Alice remains free to roam the world or 'non-place' she now inhabits, her place within the landscape outside The Hive remains dangerous. For Alice, the landscape remains incomplete: she still has her job to do. As she rides off into the distant crumbling landscape, and being pursued by gigantic zombie-bird hybrids, she smiles. Unlike The Hive which remains a memory (and those memories reflect the danger of the past), this new world, whilst remaining dangerous, offers hope for Alice. It is this 'non-place' that has now become 'place' for her. In other words, Alice has redefined herself through these landscapes, where she has pioneered a new identity and where her place in the landscape is assured.

Mulvey argues that scopophilic viewing of the individual provides emphasis on the pleasurable aspects of looking, whilst fetishistic 'looking' completely objectifies the woman who is being looked at. However, it does not only apply to the individual character. Whilst Alice remains a subject in the narrative, and as such has movement and emotions that can then create change within the environment, objects remain passive. Things are done to them, and unless they are deemed 'important' enough within the narrative, they remain without meaning. Whilst Freud sees fetish as a substitute for 'normal' sex, Mulvey sees fetishization as the fantasy of men who watch the female on the screen.[14] If this is the case, then Alice becomes an object, and likewise so do the objects she holds and uses.

The use of guns and other assorted weaponry is in evidence throughout the entire franchise. Umbrella Corporation soldiers use heavy-duty, black machine guns as part of their job. Alice uses her weapons as if they are seen as an extension of herself. She picks up guns, loads them quickly, fires with deadly accuracy and is also at ease using knives, assorted blunt instruments and anything that can help her escape her situation. Across the franchise, she uses the following: Mossbert 500 shotgun; Heckler & Koch MP5K submachine guns; Para-Ordnance P-14 pistols; Para-Ordnance Nite-Tac pistols; Brügger & Thomet MP-9s; Smith & Wesson Model 460V revolvers; Kukri knives; straight-bladed odachi blades; a fountainpen; and, finally, a pair of 10-gauge double-barrelled shotguns loaded with quarters, that kill zombies with American currency.[15] When Project Alice says, 'We're going to kill every last one of them. Grab some gear. This is what I do' (*Resident Evil: The Final Chapter*), her instructions clearly show a female action hero completely in control of both herself and the weapons at her disposal *and* those around her.

The way that she uses weapons clearly demonstrates that she is skilled in the art of weaponry. However, the way that she is placed within the screen whilst using these guns and so on clearly fetishize the weaponry through which she expresses her outer strength. For example, in the final fight scene in *Resident Evil: Retribution*, when Alice is confronted by Jill Valentine (Sienna Guillory), the camera remains fairly static, concentrating on Alice as the main focus of the scene. During this sequence, Alice shoots and stabs at Valentine, but this is often seen in slow motion, emphasizing both the weapons on display and Alice as an object within the cinematic plane. However, because of the way that Alice is often photographed, where she was once objectified by men, her expertise at handling weapons (and using herself as a weapon) ensures that with each kill she

---

[14]Dapolito (2016, p. 13).
[15]IMFDB *Resident Evil: Afterlife* (2010).

remains in charge whilst claiming the subject position within the narrative whilst simultaneously punishing those around her who once objectified her.

The actress who portrays Project Alice is Milla Jovovich. She is petite, slim and almost androgynous in her outline. The films accentuate this androgyny, despite Alice's very infrequent scenes of nudity (when she is strapped to a gurney, or in a coma in her shower), in which only a small amount of her flesh is displayed. What makes Project Alice so interesting is this androgyny which is then objectified and fetishized through her costume. Costume/dress has no actual meanings *per se*, but is given agency when worn by individuals, and therefore becomes one of the major social constructions of identity.[16] Whilst the skin becomes hidden within the cocoon of clothing, the garments become an accepted face of aspirations, dreams, realities and fantasies.[17]

It is in the category of fantasy that Alice's objectification through her clothing takes form. The first appearance of Alice is of her lying on the tiled floor of her shower, unconscious and wrapped in a shower curtain. When she emerges from her bedroom fully dressed, she is wearing a red dress with plunging neckline and thin straps. The left side of the dress is cut to hip level, with the right side falling to below the knee. Underneath the dress she wears a black mini-skirt and heavy black boots. In *Apocalypse* she wears a cropped orange tank with spaghetti straps; olive mesh tank to the level of a mini-skirt; ripped, bootcut grey jeans; gun holster; black leather cowboy boots with heel. Her outfit is further fetishized in *Extinction*: Alice wears a sand-coloured tank, short-sleeved brown shirt, brown chaps, brown stockings and suspenders, a dark scarf, fingerless gloves and light brown duster coat. The opening sequence of *Afterlife* sees Alice's clones wearing skin-tight, black PVC catsuits. When the real Alice is seen, she is wearing a large green coat that covers her brown leather T-shirt, black military corset, black leggings, green leg warmers and black boots. Despite her return to (false) motherhood in *Retribution*, Alice wears a black spandex body suit, topped off with a tight bustier-cut leather vest with silver buckles, and black high boots with wedge heels. For her final adventure, Alice wears a tattered green army jacket replete with US army badge; navy blue crop top, black denims, black shiny boots and a camo vest harness that buckles down to leg holsters. Across the franchise her hair colour and length changes from strawberry blonde and long to brown, brunette and short.

Interestingly, unlike her male counterparts in the franchise, Alice changes her outfits both within each film and across the movies on numerous occasions. In some ways, this could reflect the change within Alice herself. Of course, in other AHS films, especially those in the Marvel Cinematic Universe, the hero/heroines usually have two clothing identities: their 'human' everyday clothes and their 'superhero' guises. This clearly differentiates between their different personas.

---

[16]Turner (1980); Fisher and Loren (2003).
[17]Butler (1993).

For Alice, the clothes come to represent both her sex and her sexuality, whilst also becoming part of her 'shield', through which she can fight and survive.

In her article 'Where Do Women Spectators Fit into All of This?' Doane (1982) suggests that women have two outlets for their sexuality through costumery: transvestitism or masquerade.[18] In the case of Alice, the masquerade remains important. Covered at first in a shower curtain and then through a variety of more-and-more fetishized costumes, she appeals to a variety of both hetero/homosexual/transgendered audiences through both the Gaze and through empowerment. This means that Alice becomes both subject and object simultaneously, where her sexualization is linked through her exceptionally overloaded sexualized costumes to her aggression, whilst her femininity is brought to the fore when dressed in jeans and shirt in the domestic household.

As a character, Alice's arc is convoluted. In the first film, she remains in a state of limbo without memory of her actions. This is accentuated through scenes of her questioning her own reasoning and that of the soldiers around her. As the narrative progresses through the franchise, and she moves deeper into The Hive to find out the true meaning of her identity, each film gives over a new perspective to her character. She becomes a mother (to Rebecca and, to an extent, the children she rescues in *Afterlife*), (false) wife to Carlos, friend, and eventually the seeming-saviour of humankind. In all instances, she remains pivotal to both the narrative and the image, forming a strong image of femininity that clearly demonstrates how important she is to the canon of female action heroes.

This comes to the fore in arguably two key scenes of the series. In the first movie, Alice is trapped in The Hive and cornered in a laboratory with seven ferocious zombie Rottweilers. Through a series of wide, medium and close-ups, the spectacle of Project Alice becomes apparent: she is sexualized through her revealing costume, but then masculinized through her shooting the dogs, whilst finally disposing of the last one by drop-kicking it onto a shard of glass. Here, the camera clearly showcases her feminine form but projects traditional–masculine traits through her physicality. In *The Final Chapter*, when confronted by the Red Queen (itself a projection of Alicia and the real-life daughter of Jovovich), Alice is given a choice: she can take on the memories of Alicia or remain 'anonymous' with only her name and recent history to be remembered.

> *Red Queen*: Alica Marcus was right about you. You are better than all of them.

> *Alice*: I was one of them. I was created by Umbrella. Just an instrument for them.

---

[18]Doane (1982).

Red Queen: No. You became something more than they could ever have anticipated. You became more human than they ever could be. You have one more step to make.

Alice: What do you mean?

Red Queen: Before she died, Alicia Marcus downloaded her memories for you. The childhood you never had, combined with the woman she could never become.

As images of Alicia's childhood envelope Alice, the camera goes to a close-up of her. She is struggling to remain herself. This is an interesting idea: for Alice, she is struggling to remain an individual, and one that is not tied to Umbrella and the society that created her. This remains at the core of Project Alice within the AHS canon. That is, she is objectified through her beauty, femininity and costumes but simultaneously remains the subject through which ideologies rest. Whilst Mulvey and Doane could argue that the patriarchal ideology remains intact where scopophilia remains, it has to be counter argued. Project Alice, in the final part of her narrative, is no longer an object. She becomes the subject through which Alice projects strong ideas of motherhood, femininity, inner strength and her own purpose and being without the interference of outside forces.

Like other AHS heroines, her trajectory is from 'normal' through 'supernormal' to 'hero'. At the end of the franchise, when Alicia offers up her memories so that Alice can now lead a 'normal' life, Project Alice refuses. She comes to represent a new form of AHS heroine, where her convoluted and confusing character arc, housed within the numerous locale's *mise-en-scéne*, has laid a foundation of intelligence, beauty, danger and skill which subverts any 'traditional' rules of AHS heroines. Her sexless female form, despite the fetishization her outfits give her, means that she remains completely androgynous and therefore 'safe' within the confines of her own sexuality. Whereas Ripley's future is seemingly one of happiness at approaching a new Earth and a new dawn for her (and bearing in mind that Ripley was a mother to both human and alien offspring), and Sarah Connor's future is pre-determined as a saviour of humankind through her son, Alice's conclusion remains tantalizingly open-ended. Humankind still needs Alice. It is this, coupled with her actions throughout the six movies, where she moves from object to subject, that makes her so important to the AHS-heroine canon.

As she rides off into the sunset, much like a John Ford cowboy in that most masculine of genres, Alice does not become a representation of either women or men *per se*. As a character, she comes to represent *herself*, which is confirmed by the last words she says:

When the T-Virus spread across the Earth, it did so at the speed of the modern world, carried by jet-liners across the globe. The anti-virus is airborne, spread by the winds. It could take years to reach every corner of the Earth. Until then, my work is not done. My name is Alice.

From a theoretical standpoint, whilst Mulvey would insist that Alice remains a fantasy figure of the Male Gaze, and Doan may suggest that she remains part of a masquerade, Alice fulfils neither category. She is a character who appears to have no sexual feelings for other characters, neither do there appear to be any such feelings for her from others, thus remaining completely androgynous (or, at least, asexual) throughout the franchise. What Alice does reflect though is the idea that whilst she is objectified through her outfits and their fetishization, she stands apart from her male counterparts within the franchise. She remains an incredibly strong character that, whilst altering over the series and bordering on both masculine and feminine traits, is capable of great feats of strength, leadership, compassion, honesty, integrity and bravery. This is why Project Alice remains one of *the* most important — though neglected — heroines in AHS films.

References

Altman, R. (1984). A semantic/syntactic approach to film genre. *Cinema Journal, 23*(3), 6−17.

Anderson, P. W. S. (2001). Resident evil director explains character and story line changes. *News Spong*. January, 26. Retrieved from htttp://news.spong.com/article/ 1837. Accessed on April 1, 2018.

Andrade, J. (2003). *The gender politics of female action heroes in television films.* Retrieved from https://docs.google.com/viewer?url=https%3A%2F%2Fdigital.lib. washington.edu%2Fdspace%2Fbitstream%2Fhandle%2F1773%2F2099%2Fandrade03. doc%3Fsequence%3D1. Accessed on April 1, 2018.

Augé, M. (1995). *Non-places: Introduction to an anthropology of supermodernity* (p. 79). London: Verso.

Butler, J. (1993). *Bodies that matter: On the discursive limits of sex.* New York, NY: Routledge.

Cox, D. (2013, December 12). *Are female action heroes good role models for young women?* Retrieved from https://www.theguardian.com/film/filmblog/2013/dec/12/ female-action-heroes-katniss-role-models-women. Accessed on April 1, 2018.

Dapolito, M. A. (2016). A contemporary analysis of action films with female leads. *Inquiries Journal, 8*(09), 1−2.

Doane, M. A. (1982). Film and masquerade: Theorising the female spectator. *Screen, 23*, 74−88.

Fisher, G., & Loren, D. (2003). Embodying identity in archaeology: Introduction. In *Cambridge Archaeological Journal, 13*(2), 225−230.

Gilpatric, K. (2010). Violent female action characters in contemporary American cinema. *Sex Roles*, June 2010, *62*(11−12), 734−746.

IMFDB *Resident evil: Afterlife* (2010). Retrieved from http://www.imfdb.org/index. php/Resident_Evil:_Afterlife. Accessed on April 1, 2018.

Inness, S. (1999). *Tough girls: Women warriors and wonder women in popular culture* (p. 5). Philadelphia, PA: University of Pennsylvania Press.

Jeffords, S. (1993). *Hard bodies: Hollywood masculinity in the regan era*. London: Rutgers University Press.

Kuhn, A. (1982). *Women's pictures: Feminism and cinema* (2nd ed.). London: Routledge & K. Paul.

Mulvey, L. (1975). Visual pleasure and narrative cinema. *Screen*, Autumn, *16*(3), 3.

Schubert, R. (2007). *Super bitches and action babes*. Jefferson, NC: McFarland & Co.

Tasker, Y. (1993). *Spectacular bodies: Gender, genre and the action cinema*. London: Routledge.

Tasker, Y. (1998). Action women: Muscles, mothers and others. In Y. Tasker (Ed.), *Working girls: Gender and sexuality in popular cinema* (pp. 65–88). London: Routledge.

Turner, S. (1980). The social skin. In J. Cherfas & R. Lewin (Eds.), *Not work alone: A cross-cultural view of activities superfluous to survival*. Beverly Hills, CA: Sage.

Chapter 14

The Final Girls (2015) as a Video Essay: A Metalinguistic Play with Genre and Gender Conventions

Emilio Audissino

The recent years have seen some redefinition of the gender roles once tradition-ally assigned in Hollywood cinema. For example, the 2013 remake of *The Evil Dead* (1981) replaced the hero Ash with the heroine Mia; the 2015 *Star Wars* sequel *The Force Awakens* retold the story of Episode IV (*A New Hope*, 1977) by re-casting the Luke Skywalker figure into the girl Rey; the 2016 reboot of *Ghostbusters* (1984) replaced the original all-male *Saturday Night Live* cast with an all-female *Saturday Night Live* cast, and the 1980s inept and flirtatious female secretary Janine became the equally inept and flirtatious male secretary Kevin. And female characters are more often the leads in what used to be the reservoir of male 'bad-ass' heroism, action/adventure movies: *Cutthroat Island* (1995), *The Hunger Games* (2012), *Atomic Blonde* (2017) and *Ocean's 8* (2018) – the all-female version of the 'heist classic' *Ocean's 11* (1960, remade in 2001 as *Ocean's Eleven*). Of all the film genres, horror has been ahead of time in the presentation of a subversion of gender roles and relations, especially in the subgenre called 'slasher'. In this chapter, after a preliminary summary of Laura Mulvey's femin-ist account of film identification, I present the identifying characteristics of this subgenre, with particular attention to the predominance of the lead female char-acter that eventually defeats the monster, identified as the 'Final Girl' by Carol J. Clover in her 1992 influential book *Men, Women, and Chain Saws* (Clover, 2015). Then I examine the 2015 film *The Final Girls* (directed by Todd Strauss-Schulson), a comedy/horror that pays overt homage to the slasher genre and echoes many theories and classifications of Clover's book, starting from her notion of 'Final Girl'.

Gender and Contemporary Horror in Film, 219–235
doi:10.1108/978-1-78769-897-020191015

14.1. Slasher Horror and Film Theory

The golden age of the slasher film can be placed between the 1970s and the 1980s.[1] Adapting Petridis's periodization (Petridis, 2014), we can say that this 'classic period' was followed by a 'post-slasher period' (1990s) marked by a high degree of sardonic self-referencing, as in the case of the *Scream* franchise (1996, 1997, 2000, 2011) and *New Nightmare* (1994), to the point that these films seem to be constructed to overtly pay homage to the classic/golden period or, often, even to parody its cliches.[2] The 'neo-slasher period' followed (2000s onward), in which the almost parodical spirit of the 'post-slasher period' is lost in favour of a return to the arresting horror and gore of the classical models, mostly in higher-budget remakes – for example *Halloween* (2007, original 1978) and *Friday the 13th* (2009, original 1980). If horror is a familiar and formulaic genre, the slasher subgenre is perhaps even more so. The typical slasher's story features 'a serial killer who is spreading fear in a middle-class community by killing innocent people. [...] The methods of killing are through knives, axes, hammers or any kind of blade' (Petridis, 2014, pp. 76–77). The victims are typically teenagers and are killed while engaged in sexual intercourse or immediately afterwards. An explanation of this equation sex = death has been provided in sociological terms: a reaction of the conservative Reaganite era to the 1970s liberated mores, and a metaphor of the AIDS epidemic that was spreading death through sex (Petridis, 2014, pp. 78–79). Carol J. Clover prefers a psychonalytical explanation to a sociological one. In particular, her 1992 study examines the gender dynamics of the low-budget horror films of the 1970s and 1980s, 'the relationship of the "majority viewer" (the younger male) to the female victim-heroes who have become such a conspicuous screen presence in certain sectors of horror' (Clover, 2015, pp. 6–7). Revising the classical feminist film theory in the wake of Laura Mulvey's development of Christian Metz's psychoanalytic

---

[1]Dika (1990) offers a narrow definition of slasher horror film focused on a cycle of films released between 1978 and 1984 that centre on mysterious stalkers that slash their victims with blades – thus excluding *The Texas Chainsaw Massacre* (1974). Workland (2007) also indicates 1978, the release date of *Halloween*, as the inaugural year. Others, like Petridis (2014) and Clover (2015), include *The Texas Chainsaw Massacre* in the canon and choose 1974 – the release date of this film and the Canadian stalker-shocker *Black Christmas* – as the start of the classic period, with Clover (2015) setting 1986 as the closing year (p. 26), a periodization adopted by Rockoff 2011. On the slasher see also Clayton (2015), Normanton (2012), Nowell (2010) and Robinson (2010). For a contextualization of the slasher genre within the broader American horror cinema, see Maddrey (2004).

[2]Spoof traits can already be spotted in the late classic period, for example in *The Texas Chainsaw Massacre 2* (1986), in the comic moment at the radio station when Leatherface's chainsaw has a power fail just when he is about to attack the heroine (read: sudden impotency) – appropriately, the classification of this film on the Internet Movie Database is 'comedy/horror', while the first film from 1974 is classified as a straight 'horror'.

account of spectatorship,[3] Clover offers a more flexible reading of the identification processes at work.[4] Before addressing Clover's theory, a quick overview of the subtended traditional account of gendered identification in film-viewing may be required.

The Mulvey theory – based on the Metzian interplay between Primary Identification (with the camera's eye) and Secondary Identification (with characters) – claims that the 'cinematic apparatus' (film technique) expresses the inherent patriarchal ideology of the System by assigning the active 'Gaze' to the male and making females the passive objects of such Gaze. If the Gaze is the optical correlative of the Phallus – the penis symbolically invested with power and exercising a dominion – the one who has the Gaze in the optical medium of cinema is the one who exerts the power. Patriarchal ideology assigns both the Gaze and the Phallus to men, and *they* retain the power, in real life as well as in films. Films are designed for a male audience, to satisfy men by constructing a gendered system of gaze dynamics and role-based storytelling in which the male is the active masculine hero and the female the passive feminine subject of his desire. The narrative is set and kept in motion by the male, while the female represents a temporary stop to its progression. The female is introduced as a moment of sheer spectacle, she is there to offer the view of her body to the male gaze of the camera. But the female body is at the same time seductive and threatening. In Freudian terms, it presents a 'Lack', the absence of the penis; the vagina looks like the open wound that results from emasculation, a sight that in men activates the fear of castration. In Lacanian terms, the female represents the 'Imaginary', a stage of the psychic life that precedes the 'Symbolic', the domain of order, language and rationality, the domain of men. Whether one sees the penis-less female body as an image of castration or as a threat of the Imaginary to the Symbolic sociocultural domain of men, either way the female represents a potential menace to male supremacy. To domesticate such menace and make the female image an anxiety-free commodity for the male viewer, two strategies are adopted in film. The female is fetishized by the camera, and thus turned from an active character of the narrative into a passive object of visual pleasure, with the fetishizing camera concentrating on selected parts of her body (legs, feet, bosom …) to distract from and substitute for the 'Lack'. Alternatively, the narration builds

---

[3]Mulvey (1975) and Metz (1986).
[4]Psychoanalytical film theory has been questioned on the grounds of its lack of empirical evidence, free-association thinking and generalization of single and limited case studies (see Carroll, 1988, pp. 9–88). Psychoanalysis tends to depict a passive spectator that does not correspond to the actual one (see Prince, 1996), and most film scholars prefer an empathy/cognitivism-based approach over the identification/ psychoanalytic one (for example, Neill, 1996, or Smith, 1995). Feminist approaches not based on psychoanalysis have also been proposed (for example Freeland, 1996), which also contains a criticism of Clover's theory, deemed to be too reliant on psycho-sexual models.

a plot in which she transgresses – typically by taking possession of the Gaze and becoming an active part of the narrative in some investigation or quest – and then she is punished, sadistically, for her transgression, which brings her back under the male control of the 'Symbolic' and the Phallus. If films are made for a male audience, the only way for a female viewer to identify with the characters is to 'transvestite' as a man, thus embracing the identification patterns of the film.[5]

Clover questions this binary and impermeable separation. While the classic horror films did seem to adhere mostly to this dynamics – think of the 'damsel in distress', the screaming and helpless girl who is abducted by some monster and has to be saved by the fearless male hero – the new horror films do not. A considerable number of post-1970 horrors feature females in active and reso-lutive roles: 'The women's movement has given many things to popular culture […]. One of its main donations to horror, I think, is the image of an angry woman – a woman so angry that she can be imagined as a credible perpetrator (I stress 'credible') of the kind of violence on which […] the status of the full protagonist rests' (Clover, 2015, p. 17). Since the numbers show that the majority of viewers of these films are young male (Clover, 2015, p. 23), Clover wonders how these male teenagers could engage with these stories if identifica-tion is classically described as happening between the male viewer and the male character through the male gaze of the camera. How can these films be so popular with teenage males if their protagonists are females? Clover notes that the horror genre is not necessarily sadistically misogynist as most critics have simplistically claimed (Clover, 2015, p. 19) and raises the problem of the clas-sical accounts of male spectatorship focusing too much on fetishism and sad-ism but, curiously, neglecting masochism altogether. In these 'gender bender' films, one of the male viewer's pleasures is to masochistically identify with the victim, and since the victim is traditionally the female, these films make it pos-sible for the male viewer to experience, to some extent, the female condition (Clover, 2015, p. 212 ff, and 222 in particular). Although Clover's book does not focus exclusively on the slasher but also on other post-1970 horror subgenres – like the 'rape revenge' and the 'possession' film – it is her take on the slasher that has become particularly popular, as she has distilled its main defining elements. Since my analysis of *The Final Girls* is strongly based on Clover's book, I deem it useful to provide below a list that presents and quickly describes those 'Clover Categories' that are openly showcased in the film (in **bold** hereafter, for easier cross-reference). I am also providing as many quotations as possible of Clover's own wording regarding the essential pas-sages of her categorization, for those who might not have her book within immediate reach.

---

[5]I have presented here a rough summary of the initial theory, soon criticized by fem-inist scholars as too rigid (see Doane, 1990; Gaines 1990). Mulvey herself revised her theory (Mulvey, 2009, pp. 31–40).

14.1.1.   *The Victims*

While once the victims in horror films were mostly adults, now they are teen-agers and 'sexual transgressor of both sexes [that] are scheduled for early destruction' (Clover, 2015, p. 33). Indeed, 'killing those who seek or engage in unauthorized sex amount to a generic imperative of the slasher film. It is an imperative that crosses gender lines, affecting males as well females.' (Clover, 2015, p. 34). Yet, while boys are dispatched because they 'make mistakes' (Clover, 2015, p. 33) – for example, they trespass upon the killer's turf – on the contrary girls 'die [...] because they are female'. (Clover, 2015, p. 34). More importantly, the murders of the male characters are quick and shown from a dis-tance, while the killing of a female is showcased in closer and richer detail, and at length (Clover, 2015, p. 35), making a spectacle of the tortured female body, which exposes the nature of the slasher as a substitute for porn targeted at young teenage males (Clover, 2015, p. 29).

14.1.2.   *The Killer*

The villain is mostly male,[6] but a 'male in gender distress', like *Psycho*'s Norman Bates (Clover, 2015, p. 27). The root of the villain's killing drive – a 'psychosexual fury' (Clover, 2015, p. 27) – can almost invariably be found in some traumatic experience that has impeded a regular development. They are anatomical male but they have not reached a psycho-sexual maturity; they may have the penis but have not acquired the Phallus. They replace the acts of sex they cannot perform with acts of violence – perhaps enviously, against people who do have a sex life – and they replace the missing Phallus with phallic weapons – machetes, chainsaws, knives [...] – with which they exert their power by penetrating the victims' bodies.[7] To mask this gender uncertainty – in order not to undermine the threat he must represent – the psychokiller is compensated with almost 'superhuman' qualities, he is seemingly indestructible (Clover, 2015, p. 30).

14.1.3.   *Weapons*

The preferred means of death are blades of various natures – knives, hatchets, razors, etc. 'Guns have no place in slasher films' (Clover, 2015, p. 31). Such blades and implements, contrary to firearms, entail a close proximity to the vic-tim, an invasion of the intimate space, in proxemic terms. 'Knives and needles, like teeth, beaks, fangs, and claws, are personal extensions of the body that bring

---

[6]With the notable exception of Jason's mother in *Friday the 13th*.
[7]It is this displacement of sex onto violence that facilitates cross-gender identifica-tion: 'One reason the slasher film can go as far as it does in playing with gender is that it deals with genital behavior only indirectly, through the metaphor of violence; thus women as well as men can come by knives or power drills, and men as well as women can have holes drilled or bored into them' (Clover, 2015, p. 157).

attacker and attacked into primitive, animalistic embrace' (Clover, 2015, p. 32), an extension of the body with which the victims can be penetrated: 'closeness and tactility are also at issue [...] a fascination with flesh or meat itself as that which is hidden from view' (Clover, 2015, p. 32).

14.1.4. Shock

The slasher presents not only an alternation of tones and moods – one scene may be raunchy and look as if lifted from a college-lampoon film like *Porky's* (1981); another scene may have the mawkish tone of a teenager sentimental film; another may be exaggeratedly gore as if belonging to a grand-guignolesque shocker. It also oscillates between moments in which the narration constructs a serious engagement with the events and the characters – as when we follow with anticipation the final showdown between the survivor and the killer – and others in which the excessive staging and acting resemble a spoof of the violence that is shown (Clover, 2015, p. 41). This oscillation of moods and registers is punctuated with sudden and shocking moments of violence, which must first catch viewers unprepared and startle them, and secondly shock them with the graphic details of the slaughter. Another element that derives from this, though not openly discussed by Clover, is the 'body count', slasher's main formal principle, in Conrich's words, 'the reduction of the story [to] a recounting of the methodical slaughter of each helpless individual' (Conrich, 2009, pp. 174, 179). The typical slasher is structured around a string of shocking killings, and *those* are the set pieces the audience is waiting for – like a musical is structured around a string of dance numbers and songs, and a porn around a string of coital activities. Similarly, the body count is one of the slasher's biggest attractives, and the higher the count, the better the draw.[8]

14.1.5. Terrible Place

A recurring trope of the slasher is some dilapidated mansion, but often a cabin, or any other typically seedy place where the villain has his lair. It looks like an abandoned place, decrepit, dark, covered in cobwebs, dust, mould and moist stains. Rusty chains and ominous, often blood-stained tools – meat hooks, saws, hatchets ... – provide the décor. The trespassing teenager who happens to enter the terrible place is bound to die, horribly (Clover, 2015, pp. 30–31).

---

[8]As early as 1981 the 'body count' and other hallmarks of the slasher film had reached so high a level of codification and recurrence as to be suitable targets for parody. In *Student Bodies* (1981) – a spoof comedy that particularly pokes fun at *Prom Night* (1980) – after each murder we are shown a number appearing onscreen so as to keep track of the progression of the body count.

14.1.6. The Final Girl

Typically, the only survivor of the group of teenagers is a girl who eventually manages to vanquish the villain. This female survivor displays precise and recognizable characteristics: 'The Final Girl [...] is presented from the outset as the main character. The practiced viewer distinguishes her from her friends minutes into the film' (Clover, 2015, p. 39). Like the killer, she is equally shifting and undetermined in her gender. She often acts like a masculine-gendered person: 'She is a Girl Scout, the bookworm, the mechanic. Unlike her girlfriends [...] she is not sexually active. [...] Above all, she is intelligent and resourceful in a pinch' (Clover, 2015, p. 39). Anatomically female, nevertheless she is 'boyish' (Clover, 2015, p. 39), even androgynous and often sports a gender-ambiguous name – Stevie, Marti, Terry, Will, Joey [...]; in clothing, she chooses quasi-shabby comfort (check shirts and jeans) over sexy apparel; she has an interest and a penchant for occupations that are typically men's business; she is serious, perceptive and focused, unlike her vacuous and vain female co-protagonists; she does not appear to be interested in a sentimental relationship or even in sex at all; in most cases, she is a virgin, or so we infer.[9] Final Girls prove themselves tougher and apter than 'their cringing male counterparts' (Clover, 2015, p. 36). She survives those 'butch types' who would like to solve the situation through manly force and dexterity – 'the comic ineptitude and failure of would-be 'woodsmen' is a repeated theme' (Clover, 2015, p. 38) – but she also survives the 'nerdy types' who think they can defeat the monster through a logical plan: 'traditional masculinity [...] does not fare well in the slasher film; the man who insists on taking charge, or who believes that logic or appeals to authority can solve the problem, or (above all) who tries to act the hero, is dead meat' (Clover, 2015, p. 65). The Final Girl is the absolute protagonist of the final act (Clover, 2015, p. 36).

14.1.7. The Body

The body in is not only the 'dead meat' to be sacrificed on the altar of the body count, or the female body to be displayed in the 'pornographic' murders. The body is also the anatomical site where the fluctuation of genders takes place. The killer's body may be male but his psychosexual identity is slippery: he may handle phallic weapons but in many instances he lives in a 'terrible place' whose dark and humid quality makes it look like a uterus (Clover, 2015, p. 48). Similarly, the Final Girl is somewhat amorphous: she has a female body but 'just as the killer is not fully masculine, she is not fully feminine' (Clover, 2015, p. 40). When she eventually defeats the killer, from victim, she becomes hero;

---

[9]This cliché was already so crystallized in 1981 as to become the object of parody in, again, *Student Bodies*, in which, the Final Girl is portrayed as so extremely sexphobic as to carry a set of 'NO' brooch badges pinned on the various layers of her clothes, the one on the brassiere being the biggest one.

from feminine, she becomes masculine: 'The Final Girl has not just manned herself; she specifically unmans an oppressor whose masculinity was in question to begin with. [...] It is the male killer's tragedy that his incipient femininity is not reversed but completed (castration) and the Final Girl's victory that her incipient masculinity is not thwarted but realized (phallicization)' (Clover, 2015, pp. 49–50).

Of all the elements analysed in the slasher, the Final Girl has proven so successful as to 'hijack' all the other points in Clover's book. The success of the Final Girl notion has even caused her study to be mistaken by the general public for, reductively, a book 'about slasher movies and their feminist heroes' (Clover, 2015, p. x). In the new foreword to the 2015 reprint, Clover sums up the fortune and misunderstanding of her Final Girl:

> The fate of that trope since then has largely determined, for better or worse, the intellectual and more broadly cultural trajectory of the book itself, I say 'for worse' not because of the Final Girl's appropriations in rock and rap music, novels, plays, films, and the like, but because, in the course of that history, she has eclipsed other figures and issues in the book and, more to the point, has in her wanderings become a rough sketch of her former self. Detached from her low-budget origins and messier meanings, she now circulates in these mostly cleaner and more upscale venues as a 'female avenger,' 'triumphant feminist hero,' and the like. (Clover, 2015, p. x)[10]

In the original formulation, the Final Girl is described as a 'female victim-hero' (Clover, 2015, p. 4), incarnating both roles and both genders at the same time: feminine-gendered victim and masculine-gendered hero. She is not simplistically heroic but she is also 'abject terror personified' (Clover, 2015, p. 35). Her eventual victory seems like a stroke of luck or a desperate extreme reaction triggered by survival instinct, and it comes after an exhausting and scarring experience: 'she is the one who encounters the mutilated bodies of her friends and perceives the full extent of the preceding horror and of her own peril; who is chased, cornered, wounded; whom we see scream, stagger, fall, rise, and scream again' (Clover, 2015, p. 35). From a mobile victim/hero character in which the problematic gender tensions converge, the Final Girl has been reduced to a crystallized type. The 2015 comedy/horror *The Final Girls* not only pays overt homage to the slasher genre but it is so systematic in its staging, articulation and even demonstration of the slasher's conventions that it could almost be called a 'video essay' about

---

[10]An example of this misunderstanding is the 2015 film *Final Girl* (Tyler Shields) that, despite the tip-of-the-hat title, is not about the Cloverian Final Girl but rather about a trained Nikita-like avenger girl who terminates a gang of sadistic killer boys.

Clover's study.[11] I have found no evidence that the filmmakers did read Clover's book; yet, the title itself and the precision with which the 'Clover Categories' are almost illustrated make me suspect that a close familiarity with this renowned book is highly probable.

14.2.   The Final Girls: Intertextuality, Metalanguage and Film Theory

Resuming the periodization previously presented, the 2010s saw a return to the 'post-slasher' parody/horror mix, in films like *The Cabin in the Woods* (2012) and *Tucker and Dale vs Evil* (2010). *The Final Girls* is a pre-eminent representative of this trend. Clover, notes that 'horror is the most self-reflexive of cinematic genres' (Clover, 2015, p. 16). The very concept at the basis of the *The Final Girls* is as self-reflexive as possible: a group of 2009 teenagers – Max (the lonely shy girl), Gertie (Max's best friend, the extroverted outspoken girl), Vicki (the sexually active beauty queen), Duncan (the nerd) and Chris (the handsome guy) – get magically trapped inside a fictional 1986 slasher, *Camp Bloodbath*, and their only chance to survive is to apply their knowledge of the slasher film's rules and conventions. Most characters, locales and events are intertextual nods to the slasher classics; for example, Tina and Nancy are named after characters from *A Nightmare on Elm Street* (1984), Billy the killer from *Black Christmas* (1974), Billy's past trauma echoes the one in *The Burning* (1981), the summer camp setting is lifted from *Friday the 13th*, and the killer's appearance is halfway between that from *Halloween* and that of *Friday 13th Part II*. The 'Clover Categories' are featured too. The **psychokiller**, one character recounts, 'was always picked up for being different, ugly'. He was a lonely boy bullied by the popular boys – Billy, as a victim, was gendered feminine – and his foundational trauma was precisely a humiliating prank gone wrong. He is a textbook case of castration compensated with a violent use of **phallic weaponry** – a long machete. His home is as dark and humid as possible, a veritable visualization of Clover's 'intrauterine' **Terrible Place**. And, obviously, he is eerily unstoppable: neither being impaled on antlers, nor being hit by arrows, nor being set on fire, nor being stabbed repeatedly can halt his fury. The **victims** are all teenagers, and the golden rule of the slasher is amply paraded: as 2009 Duncan, the slasher expert, explains to his film-stranded friends, 'Everyone who has sex in this movie dies', and later 2009 Max restates the inescapable equation, 'the moment a top comes off, Billy [the psychokiller] shows up'. *Quod erat demonstrandum*, the very first character slated to die in *Camp Bloodbath* is indeed 1986 Mimi, a flower child, the quintessential symbol of sexual liberation. Though strongly verging on comedy and metalinguistic/intertextual parody, the film has its moments of **shock**

---

[11]A video – or videographic – essay is a research output that, instead of coming in the traditional written form, comes in audiovisual forms. See Keathley and Mittell (2016) and Kiss and van den Berg (2016).

that catch us off guard: for example, Duncan is the first to die within the 2009 group, unexpectedly, because up to that point the film-stranded 2009 characters thought they were untouchable observers of the *Camp Bloodbath* events; later, the sudden deaths of 2009 Vicki and 2009 Gertie are also rendered in a serious tone.

The circumstances of the screen trespassing comply with another generic trope: 'horror film characters are forever watching horror movies [...], and not a few horror plots turn on the horrifying consequences of looking at horror' (Clover, 2015, p. 167). Indeed, as 2009 Max approaches the film theatre to take part in the viewing of *Camp Bloodbath*, menacing non-diegetic music alerts us of the upcoming 'horrifying consequences'. The whole sequence set in the film theatre is endowed with an ominous paranormal halo. We are shown the viewers in their seats through a mobile camera that obtrusively glides across the room, offering a bird's eye view of the audience (a ghost's eye view?), as if some supernatural presence were hovering over. Indeed, something eerie happens: a fire suddenly breaks out. The accident is triggered by a chain of uncannily coordinated events reminiscent of the deadly butterfly effects of *Final Destination* (2000). There is also a strange coincidence of action between what is happening within the projected film and what is happening in the film theatre, a correlation that reminds of Jung's Synchronicity — the existence of 'meaningful coincidence' between 'acausal parallelism' that can reveal the presence of a paranormal dimension (Jung, 1973, p. 8). In the film, 1986 Nancy lights up a Zippo, and a 2009 viewer in the theatre does the same simultaneously; 1986 Kurt takes a mouthful of beer in the film, and a 2009 viewer takes one of vodka in the theatre; the vodka bottle slips off the hands and lands onto the floor, rolling all over under the seats, spreading the liquor around and terminating its route on the velour curtains. When one 2009 viewer drops some cigarette ember on the floor, a flame trail is ignited that reaches the curtains right in front of 2009 Max — on her way to walk out of the screening — thus blocking her exit. The fire instantly propagates all around. As the 2009 viewers scream, 1986 Nancy screams onscreen at the sight of Billy the psychokiller about to take her life. In the turmoil, 2009 Max bumps into another viewer, who drops a machete. It is with that blade that Max opens an emergency exit into the screen, slashing the film's body exactly as, onscreen, Billy slashes Nancy's. The narration in this sequence seems to suggest that Max is destined by some higher force to enter into the film *Camp Bloodbath*.

The screen-crossing trope is hardly new. The permeability of the film screen is as old as cinema — just think of Lumière's *L'arrivée d'un train à la Ciotat* (1895), or the projectionist entering into the film in Buster Keaton's *Sherlock Jr.* (1924). The trope has continued to resurface, with other examples including *The Purple Rose of Cairo* (1985) — with film characters exiting the screen — and more recently, *Pleasantville* (1998) — with viewers entering the screen. It has been already exploited in the horror genre too, for instance in *Demons* (1985) — with zombies exiting the screen — and *Poltergeist* (1982) — with little Carol Anne sucked into the TV screen. Nevertheless, *The Final Girls* substantiates it with an emotionally-charged background story. *Camp Bloodbath*'s 1986 Nancy was played by the deceased mother of 2009 Max, Amanda, and the date of the screening coincides exactly with the third anniversary of Amanda's death. *The Final Girls* opens with a trailer of *Camp Bloodbath*, which is soon revealed to be watched on a smartphone by Max, waiting in a car, twenty years after the film's release. Her mother Amanda shows up and we recognize the screaming 1986 Nancy from the trailer. Amanda, a single mother, drives her daughter back home, after another unsuccessful audition – we learn that she is a struggling actress regretting the *Camp Bloodbath* role which potentially hindered a legitimate career. A car accident ensues, in which Amanda dies. Before the accident, a delayed dialogue hook anticipates the plot's development: Max worries about her mother's troubled sentimental relationships, and Amanda sweetly replies, 'Look at you, taking care of me!' Indeed, in her screen-crossing adventure, 2009 Max will not strive simply to save herself but also to save 1986 Nancy, her mother's screen character. Nancy – 'the shy girl with the clipboard and the guitar' – is supposed to die in *Camp Bloodbath* as soon as she loses her virginity to 1986 Kurt, as per the slasher film's rules. Hence, 2009 Max must prevent 1986 Nancy from having sex with 1986 Kurt – a 'troubled relationship' that mirrors the ones the actress Amanda had in real life. 'Sex can kill you!' 2009 Max warns 1986 Nancy, who replies, 'You sound like my mom!' The prefigured inversion of role is fully realized here: Max is acting parentally and hyper-protectively towards the younger version of her mother.

The mother–daughter inversion of roles is further symbolized by the citation of the Persephone myth, earlier in the film: Persephone was abducted and trapped in the underworld, and her mother Demeter travelled to Hades in the desperate attempt to take her back. Here, 2009 Max is like Demeter; she too wants her mother/daughter back. Still grieving and processing the loss, Max is reluctant to attend the *Camp Bloodbath* screening but, once there, she finds a bitter-sweet solace when she sees her mother Amanda 'living' again onscreen in the Nancy character. Once trapped inside the film, 2009 Max is under the delusion that the Nancy character *is* her mother, and that taking her outside of the film is a way to move the time backwards, before Amanda's death. The door through which Max's Demeter-like journey begins is highly symbolical. The only escape route from the fire that is devouring the theatre is through the back-door behind the screen. Max cuts a slit in the screen on which the image of her mother is projected on that precise moment.

Clover's book abound in psychoanalytical references, and this image of the screen with the mother and an aperture is highly 'vaginal': in a regression fantasy, Max re-enters into her mother's womb.[12] This is not the only allusion to the psychoanalytical territory. In another scene where the screen-crossers wonder if the experience they are living can be a collective dream, 2009 Duncan casually exposes – a slip of tongue – a very sexually-charged dream: 'If this is a dream,

---

[12]For example, Clover links the vaginal figures to the openness to the supernatural in her analysis of possession film (pp. 100–113). But the screen as a womb reminds of Baudry's idea of the screen as feminine, as the mother's bosom, to which the child/spectator wishes to reunite: see Baudry (1980) and also Mayne (1990, pp. 38–39).

then there's a very strong chance that my dad's going to come up to us naked and offer us some pecan pie. But don't take any. It's not pecan pie'. This seems a parody of Freud's noted 1919 case study 'A Child Is Being Beaten', a repressed male homoerotic/masochist fantasy amply referred to by Clover (pp. 13–16, 212–218).

The discourse about gender roles is closely linked to the metalinguistic/intertextual display. Like a time-travel film, the 1986 teenagers of *Camp Bloodbath* come in contact with the 2009 teenagers, and the encounter allows for a comparison of how gender representation has changed since. *Camp Bloodbath*'s Nina is the 1986 stereotype of the uninhibited girl with an active sex life. She is presented as a sexual object, and happy about it, to the point that she seems to have problems in keeping her clothes on. If she is sexy, ergo, she must be dumb and slutty: warned by the 2009 screen-crossers to keep her top on to prevent Billy from killing her, the one thing that actually worries her is: 'But why does he hate my boobs? Because they're not big?' Nina's counterpart is 2009 Vicki. She is the most popular girl, uninhibited, with a growing track record of relationships. She is depicted as mean or haughty at times but shows no signs of 'sluttishness,' and she is intelligent and as dedicated to study and achievements as she is to boys – she is applying for Cornell and Stanford, and takes Adderall (an amphetamine-like drug) to boost her cognitive performance. While 1986 Nina would naturally giggle at the boys' gross compliments – 'What's up, funbags?' is 1986 Kurt's way of greeting girls – 2009 Vicki is contemptuous of such expressions and she speaks up her feminist awareness: 'Funbags [...] Right [...] Yay, feminism!' The male terms of comparison are 1986 Kurt and 2009 Chris. 1986 Kurt is a concentrate of retro sexist and macho ethos. Constantly bragging about his sexual prowess and making lewd compliments to any girl he stumbles upon, coitus seems to be Kurt's *idée fixe*, and the more sexual trophies he collects, the more man he proves to be: 'These girls are slamming! And I am going to do all of them'. 1986 Kurt is as hard-wired to objectify women as 1986 Nina is hard-wired to be objectified. As 2009 Vicki is the mirror of 1986 Nina, so 2009 Chris is of 1986 Kurt. 2009 Chris looks manly and handsome – much more so than 1986 Kurt – seemingly a perfect candidate to occupy the male-dominant position. Yet, from the very beginning we understand that he has a romantic interest for 2009 Max but he never makes any overt move on her. He is depicted as shy and respectful of Max's feelings. The dialogue between him and Kurt, who is inspecting an issue of *PlayMan*, further presents the difference between the monolithic phallic mindset of 1986 Kurt and 2009 Chris's more open outlook:

> Kurt: Look at that pair on her!
>
> Chris: Yeah, but look at those articles. I could read those all night long.
>
> Kurt: What are you, a fag? You don't like some nice big hoots?
>
> Chris: My dads are gay. So, shut the hell up.
>
> Kurt: Yeah, right! Gay guys can't have kids!

When the 2009 screen-crossers help the 1986 residents to set a trap for Billy, 2009 Chris is not afraid to confess to 2009 Max, 'I'm really scared.' Clover states that, 'if action cinema mourns the passing of the "real man", horror in general urges it along' (Clover, 2015, p. 99). 2009 Chris is not a 'real man' for the 1980s action-film standards, but he is a more complete man, one that not only is not abusive but sympathetic to women; one that is also liberated from the male's own traditional 'butch' gender role and is thus able to connect with and be frank about his emotions. *The Final Girls* seems to portray those 'new male viewers' that, for a series of socio-cultural reasons (Clover, 2015, p. 231), have developed a less rigid understanding of gender and role identification, and 2009 Chris's case and his experience with same-sex parents reminds of one specific item in Clover's explanations: 'an increased openness, among young people, to bisexual aesthetic, if not bisexual practices' (Clover, 2015, p. 231). The 'new man' is also portrayed – though comically – in the 2009 Duncan character. Besides Duncan's already mentioned Freudian dream that speaks of bisexuality and masochism, other dialogue lines confirm his fluid gender identity. In one of the outtakes that are shown within the end credits, Duncan plainly admits: 'Ever since I was a little boy, I've dreamed of being the Final Girl', and Clover reminds us that:

> The Final Girl is [...] a congenial double for the adolescent male. She is feminine enough to act out in a gratifying way, a way unapproved for adult males, the terrors and masochistic pleasures of the underlying fantasy, but not so feminine as to disturb the structures of male competence and sexuality. [...] The Final Girl is a male surrogate in things Oedipal, a homoerotic stand-in, the audience incorporate. (Clover, 2015, pp. 51, 53)

The film also shows sexual equality in its depiction of death, as it neutralizes the discrepancy noted by Clover between the quick and distant portrayal of male deaths and the detailed and prolonged one of female deaths. There is no special treatment of the female murders as a spectacle, but both sexes are treated similarly. In the 'final act,' we have a vivid instance of the typical slasher film's 'gender rezoning' signalled by Clover: when 2009 Max takes up the role of the Final Girl, decidedly shifting towards the masculine-gendered hero.

The film title is a plural: *The Final Girls*. Who are these girls, specifically? From the fictional *Camp Bloodbath* trailer that opens the film, we are informed that the designated Final Girl is a brunette – 1986 Paula, we will learn later. She closes the trailer, dishevelled and brandishing a machete, saying: 'You just messed with the wrong virgin.' When the 2009 screen-crossers, after the initial disorientation, realize they are within the film, and also that they are potential victims, they understand that the only way to get out of the film alive is to play by the slasher film's rules. Unlike the 1986 characters, they seem to live in-between the diegetic and the non-diegetic level, halfway between characters and spectators. They have an awareness of being in a film; they can hear the non-diegetic music, in particular Billy's motif alerts them that the psychokiller is approaching; they can interact with non-diegetic film elements, for example they can climb over the intertitles.

They also exert some control over the film itself, to the point that they can bend its course: they can trigger a flashback just by pronouncing the dialogue line scripted to launch it. But to a point: the film's denouement *cannot* be changed. As 2009 Duncan explains, 'Movies like this end after the Final Girl kills the main bad guy and the credits roll.' The plan then seems straightforward: they have to follow the Final Girl. 1986 Paula arrives, driving a 'bad-ass' car − plate: 'Paula-1. Freedom and Glory' − dressed in tank-top, leather jacket, jeans and combat boots, sunglasses and cigarette in her mouth. She is as beautiful and sexy as a girl, and as tough as a boy, and she is a virgin: Final Girl incarnate. We are led to think, at this point, that the two titular Final Girls are 1986 Paula and 2009 Max, who will probably have some assisting role. But the screen-crossers alter the course of the film and 1986 Paula dies. A new Final Girl has to be appointed. 2009 Vicki applies for, but her candidature is immediately rejected: 'You're not a virgin.' Neither is 2009 Gertie, so 2009 Max is the only choice. But since 1986 Nancy was 'saved' from having sex with 1986 Kurt, she is a virgin too. 1986 Paula is thus replaced with *two* Final Girls, 1986 Nancy and 2009 Max, mother and daughter − in the complex reverse-role dynamics we have seen. In his only 'traditionally virile' endeavour, 2009 Chris devises an elaborate plan by which he think he can kill Billy: a *booby* trap whose decoy, much appropriately, is 1986 Tina removing her top and 'flashing'. Of course, the scheme turns out to be a total failure: as Clover warns, 'the man who insists on taking charge [...] is dead meat' (Clover, 2015, p. 65). Actually 2009 Chris survives, and flees with the other two survivors, the two Final Girls, but from that point on, after the breakdown of his masculine initiative, he takes on a passive role, he is femininized: 'Sex, in this universe, proceeds from gender, not the other way around. A figure does not cry and cower because she is a woman; she is a woman because she cries and cowers. [...] Those who save themselves are male, and those who are saved by others are female.' (Clover, 2015, pp. 13−59). In the following scene, 2009 Chris is stabbed by Billy and 1986 Nancy is abducted. 2009 Max, who has already taken possession of the phallic machete, assumes a protective masculine role − the 'saver' − and carries the wounded body of 2009 Chris − the 'saved' − across the woods, to put him to rest inside an abandoned church. Then, she leaves to rescue 1986 Nancy, after reassuring a cringing 2009 Chris who sobs: 'Max, I don't want to die alone.'

2009 Max finds 1986 Nancy in the Terrible Place, Billy's lair. An inversion of roles happens here, as 2009 Max is wounded and 1986 Nancy saves her from Billy's fatal blow. Now it is 1986 Nancy that carries 2009 Max across the woods, to the church. Max is dying, and the reason is simple: there can be just *one* Final Girl. Nancy knows there is only one thing to do: 'You're not the Final Girl yet, Max. Because of me. I'm still alive'. Max tries to resist Nancy's decision but the rule cannot be circumvented, 'That's not what I'm supposed to be, remember?' [...] You have to let me go,' says Nancy. Max sobs, 'I wanted to save you' but Nancy replies, 'You did, Max!' And Nancy courageously walks outside to meet Billy and her demise, on the notes of Kim Carnes's 1981 song *Bette Davis Eyes*, which we had heard in the prologue, during the car dialogue between mother and daughter, identified as Amanda's favourite song. On that first appearance, the song may have looked as a device to colour Amanda's character with the proper 1980s nostalgia. Here its deeper meaning is made evident: the song speaks of an independent, active woman in control of her life – dedicated to Bette Davis, one of the strongest women of the classical Hollywood cinema – and prefigures some of the qualities of the heroic Final Girl: 'Her hands are never cold / She'll take a tumble on you, roll you like you were dice / She's ferocious [...].'[13] 1986 Nancy, in a way, is indeed a Final Girl in *ethos*, exactly the 'victim/hero' as described by Clover. Nancy's *heroic* sacrifice is a seminal step to the elimination of the villain. And Max has indeed saved her: Nancy has been freed from the externally determined role of the terrorized helpless victim under the male control – the damsel in distress – and given the active role of the self-determined woman. She is killed, but she is because *she* has so decided, and she offers herself without giving the sadist the satisfaction of hearing a single terrorized scream, unlike the previous scripted image of her seen in the original *Camp Bloodbath*.

As soon as 1986 Nancy dies, 2009 Max heals, ready to build on what the first Final Girl has set up. The investiture is represented emphatically, introduced by a supernatural-looking thunderstorm. As if endowed with some magical powers, Max rises, and the music accompanies with a virile synth-horns motif her picking up and confidently swinging the machete. Chris, still passively on the ground, powerless, looks up to her in admiration. Max steps out of the church to solemnly utter 1986 Paula's Final Girl's motto, though in a more contemporary wording: 'You just fucked with the wrong virgin.' In a highly choreographed showdown, Max seems as indestructible as Billy and eventually manages to chop his head off. This final duel is represented in such exaggerated terms – with kung fu and wuxia acrobatics and even a knife-dodging stunt reminiscent of the dodged bullet in *The Matrix* (1999) – that the whole scene betrays its parodical intent. It presents precisely that stereotypical byproduct of the Final Girl – 'female avenger and triumphant feminist hero' (Clover, 2015, p. x) – that Clover says has come to 'hijack' the original more ambiguous formulation (Clover, 2015, p. 63).

14.3.   The End?

As soon as Billy is defeated, the end credits roll and Max and Chris reunite and watch the titles rising from behind the hills, like a sunrise, in a highly metalinguistic moment.

Finally, they kiss. As the film *Camp Bloodbath* literally ends – we see the tail of the filmstrip running behind them – they cross over to wake up in a hospital

---

[13]By Donna Weiss and Jackie De Shannon, © 1981, Warner/Chappell Music, Inc, Karen Schauben Publishing.

room, where they find all the 2009 gang — Duncan, Vicki and Gertie — alive and well. Is it the end? They suddenly hear again the infamous Billy musical motif, announcing that he is in the premises. Worryingly, they peek out of their room and notice 1980s elements around — a Rubik cube, a Gizmo puppet, a Tab Cola, a doctor serenely harassing a complacent nurse … — and Duncan realizes: 'Of course! The sequel!' They are still inside a film: Billy breaks in from a window, accompanied by the title 'Camp Bloodbath 2: Cruel Summer'. As Max grabs her drip-feed stand like a spear and launches an attack on Billy, *The Final Girls* ends. The film has carried on with its metalinguistic/intertextual play to the very end: the twist finale is another trope of horror films in general — 'when you thought it was safe to […]' — as well as the surprise return of the supposedly defeated monster — think of *A Nightmare on Elm Street*. In particular, this is an overt homage to *Halloween 2* (1981), in which the Final Girl Laurie is tracked down by the psychokiller in the hospital where she is recovering from the previous fight. And Alice, the Final Girl from *Friday the 13th*, defeats the deranged Mrs Voorhees in the series' first instalment only to be brutally murdered at the beginning of *Part 2* by Jason, Mrs Voorhees's son. In the perpetual return of the villain and, consequently, the short-lived and only temporary victory of the Final Girl we can see more than the mere need to prolong a profitable franchise. If we interpret the Final Girl as a feminist symbol of fight against the phallic threats of the psychokiller, then the meaning is that the Final Girl might have won one battle, not the war. The slasher may be rich in gender-crossing dynamics and offer some sort of feminist victory, but it presents these in the form of a pattern bound to be cyclically repeated. There will always be a struggling Final Girl and a threatening male killer, and if the outcome is her victory, this outcome is only temporary, the cycle is likely to start over soon. Feminism has won some battles, but the war is still far from being over. The years might have brought more sympathetic and open male figures — like 2009 Chris — and a rezoning of gender, with softer and more fluid borders, but much is still to be done. Max has not even had the time to heal from one battle that she is called back to service. The fight is, seemingly, endless.

References

Baudry, J.-L. (1980). The apparatus. In T. H. K. Cha (Ed.), *Apparatus* (pp. 41–46). New York, NY: Tanam Press.

Carroll, N. (1988). *Mystifying movies. Fads and fallacies in contemporary film theory*. New York, NY: Columbia University Press.

Clayton, W. (Ed.). (2015). *Style and form in the Hollywood slasher film*. Basingstoke: Palgrave Macmillan.

Clover, C. (2015). *Men, women, and chain saws. Gender in the modern horror film* *[1992]*. Princeton, NJ: Princeton University Press.

Conrich, I. (2009). The *Friday the 13th* films and the cultural function of a modern Grand Guignol. In I. Conrich (Ed.), *Horror zone: The cultural experience of contemporary horror cinema* (pp. 173–188). London: I.B. Tauris.

Dika, V. (1990). *Games of terror: Halloween, Friday the 13th, and the films of the stalker cycle.* Madison, NJ: Fairleigh Dickinson University Press.

Doane, M. A. (1990). Film and the masquerade, theorizing the female spectator. [1982]. In P. Erens (Ed.), *Issues in feminist film criticism* (pp. 41−57). Bloomington, IN: Indiana University Press.

Freeland, C. A. (1996). Feminist frameworks for horror films. In D. Bordwell & N. Carroll (Eds.), *Post-theory. Reconstructing film studies* (pp. 195−218). Madison, WI: University of Wisconsin Press.

Gaines, J. (1990 [1984]). Women and representation: Can we enjoy alternative pleasure?. In P. Erens (Ed.), *Issues in feminist film criticism* (pp. 75−92). Bloomington, IN: Indiana University Press.

Jung, C. G. (1973 [1952]). *Synchronicity: An acausal connecting principle* (trans. R. Hull). Princeton, NJ: Princeton University Press.

Keathley, C., & Mittell, J. (2016). (Eds.), *The videographic essay: Criticism in sound and image.* Montreal: Caboose.

Kiss, M., & van den Berg, T. (2016). *Film studies in motion: From audiovisual essay to academic research video.* Los Angeles, CA: Scalar. Retrieved from http://scalar.usc.edu/works/film-studies-in-motion/index. Accessed on 25 January 2018.

Maddrey, J. (2004). *Nightmares in red, white and blue. The evolution of the American horror film.* Jefferson, NC: McFarland.

Mayne, J. (1990). *The woman at the keyhole: Feminism and women's cinema.* Bloomington, IN: Indiana University Press.

Metz, C. (1986 [1977]). *The imaginary signifier: Psychoanalysis and the cinema.* (trans. C. Britton, A. Williams, B. Brewster, & A. Guzzetti). Bloomington, IN: Indiana University Press.

Mulvey, L. (1975). Visual pleasure and narrative cinema. *Screen, 16*(3), 6−18 (1 October).

Mulvey, L. (2009 [1981]). "Afterthoughts on 'Visual Pleasure and Narrative Cinema' Inspired by King Vidor's *Duel in the Sun* (1946)", in Id. *Visual and other pleasures* (2nd ed., pp. 31−40). London: Palgrave Macmillan.

Neill, A. (1996). Empathy and (Film) fiction. In D. Bordwell & N. Carroll (Eds.), *Post-theory. Reconstructing film studies* (pp. 175−194). Madison, WI: University of Wisconsin Press.

Normanton, P. (2012). *The mammoth book of slasher movies.* London: Constable & Robinson.

Nowell, R. (2010). *Blood money: A history of the first teen slasher film cycle.* New York, NY: Continuum.

Petridis, S. (2014). A historical approach to the slasher film. *Film International, 12*(1), 76−89..

Prince, S. (1996). Psychoanalytic film theory and the problem of the missing spectator. In D. Bordwell & N. Carroll (Eds.), *Post-theory. Reconstructing film studies* (pp. 71−86). Madison, WI: University of Wisconsin Press.

Robinson, J. (2010). *Life lessons from slasher films.* Lanham, MD: Scarecrow Press.

Rockoff, A. (2011). *Going to pieces: The rise and fall of the slasher film, 1978−1986.* Jefferson, NC: McFarland.

Smith, M. (1995). *Engaging characters: Fiction, emotion, and the cinema.* Oxford: Clarendon Press.

Workland, R. (2007). *The horror film. An introduction.* Malden, MA: Blackwell.

Chapter 15

Dissecting Depictions of Black Masculinity in *Get Out*

Francesca Sobande

15.1. Introduction

It is the 23rd of January 2018 and *Get Out* (2017) has been nominated for four Oscar awards; Best Picture, Best Actor, Best Director and Best Original Screenplay. Online coverage of this news spreads quickly. Jordan Peele is only the fifth Black director in history to be nominated for the Best Director accolade. Peele's debut film – *Get Out*, even earnt a place amongst the top 10 most profitable ones in 2017. The film has been lauded as groundbreaking (Cane, 2017; Rankin, 2018) due to its focus on the horrors of racism which unfold in an unsettling US suburban context.

An abundance of film reviews pick apart the racial politics of *Get Out*: '*Get Out*: the horror film that shows it's scary to be a black man in America' (Blackwell, 2016), '*Get Out*: why racism really is terrifying' (Anderson, 2017), '*Get Out* review: a breathlessly suspenseful exposé of the horror of liberal racism' (Robey, 2017). Although much has been written about how *Get Out* deals with racism in the US (Lopez, 2017), the complexities of associated matters regarding Black masculinity and horror, are not always accounted for. While 'more recent scholarship has focused on issues of race and class in horror' (Grant, 2015, p. 5), there is still a scarcity of writing that inspects how Black people are portrayed in horror films. As such, there is much to gain from a critical textual analysis of depictions of Black masculinity in *Get Out*.

15.1.1. *Get Out*

To put it briefly, *Get Out* follows the experiences of Chris Washington (Daniel Kaluuya), who is in an interracial relationship with a young white woman named Rose Armitage (Allison Williams). Chris finds himself in danger when visiting Rose's waspish parents Dean (Bradley Whitford) and Missy (Catherine Keener), and her brother Jeremy (Caleb Landry Jones). The film, which is about 'white terror and black bodies' (Henry, 2017, p. 334), pans out in an affluent

Gender and Contemporary Horror in Film, 237–250
doi:10.1108/978-1-78769-897-020191016

and secluded predominantly white location. When Chris enters this space, his Blackness is immediately hypervisible (Du Bois, [1903] 2007), as is the difference between his class position and that of Rose and her notably wealthy family. Chris is marked as a curiosity and 'the Other', which is a societal position often ascribed to Black people (Guerrero, 1993; hooks, 1992; Kee, 2015; Lewis, 1997). However, the film is a far cry from *Guess Who's Coming to Dinner* (1967), which in contrast to *Get Out* deals with the awkwardness of interracial relationships and familial meetings, in a somewhat light-hearted way.

An introductory scene in *Get Out* features a track by Childish Gambino (A.K.A. Donald Glover) (2016), which includes haunting lyrics about staying 'woke' because 'they gon' find you' and 'catch you sleepin'. Staying woke, in this context, relates to being aware of, and challenging, sociopolitical injustices that the most marginalized groups of society face. The concept of being woke has strong links to Black liberation and anti-racist organizing, including the Black Lives Matter social justice movement (Taylor, 2016). Thus, Gambino's song quietly foreshadows horrific and neocolonial manifestations of racism that occur throughout the film.

Uncomfortable on-screen exchanges in *Get Out* are peppered with racially coded language and gestures. Ultimately, this cultivates a looming sense of doom that eventually leads to Chris's unbridled suspicion of Rose's family, their friends and the Black staff members that help around their house. Whilst this chapter is particularly based on analysis of Chris in *Get Out*, it also touches on his on-screen friendship with the character Rod Williams (Lil Rel Howery). Despite the representation of women not being the focus of this chapter, there is consideration of how Black masculinity in *Get Out*, takes shape in relation to both the absence and presence of Black women and white women.

The writing that follows outlines how *Get Out* offers complex and rarely featured representations of Black masculinity, and boyhood, in horror. It unpacks what this reveals about the racial politics of constructions of Black masculinity and interdependent gender relations, in such a film genre. This includes consideration of how inter- and intra-racial relations are implicated in the depiction of Black masculinity in *Get Out*. Even though this chapter is influenced by a strong body of academic studies of race, media, horror and identity (Blackwell, 2017; Carbado & Gulati, 2013; Carroll, 1990; Cherry, 2009; Graveyard Shift Sisters, 2018; hooks, 1992; McCollum, 2016; Means-Coleman, 2011; Wood, 2002), it also draws on related online commentary. The works of Black scholars and cultural critics are integral to my writing, including to avoid replicating the subjugation of Black voices and identities.

15.2.   Theoretical Framework

15.2.1.   Horror and the Gaze

Defining horror presents a challenge that reflects the mystery, contradictions and confusion that horror cinema provokes. Amongst well-established definitions of horror film is Wood's (2002, p. 28) description of it being based on 'the struggle for recognition of all that our civilization represses and oppresses'. This statement can open up conversations about how oppressed people may find solace in bright screens dawning horror films. Conversely, Wood's (2002) remark can also relate to how horror cinema can fuel the stereotyping of social groups, including on the grounds of gender, race and sexuality (Blackwell, 2017; Denzin, 2002; Guerrero, 1993; McCollum, 2016; Means-Coleman, 2011).

Another take on horror can be found in the words of Carroll (1990, p. 12), who affirms that horror 'is not an obscure notion' and asserts that the horrific qualities of visual content relates to 'the emotion it characteristically or rather ideally promotes; this emotion constitutes the identifying mark of horror'. When accounting for the emotion-stirring quality of horror, there is a need to address how the identities of film spectators influences what they interpret as being horrifying. Films such as *Get Out* have highlighted the importance of acknowledging the experiences of Black people as horror spectators, and whose gaze is rarely prioritized amidst the production of horror cinema.

Online articles such as 'Dear White People: A Guide to Watching "*Get Out*" with Black Audiences' (Dickerson, 2017) stress the need to critically reflect on the racial politics of watching *Get Out*, as well as ideas regarding race conveyed in the film. Furthermore, *Get Out's* nomination for a Golden Globe award for Best Musical or Comedy Motion Picture, stimulated commentary regarding the racial politics of how films are categorized. The way that *Get Out's* status as a horror film has been struggled over, speaks to its unusualness, as well as the contested nature of the horrors of racism.

This chapter focuses specifically on representations of Black masculinity in *Get Out*, but it includes consideration of the racial politics of spectator looking relations. Prior work, such as Gray's (1995, p. 142), illustrates how media depictions facilitate 'a kind of public acknowledgement, contestation, and renegotiation of blackness, especially the specific terms in which masculinities, sexuality, desire and identity have been figured in commercial culture'. Gray's observation is central to my analysis of *Get Out* and by blending academic and cultural commentary, this film can be explored in-depth.

15.2.2.   *The Horrors of Racism*

It was over 20 years ago that Guerrero (1993, p. 41) asserted that 'race is one of the most emotionally and politically charged subjects in the American social psyche and media imagination', yet such a statement is as resonant today as it was then. Rhetoric regarding the post-racial world that 44th President of the United States of America Barack Obama allegedly symbolized has been subsumed by the election of President Donald Trump. This is not to suggest that mythic claims of a post-racial America were ever anything other than fantasy. Rather, it is important to recognize the sociopolitical backdrop of *Get Out*, which is marked by the rise of publicly condoned far right politics, racist sentiments, and the construction of whiteness as innocence (Emejulu, 2016).

The horrors of racism are not always as explicit as the unexpected bang of a gun, followed by yet another Black fatality. Instead, they are also to be found in the insidious everydayness of racism, which can prompt Black people to act and present themselves in raced, classed and gendered ways, that may be perceived as being intentionally 'racially palatable'. Carbado and Gulati (2013, p. 1) assert that being Black in primarily white settings 'is like being an actor on stage. There are roles one has to perform, storylines one is expected to follow, and dramas and subplots one should avoid at all cost.' Consequently, to be Black in a predominantly white institution can involve strategic and self-preservationist approaches to racial performance; amounting to a form of 'Working Identity' (Carbado & Gulati, 2013, p. 3). It is through taking up this conceptualization that depictions of Black masculinity in *Get Out* are examined in this chapter.

This work is underpinned by critical race theory, which enables articulation of how Black people are societally framed as embodying Otherness (Du Bois, [1903] 2007; Guerrero, 1993; hooks, 1992; Kee, 2015; Lewis, 1997). This notion of Otherness captures how Black individuals are often treated as a marker of difference and deviance, in comparison with the normative status of white identities (Dyer, 1997). DuBois' ([1903] 2007) related notion of double-consciousness encompasses how the self-image and lives of Black people are impacted by white supremacy (Wekker, 2016), and which results in their constant awareness and anticipation of racist perceptions of them.

15.2.3.   *The Racism of Horror*

There are many 'familiar racial tropes circulating endlessly through US visual media: as a defenceless victim inducted into the brutal history of anti-Black violence or as a frightening "thug," symbolic of an ongoing threat posed by Black men to White middle-class society' (Kee, 2015, p. 47). Although the debated genre of Black film (Diawara, 1993; Leonard, 2006; Mask, 2014), often focuses on the lives of Black men (Fisher, 2006), horror cinema has rarely engaged with their experiences in well-developed ways. Even when not depicted as part of physically violent scenes, Black characters in horror films are often still subject to symbolic forms of violence, through the use of rhetorical and visual cues that invoke racist and colonial ideologies. Further still, Black people in horror are often killed early on, as Jada Pinkett's character Maureen said at the beginning of *Scream II* (1997).

When scrutinizing how issues of race are embedded in those concerning horror film, Blackwell (2015) asks: 'What does it look like when a horror film takes on the horrors of racism and race relations?' An answer to this question can be provided by analysing *Get Out*. The film defies conventional categories and sits at the edges of genres, including satire, black comedy, psychological thriller and coming-of-age drama. The concept of horror at the core of my analysis encompasses the horror of lived realities, as well as fictional filmic plots, where previously 'the scene of Black annihilation promised a *horror* show' (Means-Coleman, 2011, p. 1).

The stereotypical ways that Black men are portrayed in horror film includes the prevalence of hypermasculine and hypersexualized representations, as well as the images of Black pain and trauma that can be reminiscent of Black lynchings (Kee, 2015). In other words, the humanity of Black men has scarcely been treated with nuance in horror cinema, nor has that of Black women. Moreover, discussion of issues related to gender and horror frequently involve reflection on masculinities and/or femininities, but it is still uncommon for this to entail detailed analysis of the entanglements of race and gender. For this reason, my work attends to some of the ways that issues regarding race *and* gender intersect amidst the depiction of Black masculinity in *Get Out*.

15.3.   Where Is My Mind? *Get Out* and the Humanity of Black Men in Horror

Tension building at the heart of *Get Out* focuses on the psyche of Chris, including buried childhood memories that resurface when visiting the wealthy white family of his girlfriend Rose. Uncomfortable on-screen conversations between Chris and Rose's brother Jeremy, bring up long-standing racist stereotypes regarding the perceived aggressive and 'bestial' nature of Black men (hooks, 2004a, 2004b). This includes a scene featuring Jeremy suggesting that Chris's 'genetic makeup' would make him a great Mixed Martial Arts (MMA) fighter. Apart from such an exchange, and a few tense fights that Chris emerges from victorious, this is where any emphasis on his physical strength ends. Instead, the prominence of issues related to Chris's mind indicates a focus on the humanity of Black men in *Get Out*.

The representation of Black men throughout cinematic history has been dogged by monolithic imagery (Bogle, 1973; Chan, 1998; Guerrero, 1993) which positions such men as being 'primitive' and/or serving a purely comical purpose. For example, *Scary Movie* 2 (2001), which is the second in the spoof film series, includes a scene featuring a Black man named Shorty being attacked by a marijuana monster, which rolls him up and smokes him. This is an all too familiar representation of Black men in film, often portrayed as hyperbolic and humorous characters who lack a wide spectrum of emotions, and whose minds are seldom of cinematic interest.

The physicality of Chris in *Get Out* is partly why he appeals to Rose's parents – Missy and Dean. Through hypnosis and brain surgery, they plan to use Chris's body to house the consciousness of a rich white person and confine Chris's mind to 'the sunken place'. However, it is the potentially perilous state of Chris's psyche, which is at the core of this film's suspense. Chris's entry to 'the sunken place', which plays a central role in *Get Out*, is facilitated by hypnosis therapy led by Missy. This results in Chris's mind becoming detached from his embodiment, which prohibits him from physically responding to his surroundings.

When Chris first becomes trapped in 'the sunken place', he is still able to see a blurred impression of Missy, as well as hear her speak to him, although he is unable to reply. This scene involves filmic techniques that create a strong sense of distance between Chris and the image of Missy, who towers over him. Visually, such imagery echoes Du Bois's ([1903] 2007, p. 12) summary of the 'double-consciousness' of Black people, which is described as being a 'sense of always looking at one's self through the eyes of others, of measuring one's soul by the tape of a world that looks on in amused contempt and pity'. Chris is momentarily powerless to the words of Missy, who stares at him with anthropological but detached interest.

Get Out includes an emphasis on Chris's life and humanity. He is not fighting to merely avoid a gory death that Black men often meet in horror films, and which treat them as a canvas for torture. Instead, Chris fights to maintain control over his personhood and to avoid essentially becoming a living corpse, whose body would be controlled by a white person with much socioeconomic privilege. Chris is fighting to live, rather than simply exist. The philosophical distinction between existing and living is an important one here, particularly given that the lives of Black men, and Black women for that matter, are rarely treated in multifaceted ways as part of mainstream horror cinema (Graveyard Shift Sisters, 2018; Means-Coleman, 2011).

To live, implies a form of humanity – or more simply, it implies an ability to sense, to feel, and to possibly have certain rights. The focus of *Get Out* on Chris's psyche establishes the film as offering depictions of Black men in horror that are extremely uncommon. *Get Out* directs the audience's concern for a Black man's mind, instead of entertaining them with objectifying images. Throughout the film, the ever present monster to be feared is systemic racism. The plot of *Get Out* parallels aspects of the daily realities of Black people in the US and further afield, who may find themselves trying to resist state surveillance, societal disenfranchisement and physical violence that is inflicted on them (Taylor, 2016).

Chris's humanness is what is at stake throughout the film. His paralysis, when in 'the sunken place', is symbolic of how systemic racism compromises both the mental and physical well-being of Black men. *Get Out* plays with long-standing stereotypes to do with gender, race and interracial gender relations. As Daniels (2016, p. 73) acknowledges, racist images of Black men and Black women are 'constructed in relation to those of white men and white women'. Resisting stereotypes, *Get Out* flips normative notions of the presumed innocence of white women, such as Rose and Missy, in comparison with Black men, such as Chris, and who are often portrayed as aggressive, sly and predatory (Daniels, 2016).

The image of Chris floating in a dark abyss ('the sunken place'), peering powerlessly up at Missy, could not be further from how Black men have been framed throughout history as posing a risk to white people; specifically, white women and their perceived 'purity'. Chris's vulnerability, as visualized in the scene where he finds himself in 'the sunken place', juxtaposes with the monstrous actions of Missy, Rose and the rest of their family. This contrast captures the fragility of a Black man's life in a white supremacist society, within which white femininity is often synonymous with an innocence that may be weaponized in racist ways. It only takes recalling the lynching of 14-year-old Emmett Louis Till in Mississippi in 1955, in response to the false accusations of a white woman, to observe how the horrors of racism are connected to gendered inter-racial relations.

The prospect of Chris physically dying is not what sparks *Get Out's* fright factor. Instead, it is the prospect of him being dehumanized in a way that would result in his self-dispossession. This has associations with how 'the psychic residue of slavery continues to taint subtly all black-white social relations and transactions' (Guerrero, 1993, p. 42). The creepy possibility of Chris's body being inhabited by another conjures up imagery and ideas related to colonization. It echoes the enslavement of Black people, who, just as in *Get Out*, have been treated as property and possessions to be auctioned and used, rather than humans to be respected (Du Bois', ([1903] 2007).

15.4. Black Boyhood and Vulnerability

Get Out focuses on Chris's paranoia and pain in the present, as he navigates interacting with Rose's family and friends. However, via brief flashbacks to Chris's past, we learn of a pivotal moment in his life — the death of his mother when he was a young child. Flashback scenes of Chris feature a young Black boy sitting in front of a television screen, which glows whilst he waits for his mother, with no knowledge that she has died in a road accident. The implication is that this tragedy marked the death of Chris's mother and that of his childhood. The latter of these is a life-stage that Black boys are often denied, due to their societal framing as men to be feared from a very young age.

The childhood of Black boys is one that is often represented in film as involving tragic circumstances, particularly those related to criminal and gang activity (Fisher, 2006; Guerrero, 1993). However, the emotional vulnerability of Black boys has certainly not been the source of much horror material. In *Get Out*, Chris blames himself for his inaction as a child, who he believes could have alerted someone sooner about his mother's missing presence. Chris's state of paralysis on the day that his mother died, is mirrored by his potential mental and physical immobilization as a young man in the present, who finds himself in 'the sunken place', led by Missy, and who asks in a hushed voice: 'where was your mom?'

Chris's initial response to Missy's question is a muted one, although his discomfort is clear. He speaks of having 'just sat there', whilst waiting for his mother to return. When being asked why he did not call or seek out someone else, Chris replies by saying that he thought if he did 'it would make it real'. The sense of escapism and denial that these words encompass suggest Chris has continued to repress his emotions since childhood. This is all too commonly a trait deemed essential to hegemonic Black masculinity. These expectations are particularly enabled by the prospect of Black men's emotions being interpreted as aggression (Bryan & Lindo, 2017; hooks, 2004a, 2004b) and with fatal consequences.

As tears start to streak Chris's face whilst undergoing hypnosis, his hands clench the arms of the chair he sits in and his fingers fidget. Images of Chris crying in this particular scene have become synonymous with *Get Out*, which foregrounds the emotional rather than physical pain of a young Black man. Whilst Chris cries, the scene cuts back to the same mannerisms as a child, when awaiting the return of a mother who never arrived. As a young boy in that situation, Chris had nervously clawed away at woodwork and repressed his distress, despite the absence of his outward displays of emotion. The risks posed to Chris by 'the sunken place' are evident, however, the emotional breakthrough he experiences when introduced to it, is one that seemed necessary. That it was stimulated in such an invasive way is representative of how the mental and physical well-being of Black men is disregarded in society.

15.5.   Breaking Barriers for Black Men in Horror (but not Black Women?)

Reflecting on whose and what fears tend to be emphasized as part of horror film, illuminates how such cinema is shaped by intersecting issues concerning race and gender. Chantal (2017) has spoken about the fact that in *Get Out* he wanted to communicate 'my truth as a Black man [...] my perspective that I haven't seen in film before'. As well as this, on numerous occasions Peele has disclosed his desire to make material that attracts Black filmgoers. Whilst *Get Out* has a crossover appeal which prevents it from solely being defined as Black film, that it was directed by a Black man, for the gaze of Black spectators, is significant.

The treatment of Chris's character smashes the stereotype of a Black man being a meagre plot device to leverage the heroic nature of a leading white character. The character of Chris may have carved out further space for Black men to take up different parts in horror films, including as (anti-)heroes, or in future, individuals with different gender identities and sexualities. That said, due to the intersections of racism and sexism (Crenshaw, 2017), it may be much more time until Black women receive the same critical acclaim in mainstream horror.

The absence of Chris's mother, paired with the character of Georgina (Betty Gabriel), leaves much to be desired in terms of how Black women are (not) depicted in *Get Out*. Georgina is more of a background character than a central one, and initially appears to be a demure but socially detached Black staff member in Dean and Missy's home. Georgina's presence is a striking one. She conveys a conflicted character who arguably symbolizes the sickness of both a racist and sexist society, within which her subtle cries for help go unnoticed.

On the surface, Georgina's character fails to provide a developed portrayal of a Black woman. On closer inspection though, her painful containment of visceral suffering, which surfaces in outbursts, captures how Black women are especially susceptible to systemic oppression due to the intersecting axis of racism and gender. Georgina, who initially seems to provide help around the home of Missy and Dean, in fact turns out to provide an embodied home herself, to the consciousness of Dean's mother – Marianne. Georgina's vacant stares and sudden moments of agitation throughout *Get Out*, are a subtle indication of the tensions that lie within her.

Georgina's response to Chris initially seems to range from cold and clinical to frazzled and quietly furious; seemingly portraying Black women as emotionless and uneasy. Prior to the revelation that Georgina's body houses Marianne, she moves through the film with a simultaneously strong and subservient demeanour. This would do little to challenge stereotypes regarding Black women, were it not for the fact that Georgina's body contains the consciousness of an elderly white woman, as well as the more deeply buried soul of the Black woman whose body it is.

There is a sharp contrast between the character of Chris, whose emotions are more freely expressed as the film progresses, and Georgina, who appears to maintain an artificial calmness for much longer than him. Such differences may be interpreted as mirroring the particular pressures to appear pristine, and to placate, which can be placed on Black women. Indeed, Georgina's character represents that of a Black woman whose body is inhabited by her own soul and that of a white woman. Nevertheless, as the only distinct representation of a Black woman in *Get Out*, Georgina's character is still a vehicle through which to reinforce or resist stereotypes specifically related to Black women.

There is no shortage of examples of how Chris exerts his agency in *Get Out*, but the same cannot be said of Georgina. This is precisely one of the reasons why her character is so impactful; she portrays a Black woman whose soul has become restricted to 'the sunken place'. Despite the dire fate that could await Chris, Georgina appears to be in an even grimmer state. Her stilted smile, constant serving, and understated pleas for help, can be interpreted as reflecting a form of deferential and degrading 'Working Identity' (Carbado & Gulati, 2013, p. 3), which Black women may feel forced to adopt when situated in primarily white institutional environments.

The awkward dynamic between Georgina and Chris leads him to speak to Rose about it; eventually insinuating that Georgina may be acting bizarrely because some Black women have an issue with Black men dating white women. This relatively fleeting moment places Black women as being in competition with white women, for the affections of Black men. This is a reminder of how despite the character of Chris pushing against stereotypes, he still upholds certain heteronormative, raced and gendered notions of Black masculinity, including via its positioning in relation to both Black and white femininity.

15.6.   The Terrifying Risks Involved in Respectability Politics

Whilst not all images of Black men in films connote a 'one-sided caricature' (Sanneh, 2001, p. 42), more varied representations are still considerably limited. This is especially true of the horror genre, which can perpetuate how Black people 'are transported into a media hyperspace where they are magnified into a spectacle of hyperblackness' (Shary, 2002, p. 124). Rather than Chris serving as a mythical monster in *Get Out*, or a short-lived prop for an otherwise white cast, his character is complex. This is not to suggest that Chris represents a faultless or idealized image of Black men. Far from it, one of his potential flaws is his initial reluctance to critically question and act on the racist undertones of moments that occur.

Peele has spoken openly about having written *Get Out* during a period when Barack Obama was the President of the United States of America, and when it felt as though people were embracing 'a post-racial lie'; denying that racism existed any longer (Carbado & Gulati, 2013). As Chantal (2017) notes, Peele has also explained that *Get Out* is very much about the idea of staying woke, including when saying: 'I wanted to make sure that this movie satisfied the Black Horror movie audience need for characters to be smart and do things that intelligent, observant people do.' Peele even describes Chris as being 'woke'. However, Chris's ambivalence regarding early indications of racism at the Armitage household prolongs the point at which he finally *does* get out.

Chris's failure to readily act on his suspicions reflects the normalization of racism in society. It symbolizes how many Black people unflinchingly endure countless racist instances in silence. More pertinently, for much of the film, Chris embodies a relatively composed and courteous manner, even in the face of potential bigotry. Chris's emotional concealment captures the performance of raced, gendered and classed respectability politics, that Black men may find themselves undertaking as a survival strategy in white middle-class settings. Therefore, Chris's initial willingness to overlook moments of racism is not as much a character flaw as it is a product of race relations in the US and beyond.

Chris's internal battle about the prospect of being confronted by the racist and morbid inclinations of Rose and her family, also speaks to the double-consciousness of Black people (Du Bois, [1903] 2007). This is indicated when Chris asks Rose if she has informed her parents that he is Black, before meeting them. Chris's efforts to avoid seeming alarmed and aggravated throughout the film, can also be read as exemplifying the lengths that Black men may go to when trying to evade being interpreted as aggressive, as part of the self-management of their 'Working Identity' (Carbado & Gulati, 2013).

As *Get Out* progresses, the sinister and surreptitious motive behind Chris's invitation to the estate of Missy and Dean is slowly revealed. This forces Chris to quit expending energy on performing a politeness and potential racial palatability that masks his true perception of them. Chris's gradual shift in approach is portrayed without insinuating a descent into madness, and which could have perpetuated stereotypes reminiscent of Shakespeare's tragically destined Black male protagonist – Othello.

The proverbial demon that Chris comes up against in *Get Out* is one that horror cinema has rarely dared to deal with in ways that unapologetically centre complex Black characters. That demon is white supremacy, and which is at the root of Chris being treated as nothing more than a body to be auctioned off by Rose and her family. Chris's survival instinct in *Get Out* ultimately reminds him and the audience that, when as a Black person you are faced with the scary reality of racism, 'your silence will not protect you' (Lorde, 2017).

By the end of the film, Chris's friend Rodney has come to his rescue. The pair are on-screen proof of *Get Out's* refusal to subscribe to the 'Black people die first' approach that often underpins horror cinema. Furthermore, although Chris's friend Rodney is a humorous character that provides light relief via his comical cynicism and unabashed manner, Rodney's determination to protect Chris is a rare representation of friendship between Black men in the horror genre. Instead of being treated as Black bodies, or demonic Others to be feared, both the characters of Chris and Rodney contribute to constructions of Black masculinity in *Get Out*, which dismiss tired stereotypes.

15.7. Conclusion

To return to the words of Wood (2002), horror has the capacity to stimulate depictions and dialogue related to oppressive experiences, as well as repressed emotions. Thus, horror cinema can provide a visual site within which ideas related to the lives of Black men, and boys, can be scrutinized, struggled over, and move beyond merely replicating 'sensationalized models of masculinity' (Watkins, 1998, p. 202). In addition to exemplifying the genre-bending nature of horror in the twenty-first century, *Get Out* offers representations of Black masculinity that resist stereotypical comedic tropes, or images of enraged Black men. This includes the portrayal of a strong friendship between Chris and Rodney, as well as the emotional fragility of Chris, whose childhood trauma has been unresolved.

Get Out points to the idea that the survival of a young Black man in a primarily white and middle-class setting is far from simply being dependent on a racially palatable performance of his 'Working Identity' (Carbado & Gulati, 2013, p. 3). Films featuring Black people in leading roles continue to expand and evolve definitions of horror. This includes Spike Lee's film *Da Sweet Blood of Jesus* (2015), and Michael O'Shea's *The Transfiguration* (2016), which add to representations of Black masculinity amidst plots based on vampiric tendencies.That said, much of such cinema continues to exclude Black women from the leading line-up, suggesting a need for more scrutiny of the intersecting ways that both racism and sexism (Crenshaw, 2017) continue to inform the making of horror films.

Horror reflects and reinforces issues regarding race and racism, including by depicting how Black people navigate nightmarish racist realities. Whilst paranormal themes play a part in *Get Out*, its key trope is the threat and fear of one's body being inhabited and controlled by another (i.e. the end result of racism). Further still, it is the relative absurdity of Black people's bodies becoming occupied by the souls of wealthy white people, in hand with the pervasiveness of racism, which makes for *Get Out's* chilling feel. It is therefore amidst a space between the familiar and the unknown – the (un)familiar, that the potency of this film emerges. The real monsters that lurk in the content of such cinema are not visible or tangible entities. It is the illusory nature of pressures and problems related to the lives and treatment of Black boys and men, which is the most haunting feature of all in *Get Out*.

References

Anderson, V. (2017). *Get Out*: Why racism really is terrifying. *The Independent*, 26 March. Retrieved from http://www.independent.co.uk/arts-entertainment/films/features/get-out-why-racism-really-is-terrifyinga7645296.html. Accessed on November 28, 2017.

Blackwell, A. (2015). Black (fear) on both sides: Thinking about race in horror films. *Comingsoon.net*, 10 February. Retrieved from http://www.comingsoon.net/horror/news/744889-black-fear-sides-thinking-race-horror-films. Accessed October 10, 2018.

Blackwell, A. (2016). *Get Out*: The horror film that shows it's scary to be a Black man in America. *The Guardian*, 6 October. Retrieved from https://www.theguardian.com/film/filmblog/2016/oct/06/get-out-horror-film-jordan-peele-black-men. Accessed on November 20, 2017.

Blackwell, A. (2017). On our terms: A Black [women's] horror film aesthetic. *Bitch Flicks*, 1 November. Retrieved from http://www.btchflcks.com/2017/11/black-womens-horror-film-aesthetic.html#.WyI6UkgvyUk. Accessed on May 3, 2018.

Bogle, D. (1973). *Toms, coons, mulattoes, mammies & bucks: An interpretive history of Blacks in American films*. New York, NY: Viking Press.

Bryan, R., & Lindo, J. (2017). *Black boy feelings* — Volume 1. Boyhood. Brooklyn, NY: Black Boy Feelings.

Cane, C. (2017). Why Jordan Peele's '*Get Out*' just made history. *Cable Network News*, 15 March. Retrieved from https://edition.cnn.com/2017/03/14/opinions/jordan-peelemakes-movie-history-with-get-out-cane/index.html. Accessed on 25 November 2017.

Carbado, D. W., & Gulati, M. (2013). *Acting White? Rethinking race in post-racial America*. New York, NY: Oxford University Press.

Carroll, N. (1990). *The philosophy of horror or paradoxes of the heart*. New York, NY: Routledge.

Chan, K. (1998). The construction of Black male identity in Black action films of the nineties. *Society for Cinema & Media Studies*, *37*(2), 35–48.

Chantal, N. (2017). Jordan Peele, Childish Gambino's Gotham Film awards a win for #StayWoke push. *Rollingout*, November 30. Retrieved from https://rollingout.com/2017/11/30/jordan-peele-childish-gambinos-gotham-film-awards-win-staywoke-push. Accessed on June 17, 2018.

Cherry, B. (2009). *Horror*. New York, NY: Routledge.

Crenshaw, K. (2017). *On intersectionality: The essential writings of Kimberlé Crenshaw*. New York, NY: Free Press.

Da Sweet Blood of Jesus. (2015). [Film] Directed by S. Lee. USA: 40 Acres and a Mule Filmworks.

Daniels, J. (2016). *White lies: Race, class, gender and sexuality in white supremacist discourse*. New York, NY: Routledge.

Denzin, N. K. (2002). *Reading race: Hollywood and the cinema of racial violence*. London: Sage.

Diawara, M. (1993). *Black cinema*. New York, NY: Routledge.

Dickerson, J. (2017). Dear White People: A guide to watching '*Get Out*' with Black audiences. *Medium*, 27 February. Retrieved from https://medium.com/@TheRealPRLady/dear-white-people-a-guide-to-watching-get-out-with-black-audiences-4d49e82f0d65. Accessed on April 10, 2018.

Du Bois, W. E. B. ([1903] 2007). *The souls of Black folk*. Oxford: Oxford University Press.

Dyer, R. (1997). *White: Essays on race and culture*. New York, NY: Routledge.

Emejulu, A. (2016). On the hideous whiteness of Brexit: 'Let us be honest about our past and our present if we truly seek to dismantle white supremacy'. *Verso*, 28 June. Retrieved from https://www.versobooks.com/blogs/2733-on-the-hideous-whiteness-of-brexit-let-us-be-honest-about-our-past-and-our-present-if-we-truly-seek-to-dismantle-white-supremacy. Accessed on April 12, 2018.

Fisher, C. A. (2006). *Black on Black: Urban youth films and the multicultural audience*. Oxford: Scarecrow Press.

Get Out. (2017). [Film] Directed by J. Peele. USA: Blumhouse Productions and Monkeypaw Productions.

Grant, K. B. (2015). *The dread of difference: Gender and the horror film*. Austin, TX: University of Texas Press.

Graveyard Shift Sisters. (2018). *Our vision*. Retrieved from http://www.graveyardshiftsisters.com/p/mission.html. Accessed on April 20, 2018.

Gray, H. (1995). *Watching race: Television and struggle for blackness*. Minneapolis, MN: University of Minnesota Press.

Guerrero, E. (1993). *Framing Blackness: The African American image in film*. Philadelphia, PA: Temple University Press.

Henry, K. L. Jr. (2017). A review of *Get Out*: On White terror and the Black body. *Equity & Excellence in Education*, *50*(3), 333–335. doi:10.1080/10665684.2017.1336952

hooks, b. (1992). *Black looks: Race and representation*. Boston, MA: South End Press.

hooks, b. (2004a). *We real cool: Black men and masculinity*. New York, NY: Routledge.

hooks, b. (2004b). *The will to change: Men, masculinity, and love*. New York, NY: Atria Books.

Kee, J. B. (2015). Black masculinities and postmodern horror: Race, gender, and Abjection. *Visual Culture & Gender*, *10*, 47–56.

Leonard, D. J. (2006). *Screens fade to black: Contemporary African American cinema*. Westport, CT: Praeger Publishers.

Lewis, G. (1997). *Living the differences: Ethnicity, gender and social work*. PhD thesis. The Open University.

Lopez, R. (2017). Jordan Peele on how he tackled systemic racism as horror in '*Get Out*'. *Variety*, 1 November. Retrieved from http://variety.com/2017/film/news/jordan-peele-get-out-systemic-racism-1202604824/. Accessed on November 15, 2017.

Lorde, A. (2017). *Your silence will not protect you: Essays and poems*. London: Silver Press.

Mask, M. (2014). *Contemporary Black American cinema: Race, gender and sexuality at the movies*. New York, NY: Routledge.

McCollum, V. (2016). *Post-9/11 heartland horror: Rural horror films in an era of urban terrorism*. New York, NY: Routledge.

Means-Coleman, R. R. (2011). *Horror Noire: Blacks in American horror films from the 1890s to present*. New York, NY: Routledge.

Rankin, S. (2018). Why *Get Out* was the most important movie of award season. *News*, 4 January. Retrieved from http://www.eonline.com/uk/news/903509/why-get-out-was-the-most-important-movie-of-award-season. Accessed on January 10, 2018.

Robey, T. (2017). *Get Out* review: A breathlessly suspenseful exposé of the horror of liberal racism. *The Telegraph*, 17 March. Retrieved from http://www.telegraph.co.uk/films/0/get-review-breathlessly-suspenseful-expose-horror-liberal-racism/. Accessed on November 10, 2018.

Sanneh, K. (2001). Black in the box: In defence of African American television. *Transition*, *10*(4), 38–65.

Scary Movie 2. (2001). [Film] Directed by K. Ivory Wayans. USA: Miramax Films.

Shary, T. (2002). *Generation multiplex: The image of youth in contemporary American Cinema* (pp. 1–135). Austin, TX: University of Texas Press.

Taylor, K. Y. (2016). *From #BlackLivesMatter to Black liberation*. Chicago, IL: Haymarket Books.

The Transfiguration. (2016). [Film] Directed by M. O'Shea. USA: Transfiguration Productions.

Watkins, C. (1998). *Representing: Hip hop culture and the production of Black cinema*. Chicago, IL: University of Chicago Press.

Wekker, G. (2016). *White innocence: Paradoxes of colonialism and race*. London: Duke University Press.

Wood, R. (2002). The American nightmare: Horror in the 70s. In M. Jancovich (Ed.), *Horror, the film reader* (pp. 25–32). London: Routledge.

Index

Printed in the United States
By Bookmasters